SEXUAL
JUSTICE

SEXUAL JUSTICE

Democratic Citizenship

and the

Politics of Desire

Morris B. Kaplan

ROUTLEDGE
New York   London

Published in 1997 by
Routledge
29 West 35th Street
New York, NY 10001

Published in Great Britain by
Routledge
11 New Fetter Lane
London EC4P 4EE

Copyright © 1997 by Routledge

Printed in the United States of America on acid-free paper.

Library of Congress Cataloging-in-Publication Data

Kaplan, Morris B.
    Sexual justice: democratic citizenship and the politics of desire /
Morris B. Kaplan.
      p. cm.
    Includes bibliographical references and index.
    ISBN 0-415-90514-1 (hb). — ISBN 0-415-90515-X (pb)
    1. Gay rights—United States.   2. Gays—Legal status, laws, etc.—United States.   3. Homosexuality—Law and legislation—United States.   I. Title.
HQ76.8.U5K36   1996
323.3'264'0973—dc20   96-30436
                                                 CIP

*This book is dedicated to the memory of
my father, Harry Kaplan and of my teachers,
Nathaniel Lawrence and Laszlo Versenyi.*

TABLE OF CONTENTS

PREFACE

PERSONAL AND POLITICAL

$\bowtie$

I started work on this book in 1988, shortly after my return to college teaching from almost fifteen years as a practicing attorney in New York City. It originated in a conversation with an aspiring young gay philosopher whom I had just met. He asked whether I thought there were philosophical issues that one needed to consider simply by virtue of being gay. The conversation went on with minimal interruption for three days. In an important sense, it continues. *Sexual Justice: Democratic Citizenship and the Politics of Desire* is one result of the thinking, writing, and dialogue that began for me on an August weekend in the Berkshires. My research and reflection initially engaged issues in constitutional law and jurisprudence bearing on privacy rights and political equality. However, I soon saw that doing justice to the topic of sexual citizenship required me to cast a much broader net — encompassing law, philosophy, psychoanalysis, history, and literature. I found myself returning to texts and thinkers that have informed my own reflections on political and social matters over several decades. I found it necessary to articulate the role of desire in individual self-making and to chart the vicissitudes of equality and difference in modern democracy. Plato, Freud, Thoreau, Arendt, Rawls, and Foucault became important resources for my efforts to apply democratic ideals of freedom and equality to the politics of desire. I concluded that it is impossible to theorize lesbian and gay rights and liberation without considering institutions of gender subordination and what Adrienne Rich has called "compulsory heterosexuality." Although this book primarily engages the work of male and heterosexual thinkers and focuses on the analysis of masculine desire and sexuality, I have tried to read texts and historical institutions as a queer and a feminist, sensitive to pressures towards normalization and the erasure of sexual difference.

As I completed final revisions of this manuscript I discovered that I had inadvertently written a kind of disguised autobiography. This should not be so surprising given the intimate nature of the issues with which I am concerned. However, since the book proceeds through a series of rather austere philosophical arguments and sometimes dense literary and historical interpretations, it may be helpful if I reveal up front the personal, political, and intellectual history from which it emerges.

My initial research drew on my legal training and experience to examine critically the Supreme Court's then recent decision in *Bowers v. Hardwick*. That case brought an end to expectations that appeals to constitutional rights of privacy would invalidate the sodomy laws by which same-sex activities by adults — even in private — are defined as crimes in one half of the United States. My research into the legal background led me into the contested terrain of privacy rights more generally and eventually back to fundamental issues in the theory and practice of American democracy. Despite the setback in *Hardwick*, I concluded that the commitments to liberty and equality that underlie the constitutional scheme provide continuing resources for the movement for lesbian and gay rights and liberation.

I came to realize that equality for sexual minorities includes a lot more than just freedom from harassment by criminal laws and police. Lesbian and gay oppression results from pervasive legal disabilities that sanction and reinforce social discrimination and subordination. Indeed, the legal and social status of homosexuals in our society amounts to a condition of second-class citizenship. Democratic citizenship extends beyond formal equality before the law and access to abstract rights. Citizenship is a political status; democratic equality entails the ability to participate on the same terms as others in collectively shaping the conditions of common life. Political equality for unpopular minorities can be secured only if they are protected against retaliation for exercising their civil rights by laws that prohibit discrimination against them in employment, housing, education, and other critical areas of social and economic activity. Only nine states currently provide such protection to lesbian and gay citizens.

Despite this fact, recent years have witnessed an extraordinary upsurge in concerted activity by lesbian and gay citizens asserting their right to democratic equality. For someone like me, who came of age in the activist 1960s, the emergence of a highly visible lesbian and gay politics is an astonishing and heartening development. Partly in response to the AIDS epidemic, but with implications that resonate throughout society, individuals have come out of the closet and joined in a social and political movement that reaches from local organization of community services to the mobilization of national demonstrations and lobbying campaigns. One momentous effect of the emergence of a queer politics has been to transform the social circumstances and ways of life available to lesbian and gay citizens. Although the situation varies across the country, it has become increasingly easy to come out, especially in urban centers and on university campuses, and to lead an openly gay life. Political and social organizations, programs in lesbian and gay studies, and centers for counseling, health care, or entertainment provide a context in which lesbians and gay men form friendships, partnerships, and alliances. Same-sex couples now celebrate mutual commitment ceremonies in the company of family and friends. We organize on behalf of demands for a right to marry or negotiate with employers to secure benefits for domestic partners. Lesbians are bearing children in a mini-"baby boom," and queers construct "families we choose" as alternatives to the traditional variety.

When I was in college, graduate school, and law school during the 1960s, lesbian and gay students were largely invisible. Queer faculty remained in the closet.

Democratic politics coalesced around the efforts of African Americans and their allies in the Civil Rights Movement, citizens of all sorts opposed to the war in Vietnam, and students concerned with their universities' responses to both issues. The Women's Movement was just beginning. Lesbian and gay politics? Unthinkable. At least the people I knew and I didn't think of it. Very much caught up in efforts to realize the promises of American democracy, I saw my own sexual frustrations and confusions as personal matters irrelevant to broader political concerns.

I was not alone. Many of my friends from college later turned out to be gay. Back then, we recognized each other as having something important in common, although few of us seemed very clear about what that was and what it might imply for our future lives. In the intense same-sex atmosphere of what was then called a "boys'" school in the middle of nowhere, it was not easy to know what our crushes meant or whether our sexual experimentation expressed more than the needs of horny male adolescents. Of course, there were other signs — some alienation from fraternity life and college sports, a tendency to get caught up with books and the arts, an enthusiasm for Judy Garland, Ethel Merman, and Marlene Dietrich. Late at night, after lots of drinks, we would confess our latest unrequited loves and complain about our sexual frustrations. Only in recent years have I learned that many of us were having more sex than we then admitted, much of it with guys who had not much in common with our little group of friends. I don't think we ever gave a name to the cluster of qualities we shared; I know that we didn't think of ourselves as "gay" and suspect that we thought of "homosexuality" as both a social disgrace and a dreadful disease. Most of us were terribly naive about sex, assumed that our alienation resulted from being liberal intellectuals surrounded by conservative jocks, and expected that we would become magically interested in "girls" when we graduated from our all-male enclave. I, at least, viewed the latter prospect with some regret.

Don't get me wrong. My experience of college and university life in the 1960s was by no means primarily one of frustration and confusion. Late night soul-searching and occasional groping was a background theme that sometimes erupted into agony and disorientation. Most of my time was taken up with two pre-occupations that have continued in some form throughout my life — the study of philosophy and participation in democratic politics. Since it has become intellectually fashionable and politically popular to trash the movements for social change of the 1960s, let me state unequivocally: it was a great time to be alive, and "very Heaven to be young." I'll go further. It was a great moment for American democracy, fraught with conflict and contestation, but filled with promise and hope. Many of the aspirations of African Americans, war protesters, students, the poor, and others have been disappointed. But the ideals of freedom and equality that animate active democratic citizenship have not been discredited by the contingencies of subsequent history. *Sexual Justice* is an effort to recuperate the positive sense of democratic equality celebrated in the Sixties and to show what it requires in the domain of sexual citizenship.

My own political engagements with the "Movement" began with efforts to dislodge a fraternity system from its place at the heart of my college's social system. They went from early opposition to nuclear testing in the atmosphere to draft counseling and resistance to the Vietnam War, from support for efforts at desegregation in the South to teaching at historically black colleges and helping to organize educational projects for poor youth in the inner cities of the North. Fellow students and faculty at both college and university were caught up in a whole range of such efforts. Many of us saw our study of ethics and political theory, our teaching of undergraduates and tutoring of younger students, and our more explicitly political activities as inseparable components of thoughtful democratic citizenship. We argued intensely and at length, organized in the university and surrounding communities, marched and demonstrated, read Thoreau on civil disobedience and Arendt on action in the public sphere. In all of these settings, I became increasingly aware that my own attractions to other men were a powerful source of political and intellectual energy. Although I knew others for whom this was true, on this topic we were uncharacteristically reticent. It remained a private matter for intimate conversation with friends, quite separate from political analysis and organization.

My study and teaching of philosophy provided occasion for reflection on the ways that my erotic desires and attachments informed my political and intellectual activities. After all, I had first been attracted to philosophy through reading Plato as a freshman in college. Many of my most intense experiences involved long, intense conversations with other young men late into the night at college and after. Searching together for some reasonable basis on which to conduct our lives and affect the society we lived in seemed integral to forming fast friendships. I read and reread Plato's dialogues on friendship, wrote papers on the *Symposium* in college and graduate school, and agonized over whether Platonic love was sexual or celibate. For Plato, eros is the motive force in individual ethical development and a pervasive factor in community life. As years passed during which I seemed less and less able to integrate the intensity of my own sexual longings with the more public dimensions of friendship, philosophy, and politics, I turned to modern studies of sexuality as well. Oddly enough, the two most compelling courses I took in law school were taught by psychoanalysts and involved the serious study of texts of Freud and his followers. When sexual and emotional discontents threatened utterly to disrupt my intellectual work, personal friendships, and political activity, I was lucky enough to find help in psychoanalytically informed therapy.

After a somewhat turbulent period of false starts and interruptions, I abandoned teaching and the academic study of philosophy to complete law school. Moving to New York, I went to work as a trial attorney with the Legal Aid Society and settled down for a challenging and satisfying engagement that lasted almost thirteen years. The practice of law on behalf of poor people in the Family and Criminal Courts of New York taught me an enormous amount about conditions in our society and the institutions through which it is governed. Nothing in my education had prepared me for the harsh realities of urban poverty or the bureaucratized callousness and stupidity of the "justice system." When I came later to read Foucault, I felt the shock of recognition. The trial courts of New York have an uncanny resemblance to Hobbes's description of the state of nature —"the war of all against all." I survived and flourished in an adverse and conflictual environment by becoming active in the Association of Legal Aid Attorneys, District 65/United Auto Workers, the union through which staff attorneys defended our professional independence and exercised some control over our working conditions.

In 1981, I found myself rereading Hannah Arendt as I participated in an eleven-week strike to protest the firing of a diligent lawyer who had challenged the size of his caseload. My work on this book is shaped as much by those experiences as by the academic study of constitutional law and jurisprudence. Despite the power and importance of the rule of law in modern democracies, ideals of freedom and equality must be realized through continual political efforts to develop and maintain institutions that respond to social inequities and individual dissent.

Coming to New York also marked my coming out. My friends and family had long known of my inner struggles around desire and intimacy. New York meant *coming into* a rich, diverse, and politically active community of lesbians, gay men, and queers of all sorts. There were a number of out lesbians and gay men on the staff of the Legal Aid Society. Many of us also became involved in the struggle for lesbian and gay rights. I missed the Stonewall Rebellion but was able to join in efforts to combat Anita Bryant's "Save Our Children" campaign to roll back gains in lesbian and gay equality, and I became involved in the perennial project of getting a civil rights bill passed by the New York City Council. In those days, there was a lot of political energy as well as the first stirrings of distinctively lesbian and gay intellectual milieu through groups like the Gay Academic Union and the Committee of Lesbian and Gay Socialists.

Coming out in the 1970s in New York and elsewhere also meant entry — for gay men at least — into a wide variety of sexual venues. I arrived in the city well before the advent of the AIDS epidemic and enjoyed a period of erotic freedom and community more exciting than anything I had ever imagined. The combination of political mobilization, personal friendship, and sexual experimentation that marked the period has been eclipsed by the terrible suffering of so many in the wake of AIDS. I refuse to turn that dreadful contingency into a moral judgment of the lives we led and enjoyed.

In 1987, I took a leave of absence from the Legal Aid Society to return to teaching philosophy at Purchase College in the State University of New York, where I continue to teach. It is my great good luck that the leave turned into a career change. Shortly after coming to Purchase, I began work on this book. It is inconceivable to me that I might have undertaken this project at an earlier time. Returning after an absence of over fifteen years, I found the academy transformed. When I left university teaching in 1971, political and social philosophy played virtually no role in the philosophy curriculum; normative political theory was a largely historical endeavor within political science departments. (Rawls's *A Theory of Justice*, which gave new life to the academic study of political philosophy, was first published in 1971.) Feminism had not yet arrived as an intellectual movement in the academy. Although the campuses had been centers of ferment for political and social change, this fact was not much reflected in courses of study or in the work of scholars. Today feminism has installed the critical study of gender across the curriculum. Lesbian and gay studies have been introduced on many campuses. Sexuality as a topic figures in history, literature, politics, and philosophy courses. "Theory" has emerged as a concern that runs across disciplinary lines and engages students and professors of all sorts in the study of critical texts in the European philosophical tradition. Much of this work, even when it is not explicitly feminist, is sensitive to the construction of forms of desire and identity. In addition to interdisciplinary attention to general issues in social and cultural theory, many scholars have moved to historicize studies in the humanities and social sciences.

When I first returned to college teaching, I was struck by the proliferation of critical vocabularies and the widespread engagement with political issues. As I worked on this book, I was able to draw on the research of scholars in many disciplines concerned to promote the serious study of sexuality, gender, and culture. Students respond to these issues with intelligence and enthusiasm and are willing to wrestle with austere and difficult texts that address their deep personal concerns. This is not the place to enter the lists in the culture wars and the ongoing debate about multiculturalism. I could not have written *Sexual Justice* in the absence of these developments. This work synthesizes material from law, philosophy, psychoanalysis, literature, and history; it connects with feminist interrogations of the sex/gender system and of the culture of compulsory heterosexuality. It gains focus and energy from my own personal and political engagement with lesbian and gay politics and queer theory.

When I was in college and graduate school, I encountered no critical discussions of the ethics and politics of desire and identity. It was not only lesbian and gay faculty and students who were confined to the closet; desire itself was consigned to the bull session and the locker room. At a time of life when one's erotic drives and development are a matter of the greatest urgency, students of my generation were left to our own devices. The humanistic tradition so often invoked by conservative critics of educational change is not so blind — as I hope this book will demonstrate, some of the greatest writers we know made the vicissitudes of desire central to their own theoretical reflections. Texts from Plato to Thoreau to Freud and beyond interrogate the conventions by which our erotic lives are organized and recognize the power of our longings to shape and disrupt our communities. I offer this book as a contribution to a very old and ongoing philosophical dialogue about how our desires shape the persons we become and to a contemporary debate about how our political practices can deliver on the democratic promise of liberty and equality for all.

ACKNOWLEDGMENTS

$\rm A$ major theme of this book is the centrality of friendship and intimacy to individual development and the extent to which even the most personal relations develop against a background of diverse communities and institutions. These linkages are as true in the intellectual as in the erotic domain, if we can separate the two. Writing *Sexual Justice* has been very much a collaborative effort in which I find it hard to separate my own efforts from the multiple dialogues and exchanges through which the work developed. Not all of those who contributed are aware of the fact. I have drawn on over thirty years of intellectual, personal, and political engagements to work out these arguments and interpretations.

Some have a more direct responsibility. Ed Stein first raised with me the question regarding the philosophical significance of being gay. He encouraged me to undertake my first investigations of gay rights and privacy rights and has supported all of my efforts since. He is a careful critic, a committed scholar, and a generous friend. Ed has read and responded to everything I have written, a lot of it on several occasions. I have learned an enormous amount from conversation with him and from studying his own work in lesbian and gay studies. Early on, I attended the Third Conference on Lesbian and Gay Studies at Yale University. There I first heard Judith Butler, one of the most impressive philosophers working in the United States today. I am indebted to her for encouraging and supporting this project from very early on as well as for the extraordinary power of her conversation and published work from which I continue to profit. My old friend Seyla Benhabib welcomed me back to the academy by publishing my work in *Praxis International* and urging me to develop it further. Alan Ryan lent his learning and intelligence to the project in many fine conversations over meals on both coasts. In their very different ways, these thinkers continually demonstrate that first-rate philosophical work is capable of addressing ethical and political issues of the utmost importance. I hope that this book will not disappoint them.

Maureen MacGrogan at Routledge has been everything I dream of in an editor, allowing me the freedom to work at my own pace and in my own directions while continually offering support, encouragement, and the occasional nudge to get on with it. I cannot imagine that I should have written the book if I had not contracted with her to produce it. At Routledge, Alison Shonkwiler (now at Cornell University Press), Laska Jimsen, and Ronda Angel were consistently helpful and fun.

I am especially grateful to Ed Stein, Cheshire Calhoun and a third, anonymous reader who went over an earlier draft of this book in great detail and provided concrete and constructive criticism of its organizational difficulties. Ron Caldwell went way beyond the role of copy-editor in cleaning up my prose and raising questions of organization and substance as well. My friend Bill Torbert interrupted his own busy life to read two complete drafts and offer some very helpful proposals from a "general reader." Many friends and colleagues have been generous in reading and offering advice on earlier drafts of specific chapters. Many thanks to those who read and responded to one or more: Robert Anderson, Seyla Benhabib, Jane Bennett, Judith Butler, Marcos Bisticas-Cocoves, Ken Dove, Wayne Dynes, Richard Eldredge, Frank Farrell, Don Gifford, Cheryl Hall, Janet Halley, Ellen Haring, Bonnie Honig, George Kateb, Michael Koessel, Smadar Lavie, Pericles Lewis, Peter Lipton, Tamsin Lorraine, Jason Mayerfeld, Sharon Meagher, Meredith Michaels, Richard Mohr, Linda Nicholson, Sean O' Connell, Dan Ortiz, Paul Robinson, Alan Ryan, Tom Schmid, Charles Shepardson, Michael Sherman, David Stern, and Rosemarie Tong.

I have been lucky in my work as well as in my friends. Purchase College has provided an extremely congenial and stimulating environment in which to study and teach. My colleagues in the Philosophy Board of Study have supported me both personally and intellectually; one could not wish for finer colleagues and friends than Naomi Block (now retired), Ken Dove, Frank Farrell, Casey Haskins, and Marjorie Miller. Gari LaGuardia, who presides with remarkable equanimity and good spirit over the Humanities Division, has been the good angel of my return to academe, providing both personal and institutional support for my teaching and research. I feel a special debt to those friends and colleagues who joined together to form the Lesbian and Gay Studies Program: Deb Amory, Bill Baskin, Kim Christensen, Steve Dubin, Naomi Holoch, Susanne Kessler, Eric Nicholson, and Esther Newton. For three years Esther and I have taught together courses on sexual orientation that have combined pedagogy, learning, and good fellowship. A "founding mother" of lesbian and gay studies, Esther has been a great colleague and a good friend. Many of my colleagues in Humanities have been encouraging and often helpful to my work, especially Bell Chevigny, Geoff Field, Maria Gagliardo, Jay Novick, Michael O'Loughlin, Lee Schlesinger, Richard Stack, Bob Stein, Nina Strauss, and Louise Yellin.

I have spent most of January over the last ten years teaching in the Williams College Winter Study program. The students and faculty there have provided another important community that has encouraged and supported my work. I am especially grateful to Laurie Benjamin, Tim Cook, David Eppel, Sam Fleischacker, Steven Gerrard, Don Gifford, Honora Gifford, Tom Kohut, Diana Lipton, Peter Lipton, Jane Nichols, Dan O'Connor, Mary O'Connor, Clara Claiborne Park, David Park, Jorge Pedraza, Chris Pye, Mark Reinhardt, Jack Savacool, Jana Sawicki, Kurt Tauber, Jack Yaeger, Chris Waters, and Alan White.

During the years that this book has been in process I have lectured and presented papers in many academic milieus. My own thinking has been advanced by the lively discussions in which I participated. Thanks for invitations to: California State University at San Jose Philosophy Department; Columbia University Seminar on Homosexualities; Harvard University Center for European Studies

Conference on Hannah Arendt; Jing Lyman Lecture Series at Stanford University; Massachusetts Institute of Technology Lesbian and Gay Studies Series; Purchase College SUNY Humanities Colloquium; Stanford Humanities Center; the course in Philosophy and Social Sciences at the Institute of Philosophy, Prague; Stanford Law School; State University of New York at Buffalo Law School; State University of New York at Stony Brook Philosophy Department; University of California at Santa Cruz, Philosophy, History of Consciousness, Women's Studies, and Cultural Studies Boards of Study; the University of Washington Political Science Colloquium; Willamette University Philosophy Department; and Williams College Philosophy Department. Special thanks to Ken Baynes, Seyla Benhabib, Jean Cohen, Christoph Cox, Christine DiStefano, Carla Freccero, Steven Gerrard, Janet Halley, David Halperin, Charles Junkerman, the late Muhammud Kenyatta, Eva Kittay, Wanda Korn, Gari LaGuardia, Rita Manning, Sally Markowitz, Jason Mayerfeld, Eugene Rice, Bill Shaw, Ed Stein, Randolph Trumbach, Molly Whalen, and Alan White.

I have also presented some of this work at meetings of various professional associations; the American Philosophical Association, Pacific Division; the American Political Science Association; Fourth Annual Lesbian and Gay Studies Conference at Harvard University; the New York State Political Science Association; the Society for Lesbian and Gay Philosophy; and the Society for Systematic Philosophy. Special thanks to Bob Anderson, Seyla Benhabib, Mark Blasius, Cheshire Calhoun, Joan Cocks, Cheryl Hall, David Johnson, Meredith Michaels, Richard Mohr, Melissa Orlie, Ed Stein, Rosemarie Tong, Nancy Tuana, James Wilkinson, and Richard Winfield.

Friendships and communities require support from more impersonal institutions, including the state, if they are to flourish. My research, conversation, and writing in the course of this project have been sustained by assistance from the Purchase College President's Junior Faculty Development Fund, the Rockefeller Foundation Fellowship in Legal Humanities at the Stanford Humanities Center, the American Council for Learned Societies, and the National Endowment for the Humanities. The Stanford Humanities Center is an institution unique in my experience. It provided a comfortable and stimulating environment during the academic year 1993–94 when I made major progress on this project; I can't imagine that I could have done it without that opportunity.

I am grateful to Wanda Korn and Charles Junkerman, who directed the Center at the time; Susan Sebbard and Sue Dambrau went out of their way to be helpful. The Graduate Student and Faculty Fellows contributed in many ways, direct and indirect, to my own efforts, especially Vilashini Coopan, Richard Eldredge, Susan Gillman, Hans-Ulrich Gumbrecht, Jonathan Ivry, and Pericles Lewis. Outside the Center, Janet Halley of the Stanford Law School and Paul Robinson of the History Department were especially generous with their time and attention. The students in my seminar on "The History and Politics of Sexuality" were consistently engaging. My stay in the Bay area was made productive and pleasurable by many friends outside of Stanford as well: especially Jane Bennett, Jim Blume, Wendy Brown, Judith Butler, Bill Connolly, Bonnie Hong, Stanley Hutter, John Jobeless, Tim Lull, Mary Carlton Lull, Steven Meyer, Alan Schlosser, and Wayne Thomas.

My return to academic life has been facilitated by an institution funded by the federal government. Through their summer seminars and institutes, the National Endowment for the Humanities has for many years provided opportunities for college and university teachers to come together for weeks of discussion and research with each other and with some of the most distinguished scholars in their fields. NEH has offered a "life-line" to overworked and underpaid teachers and scholars from all over the country. I have benefited enormously from these programs: in 1991, Alan Ryan's seminar at Princeton on seventeenth century political thought; in 1992, the Institute on Ethics organized by David Hoy, Hubert Dreyfus, and Jocelyn Hoy at U.C. Santa Cruz; in 1993, the Institute on Ethics and Aesthetics organized by Anthony Cascardi and Charles Altieri at U.C. Berkeley. I am grateful to the many fine scholars and teachers that I met in these settings as organizers, guest lecturers, and fellow participants. Some of them are now among my closest friends and colleagues. It is very sad that the know-nothings now in control of the United States Congress have targeted such a useful and inexpensive agency as NEH which has done so much to contribute to the quality of education by enabling our college teachers to remain intellectually alive.

During my years as a trial attorney, I was associated with another agency recently under attack — the Legal Aid Society of New York. My experience in the criminal and family courts of New York and with the Association of Legal Aid Attorneys informs my reflections in large ways and small that may not be evident in what follows. However, I believe that this book is a much better one as a result of those years and that experience. I am grateful to the many colleagues whose dedicated efforts did so much to sustain my own. Special thanks to those who became good friends: Janet Fink, Carol Gerstl, Karen Goldstein, Nan Kripke, Joseph Opper, Dennis Parker, Steven Pokart, Gary Sloman, Mara Thorpe, and Mark Whalen.

So many people have contributed to my writing this book that I fear I have not named them all. I have been supported by the interest and enthusiasm of friends, family, colleagues, students, and others with whom I have spoken over the last five years or more. I hope I will be forgiven for chance omissions. Closer to home, I have been supported in good times and bad by a circle of friends, both long-standing and recent, and a family so nourishing that I no longer distinguish between them. My deepest thanks to: Bob Anderson, Ken Dove, Robin Faine, Frank Farrell, David Gerber, Gari LaGuardia, my sister Barbara J. Kaplan, my nieces Judith and Leslie Kaplan, Mary Lawrence, Steve Linn, Brett McDonnell, Jennifer Middleton, my mother Sylvia Kaplan Radolan, my stepfather Joseph Radolan, my sister Susan Kaplan Rosenberg, my niece Stacey Rosenberg, Paul Rubin, Ed Stein, Bill Torbert, and Jim Walsh. Special thanks also to Donald Moss,

Thomas Wehr, and especially Harrison Eddy who helped me get through some very difficult times.

Finally, my life has been shaped perhaps more than most by a succession of fine teachers who have provoked and inspired me: at Williams, Don Gifford, Grover Marshall, Neill Megaw, Dan O'Connor, Kurt Tauber, and Alan Wilde; in the Yale Philosophy Department, Richard Bernstein, the late Robert Brumbaugh, the late Alexander Passerin d'Entrèves, George Schrader, Rulon Wells, and Paul Weiss; at the Yale Law School, Joseph Goldstein, Jay Katz, and Eugene V. Rostow. The book is dedicated to the memory of Nathaniel Lawrence and Laszlo Versenyi, two teachers at Williams who launched me on a course that, however erratically pursued, has become my life — and of my father, who first urged me to stop and think.

DEMOCRACY, DIFFERENCE, AND DESIRE

In late May of 1996, as I completed copy-editing the manuscript of this book, the movement for lesbian and gay rights and liberation won its first major victory in the United States Supreme Court. In *Romer v. Evans*, the Court, with a surprisingly strong six-to-three majority, ruled that Amendment 2 to the Colorado Constitution, the result of a state-wide referendum, violated the U. S. Constitution's guarantee of equal protection of the laws. That amendment repealed those provisions in the laws of some cities that extended civil rights protection to citizens discriminated against by reason of their sexual orientation and prohibited all state legislative, executive, or judicial actions designed to protect lesbian and gay citizens. Citing the nineteenth-century Justice Harlan's admonition that "the Constitution neither knows nor tolerates classes among citizens," the Court, in an opinion by Justice Anthony Kennedy, held that no rational relationship existed between the denial of protection to the class of citizens of "homosexual, lesbian or bisexual orientation" and any legitimate interest of the state. Indeed, the Court held that " . . . the amendment seems inexplicable by anything but animus towards the class that it affects. . . ."[1]

The Supreme Court has vindicated decades of struggles for the equality of lesbian and gay citizens. Although the full legal implications of the decision will become clear only through subsequent litigation, its political and ethical salience is evident. The Court has spoken with a powerful voice on two of the most important matters currently at issue in American democracy: the entitlement of homosexuals to full citizenship under the U. S. Constitution and the character of anti-discrimination protection as a condition of democratic equality rather than a "special right" granted to favored minorities. The Court held in the most unequivocal terms that no legitimate state interest could support the broad denial of rights to lesbian and gay citizens in Colorado's Amendment 2: ". . . laws of the kind currently before us raise the inevitable inference that the disadvantage imposed is born of animosity towards the class of persons affected." Citing an earlier case, the Court concludes, ". . . a bare . . . desire to harm a politically unpopular group cannot constitute a legitimate governmental interest." Although the holding directly affects only the Colorado amendment and similar laws under consideration in other states, the Court's rationale reaches much further. Quite simply, it has declared that the disapproval of homosexuality by popular majorities cannot justify differential treatment of lesbian and gay citizens under the law.

Equally important, the Court's holding should go far to discredit the current rhetoric mounted in opposition to civil rights protection — not only for lesbians and gays, but for African Americans, women, and other historically disadvantaged groups. In the popular mind, stirred up by right wing ideologues, civil rights laws have become synonymous with affirmative action, which is identified with quotas and other policies alleged to injure hardworking, meritorious white men. The issue in Colorado turned on whether or not cities or other governmental agencies could undertake to provide remedies for citizens discriminated against by reason of their sexual orientation. Such laws create no favored status for anyone, rather they enable citizens who have been treated unfairly to seek redress through the government. (In section VII of Chapter One, I argue that such protection is fundamental to equal citizenship for lesbians and gay men.) The Supreme Court in *Romer v. Evans* decisively rejects the characterization of anti-discrimination laws as creating "special rights" for homosexuals: "To the contrary, the amendment imposes a special disability upon these persons alone. Homosexuals are forbidden the safeguards that others enjoy or may seek without constraint." Indeed the Court reminds us that most Americans simply assume that they are protected against invidious discrimination in employment, housing, public accommodations, and the like: "These are protections taken for granted by most people either because they already have them or do not need them; these are protections against exclusion from an almost limitless number of transactions and endeavors that constitute ordinary civic life in a free society."

On behalf of the three Justices who dissented from the decision, Justice Scalia claims that "The Court has mistaken a Kulturkampf for a fit of spite." It's not easy to ascertain exactly what constitutional status Scalia envisions for this Kulturkampf, but he makes it very clear what side the dissenters are on. His allusion appears to be, not to Bismarck, but to Patrick Buchanan, who declared a cultural war at the Republican Convention of 1992. Writing with a vehemence unusual even for him, Scalia argues: "This Court has no business imposing upon all Americans the resolution favored by the elite class from which the Members of this institution are selected, pronouncing that animosity towards homosexuality . . . is evil. I vigorously dissent." He describes Amendment 2 in these terms: ". . . a modest attempt by seemingly tolerant Coloradans to preserve traditional sexual mores against the efforts of a politically powerful minority to revise those mores through use of the laws." Later Scalia writes, "It is also nothing short of preposterous to call 'politically unpopular' a group which enjoys enormous influence on American media and politics. . . ." This rhetoric is familiar, albeit unusual in opinions by Justices of the United States Supreme Court. (In Chapter Seven, I explore the shared genealogy of homophobia and anti-Semitism in nineteenth-century Europe.)

The juxtaposition of the opinion of the Court with Scalia's dissent displays the collision of fundamental conceptions of democratic equality with intensely held feelings about morality and traditional values. In the discussions that have followed the Court's decisions, more temperate dissent has been expressed in the language of majoritarian democracy. Thus, the attorney-general of Colorado announced that the Supreme Court had just deprived the citizens of her state of their democratic right to govern themselves. In terms of political theory, the conflicting conceptions of democracy at work in this debate have a long history. Ancient democracies were founded on the primacy of majority rule (among the small group privileged to be "citizens") and recognized no limits on their capacity to impose their will on minorities or individuals. The United States Constitution enacted a different notion of democracy for which the ideal of equality restrained the authority of the government and of popular majorities to override fundamental rights of individuals and dissenting minorities.

The concept of democratic citizenship articulated by the founders of modern democracy has figured importantly in the struggles of disadvantaged and excluded groups over the last hundreds of years to achieve the equality promised. Justice Harlan's condemnation of two classes of citizenship, with which the opinion of the Court in *Romer v. Evans* begins, was articulated in his *dissenting* opinion in *Plessy v. Ferguson*, which legitimized the rule of "separate but equal" for African Americans in the South. Not until 1954 with *Brown v. Board of Education* did the Supreme Court recognize the extent to which *separate* meant *unequal* in the public sphere for a minority once subjected to slavery and denied even minimal protections of citizenship. In *Romer v. Evans*, the Supreme Court declares that homosexuals cannot be consigned to second-class citizenship. But we already suffer from pervasive legal disabilities.

In *Sexual Justice: Democratic Citizenship and the Politics of Desire* I argue that the achievement of equality for lesbian and gay citizens is part of the unfinished business of modern democracy. This task requires a robust conception of lesbian and gay rights that emphasizes protection against discrimination and advocates recognition of queer relationships, families, and associations. Insisting on the centrality of sexual desire in human flourishing and on the variety of its forms, I argue that respect for individual freedom requires the existence of a plurality of voluntary "intimate associations" through which individuals shape their lives and define their personal identities. Equality for lesbian and gay citizens entails the end of laws by which private sexual activities between adults of the same sex are defined as crimes; it requires the extension of civil rights laws to protect queer citizens against retaliation for exercising their freedom to associate openly with others in both social and political contexts. Such a conception of lesbian and gay rights depends on a strong reading of the demands of democratic citizenship and the exigencies of desire in individual self-making. The importance of personal liberty in shaping one's desires to determine the course of a life must be articulated in relation to the political freedom of citizens collectively to decide the forms of their common life.

Political philosophy in the West began with sustained critical reflections on both democracy and desire in the dialogues of Plato. *Sexual Justice*, like the culture it reflects, is haunted by figures from ancient Athens. I consider Athenian pederasty as an institution of same-sex relations between men, the complex and ambiguous celebration of male homoerotic love in the *Symposium*, the deployment of Greek models in the nineteenth-century elaboration of modern homosexuality, and the influence of Socrates' collision with his city in developing conceptions of civil disobedience as an aspect of democratic citizenship.

The Greek legacy is problematic for reflections on the situation of contemporary lesbian and gay citizens and for spelling out the aspirations of modern democracy. Benjamin Constant's famous distinction between the "liberty of the ancients" and the "liberty of the moderns" provides some clarification here. He urged that democracy for the ancient Greeks recognized the centrality of the freedom to participate directly and actively in deciding matters of public policy. Citizens joined together in courts and assembly to debate and decide the direction of their city's international and domestic relations. Public life provided an arena for vigorous self-assertion and contestation. However, the ancient city exercised a profound influence on the conduct of its citizens' lives; public freedom was conjoined with individual submission to the ethical authority of the community in matters such as religion, opinion, and personal honor. The reach of the city's laws was not constrained by recognition of individual rights nor even by the demands of procedural regularity. Penalties were harsh and decisions unpredictable. Constant also emphasizes that the equality of citizens was constructed on the basis of the subordination of others to the status of slavery. Women were completely excluded from the public domain of citizenship.

By contrast, the liberty of modern democracy extends considerable protection to the private individual. Freedom of choice in matters of opinion, religion, choice of profession, and personal ethos is defended as a central democratic value. Courts and legislatures are constrained by constitutional definitions of the scope of governmental power and the requirements of due process of law. Although Constant defends the liberty of the moderns as superior to that of the ancients under the conditions of life in nineteenth-century Europe, he recognizes something is lost. Establishing the rule of law and the institutions of representative democracy displaces the public freedom enjoyed by the ancients. The protection of private liberty and enjoyment is accompanied by the restriction of most individuals to the domain of privacy. Active participation in public life becomes a prerogative of the few. On the other hand, the institution of slavery becomes intolerable for modern democracy. For Constant, the contrast between the two forms of liberty and of democracy is linked to broader historical contingencies, such as the vastly increased scale of political organization and the growing role of commerce, rather than war, as the medium of international relations.[1]

The defense of lesbian and gay rights necessarily appeals to fundamental conceptions of individual liberty as established in constitutional texts and practices within modern democracy. It invokes liberal conceptions of personal freedom and moral autonomy. However, the distinctive theme of my argument in this book is the insistence that abstract rights can be vindicated only through collective political struggle and must be established in social and ethical institutions. The integrity of a private sphere of individual decision-making will be protected only to the extent that it is recognized as such by political and legal authorities and respected by popular opinion. This is especially true where the liberties in question are those of an unpopular minority. Implicit in the distinction between ancient and modern democracy is a transformation in the conception of political equality as well as that of liberty. Not only did the ancients maintain slavery, but the status of citizenship itself was available only to a small minority. Women, children, foreigners, resident aliens, and manual laborers were excluded from citizenship; they enjoyed neither public nor individual liberty. In principle, modern democratic citizenship extends to all persons. However, the history of the last two hundred years and more reveals the extent to which the abstract principle of universal equality is inherently contested and will be established as a political reality only through political struggle. We cannot simply rejoice in the triumph of modern liberty. Indeed, to the extent that the formal proclamation of human rights and equal liberties may substitute for its embodiment in concrete forms of life, we must reassert ancient conceptions of public freedom and active citizenship as necessary to establish and maintain equal rights.

With respect to the social status of same-sex relations and the politics of desire, the contrast between ancients and moderns presents different but related hazards. For many male homosexuals over the course of decades — if not centuries — the example of Greek pederasty has been a source of legitimation and inspiration. However, like the status of citizenship, the institution of male same-sex love was imbricated with pervasive inequality in ancient democracies. The love of men for youth was inherently asymmetrical, with an older, active lover pursuing a younger, passive beloved; hierarchy rather than mutuality was the rule. Even more important, it is very hard to understand the importance of pederasty as a social form without recognizing how profoundly it was linked with a culture of misogyny and a polity that systematically subordinated women. Quite simply, adult males celebrated younger men because women were denied education, relegated to the household, and denied access to the public arena of citizenship so crucial to the Greek ethos. A citizen had the *duty* to marry and have children to carry on his line and his city's public life; friendship between older and younger men was the scene of romance. The pervasive sexism of the ancient city is contrary to principles of modern democratic equality. It is certainly unacceptable to a contemporary defense of the rights of sexual minorities.

Throughout this book, I advance arguments that support *lesbian and gay rights*.

With this locution, I do mean to elide the importance of differences between the political, social, and personal situations of homosexual men and women. Indeed, my analysis consistently returns to the links between the marginalization of same-sex love and the preservation of gender hierarchy. As Adrienne Rich and others have argued so powerfully, "compulsory heterosexuality" is an important instrument in the oppression of women. To that extent, lesbian and gay rights and liberation are in the service of women's liberation as well. However, precisely because of the pervasiveness of sexism, some gay men have access to privileges that are inaccessible to most lesbians. Even more important, as the example of Greek pederasty reveals, some historical and current forms of male homosexuality are themselves deeply implicated in misogyny and sexism.

In recent years, "queer" has emerged as a category describing innovations in both the theory and practice of the politics of sexuality. By now the meanings of that term, too, have proliferated and been subject to ongoing debate. Some of the issues in that debate have genuine political and intellectual significance, but they are not the subject of this book. I have adopted the term and sometimes use it interchangeably with "lesbian and gay," both for stylistic reasons and because I want to acknowledge that some nonconforming sexualities are marginalized even within movements of lesbian and gay rights and liberation. To the extent that "queer politics" embraces the cause of transgendered and transsexual people, boy-lovers, bisexuals, consensual sadomasochists, leatherfolk, and other sexual minorities, it is an important reminder of the range of sexual discrimination and the realities of modern pluralism.[3] To the extent that it becomes a means of effacing the specificities of lesbian and gay oppression or of subordinating the concerns of lesbians to an amorphous celebration of nonconformity, it may be misleading.

The very vagueness of the term has political advantages. "Queer" must necessarily be defined in opposition to dominant norms. In a society of compulsory heterosexuality, such nonconformity is indeed manifested by lesbians, gay men, and various others. However, especially as some of these groups make progress, they become vulnerable to risks of imposing exclusions of their own to defend their limited gains. Drag queens or boy-lovers may become "queers" within the lesbian and gay movement. Such tendencies conflict with the egalitarian and contestatory character of modern democratic aspiration. Nonconformity, "queerness" of a sort, is a positive value as an assertion of the priority of individual liberty and moral autonomy. Given the centrality of desire is ethical self-making, the activities of sexual nonconformists are especially important in challenging the limits of social regulation. However, independence of any sort is costly to maintain; lesbians and gay men are as liable as anyone else to settle for less than full freedom and equality. "Queer" affirmation should remind us of the risks and temptations of sexual and social conformity and the necessity for concrete specification and real pluralism in defining personal identities and political struggles.

Throughout this book, I am concerned to show that figures of male same-sex love have informed traditional understandings of the dynamic of sexuality more generally and are imbricated with models of democratic citizenship, agonistic politics, and social solidarity. In these cases, the recovery of masculine homoeroticism reveals the absence of women and the silence of feminine desire. Then why lesbian and gay rights? Because I believe that universality and abstraction necessary in clarifying the demands of democratic liberty and equality may be deployed on behalf of a critique of the exclusions that continue to define our political culture. In addition, by extending the range of rights to include the recognition of queer relations and families and by situating the vindication of equality within the domain of democratic contestation, I hope to open rather than close a public dialogue about what equality really requires. Most of the authors I consider are men; the institutions, masculine. Given our history, this is not accidental. My analysis works to expose the pervasiveness and depth of sexual difference as a determinate force in figuring both the vicissitudes of desire and the demands of democracy. My work is indebted to a wealth of recent feminist scholarship; I hope that I have been true to its spirit in recognizing the extent to which sexist assumptions are at work even in defense of the legitimacy of different sexualities.

The arguments of *Sexual Justice* develop through a series of engagements with specific issues and texts. My approach is eclectic, pluralist, and pragmatic: each chapter takes on another aspect of the general problematic and provides a new context for what has gone before. *Sexual Justice* does not purport to develop a comprehensive theory of justice along the lines of, say John Rawls's *A Theory of Justice*. Nor does it consist of an attempt to apply an already-developed theory to the issues specifically raised by the contemporary movement for lesbian and gay rights. Instead I have drawn on a variety of philosophical reflections on justice — some in the form of general theories, others embodied in essays, speeches, dramatic dialogues, scientific treatises, or historical studies. My purpose is to show how the question of social justice for sexual minorities brings into focus a wide range of concerns that have informed two millennia of sustained reflection on the nature of justice, the role of desire in individual self-making, and the scope of democratic citizenship. The most explicitly theoretical treatment of justice appears in Chapter One, where I examine the jurisprudence of the constitutional right of privacy in relation to philosophical analyses of "law, liberty, and morality." and the Rawlsian principle of equal liberty. Readers familiar with that literature will not be surprised to find arguments of John S. Mill, H. L. A. Hart, Sir Patrick Devlin, and John Rawls brought to bear on evaluating a range of claims to equality advanced by defenders of lesbian and gay rights. Indeed, I deploy these arguments critically to support an expansive conception of what justice requires in regard to homosexual citizens — not only the decriminalization of same-sex activities but also protection against invidious discrimination and the legal recognition of same-sex partnerships and lesbian and gay community institutions. I articulate a general framework for understanding the right relationships between queer citizens and the state in modern constitutional democracies, with their commitments to liberty, equality, and community.

But justice applies to more than the relationship between the individual citizen and the political community. In a tradition as old as Plato's *Republic*, justice is an individual virtue as well as a political ideal, bearing on the right relations of the individual to her own desires. Moreover, both "justice in the city" and "justice in the soul" must be realized in specific cultures under contingent historical circumstances. Democracy is a distinct historical phenomenon with important variations across periods and civilizations; the forms of desire, too, must be situated within diverse contexts that construct forms of personal and sexual identity. Following a lead from Hannah Arendt, I undertake here "to see historically and to think politically" about the role of desire in self-making and about democratic citizenship.

Chapter Two takes up the theme of "historicizing sexuality" and uses two case studies to exhibit the complexities that such an endeavor generates. Greek pederasty and the emergence of "modern homosexuality" in nineteenth-century Europe are topics directly relevant to any enquiry into the construction of sexual identities; they also provide rich examples for thinking more generally about situating forms of desire in their cultural and historical contexts. The first two chapters comprise Part One: "Principles." The principles in question are the normative ideals of modern democracy and the interpretive methodology that informs my general argument.

The historical narration and political interpretation of Chapter Two are a necessary supplement to the normative argumentation of Chapter One as a general introduction to the themes of this book. Both universal principles of human rights and the abstract persons to whom they apply must be situated in concrete institutional contexts within which distinctive sexual subjectivities emerge and personal desires bump up against social constraints. The movement from moral abstraction to historical context, from cultural conventions to individual desire and back again, will be repeated throughout the book.

Part Two, "Psyches," shifts focus from abstract ideals and historical political structures to what Plato called justice in the soul, turning on questions about the individual's relation to himself and his own desires. I examine two canonical texts on eros and sexuality in which specific manifestations of male homosexuality inform efforts to develop universal theories about the relations of desire to cultural conventions and to individual self-making. Chapter Three offers a sustained reading of Plato's *Symposium* as a reflection on the ethos of Greek pederasty that moves toward a more general portrayal of the relations among eros, identity, and political community. In Chapter Four I bear down hard on Freud's *Three Essays on the Theory of Sexuality* to show how his engagement with "third sex" theorists and other defenders of male same-sex love in nineteenth century Europe shaped the psychoanalytic account of sexuality as such. Both of these texts take masculine desire as their starting point. Although they problematize the assumptions about masculinity and the naturalness of desire embodied in contemporary cultures of compulsory heterosexuality, they generate troubling questions when it comes to their treatment of lesbianism and feminine desire more generally. My arguments in these chapters connect with feminist concerns about the sexist underpinnings of Greek pederasty, cultural equations of femininity with passivity, and the incapacity of nineteenth-century medicine to imagine an autonomous female sexuality.

Part Three, "Politics," situates democratic norms and erotic self-formation in the context of active citizenship and contestatory politics. These chapters take up the vicissitudes of sexual citizenship in three distinct historical contexts to show how the deliberate shaping of desire may both reflect a social situation and generate resistance to conventional norms. In Chapter Five, I use Hannah Arendt's analysis of the dilemmas of Jewish emancipation in Europe and her reading of Marcel Proust to draw some cautionary lessons for contemporary queer politics; in particular, I focus on the interplay of political equality and social difference in the historical construction of abject, naturalized, inherent conditions — "Jewishness" and "homosexuality." For Arendt, this ideological process short-circuited the democratic affirmation of plurality through contestatory politics and justified the oppression of both groups. In Chapter Six, I examine democratic citizenship from the perspective of the ethics of self-making in a reading of Thoreau's "Civil Disobedience" and other texts. I show that his affirmation of the necessity of resistance to civil authority is grounded in a recognition that democracy resides in the individual's deliberate shaping of his own desires. Thoreau's insistence on the centrality of individual integrity moves toward a celebration of agonistic friendships that are figured as both homoerotic idylls and impossible ideals.

Sexual Justice concludes with a critical interrogation of the ethics and politics at work in demands for the recognition of same-sex marriage. My argument returns to its starting point in constitutional rights of privacy and democratic ideals of liberty, equality, and community. Using Justice Blackmun's dissenting opinion in *Bowers v. Hardwick*, I argue that lesbian and gay rights are grounded in a freedom of intimate association that acknowledges the legitimacy of a plurality of forms of erotic life. Intimate relations with others are an important aspect of human flourishing and a site for the shaping of individual identities; they are also situated within the broader freedoms of democratic politics. Examining the historical role of marriage as a support for patriarchy and gender subordination, I contend that same sex marriage may be a site of resistance and subversion. In a regime of compulsory heterosexuality, same-sex marriage may be reconceived as a form of civil disobedience. I develop this argument by drawing on arguments from Plato, Thoreau, Arendt, and Rawls. The chapter and the book conclude with a defense of the ethical legitimacy of a plurality of forms of erotic life and of diverse institutions to support them. My example is the gay male bathhouse or sex club considered as a site of sexual experimentation, erotic community, and safer sex education in the age of AIDS.

PART ONE

PRINCIPLES

CHAPTER ONE

THEORIZING LESBIAN AND GAY RIGHTS

✎

Liberty, Equality, and Community[1]

S*exual Justice* defends a robust conception of lesbian and gay rights that includes decriminalization of same-sex activities between adults, the protection of lesbian and gay citizens against discrimination, and the recognition of lesbian and gay relationships, queer families, and community institutions. In this chapter, I present an argument as to the principles at issue in the appeal to human rights. My immediate concern is to show how much is required by established democratic norms of liberty, equality, and moral pluralism and by constitutionally recognized rights of privacy. This discussion necessarily abstracts from the specificity of lesbian and gay forms of life to articulate claims in the universalizing languages of democratic theory and constitutional law. However, my purpose is to go beyond the thin conceptions of legal personality and negative freedom that inform liberal theory and to insist on the concrete social dimension of the assertion of equal citizenship by lesbians and gays. Democratic citizenship is embodied in a plurality of voluntary associations and community institutions that result from the exercise of situated freedoms by specific individuals and groups. Analysis of the principles underlying claims to lesbian and gay rights is politically salient because of the emergence of an increasingly visible political and social movement of queer citizens since the 1960s. That movement would have been inconceivable in the absence of the struggles for equality by African Americans, women, and other groups historically excluded from the American democracy. General norms of liberty and equality must be realized through social interaction that transcends the terms of legal entitlement and prohibition while at the same time requiring legal protection and support; continuing contestation of the limits and uses of state power must inform any exercise of active citizenship in modern democracies. Forms of erotic life especially are deeply imbricated in the cultural organization of family relations and individual self-formation. My effort to theorize lesbian and gay rights and liberation moves between abstract universal norms and historically situated forms of life. This chapter focuses on the general structure of normative arguments about equal citizenship for sexual minorities.

I analyze lesbian and gay rights in terms of three kinds of claims: for the decriminalization of private, consensual homosexual acts between adults; for protection against invidious discrimination; and, for the recognition of the ethical and social status of lesbian and gay relationships and associations. Each of these claims brings into play its own conceptualization of the right relations between the democratic state and its citizens, between legal norms and social forms of life. By emphasizing the second and third class of claims, I will formulate a more general ethical framework in which norms of liberty, equality, and community are mutually articulated in a conception of democratic citizenship that includes erotic self-formation as well as political association and contestation.

I. What Are "Lesbian and Gay Rights"?[2]

Claims of lesbian and gay rights encompass a range of arguments regarding the right relationships between gay people and the state. As the movement for these rights has developed in the United States since the 1960s, claims have come to include disparate demands on the political order, supported by diverse and potentially conflicting conceptions of the scope and limits of legitimate state action. This political situation has been exacerbated and made more urgent by the impact of the AIDS epidemic. However, it remains important to identify and clarify the divergent strands of a movement for lesbian and gay rights. It may be useful to indicate three primary categories for such claims: 1) decriminalization of homosexual activities between consenting adults; 2) the prohibition of discrimination against lesbians and gays in employment, housing, education, and public accommodations; and 3) the legal and social recognition of the ethical status of lesbian and gay relationships and community institutions.

Approximately one-half of the states continue to prohibit specified sexual activities (usually anal and oral intercourse) even when pursued in private between consenting adults; some jurisdictions proscribe such activities among "persons," others specifically target "persons of the same sex." Moral and political opposition to such criminalizing of intimate sexual behavior is generally articulated in terms derived from John Stuart Mill's classic essay *On Liberty*. Legal strategies seeking to invalidate such legislation as an unconstitutional infringement of individual "rights of privacy" culminated in the Supreme Court's five-to-four decision of *Bowers v. Hardwick*, when the Court refused to overturn Georgia's laws banning consensual sodomy.[3] Litigation in state courts premised on the provisions of state constitutions has met with some success.[4] The claim underlying demands for decriminalization is an individual's right "to be let alone." At issue is the limitation of the state's authority to regulate individual behavior between consenting adults in which no one is harmed. A number of important academic debates, to be considered below, have in recent decades used the example of consensual homosexual relations among adults in private as a lens through which to consider the limits on the coercive authority of the state. In political terms, libertarians of the right sometimes join with traditionally liberal civil libertarians in condemning state intrusion into the domain of private sexual behavior between consenting adults.[5]

A somewhat different range of concerns informs opposition to invidious discrimination against lesbians and gays. Here the movement for lesbian and gay rights joins African Americans, women, religious and ethnic minorities, and the disabled in seeking the protections provided to some of these groups by the United States Congress in the Civil Rights Acts of 1964 and 1965 and by subsequent similar enactments by states and localities. When couched in constitutional terms, these claims invoke the "Equal Protection Clause" of the Fourteenth Amendment, whereas privacy claims depend on the "Due Process Clause." Currently fashionable libertarian advocacy of "minimal government" and some versions of liberalism that reject the criminalization of private homosexual behavior nonetheless oppose the extension of civil rights protections as an unjustifiable intrusion into private decisionmaking by employers, landlords, and others.[6] Only nine states include sexual orientation among the categories protected against discrimination in their civil rights laws.[7] The federal civil rights laws do not include sexual orientation as a protected category (although the Clinton administration supported proposals to do so in a 1995 bill with virtually no chance for passage in the 104th United States Congress). Civil rights legislation in general prohibits discrimination against specified groups in employment, housing, education, and public accommodations and provides a range of remedies from injunctive relief through compensatory damages to punitive damages. Claims by lesbians and gays for such protection envision a more positive role of the state in assuring these rights. Indeed, libertarians and other defenders of a minimal state are correct in seeing that the demand for protection against discrimination asks the state to prohibit individuals from exercising their prejudices against queers when they occupy positions empowered to dispense jobs, housing, or other economic opportunities. However, their objection conflates individual freedom of association, the right to choose your friends, with the collective economic and social power of large-scale employers, financial institutions, real estate enterprises, and the like; it engages not only questions about private property, but also the legal fiction that corporations are persons. The philosopher Richard Mohr, no friend to state power, has effectively marshaled the arguments favoring the inclusion of lesbians and gays in civil rights legislation, emphasizing the crucial importance of such legislation as a guarantor of fundamental political rights.[8] He describes the role of the state in this context as that of a "civil shield." I shall return to the links between civil rights protections and democratic citizenship in the concluding section of this chapter.

The highly contested political character of this issue, in a period of widespread reaction against all civil rights legislation — and growing moral panic about homosexuality — is evidenced by efforts in Oregon, Colorado, and elsewhere to forbid by referendum the enactment of laws to protect homosexuals against discrimination. These campaigns have invidiously labeled as demands for "special rights" the efforts of lesbian and gay citizens to gain equal citizenship. These referenda themselves raise fundamental questions as to the authority of popular majorities to deny to some groups equal access to normal political processes. (In May 1996, the Supreme Court invalidated Proposition Two amending the Colorado Constitution as a violation of the U. S. Constitution's guarantee of "equal protection of the laws" to lesbian and gay citizens.[9] *Romer v. Evans* is discussed in the Introduction.)

A related but distinct class of claims emerge when we turn to the growing demand on states and the law for recognition of the status of lesbian and gay relationships, institutions, and communal needs. Among the practical issues addressed here are: the right of lesbians and gays to marry or otherwise establish domestic partnerships; the entitlement of lesbian and gay partners to the benefits of health insurance, lease or rent stabilization privileges provided spouses or family members, or the dignity of recognition within the institutions that provide care for the sick and dying; the recognition of lesbian mothers and gay fathers as fit custodians of their own children and of lesbians and gay men generally as potential foster or adoptive parents; the demands of lesbian and gay organizations for official status in public schools, universities, or professional associations; the rights of queers to gather at bars, bathhouses, and social clubs without police harassment; the status of lesbian and gay institutions in the politics and provision of healthcare during the AIDS crisis. These are among the most controversial claims, and some advocates of liberal tolerance see them as going too far. During the 1996 Presidential campaign, President Bill Clinton, who supported federal civil rights protections for lesbians and gay men, emphasized his opposition to same-sex marriage. Nonetheless, litigation challenging the denial of marital status to same-sex couples is proceeding in several jurisdictions; the Supreme Court of the State of Hawaii in *Baehr v. Lewin* held that this exclusion violates a state constitutional ban on discrimination based on sex and must survive "strict scrutiny" if it is to be upheld.[10] Efforts to secure recognition of same-sex domestic partnerships have met with some success from local governments and in negotiating agreements with private employers. Moreover, throughout the country, lesbians and gay men in increasing numbers are sharing "commitment ceremonies" with their families and friends, bearing and adopting children, and establishing families of their own.[11] The ethical and social attitudes underlying these claims present a provocative and unstable juncture of conservative and radical impulses.

At issue is the demand for the recognition and respect of lesbian and gay relations and institutions within the broader legal, social, and ethical context. The state functions in this context not only as a civil shield protecting lesbians and gay men against invidious discrimination by private citizens, but also as a positive agency for actualizing the aspirations of queer citizens. Moreover, the rights in question are not simply those of individuals, but of couples, families, and voluntary associations. Ultimately what is at stake is the moral legitimacy and ethical validity of lesbian and gay ways of life. These claims reveal the political and philosophical heart of the movement for lesbian and gay rights. Far from being "icing on the cake," such demands are the real "bread and butter" underlying more abstract and formal conceptualizations of lesbian and gay rights. These issues provide a focal point for comprehending the resistance to lesbian and gay rights as well as a perhaps surprising locus for potential reconciliation between lesbian and gay rights and traditionally formulated "family values" and community norms. Indeed, attention to the ethical and social status of lesbian/gay relationships and institutions requires us to probe and to clarify the problematic role of "community" in contemporary democratic theory and practice.

II. Uses and Limits of the Constitutional Right of Privacy

In this section I consider the development of a constitutional right of privacy insofar as it bears on the question of lesbian and gay rights. A full blown conception of lesbian/gay rights requires that we go beyond a right of privacy narrowly construed as a negative "right to be left alone." Such a limited conception of privacy rights at best grounds arguments against the criminalization of private consensual homosexual acts between adults; it has little bearing on the regulation of discrimination or on the recognition of lesbian and gay partnerships and institutions. Nonetheless, the recognition of a positive constitutional right of privacy with its implication of the equal enjoyment of such rights by all citizens is a necessary component in a full blown articulation of lesbian and gay rights. An account of liberty as personal autonomy inextricably linked to freedom of association explicates the right of privacy as encompassing basic principles concerning limited government, political neutrality, and democratic pluralism, and locates it within the context of political theory and constitutional morality. Unfortunately — although not decisive in philosophical terms — the constitutional right of privacy has become problematic in relation to the politics of the Supreme Court. Still, the jurisprudence developed in the privacy cases sheds important light on the relations between lesbian and gay rights and constitutional principles.

The great irony of the privacy jurisprudence is that it receives its most articulate and theoretically substantial formulation in Justice Harry Blackmun's *dissenting* opinion in *Bowers v. Hardwick*.[12] In that case, the Court refused to invalidate Georgia's consensual sodomy laws as a violation of constitutionally based privacy rights (at least insofar as the law applied to homosexuals). The constitutional right of privacy was first formulated in *Griswold v. Connecticut*, in which the Court invalidated a state ban on the possession and use of contraceptive devices and substances.[13] Although the result was supported by a majority of seven-to-two, the Justices offered quite diverse statements of the Connecticut decision's rationale. As a result, the constitutional right of privacy has been the subject of a vigorous and heated academic and political debate, most dramatically in the televised public hearings on President Ronald Reagan's nomination of Judge Robert Bork to the Supreme Court. There is little doubt that the U. S. Senate's eventual rejection of the Bork nomination was influenced importantly by the nominee's insistence that rights of privacy many citizens take for granted are the result of an illegitimate and indefensible extension of judicial power. Notwithstanding the criticisms of Bork and others, especially in the legal academy, the right of privacy has been applied since 1965 to invalidate state laws aimed at regulating a variety of activities: the enjoyment of "obscene" materials in the home, in *Stanley v. Georgia*;[14] the availability of contraception to unmarried adults in *Eisenstadt v. Baird*[15] and to minors; and, of course, the right of a woman to terminate her pregnancy by abortion in *Roe v. Wade*.[16]

The *Griswold* line of cases has been vehemently criticized as an instance of unprincipled judicial legislation with no support in the text or history of the Constitution. Full consideration of these arguments goes to the heart of contemporary constitutional theory and is beyond the scope of this book. However, it is important to recognize this background in evaluating the Court's decision of *Bowers v. Hardwick*. Simply stated, to see the Court's retreat here as an instance of homophobia may be the *optimistic* view of the matter: one cannot rule out the possibility that the right of privacy as such no longer commands the support of a majority of Justices of the Supreme Court. If so, the implications extend quite beyond lesbian and gay rights — the Court's recent vacillations on a woman's right to abortion are further evidence in this regard. Political preferences aside, what is to be said on behalf of the constitutional right of privacy? What place does it play in a sound scheme of constitutional rights? What are its possibilities and limitations as a basis for lesbian and gay rights?

In his classic dissenting opinion in *Olmstead v. United States*, Justice Louis D. Brandeis identified the right of privacy as "the most comprehensive of rights and the right most valued by civilized men"; he defined it as "the right to be left alone."[17] We must distinguish between privacy rights as defined by common law or by particular state or federal legislation and a right of privacy guaranteed by the United States Constitution. The latter, as formulated in *Griswold*, comes into play when a litigant seeks to have federal courts invalidate state legislation as an infringement of the Due Process Clause of the Fourteenth Amendment. It is noteworthy that in his concurring opinion in *Griswold*, the great conservative jurist John M. Harlan found the issue relatively unproblematic: the Connecticut law is invalid because it constitutes state interference in marital relations that have been insulated against government intervention by generations of history and tradition. Harlan found that the freedom of married couples to decide whether or not to have children is "implicit in the concept of ordered liberty," citing Justice Benjamin Cardozo. The decision was not so easy to justify for Justice William O. Douglas and his allies on the Court who had effectively extended the reach of the Due Process Clause by insisting that the Fourteenth Amendment incorporated and applied to the states the specific provisions of the Bill of Rights. The "incorporation" doctrine was intended to protect individual rights at the same time that it limited the discretion of the Supreme Court by emphasizing that these rights are grounded in a literal reading of the text of the Constitution. This *liberal* literalism was developed as a corrective to the expansive and indeterminate reading of the Fourteenth Amendment by which an earlier, conservative Court had employed doctrines of "substantive due process" to invalidate New Deal legislation. Justice Hugo Black, a leading proponent of the incorporationist view and a great defender of individual rights, actually dissents in *Griswold* on the ground that he can find no textual basis for a constitutional right of privacy.

The political context of contemporary controversies over "strict construction" and "original intent" has served to obscure the fact that an earlier generation of constitutional fundamentalists like Black urged a literal reading of the constitution to limit state action and expand the range of protected individual rights. Rejecting doctrines of "substantive due process" in favor of a thoroughgoing textualism, Justice Black is unable to find support for a constitutional right of privacy in the specific language of the Bill of Rights. For Douglas, who wrote the opinion of the Court in *Griswold*, the task is to identify the general principles or values underlying the specific provisions of the Bill of Rights and to recognize their force as elements of due process of law. His argument proceeds on two complementary fronts: Douglas's more general strategy is to establish that rights unenumerated in the Constitution have been recognized historically and enforced as necessary for the protection of specific rights which *are* enumerated in the Constitution; more particularly, he identifies privacy as the value protected by specific enumerated rights. Douglas especially emphasizes the linkage between privacy rights and First Amendment freedoms of association. He also identifies zones of privacy generated by the Third Amendment prohibition of the quartering soldiers in people's homes during peacetime without the consent of the owners, the Fourth Amendment prohibition of "unreasonable searches and seizures," the Fifth Amendment's protection against compulsory self-incrimination, and the Ninth Amendment. Justice Arthur Goldberg, in his concurring opinion, places particular emphasis on the Ninth Amendment, which states that the enumeration of "certain rights" in the Constitution should not be construed as to "disparage other rights which are retained by the People." The language of the Ninth Amendment stands as a continuing rebuke to those who would limit constitutional rights to those literally specified in the *other* provisions of the Bill of Rights.

In retrospect, the force of Justice Douglas's arguments was somewhat obscured by the language of his opinion which located the right of privacy in "penumbras and emanations" of the Bill of Rights. These are neither terms of art, nor especially artful terms. A generation of law professors has written its way to tenure by making fun of Douglas's rhetoric in *Griswold*. But it is not so easy to dismiss the underlying analysis which identifies personal privacy as the fundamental value underlying the prohibition of unreasonable searches and seizures, the protection against compulsory self-incrimination, the guarantee of free exercise of religion, and the proscription of quartering soldiers in people's homes. At issue is the theory of limited government that informs the constitutional framework. For the framers, this theory was critically linked to the conception of natural rights, possessed by *persons* as such, independent of any positive legal or constitutional enactments. As Senator Joseph Biden — then chairman of the Senate Judiciary Committee — insisted in his exchanges with Bork at the confirmation hearings, rights are something one is born with; they are not given to us by the government. Although such theories have been out of fashion for over a century, especially among academics, they played an important role in the philosophical defense of the American Revolution and were institutionalized in the Bills of Rights enacted as parts of the constitutions of the newly independent states and, eventually, of the United States.[18]

The Ninth Amendment emphasizes that the enumeration of specific rights to be protected against infringement by the new governments was understood as a *recognition* and *specification* rather than a positive creation of individual rights. Thus, the constitutional right of privacy appears as the belated formulation of a conception of the relation between individuals and their government that is central to the political philosophy of the Constitution. Indeed, the Federalists had initially opposed the adoption of an enumerated Bill of Rights in the Constitution as unnecessary and potentially misleading. They feared that later generations might come to view such a list as exhaustive of constitutionally protected individual rights. Alexander Hamilton insisted that the Constitution created and defined the *powers* of a limited government whereas persons naturally possessed *rights* prior to the institution of government.[19] When the Bill of Rights was adopted in the first Congress, the Ninth Amendment was adopted as a prophylaxis against the diminution of personal rights by "strict construction" of its language.

In his dissent in *Bowers v. Hardwick*, Justice Blackmun summarizes the privacy jurisprudence in terms of the protection of "zones of privacy" pertaining to both the physical spaces persons occupy and the decisions they are entitled to make in the conduct of life. Privacy rights protect both places and personal choices from arbitrary interference by political authorities. The recognition of such zones of privacy does not constitute total insulation against all public regulation; rather, the identification of fundamental rights of privacy requires that attempts by the government to intervene in private spaces and decisions be subject to critical scrutiny by courts enforcing constitutional standards. Such scrutiny seeks to strike a balance between individual rights and legitimate public objectives by considering the importance of the government's aim, the intrusiveness of the proposed means, and the availability of less restrictive alternatives. Once fundamental rights have been identified, courts have labored over generations to develop reasonable standards for striking the requisite balance. This interpretive process is inherently contestatory and subject to political and intellectual challenge, but it is just the sort of task entrusted to judges within a constitutional democracy.

The contested question in *Bowers v. Hardwick* is whether the constitutional right of privacy encompasses consensual homosexual acts between adults. The scope of privacy rights, like the reach of the Due Process Clause generally, is defined through interpretive arguments that identify and analyze competing private and public claims in regard to the values, history, and practices of the United States polity. As Cass Sunstein has stressed, adjudication under the Due Process Clause tends to be conservative in the sense of respecting history and tradition as the locus of cherished values and recognized constraints on government, whereas litigation under the Equal Protection Clause has been critical and forward looking in its application of constitutional aspirations to equality.[20] The difficulty always is to articulate persuasively the general principles that are embodied in such history, practice, and hope. The differences between Justice Byron White, who wrote the opinion of the court, and Justice Blackmun, who dissented, may be seen in the way each formulates the right at issue in the case. For White, by contesting the constitutionality of the Georgia law, Michael Hardwick asserted a constitutional right of "homosexuals to engage in sodomy." It is hardly surprising that he failed to find textual support in the Constitution for a right defined in such terms. For Blackmun, the issue involved the right of all persons to pursue happiness through freely chosen intimate associations with others.[21] In this view, such a formulation states a moral and legal principle of constitutional magnitude, integral to the framework protecting individual rights. Further, he interprets the Court's previous privacy decisions as articulating a principle of freedom of intimate association. The fundamental right of intimate association, which is infringed by the criminalization of consensual sexual conduct between adults, requires courts carefully to examine the objectives of the state in enacting such a law. Blackmun concludes that the public interests alleged by the State of Georgia could not outweigh the personal rights at issue. His analysis shifts the focus from defining the scope of an individual right of privacy to articulating the grounds and limits of public enforcement of morality in a society committed to individual liberty and moral pluralism. That question, critical for any theory of lesbian and gay rights, is the subject to which we now turn.

Let me summarize the discussion of the constitutional right of privacy so far. I am persuaded that the constitutional right of privacy enunciated in *Griswold* and its progeny has a legitimate and important place in constitutional adjudication. As Justice Blackmun argues, it is implicated in fundamental autonomy rights and freedom of association. Equal application of the relevant principles would have required the Supreme Court to invalidate Georgia's consensual sodomy law in *Bowers v. Hardwick*. At the very least, that decision is an unjustifiable retreat from the principles of the privacy cases. Such retreat may signal the willingness of a majority on the Court to abandon the constitutional right of privacy altogether. If so, it has moral and political implications not only for lesbian and gay rights, but also for sexual and reproductive freedom more generally. At the same time, it is not at all clear that a securely established constitutional right of privacy would be sufficient to encompass the full range of lesbian and gay rights discussed in Section I. In the remainder of this essay, I am concerned to explore more fully the range of ethical and political, as well as legal, principles at work in the movement for lesbian and gay rights. Further probing of the constitutional right of privacy will shed light on related aspects of our constitutional morality less vulnerable than privacy rights to shifts in academic, political, and judicial fashion. In particular, I want to show how Justice Blackmun's analysis of the right of privacy as freedom of intimate association may be developed in relation to concepts of personal autonomy, moral pluralism, and public justification deemed fundamental to our political culture.

III. The Individual Liberty/Community Morality Debate[22]

Although lesbian and gay rights are not adequately defined by opposition to the criminalization of homosexual acts between adults, the legal proscription of most lesbian and gay sexual activity is a central feature of the ethical and political situation. What distinguishes queer citizens from the members of other minority groups that have asserted their civil rights in recent decades is that lesbians and gays alone have been told that their freedom must be limited to accord with the moral standards of the community. Indeed, Justice White not only refuses to recognize the rights claimed in *Bowers v. Hardwick*, but characterizes their assertion as "facetious." Here we confront a stumbling block to the movement for lesbian and gay rights that sometimes threatens to overwhelm all other issues. Lesbians and gay men are seen as asserting individual liberties that directly conflict with the right of the community to use the criminal law to define standards of morality. In his dissent, Justice Blackmun carefully examines and rejects the claim that Georgia may prohibit private consensual sodomy between adults as part of its effort to maintain "a decent society," that is, to enforce alleged standards of community sexual morality as such. Here, constitutional analysis intersects with the debate within academic philosophy and jurisprudence concerning "law, liberty, and morality." Indeed, Justice Blackmun cites Professor H. L. A. Hart of Oxford in support of his position.

Any contemporary discussion of lesbian and gay rights must include some mention of the Hart/Devlin controversy. The debate was occasioned by the recommendations of the Wolfenden Commission in Great Britain in 1957, which included the liberalization of laws governing prostitution and the decriminalization of private, consensual homosexual acts between adults. The report specifically relies on John Stuart Mill's formulation in *On Liberty* of the proper limits of the state's authority over the individual. Mill limits the jurisdiction of the state to regulating those acts that cause or threaten harm to specific interests of concrete individuals. He rejects any authority of the state over individual or consensual activities in which no one is hurt or threatened by harm, even when the community regards such activities as immoral. In a public lecture subsequently published as *The Enforcement of Morals,* the British jurist Sir Patrick Devlin challenged both the commission's recommendations and its reliance on Mill's principle.

Devlin calls into question Mill's distinction between self-regarding and other-regarding acts as well as his limitation of legitimate state concern to those other-regarding acts that cause or threaten to cause harm to distinct individuals. He urges that the state has a right, indeed a duty, to maintain the moral fabric of society through the use of criminal sanctions, even against private consensual conduct. Notoriously, he claims that there is no more a right to private immorality than a right to commit private treason. Devlin argues that a society cannot survive without a shared morality and that the enforcement of moral standards through the criminal law is necessary social self-defense. Hence, he proposes a defense of legal moralism in utilitarian rather than moral terms. He does not appeal to the rightness of community standards, but rather to the alleged necessity of an enforced moral consensus to maintain social solidarity. In fact, the test that Devlin offers for identifying the moral principles the state is justified in enforcing is to consult the feelings of the ordinary citizen, "the man [!] on the Clapham omnibus." Devlin proposes that the intensity of such feelings of "indignation, offense, and disgust" is a proper measure of their importance in maintaining the moral fabric of the community. Although he is anything but psychoanalytic in his arguments, Devlin shares Sigmund Freud's insight that feelings of disgust in sexual matters are an important support of community morality. (See Chapter Four for an extended treatment of Freud's views.)

Devlin's argument evoked a considerable response, most notably from H. L. A. Hart in his article "Immorality and Treason," and subsequently in the lectures published as *Law, Liberty, and Morality.* Hart defends Mill's position, raising critical objections to Devlin in the process. This is not the place to rehearse the ensuing debate in detail. However, several comments are appropriate to this context. Hart insists that the moral status of criminal laws cannot be identified simply with the extent to which the conduct proscribed is felt by majority sentiment to be immoral. Rather, he emphasizes the need to subject both the private behavior in question and its proscription to examination in terms of principles of critical morality. He insists that morality as a practice includes not only the evaluation of actions or courses of conduct, but also of the standards by which such particulars are to be judged. The specific instrument of critical morality he deploys is Mill's harm principle and the more general utilitarian ethic to which it is linked. Hart is particularly acute in calling attention to the suffering caused by the application of criminal penalties, not only to those actually punished, but to their families and friends as well as to the much larger population of those who are threatened with such punishment. His analysis is invaluable in shifting the terms for an ethical evaluation of state regulation of individual sexual conduct. The criminalization of harmless consensual sexual activity between adults should not be conceived as striking a balance between symmetrical interests in individual liberty and community morality. The question must be recast to focus on the morality of using the coercive apparatus of the state to enforce homogeneity of sexual conduct on those who neither cause nor threaten harm to others. Hart locates the moral issue as much in assessing the legitimacy of the state's use and threat of harm to enforce conventional norms as in assessing the individual conduct to be prohibited. The important philosophical and political issue turns on the articulation of general standards of critical morality governing the use of force and threats of force to coerce nonconforming individuals. (These questions are the subject of Sections IV and V below.)

The issues that emerge in the Hart/Devlin controversy help to further focus this inquiry into the broader context of lesbian and gay rights. Although Devlin's account of morality seems to me fatally flawed (as Ronald Dworkin and others have argued in detail) he emphasizes a crucial general point: the law exists as an expression and implementation of the moral standards of a community.[23] Hart is correct in insisting on the need for critical moral standards which may be deployed in the evaluation of social norms and their enforcement. However, such standards of critical morality are themselves defined within the historical context of the moral practices of specific communities. One requires a more complex model of social morality that acknowledges majoritarian beliefs and attitudes but emphasizes practices of criticism and public justification within the actual institutions and historical aspirations of modern democratic regimes.[24] The political and institutional character of such practices is particularly evident when one considers the foundations and limits on the state's coercive regulation of individual conduct.[25]

Devlin's argument deploys an odd combination of emotivism and utilitarianism to justify the use of force to maintain the community's moral beliefs. He acknowledges that popular morality is rooted in intense feelings of offense and disgust rather than in considered judgment; he defends the enforcement of such attitudes on those who do not share them by appealing to a right of social self-defense. However, he does not interrogate such powerful sites of irrationality, nor does he offer any standard by which to evaluate the role of these feelings in maintaining social cohesion. In the end, he offers only the intensity of feelings as a measure of their importance.

Freud's analysis suggests that the very intensity of such feelings of disgust in sexual matters is linked to the degree to which they may be attractive and threatening to precariously achieved sexual identities. Indeed, he argues that clinical paranoia may result from the suppression of strongly felt homosexual desires. If so, the use of the state apparatus to enforce such feelings may actively contribute to the amount of hatred and violence circulating within a society. Hart insists that not all societies have a moral right to exist and to defend themselves. If the persecution of minorities who pose a "threat" to public consensus is the cost of social survival, specific regimes may forfeit any claim to moral respect. Nazi Germany, which achieved a high measure of social integration and solidarity through the systematic oppression of Jews and other groups offensive to the majority, provides a salient example. (The analogy between anti-Semitism and homophobia will be pursued further in Chapter Five.)

Hart powerfully identifies the inadequacies of Devlin's view, but his own use of the harm principle is associated with a utilitarian ethic that does not translate easily into the rights-based framework of American liberal democracy. Within the context of American institutions, including a written constitution and a Supreme Court charged with its enforcement through judicial review, critical morality is often conceptualized in quasi-legal terms. Actually, Americans are deeply ambivalent about the moral status of law, combining skepticism about government and its acts generally with something akin to reverence for the Constitution and the Supreme Court. This ambivalence is easily seen in popular attitudes toward lawyers. On the one hand, they are fast-talking shysters who make a living by putting one over on unsuspecting lay people. On the other, the most prestigious public office in the land turns out to be that of the Chief Justice of the Supreme Court, traditionally a lawyer. Alexis de Tocqueville observed quite early the central role of law and lawyers in the American democracy. Something more important is at stake here than a popular confusion between law and morality, which a healthy dose of legal positivism would remedy. Rather, the ethos of the American democracy, its politics, history, and culture, includes a "constitutional morality" that functions critically within our moral discourse and is institutionalized in the federal judiciary, especially the Supreme Court.[26] Citizens of the United States are jealous of their individual rights and of their freedom to create communities through voluntary association with like-minded others. Grounded in historical practices of limited government and moral pluralism, these specific traditions of the United States aspire to realize *universal* ideals of liberty, equality, and community.

IV. Constitutional Morality

Let us return to Justice Blackmun's dissent in *Bowers v. Hardwick*, using his legal analysis to illuminate broader ethical and political principles implicated in the question of lesbian and gay rights. Blackmun's explication of privacy rights and freedom of intimate association exhibits central features of a constitutional morality that encompasses and grounds the narrower legal argument. "Constitutional morality" here refers to the standards of critical moral reflection embodied in the history and political traditions of democracy in the United States and reflecting widely shared social aspirations toward the realization of individual liberty and civic equality. As with other democratic norms, the meaning of these terms is inherently contested and determined through political interaction at a variety of levels. The right of privacy gains plausibility as a constitutional principle because of its coherence with the theories of natural rights and limited government that inform the structure of the United States Constitution. Its reach and character is open to specification through processes of adjudication, legislation, and executive action against a background of public opinion and political debate. In his dissent,

Blackmun insists that such principles invalidate Georgia's prohibition of consensual sodomy between adults.

Blackmun's rejection of the state's rationale for the necessity of such a law to maintain "a decent society" deploys principles that explicate and clarify the reach of constitutional rights of privacy. Importantly, he invokes the First Amendment with its prohibition of the establishment of religion by the state and its guarantee of the free exercise of religion by the citizens. Although Georgia's sodomy statute was religiously "neutral," and Hardwick did not raise a conscientious defense of his sexual orientation and activity, Blackmun uses the principles underlying the First Amendment to reject the moral justification of the sodomy laws that plays such a large part in the opinions of the majority. Blackmun does not reject the validity of a moral justification of the criminal law as such, but rather emphasizes the inadequacy of the majoritarian conception of morality supporting the sodomy law. The moralistic defense fails for Blackmun because morality cannot be simply identified with the sentiments of a majority; neither the intensity nor the longevity of such sentiments immunize them from constitutional scrutiny. The derivation of such moral sentiments from a consensus of Jewish and Christian traditions actually renders them suspect under the First Amendment prohibition of the establishment of religion. However, Blackmun is not simply applying a positive constitutional prohibition, but rather articulating and applying a critical principle of public morality in democratic society.

Like other specific provisions of the Bill of Rights, the First Amendment requires interpretation in historical and philosophical terms in order to yield moral and political principles. The establishment clause must be construed in terms of the sectarian controversies of the seventeenth and eighteenth centuries, as well as the oppression of dissenting minorities by the established churches and emergent states of Europe. Ironically, the identification of religious orthodoxy with established state power was reinforced in the seventeenth century as an "erastian" solution to the problem of sectarian conflict and warfare: peace would be ensured by empowering the sovereign political authority with the last word on potentially explosive differences of religious belief.[27] By the late eighteenth century, liberal sentiment recognized the desirability of tolerance of diverse religious beliefs within the context of a securely established political order. This shift was made possible in part by the emergence of stable political structures and by a defusing of the politically subversive implications of sectarian difference. Thus, the rejection of an established religion by the Founding Fathers acknowledged the legitimacy of both an autonomous secular order of politics and a plurality of religious creeds and institutions.

The Free Exercise Clause underlines the conjunction of a secular politics with religious pluralism. Critically, the plurality of religious institutions is to be guaranteed by protecting the authority of individual decision-making in this domain. Moreover, the free exercise of religion requires rather more than an individual "right to be left alone." Religious practices require the existence of historical communities with their shared rituals and doctrines if religion is not to be reduced to a matter of mere private opinion. Freedom in religious matters has to do with observance and activity in concert with like-minded others as well as with private belief.[28]

The juxtaposition of the Free Exercise and Establishment Clauses on religion with the explicitly political activities protected in the First Amendment becomes philosophically salient when one focuses on the specifically public and associative dimensions of religious liberty. The existence of a theoretical framework for reconciling the claims of a plurality of ethical and doctrinal communities interacting within a broader polity does not by itself guarantee the achievement of a just society. As with all guarantees of abstract right, the realization of individual and communal freedom depends on contingent historical forces at work in particular societies. Marx's "On the Jewish Question" powerfully demonstrates the extent to which some formulations of religious liberty in terms of privately held personal rights actually work to promote a social homogeneity that undercuts the plurality of forms of religious expression. (In Chapter Five, I pursue the analogy between freedom of intimate association and religious freedom through Hannah Arendt's analysis of the interplay between legal principle and social reality in the dynamics of Jewish emancipation in nineteenth-century Europe.)

By insisting on the relevance of the First Amendment to the privacy issue, Blackmun develops both critical and positive aspects of constitutional morality as it may be applied more generally to contested moral issues. This argument has special relevance not only for lesbian and gay rights but also for a range of issues including women's reproductive rights and freedom of artistic and erotic expression. His analysis links up fundamental conceptions of political neutrality, moral community, and individual autonomy within a constitutional framework.

• First, religious teaching alone cannot be used to justify state action: the moral principles underlying the criminal law require justification in secular terms acceptable to a community of diverse religious and moral beliefs and varieties of *unbelief* as well.

• Second, a constitutional morality must recognize the priority of individual liberty in moral matters. Recognition of the right of individuals freely to determine their conduct is itself an element of the ethics that sustain democratic politics. Restrictions on such individual autonomy cannot be justified in majoritarian terms, but rather in terms of the need to guarantee for all the right to make such choices. The secular framework within which competing moral claims and practices must be adjudicated is conjoined with a commitment to the equality and reciprocity of persons with regard to their rights.

• Third, the rights to which each person is entitled under the dictates of constitutional morality pertain not only to her opinions and beliefs but also to her activities. Constitutional rights are not restricted to individual conscience but protect actions, often undertaken in concert with others, and the institutions to which they give rise.

Once again, Tocqueville early identified the centrality of voluntary associations in the ethos of American democracy. Justice Blackmun's analysis of the constitutional right of privacy in terms of moral and religious pluralism shows the need for reaching beyond a "right to be left alone" towards recognition of freedom of association for lesbian and gay citizens in creating and maintaining satisfying ways of life.

V. Individual Liberty, Moral Pluralism, and Principles of Justice

Blackmun's dissent in *Bowers v. Hardwick* explicates the terms of a constitutional morality that informs legal reasoning and decision-making but which is also embodied in the "unwritten constitution" of moral discourse and political practice. In terms of lesbian and gay rights, Blackmun articulates a framework that may be applicable to claims for state protection against discrimination and for public recognition of lesbian and gay relationships and institutions as well as to decriminalization of same-sex sexual conduct. In this section, I outline such an analysis in more general philosophical terms. The discovery of natural rights theories at the core of the privacy jurisprudence is not simply a matter of historical contingency. The principle that underlies the right of privacy is the affirmation of the centrality of uncoerced individual decision-making in important areas of human activity. In Kantian terms, morality requires recognition of the autonomy of the person and of her sovereignty in defining and pursuing the goods of life. Such recognition entails the right to participate in a society where each is free to join with others in creating institutions to support and sustain their efforts. Individual liberty cannot be limited to private matters but carries over to public rights of voluntary association integral to democratic citizenship. The egalitarian political implications of moral autonomy are inherent in the social contract tradition that provides a common context for Kantian ethics and the political practice of the framers of the U. S. Constitution.

The conceptual links among natural rights, social contract, and Kantian moral philosophies have been most fully articulated in the work of John Rawls, especially *A Theory of Justice* and "Kantian Constructivism in Moral Theory."[29] Rawls has also explicated the egalitarianism implied by such theories: autonomy is a characteristic of persons as such, and modern constitutional democracies are legitimated by the extent to which persons are recognized as equal in their rights. Finally, Rawls's theory emphasizes the centrality of moral pluralism among the circumstances of justice — of diverse conceptions of a good life embodied in the practices of distinct associations within society, understood as a basic structure of fair cooperation among individuals and groups. In his recent work *Political Liberalism*, Rawls emphasizes the extent to which his theory of justice is an explication of the normative assumptions of the political culture of modern democracy rather than a rational deduction of principles of justice *sub specie aeternitatis*.[30] He further argues that the conceptions of moral personality, the right, and the good that are deployed within the theory, themselves function as principles of public reason within constitutional democracy rather than as comprehensive philosophical doctrines. In the following discussion, I show how a Rawlsian analysis supplements and confirms the treatment of lesbian and gay rights developed thus far.

Rawls does not explicitly address the issue of lesbian and gay rights, nor of sexual freedom generally, except for some rather cryptic remarks in the course of an argument against perfectionism in *A Theory of Justice*.[31] However, it is not difficult to construct a Rawlsian approach to the question. The central conception must be the priority of the right over the good. Rawls takes a plurality of conceptions of the good as one of the "circumstances of justice" in the modern world. The basic structure of society as a system of cooperation among free and equal persons cannot be grounded on a unitary or comprehensive conception of the good life. Rather, the theory of justice attempts to identify those principles by which rational agents would agree to be governed regardless of the conception of the good they may hold. The "original position" is the representational device by which Rawls attempts to delineate such principles. The conception of the person employed here is meant to embody the minimal requirements of moral personality, i.e., freedom, equality, and rationality. To make plausible the original position as a situation in which rational choice is possible, Rawls introduces the notion of primary social goods that function as a kind of all-purpose means making them desirable across differing conceptions of a comprehensive good. In his later writings, Rawls appears to modify his interpretation of primary goods by developing the notion of an overlapping consensus by which a diversity of associations animated by distinct ways of life may nevertheless agree as to the desirability of some goods, such as income, food, and medical care. These important conceptions in Rawls raise many technical difficulties. Critical here is that he insists on the necessity of establishing a basic structure of social cooperation that encompasses a plurality of conceptions of the good and consequent ways of life devoted to their realization through concerted activity. The aspiration of a theory of justice is to articulate general principles of right to govern the interactions of diverse moral communities within an encompassing social framework. The constraints that bind all the members of such a "society of societies" must be justified by public argumentation that appeals across comprehensive conceptions of the good.

Rawls insists that his moral pluralism is not simply a modus vivendi to maintain peace among conflicting political and ethical communities. Rather, it is a moral requirement implicit in respect for individual autonomy. The links between political liberalism and moral pluralism are not always clearly spelled out in Rawls's work. However, there is some convergence here between Rawls's version of liberalism and the rather different approaches to ethical pluralism in the work of Isaiah Berlin and Bernard Williams. Rawls's analysis turns on the requirements of maintaining a basic structure of cooperation among free and equal moral persons. The rights of citizenship implicated in a theory of justice are derived by unpacking the conception of moral personality. For Rawls, this conception consists in: 1) a capacity for developing, pursuing, and revising a conception of the good; and 2) a capacity for recognizing the constraints of justice that must be observed if we are to cooperate with others. The earlier and best known sections of *A Theory of Justice* are devoted to showing the adequacy of Rawls's two principles of justice as a description of the most general features of such a structure of cooperation among free and equal moral persons. Thus, the neutrality of principles of justice regarding the good is a political requirement of the concept of a person as an autonomous individual capable of forming, enacting, and revising her own conception of the good in a context of social cooperation.

Although the rational agents in Rawls's original position are ignorant of their moral and social particularities — e.g., religious beliefs, gender, social class, sexual orientation — they are endowed with some general, "non-controversial truths" concerning human nature and a "thin" conception of the good, derived either from a theory of primary goods or from the political fact of overlapping consensus. Thus, although principles of justice cannot be tailored to a particular mode of sexual preference or personal morality, we know that persons will have some sexual desires and emotional needs for intimate association with others, however diverse the details might be. We know also that such desires and needs will play an important part in an individual's formulation and pursuit of a conception of the good life. (Rawls is rather vague about what the general knowledge that may be deployed in the original position includes; in Chapters Three and Four, I will use Plato and Freud to argue for the role of desire in self-making and the variety of its manifestations.) Critics from diverse perspectives have questioned the adequacy of the "thin" conception of the self Rawls deploys in his arguments. They have emphasized its character as disembodied and stripped of all defining commitments and social relations.

Abstraction, however, is the point. By constructing the self as a node of choice and using the representational device of the original position to situate it progressively in social and political contexts, Rawls focuses attention on the link between individual freedom and the need for a plurality of goods and social forms in spelling out and actualizing one's aspirations to a full life. In later chapters, I work to maintain some tension between a generalizing conception of human needs and a historically specific investigation of the politics and psychodynamics of self-formation in articulating the implications of democratic citizenship for sexual minorities.

In Rawlsian terms, the question for a theory of justice becomes whether any constraints on the fulfillment of personal sexual and associative desires would be accepted in advance by rational agents unaware of the particular configurations of desires that will animate their lives. In sexual matters as in most others, the thought experiment of imagining choice in the original position works to dramatize the requirements of mutuality among free and equal persons differently situated socially and adhering to disparate conceptions of the good life. Regarding acceptable limitations on the freedom of individuals to pursue sexual satisfaction through relations with others, it appears likely that something very like Mill's harm principle would be chosen by rational agents in the original position. Respect for the autonomy of moral persons and recognition of the range and depth of psychosexual differences requires permitting individuals to work out their erotic and emotional needs and identities in ongoing voluntary interaction with others constrained only by the insistence on mutuality and the prohibition of harm. The coercive use of public authority is justified only to protect persons against force or fraud.[32]

Justice-as-fairness has fuller implications for lesbian and gay rights than the ratification of arguments for decriminalization. The central concern for the equal treatment of persons within a framework of justice also supports the prohibition of discrimination based on sexual orientation. Again, the device of the original position demonstrates the implications of reciprocity. Uncertain whether one is in fact and from time-to-time destined to be either a bigot or a victim of prejudice, rational agents with a concern to promote their own life prospects, whoever they turn out to be, would rule out the denial of primary goods to anyone based solely on the disapproval of others. Modern social organization locates such goods within complex institutional settings: the acquisition of skills, knowledge, income, food, housing, medical care, requires access to education, jobs, housing, and other sites of opportunity. Decisions by functionaries in such settings cannot be assimilated to the exercise of free choice by individuals shaping their own lives, but are social decisions subject to constraints of fundamental fairness. Rational agents in the original position unaware of their social positioning would reject any notion that access to the goods embodied in employment, education and other institutions may be limited on the basis of social characteristics irrelevant to performance of the tasks at hand. Discrimination based on sexual orientation — like that based on sex, religion, race, disability, national origin — violates principles of fair equality of opportunity.

To take the analysis one step further, Rawls's analysis of primary goods buttresses the emphasis here on the centrality of respect and recognition of the relationships and institutions through which lesbians and gays in fact pursue their life plans. For Rawls, a unifying theme, linking goods to each other in the rational life plan of a morally autonomous person, is the primary good of self-respect, or, as he sometimes clarifies, the social bases of self-respect. The denial of legitimacy to an individual's affectional and sexual preferences pursued through consensual interaction radically undermines the self-respect of those affected. Rawls is clear that in actual societies, as opposed to the original position, persons require associations with others in order to pursue the good, to formulate, realize, and revise rational plans of life. Thus respect for the full autonomy of individual citizens entails social recognition of the associations, intimate and otherwise, through which they express their moral personality. The insistence on justifying state intervention in personal life through appeals to public reason functions to assure a political framework for the cooperation of disparate associations and to limit constraints on all the citizens to those that may be justified from the perspective of each. Moral pluralism and public justification are required by respect for individual autonomy. The use of coercive political authority to enforce a particular morality on society at large violates individual autonomy and fundamental principles of justice.

VI. Sexual Identity, Mental Health, and Moral Autonomy

The emergence of a social and political movement for equality among lesbian, gay, and other queer citizens raises important questions about the ways in which sexual identities intersect with the status of citizenship in modern democracies. We cannot avoid the question of how one's sexuality contributes to shaping a sense of individuality and of the goods to be pursued in the course of life. In applying the principle of democratic equality to lesbian and gay rights, I have urged that the desire for erotic expression and the ability freely to form intimate associations with others are frequently integral components of a full and meaningful life. This argument is vulnerable to the objection that some choices may be not only violations of conventional morality, but also destructive of the well-being of the person making them. Some argue that people should not be permitted to make choices deleterious to their own best interests. In its starkest terms, the view is that homosexuality is a form of mental illness and that same-sex desire itself, far from being an expression of autonomous choice, is a pathological symptom from which its sufferers must be protected.[33] Less dramatically, some see homosexuality as a developmental deficit that cuts off lesbians and gay men from the full maturity of genital heterosexuality in the context of monogamy and the nuclear family. Others claim that it is somehow impossible for homosexuals in our society to be happy, whether as a result of their own condition or of social prejudice. In any event, the culture is infused with attitudes that support the active discouragement if not the complete prohibition of lesbian and gay intimacies and identities. In personal terms, these feelings are captured in the complex and ambiguous responses that many otherwise liberal folks have to the prospects of their own children growing up gay. In terms of the Rawlsian argument from the original position, acceptance of these evaluations of the life prospects of homosexuals could lead one exercising rational choice behind a "veil of ignorance" as to one's own sexual orientation to support laws and policies designed to deter lesbian and gay forms of life.

As I have already argued, claims for the recognition of lesbian and gay relationships and community institutions directly challenge these objections to the legitimacy of lives that affirm same-sex desires and associations. J. S. Mill's argument in *On Liberty* rejects this kind of paternalism as strongly as it does moral conformism:

> . . . the only purpose for which power can be rightfully exercised over any member of a civilized community, against his will, is to prevent

harm to others. His own good, either physical or moral, is not a sufficient warrant. He cannot rightfully be compelled to do or forbear because it will make him happier, because, in the opinions of others, to do so would be wise or even right.[34]

This position derives from the same recognition of the centrality of individual moral autonomy as does Rawls's use of the original position to clarify the egalitarian implications of moral agency: "Over himself, over his own body and mind, the individual is sovereign."[35] At this point it should be clear why Rawls's sole mention of the legal regulation of homosexual activity occurs in the context of an argument against moral perfectionism, the view that the state is authorized to coerce its citizens into living in accordance with the requirements of a specific conception of the good life.[36] Although some readers may question the strict application of Mill's anti-paternalism in cases of suicide prevention or the involuntary treatment of self-destructive mental illnesses, it is hard to see how such reservations could be extended to the exercise of erotic choice. In those extreme cases, what is in question is the continued capacity of the individual to make any decisions at all, not the wisdom or prudence of a particular pattern of choices. Even if one acknowledges some need to restrain individuals from ending or irreversibly damaging their own agency, the freedom of individuals finally to determine what matters most to them and what sort of persons they will become is an irreducible component of moral autonomy.

Psychoanalytic theory and psychiatric practice may provide the most important contemporary locus for working through these issues; they have played an important ethical and political role in American culture, especially during the social transformations since World War II. At a time of increasing secularization, and within a constitutional context of religious pluralism, models of mental health have figured importantly as vehicles, sometimes as disguises, for ethical judgment and authority. Metaphysical embarrassment over the difficulty of sustaining claims to know the good, combined with political reservations about imposing sectarian religious moralities, has encouraged the extension of scientific and medical conceptions of health and illness to encompass a wide variety of behavioral and social matters. Not only sexual issues but also matters of substance abuse, addiction, efficiency at work, and the conduct of interpersonal relations are couched in terms of the language of mental health and illness. The use of therapeutic models of intervention to justify involuntary forms of treatment in civil settings and to reshape programs in criminal justice has been widespread and increasingly controversial. However, arguments against homosexuality grounded in notions of mental illness and health no longer command support from authorized experts in the fields of psychiatry and psychology; in 1973, the American Psychiatric Association, after protracted debate within the field and in response to challenges from lesbian and gay activists, struck homosexuality from the classification of mental disorders in the *Diagnostic and Statistical Manual*. The American Psychological

Association soon followed suit.[37] In the final analysis, the use of medical and psychological opinion about human behavior to support the coercive intervention of the state to overrule individual choice must be governed by same principles that apply to the enforcement of other ethical judgments. Whatever may be said about therapeutic approaches to sexuality when voluntarily undertaken, they cannot be used to justify overriding the wishes of a mature individual otherwise entitled to democratic liberty. This sort of medical paternalism collapses into moralism, albeit of a secular variety.[38]

In terms of the cultural influence of the discourse of mental health, it is worth noting that Sigmund Freud was at odds with his followers among psychiatrists in the United States over just this issue, seeing their insistence on the pathological status of homosexuality as a symptom of their moralizing and conformist tendencies.[39] Freud's own understanding of this question regarding the legal, medical, and ethical status of homosexuality set him against the normative judgments and normalizing practices of American psychiatry. His writing on the subject undercuts their claim to scientific and moral authority and offers reasons for a more positive evaluation of homosexuals' capacities and contributions to ethical life.[40] Equally important, his ongoing theoretical accounts of human sexuality provide grounds for a continuing critique of conventional social attitudes and a basis for constructing a positive defense of diverse sexualities. Psychoanalytic theory argues that all persons have deep needs for sexual expression and relation; that sexuality is a basic source of human motivation; and, that it is inherently multivalent and diverse, gaining its importance from complex connections with individual life histories, unconscious fantasies, and social convention. (The complex historical and theoretical issues presumed by this summary will be directly addressed in Chapters Two and Four.)

Perhaps surprisingly, given the abstraction necessary to articulate and adjudicate claims to constitutional equality and due process rights, the major opinions in *Bowers v. Hardwick* display conflicting analyses of the construction of sexual identity and the place of sexual conduct in personal life. (I shall return to this theme in greater detail in Chapter Seven. However, some comments are pertinent here.) For Blackmun, at issue in *Bowers v. Hardwick* is the right of individuals to pursue happiness and to shape personal identities through freely chosen intimate associations with others. He finds this moral and legal principle central to the scheme of constitutional protections of individual autonomy. By emphasizing the place of "intimate association" within a broader context of equal citizenship and moral pluralism, Blackmun incorporates substantive ethical concern for human flourishing into a liberal conception of personal rights. Although some have seen Blackmun as deploying an assimilationist strategy that eradicates homosexual difference and domesticates sexual desires, I read him as urging the expansion and enrichment of a generalized conception of human rights to include sexual desire and erotic expression within the context of an individual's life choices.[41] The result is to construct a thicker conception of constitutional liberty and of the range

34

of rights it entails. As a result, Blackmun translates "the alleged right to homosexual sodomy" from a decontextualized domain of possible sexual practices into the realm of emotional and interpersonal relationships. Although such scholars as Daniel Ortiz and Cheshire Calhoun see a "desexualization" of homosexual identity at work here, I discern recognition of an erotic component in all "intimate associations" and a sexual dimension to the identities to which they contribute.[42] Blackmun adumbrates a conception of legal personality in which individuals situated in diverse and overlapping social contexts become the locus for the construction of mutually interacting personal identities. "Freedom of intimate association" transcends the definition of privacy as a right of solitary individuals to be left alone and emphasizes the creation of intimate spaces within which persons can establish, maintain, revise, and transform both relationships and identities. Blackmun does not shy away from the conclusion that there may be many "right" ways to conduct one's sexual and emotional life.

On the other hand, Justice White in the opinion of the Court and Chief Justice Warren Burger in his concurring opinion construct homosexuals in terms of an invidious *difference*.[43] Despite the plain language of the Georgia statute that outlawed all sexual acts involving the sexual organs of one person and the mouth or anus of another, the Court considered the legitimacy of criminalizing "homosexual sodomy" only. Indeed, as Jonathan Goldberg emphasizes,[44] the Court sees homosexuals as so different that the same physical acts that are permissible when performed by heterosexuals may be criminalized when the actors are homosexual. A number of commentators have observed a certain slippage in the Court's reliance on history and tradition to buttress their deference to the Georgia law. (In Chapter Two, I will focus on the historical vicissitudes of legal, medical, and humanistic constructions of homosexual practice and identity.)[45] Not only did the Georgia law apply in its terms to all persons, not just homosexuals, but the historical condemnation of sodomy itself applied to a range of "unnatural acts" that shared a tendency to frustrate the procreative aspects of sexual intercourse. The definition of "homosexual sodomy" as a distinct and proper concern of legislative action reflects more recent medical and juridical discourses defining "homosexuals" as a distinct class of *persons* rather than the historical interest of state and church in restricting the sexual *acts* of all persons to marital settings in which procreation is a likely outcome.[46]

The historical prohibition of sodomy constructs human sexuality as directed toward procreation; it intersects with the alleged state interest in protecting and promoting marriage and the family unit that figures importantly in the privacy jurisprudence. The instability of such an appeal under contemporary circumstances is evidenced by the facts that the right of privacy was first articulated in overturning a state ban on contraception, and that its most far-reaching and controversial application has been in the abortion cases.[47] Constitutional rights of privacy have protected decisions by married and unmarried couples alike to use contraception and by all women to decide whether or not to terminate pregnancies through abortion. These cases have displayed an unstable tension between protecting individual autonomy in decision making and promoting the institutional integrity of marriage and the family unit.[48]

There is a related tension between disparate constructions of the *person* as bearer of fundamental rights: on the one hand, the autonomous decision maker with a fundamental right to determine the conditions of her life; on the other, a potential procreator charged with deploying her sexuality on behalf of the reproduction of the species. *Roe v. Wade* decisively resolves this tension in favor of individual decisional autonomy. Perhaps surprisingly, these tensions within the privacy jurisprudence mirror strains that Freud identifies as fundamental to modern civilization with its disparate demands for altruism from men and women in the regulation of their sexual desires and the maintenance of a reproductive imperative. (See Chapter Four for a detailed examination of the imbrication of different sexualities with a heterosexual matrix of sexual difference in psychoanalytic theory and social structure.) Seen in this light, the Supreme Court's decision in *Bowers v. Hardwick* is very much a rear-guard action, locking the barn after the horse has been stolen. The historical sexual moralities invoked by White and Burger construct sexuality in terms of an imperative of biological reproduction and a culture of familial integrity. When the Court subordinates the interests of families to the choices of individual women, the reproductive imperative itself is called into question.

What's left for traditional moralists is the struggle against an enemy whose very identity has been constructed in opposition to both families and reproduction, the "homosexual sodomite." This imputed identity is a hybrid produced from psychiatric discourses that define homosexuality as a perverted identity and religious moralities that condemn sodomy as a sinful act. (I will explore the conflicted genealogy of constructions of "modern homosexuality" in some detail in the Chapter Two.) The diverse opinions in *Hardwick* shows how deeply homosexual difference is implicated with judgments of disease and immorality, constructions of family relations and personal choice. Effectively, the Court consigns those of us marked by this difference to second-class citizenship by denying that the constitutional right of privacy applies to "homosexual sodomy."

VII. The Ambiguities of Community

It is easy to see the question of lesbian and gay rights as reflecting the contemporary controversy between deontological liberals with their fundamental commitments to individual autonomy and human rights and the communitarian critics of liberalism with their stress on social contexts and moral/religious traditions.[49] The matter is not nearly so simple. The analysis of lesbian and gay rights offered here insists on multivalent senses of community that encompass both majoritarian moralities and the voluntary associations of sexual and other nonconformists.

The simple dichotomy between individual liberty and community morality is inadequate to comprehend the complexity of these ethical and social relations. Even an exclusive focus on decriminalization requires explication of the *conflicting community values* at issue in the use of the coercive apparatus of the law to enforce majoritarian norms of sexual conduct on nonconforming adults. To seek state prohibition of discrimination against lesbians and gays is to appeal to professed community standards of fair treatment and equal citizenship, some of which are embodied in constitutional guarantees of constitutional rights. Ideals of respect for individual autonomy and insistence on the equal treatment of diverse groups are themselves incorporated in the moral discourse and social practice of modern democracy. Moreover, these ideals are articulated not only as abstract legal principles but also as norms of social interaction. The communitarian component of the movement for lesbian and gay rights becomes most clearly visible in the demand for recognition of lesbian and gay intimate associations and ethical institutions.

The conception of "community" figures here in at least three distinct ways. First, and most familiarly, "community" is identified with the dominant moral attitudes and related beliefs of historical and contemporary majorities. This is the sense represented by Devlin's "man on the Clapham omnibus" whose gut reactions are to be taken as indicators of the shared values Devlin deems necessary to the survival of society as such. We may label this sense of community as *conventional*. What defines it is the fact of agreement among a number of people. Defenders of conventional community emphasize the importance of traditions as providing individuals with values and beliefs that may orient and guide them in their activities and social relationships. These values and beliefs are transmitted by the institutions of socialization, such as childrearing, training, and education; they gain in force from the attachment of the members of the society to their fellows. The conventional communitarian is likely to emphasize the importance of feeling over intellect, tradition over reason, the local over the universal, social solidarity over individual autonomy. From such a perspective, the fact that homosexual practices have been condemned by church, synagogue, state and public opinion over the centuries is entitled to great moral weight and may justify the use of criminal sanctions to enforce conformity. Besides Devlin, contemporary communitarians like Sandel and MacIntyre have not addressed questions of lesbian and gay rights. However, their treatment of community is consistent with the conventional sense that I have defined.[50]

The inadequacy of conceptions of community as convention, especially for those sympathetic to community as a value and as a source of value, becomes clear as soon as one considers the fact of pluralism so central to modern politics. Quite simply, there are lesbian and gay communities as well as communities of fundamentalists, orthodox believers, and "moral majoritarians." Indeed, there are even liberal communities bound together by a common commitment to respecting differences and encouraging diversity. One of the transformations in the movement for lesbian and gay rights in recent years, in part a response to the AIDS epidemic, has been the emergence of a sense of distinctive group identity, shared values, and cooperative effort. This development indicates the social realities supporting the analysis of privacy rights in terms of freedom of association.[51] Lesbian and gay communities historically crystallized around bars, social clubs, bath houses, bookstores, and other recreational centers. With the development of "gay ghettos" in major urban centers, a wide range of distinctively gay institutions developed, including theaters, newspapers, community centers, clinics, political organizations, and sex clubs. The AIDS epidemic has led to a proliferation of associations devoted to healthcare, education, political mobilization, fundraising, and provision of services and support to the sick and dying. More traditional institutions like bars and sex clubs have become sites of "safer sex" education and community building. No doubt the increasing visibility of these forms of life has contributed to creating a backlash in the name of "traditional family values," the virulence of which has intensified the difficulties in dealing with the epidemic.

The fact of pluralism entails not only conflict among the shared norms of behavior and common ways of life of diverse communities, but also the need for developing a more complex model of individuality. One aspect of both communitarian and feminist critiques of liberal individualism focuses as much on its allegedly atomistic model of human nature as on any specific normative political doctrines. Both feminists and more conservative communitarians urge the need for conceiving of the individual as situated in concrete historical, social, and familial settings rather than as isolated and self-enclosed.[52] Such an understanding of human individuality underlies the insistence throughout this book that the realization of equal rights requires the legal and social recognition of the associative and communal forms of lesbian and gay life. Individuals must be seen as emerging from specific cultural contexts and developing through a history of interpersonal associations. The centrality of "coming out" as an experience that decisively shapes contemporary lesbian and gay subjectivities, helping them to overcome a history of marginalization and abjection, witnesses the crucial role of community interaction as a dimension of self-formation. Critically, as Mark Blasius and Shane Phelan have argued, "coming out" involves more than the revelation of an inner truth about oneself; rather, it is a "coming into community," an ongoing process of voluntarily joining with others in the deliberate reshaping of the shared conditions of individual life.[53]

"Community" in this sense refers to the *institutional* dimension of human activity. Taking their lead from Aristotle and Hegel, the proponents of institutional analysis emphasize the social contexts that condition and sustain individual and collective life. Clearly, the conception of community as institution overlaps and includes some components of community as convention. However, by focusing on the ways in which communities are realized in the development of concrete ways of life and modes of interaction, the emphasis on institutions escapes both the abstraction of talk about shared values and the atomism implicit in reducing community to matters of individual feeling or belief. A major defect of much communitarian analysis is its failure to recognize that in modern societies the individual is situated in a *plurality* of institutional settings, emerging from a complex of overlapping institutions and negotiating among them in the conduct of her life. Thus, one may be a lesbian, a mother, a Jew, a daughter of working-class parents, a university teacher, and a psychoanalyst. Such diversity of social roles and interpersonal contexts may subject the individual to conflicting ethical demands that go to the very heart of her personal identity. The recognition of moral personality as socially situated in a plurality of communities negotiating potentially conflicting claims leads back to acknowledgment of the centrality of individual autonomy in the shaping of a life. Personal identity under conditions of modernity must be seen as a contingent and provisional achievement subject to continuing reevaluation and revision in an ongoing history of individual choice. Liberty is a fact of life in pluralistic democracies, but it must also be protected by constitutional principle.

The potential for conflict among a plurality of communities increases if one defines each community in terms of a distinct conventional system of moral, religious, and other beliefs. Understood rather as institutions through which groups may organize their specific ways of life, communities are more easily seen as interacting and overlapping. Here, the theory of modern democracy — especially as developed in Rawls's more recent work or Berlin's ethical pluralism — emerges as something other than an individualist alternative to various communitarianisms. Instead, the liberal articulation of fundamental individual rights and constraining principles of justice is an attempt to map the conditions of coexistence for disparate ethical and religious communities within the overarching unities of modern pluralistic states. Thus, Rawls in his account of the state as a "social union of social unions" (a community of communities) is as much the liberal heir of the Federalists as of John Locke. It is in these terms that one may identify a distinctively *political* sense of community through which conflicting claims of distinct groups may be adjudicated and a basic structure of cooperation established and maintained. The arguments marshaled in support of a robust conception of lesbian and gay rights interpret modern constitutional democracy and the political morality that supports it as just such a framework both constraining and supporting the efforts of diverse moral communities to maintain their own ways of life. Finally, the respect for human equality and moral autonomy that underlies claims of individual rights locates persons in diverse and interacting social contexts and insists on the primacy of mutual respect as the governing norm in an encompassing community of right. Modern democracy provides an arena of contestation within the limits of constitutional principle: the implications of its fundamental commitment to equal citizenship are articulated and challenged through robust debate and political struggle.

VIII. Democratic Citizenship and Protection against Discrimination

The ethical principles that support modern democracy are embodied in the historical institutions and practices by which diverse nation-states have come to realize aspirations towards freedom and equality for their citizens. These principles are institutionalized in legal and constitutional structures and constraints as well as in the shared standards of critical morality by which citizens seek to challenge their societies to live up to their own highest ideals. The abstractions of moral and legal theory can be realized only through processes of political interpretation and contestation in which individuals and groups interact to define the common conditions of their social lives. The argumentation of liberal constitutional and political theory necessarily prescinds from specific contexts of conflict and debate while at the same time recognizing the extent to which its terms presume a background of institutional arrangements such as courts, legislatures, voluntary associations, and economic markets. Liberal theory has emphasized the importance of establishing encompassing frameworks to guarantee fairness in the interaction of diverse groups and individuals without explicitly theorizing the centrality of democratic participation as both a good in itself and a guarantor of other fundamental rights. Conservative communitarians have insisted on the primacy of social ties and traditions as a bulwark of ethical value, but have tended to project a unitary sense of community and morality that has no place for conflict and contestation as a component of democratic politics. (In Chapters Five and Six, I will turn to Hannah Arendt and Henry David Thoreau to develop a conception of democratic politics as rooted in the fact of human plurality and of active citizenship as a dimension of individual self-making.) In the balance of this chapter, I argue that lesbians and gays are entitled to state protection against discrimination based on their sexual orientation as a guarantee of basic rights of democratic political participation.

In recent years a number of queer writers with conservative political and social attitudes have contributed to the public discussions of lesbian and gay rights. Given the changing public climate of debate, these figures have occupied a potentially fruitful discursive location, urging some measure of toleration on those opponents of equality who share their conservative outlook and some measure of restraint on advocates of sexual minorities who link specifically queer concerns with a broader agenda of social reform. Although there are many areas of disagreement between such gay conservatives and liberal or radical activists, one important area of controversy turns on the importance of seeking protection for homosexual citizens against discrimination in employment, housing, public accommodation, and education. At a time when "affirmative action" for African Americans, women, and other protected minorities has become controversial, the very notion of government protection against discrimination has been challenged and civil rights legislation stigmatized as creating "special rights" for minorities.

40

Thus, right-wing libertarians who may agree that sodomy laws constitute unwarranted governmental interference in the private sphere also condemn civil rights laws as intrusions in private decision making.

Perhaps the most interesting and certainly the most visible among the new gay conservatives is Andrew Sullivan, former editor of *The New Republic*. His general political framework is more complex than that of libertarian defenders of minimal government; however, his criticism of antidiscrimination laws reiterates their arguments and their errors. In *Virtually Normal*, Sullivan mounts a sustained argument for reforms in the treatment of lesbians and gays under the law.[54] In relation to the current context of pervasive legal disabilities, his proposals have a sharp critical edge: he argues against the criminalization of private consensual sexual activities between adults, in favor of ending discrimination against open lesbians and gays in the military, and in favor of legal recognition of marriage between members of the same sex. However, he not only refuses to endorse the extension of civil rights protection to those discriminated against because of their sexual orientation, but also argues that all antidiscrimination legislation is a violation of liberal principles.

The principle Sullivan defends in his arguments about gay rights is that of formal equality before the law. He interprets this standard as requiring that the *government* not discriminate against unpopular social minorities in defining and distributing benefits and responsibilities. Given the extent of governmental regulation of modern life, Sullivan gets farther than one might imagine with his principle. He emphasizes same-sex marriage and the end to the ban on open homosexuals in the military, but acknowledges even more radical implications in such areas as eligibility for foster care and adoption, the contents of public school curricula, support for safer sex education, and AIDS policies more generally. I endorse the bold reach of Sullivan's conception of what formal equality requires. My objection to his argument is not that it does not go far enough, but rather that it is based on a misleading model of the relations between the state and a democratic citizenry, an inadequate understanding of corporate and social power, and a highly conformist conception of sexual ethics. Sullivan's book postulates rigid and untenable dichotomies between state and civil society, public and private spheres of activity. He assimilates modern economic organization to voluntary associations of individuals and accepts a communitarian conception of morality that is blind to the pluralism and hostile to the diversity of modern democracy.

Sullivan's treatment of political liberalism is highly ambivalent. His discussion of what he calls "prohibitionist" and "conservative" attitudes towards homosexuality and society reveal the extent of his sympathies with their approaches to ethics and politics, despite their disapproval of homosexuality. However, his argument against civil rights protections for lesbians and gays insists that anti-discrimination legislation violates *liberal* principles. He assimilates civil rights laws to laws against "hate crimes" and extends his critique to all efforts to protect oppressed minority groups, including African Americans in the 1960s. Sullivan accepts some of these efforts as applications of his favored formal equality principle: abolition of segregated schools; integration of the military; prohibition of "proactive discrimination in public spaces and accommodations"; ending bans on interracial marriage; and enforcement of voting rights. Lumping together the prohibition of discrimination in housing and employment with "forced integration" and much later efforts to control hate speech, Sullivan claims that: "In all of this, the liberal state was acting to ensure that certain kinds of citizens were preferenced over others because of their race, even if neutral tests suggested the opposite and individuals preferred other outcomes — and all as a way of ensuring that citizens were *not* treated differently because of their race."[55] (Italics in original.)

It is well beyond the scope of this book to sort out all the fallacies — historical, legal, and philosophical — in Sullivan's tendentious account of the civil rights legislation enacted in the United States during the 1960s to protect not only racial minorities but women, and religious and ethnic groups as well. Sullivan's characterizations of these developments, unsupported by any detailed argumentation or documentation seriously compromise his rhetorical stance of neutrality and reveal the extent of his conservative affiliations. However, he does not hesitate to draw this conclusion: "The liberal paradox here is obvious: liberty is restricted for some so as to enlarge it for others."[56] Moreover, Sullivan does not refer here to the liberty of a qualified candidate passed over in the course of affirmative action efforts to hire allegedly less qualified members of minority groups. In fact, courts have found such "reverse discrimination" to be prohibited by the same civil rights laws that Sullivan attacks. Rather his concern is to protect the liberty of employers, landlords, and others to discriminate against unpopular minorities; indeed, he obfuscates the issue of the power of corporate employers by interpreting employment discrimination as the freedom of association of *employees*. Sullivan's rejection of civil rights legislation as interference with freedom of contract is a return to an earlier epoch in which all manner of government regulation, affecting such matters as working hours, safety, child labor, health, and labor organization, was rejected as violating individual rights to freedom of contract under the doctrine of "substantive due process." Such arguments have indeed been revived in recent legal and economic discourse, but not by anyone identifiable as a "liberal" in the terms of American politics. Remember that Sullivan insists that liberal advocacy of civil rights laws is a paradoxical violation of liberal principles.

Defending individual freedom to avoid association with homosexuals if they choose, Sullivan writes:

> After all, liberties have been removed — the fundamental liberty in a free society to contract with whomsoever one wishes to — and with a precarious result. The law is largely unused, and it may provoke even more hostility among those who are forced to life by it. . . . For many people in Western societies, and most others, the sexual and emotional entanglement of two persons of the same gender is a moral enormity.

They find such behavior abhorrent, even threatening; and, while, in a liberal society, they may be content to leave such people alone, they draw the line at being told they cannot avoid their company in the workplace or in renting housing to them.[57]

Although Sullivan repeatedly asserts that anti-discrimination laws that cover sexual orientation are not used, he offers no documentation to support this claim, which must be viewed with some suspicion given that only nine states provide such protection and most of them only in quite recent years. The notion that employment decisions in corporate America are made by employees exercising their freedom of association bears no discernible resemblance to social realities. Moreover, even if they were, it is hard to see that such employees' interests in avoiding uncomfortable contacts should outweigh the interests of others in securing employment. In fact, arguments like this were raised regarding African Americans during the debates about civil rights legislation during the 1960s. Is it conceivable that Andrew Sullivan would defend the freedom of employers and landlords to discriminate against Jews or Roman Catholics, African Americans or Asian Americans, because of employees' discomfort with religious or racial differences?

Sullivan's argument joins a libertarian defense of the free market with a communitarian deference to the prejudices of popular majorities. Neither position is adequate to the ethical aspirations of modern democracy. J. S. Mill, who is invoked by Sullivan to support his anti-interventionist critique of civil rights laws, was among the first to recognize and deplore the deleterious effects of "tyranny of the majority." Given the extent to which power in contemporary societies is exercised by corporate entities within civil society, the authority of the state may well be required to protect unpopular minorities against retaliation for the exercise of basic rights of citizenship. Blacks were oppressed under Jim Crow not only by state laws mandating segregation but also by the deployment of white supremacist social and economic power to punish any black or white citizen so foolhardy as to attempt to change the status quo through political means. These political and social attitudes also licensed members of dominant groups to use violence and intimidation to keep minorities in their place. The underlying rationale of the anti-discrimination provisions of civil rights legislation is the recognition that formal legal equality is inadequate to provide for equal citizenship under conditions of popular hostility and pervasive social inequality. It is precisely the intensity and extent of the prejudice against homosexuality that justifies the claims of lesbian and gay citizens to protection against discrimination. Sullivan is so eager to establish a rhetorical linkage of employment and housing discrimination with "freedom of association" that he fails to acknowledge the fact that civil rights legislation routinely exempts private houses, small rooming houses, and businesses below a certain size. In addition, religious organizations are permitted to include religion among qualifications for employment without being subject to penalties for discrimination; for better or worse, most laws that prohibit discrimination based on sexual orientation also exempt religious groups.

The deficiencies of Sullivan's arguments against civil rights protection for lesbian and gay citizens become even more apparent when contrasted with the analysis offered by Judge Richard Posner, a founder of the law and economics school of jurisprudence and a vigorous defender of the free market. In a remarkable book, *Sex and Reason*, Posner offers an "economic analysis" of a range of public policy issues touching on sexuality. Appointed to the Court of Appeals for the Seventh Circuit by President Reagan, and widely rumored to have been Reagan's personal preference when he nominated Robert Bork to the Supreme Court, Posner offers arguments that treat sexual matters in terms of biology and economics, deploying rational choice theory in the service of a resolutely "scientific, nonmoral outlook." However, he does not shy away from normative argumentation and recommendation. He describes his normative perspective as libertarian, or classically liberal. With regard to homosexuality, Posner criticizes the decision in *Bowers v. Hardwick*, supports repeal of the sodomy laws, stops short of advocating marriage but recommends some form of legal status for same-sex couples, and equivocates on gays in the military.

Posner's handling of the question of civil rights protection is very telling. He treats the issue very briefly, framing the question in two distinct forms. When he asks whether it is a good idea to have a law against private discrimination in employment, Posner expresses skepticism. Without going into any detail, he refers to a published article of his *questioning the rationale of protecting any minority groups in this manner*. His argument that such efforts are at best inefficacious and at worst counter productive has no special relevance to the discussion of sexual orientation. On the other hand, when Posner reframes the question, his conclusion appears rather different:

> . . . given Title VII and cognate laws, is there any reason to exclude homosexuals from a protected category that already includes not only racial, religious and ethnic groups, but also women, the physically and mentally handicapped, all workers aged 40 and older, and, in some cases, even young healthy male WASPs? Is there less, or less harmful, or less irrational discrimination against homosexuals than against any of the members of these other groups? The answer is no.[58]

Posner separates his general reservations about the legitimacy and efficacy of antidiscrimination legislation from the question whether lesbians and gays have as much claim to such protection as those already covered. His answer is unequivocal. Moreover, he points in the right direction for any answer to such a question. The relevant factors have almost nothing to do with the "nature" of homosexuality, a topic that he takes up in a variety of other contexts. Rather, the relevant facts have to do with the prevalence of discrimination against homosexuals as a group in contemporary society. As the Supreme Court emphasized in *Romer v. Evans*,

"These are protections taken for granted by most people either because they already have them or do not need them. . . ."

Sullivan insists that anti-discrimination legislation breaches the line that should separate public from private domains of behavior: "But now the state was becoming involved in the details of *private* life. It made judgments about the nature of people's identity; it chose for its citizens the kinds of identities they had in private life, and attempted to mediate the public conflicts such identities entailed." How do civil rights laws define identities for private individuals? They enable individuals to challenge legally decisions of organizations within civil society that exercise "quasi-public" functions; only the fiction of corporate personality and the fetishizing of freedom of contract permit treating employment, educational, and housing discrimination as "private" decisions. Anti-discrimination laws provide a recourse for any person who feels that she has been denied opportunities because of characteristics irrelevant to her qualifications. Classes of people are singled out for protection because legislatures or courts have determined that they have been historically subject to unfair treatment within our society. When a citizen believes that she has been unfairly treated in a relevant way, she may exercise her rights under the law to challenge the treatment as discriminatory. No one is obliged to do so; the definition of protected classes does not construct personal or political identities but rather forbids employers, landlords, and other decision makers from using such categories as race, religion, or sex to *impose* an invidious identity on a person rather than treating her in terms of her individual character and qualities. The objectionable construction of identity in cases of discrimination results from a social history of subordinating and stigmatizing specific groups, not from the laws designed to remedy such effects.

Sullivan's claim that civil rights laws work to construct political identities is especially puzzling given his insistence that homosexual identity results from an inherent natural condition. Rather than defending democratic freedom for individuals to shape their own identities, Sullivan struggles to separate questions of identity altogether from social and political configurations. He attributes to liberal theory a conception of the person that abstracts from all historical vicissitudes:

> It [liberalism] asserted that insofar as the state was concerned, all citizens were the same, abstract individuals. These individuals, from the point of view of the liberal state, had no history, no context, no gender, no race, no private life. The state was concerned with them only when they became public personas, engaging in public activities, such as paying taxes, being drafted, going to court, or otherwise interacting with government agencies.[59]

At this point, Sullivan has stripped the individual of any cultural specification and shrunk the domain of democratic politics to conform to his definition of formal legal equality. At the same time, he has separated citizenship from any engagement with civil society and from any concrete political interaction. It is no accident that his arguments for homosexual equality depend importantly on the conception of homosexuality as an essential identity that effects only a small minority who have little or no choice in the matter. Sullivan's arguments enact a flight from freedom — from the political action of struggling minorities and from the individual shaping of erotic life. (In Chapter Two, I will argue that sexual identities are historical and cultural constructions and that the homosexual identity Sullivan postulates is a distinctively modern phenomenon.) In subsequent chapters, I contend that ethical self-making and democratic citizenship, too, are historical phenomena dependent on the outcomes of political contestation, struggle by oppressed minorities, and the actions of conscientious individuals. Civil rights laws that protect unpopular minorities against retaliation for the exercise of fundamental liberties are necessary to establish equal citizenship as a political reality.

CHAPTER TWO

HISTORICIZING SEXUALITY

⨳

Forms of Desire and the Construction

of Identities[1]

The love that dare not speak its name in this century is such a great affection of an older for a younger man as there was between David and
Jonathan, such as Plato made the very basis of his philosophy, and such
as you find in the sonnets of Michelangelo and Shakespeare. It is that
deep spiritual affection that is as pure as it is perfect.

—Oscar Wilde, in the dock (1895)[2]

We must not forget that the psychological, psychiatric, medical category
of homosexuality was constituted from that moment it was characterized . . . less by a type of sexual relations than by a certain quality of
sexual sensibility, a certain way of inverting the masculine and feminine
in oneself. Homosexuality appeared as one of the forms of sexuality
when it was transposed from the practice of sodomy onto a kind of interior androgyny, a hermaphroditism of the soul. The sodomite had been a
temporary aberration; the homosexual was now a species.

—Michel Foucault (1976)[3]

In Chapter One, I defended a robust conception of lesbian and gay rights rooted
in democratic theory and constitutional law. By emphasizing the radical implications of individual autonomy and freedom of association in the context of democratic citizenship, I argued that full equality for queer citizens requires not only
the decriminalization of same-sex activities but also protection against discrimination based on sexual orientation and recognition of lesbian and gay
relationships and community institutions. The appeal to constitutional rights of

privacy and democratic norms of liberty, equality, and the plurality of moral communities is necessarily abstract. The individuality of queer citizens and the specificity of lesbian and gay forms of life are comprehended by the universalist language of democratic equality, legal personality, fundamental rights, and freedom of association. The generality and abstraction that characterizes this legal and political discourse need not disadvantage members of oppressed and marginalized groups who fall outside the tacit definitions of normality or typicality that shape a political culture; rather, the relative emptiness and wide circulation of these concepts makes them available for critical redeployment and political contestation. The language of universalism provides an orientation and direction, articulates an aspiration, that can be realized only through the institutions, practices, and traditions of historical political communities; it is available to articulate the ethical claims of those at the margins who struggle to transform the conditions of their social lives.

This same tendency towards abstraction and generality in the formulation of political norms poses risks. The language of modern democracy may be deployed ideologically to mask profound social inequalities; its explicit normativity may be used to enforce homogeneity on diverse groups or to blame victims for their subordinate position. However, the dangers of ideological obfuscation pertain not only to democratic ideals but to any general justificatory scheme that may be applied to social realities. The corrective for these potential abuses is not to be found in developing yet another theoretical framework, but through work of a different sort. The normative arguments of Chapter One must be situated against a background of contingent historical developments. We cannot comprehend claims of equality for queer citizens without attending to such diverse and complex phenomena as the institutionalization of psychiatry and its discourse, the development of modern contraception and the "sexual revolution" that followed, the Women's Movement and the articulation of a feminist critique of gender, the Civil Rights Movement of African Americans and other marginalized social groups, the Stonewall Rebellion and the emergence of a political movement of out gays and lesbians, the devastation of the AIDS epidemic, and the proliferation of queer families.

This chapter is an exercise in *historicizing* the abstract claims and arguments about lesbian and gay rights developed earlier. It is an effort, in Hannah Arendt's terms, "to see historically and to think politically" — locating the movement for equal citizenship among lesbians and gays within the ongoing historical contexts of both modern democracy and modern sexual definition. I proceed along two distinct axes that converge in the emergence among contemporary social movements of a queer emancipatory politics: 1) the contested construction of sexuality as a locus of political and personal identification, and, 2) the modern deployment of "normalizing" powers that produce distinctive forms of subjectivity to internalize the work of social regulation. The terrain explored in this chapter has been indicated by the later work of Michel Foucault;[4] his emphases have been taken up, challenged, revised, and extended by much recent work in lesbian/gay/queer studies and feminism as well as social history and political theory more generally.[5] Rather than proceed through the explication of Foucault's texts or those he has influenced, I shall bring that perspective to bear on recuperating some representative and epochal moments from the history of male homosexuality, especially, in relation to the cultures of ancient and modern democracy. I will not attempt a historical survey here, but will provide snapshots of two important political contexts in which male same-sex desire played an important if contested social and intellectual function. Like Foucault, I revisit the institution of pederasty in ancient Athens and the emergence of the homosexual as a "new species" in nineteenth century Europe. However, in the latter case, I focus both on the definitions of "sexual inversion" within medicine, psychiatry, and early homosexual rights movements, and on a widespread humanistic discourse in which the revival of ancient Greek models of democracy and critical enquiry brought with it an impassioned defense of same-sex ties between men. My discussion is not intended to be exhaustive but rather illustrative of a historicizing reflection that situates sexual desire and individual self-making within specific social, cultural, and discursive forms of life. The second half of the chapter builds on these historical examples to theorize more explicitly the political contexts of a contemporary hermeneutics of sexuality and the distinctive institutions in which it is embodied.

I. Pedagogic Pederasty

I begin with the institution of pederasty in ancient Athens to interrogate its implications for understanding our own forms of sexual organization. What can we learn about lesbian, gay, and queer identities — and modern sexuality more generally — from the debates among essentialists and social constructionists about lesbian and gay history? What can we learn, for instance, from various attempts to answer the question, "Were there gay men in ancient Greece?" First, notice the shift from "lesbian and gay" to "gay men." Despite the illustrious figure of the poet Sappho of Lesbos, we have access to much more evidence about male sexual behavior and attitudes than about women in the fourth and fifth centuries BCE. Moreover, the sources from Greek literature, litigation, philosophy, and art so effectively marshaled and assessed by Sir Kenneth Dover in his *Greek Homosexuality*, pertain primarily to men and focus on adult citizens, primarily in Athens.[6] The data that inform the debate about sexuality in ancient Greece are skewed in terms of gender, social and political status, age, and ethnicity. This methodological point bears on the status of the available evidence, and suggests further hermeneutic difficulties. By focusing on the conduct and self-understanding of a privileged, exclusively male stratum of society to define the meaning of "Greek homosexuality," we generate strains that will inform any attempt to reach general conclusions or even to develop concrete comparisons with more recent forms of sexual life. It is useful to be reminded at the outset that sex is an aspect of human life that goes on in complex interplay with such other social forms as gender, political status, economic organization, and age. As feminist critiques of essentialism have emphasized, these factors are as much at work in contemporary configurations of sex and gender as they were at any earlier historical period.

Ancient Greek pederasty exercised great influence on the articulation of same-sex desire in late-nineteenth-century England and Germany; even Sigmund Freud's engagement with the theories of sexology and medical science about "sexual inversion" is informed by his own admiration for ancient Greek forms of life. (See Section II of this chapter and Chapter Four below.) Yet so distinguished a contemporary classicist and gay scholar as David Halperin, in defending a strong version of social constructionism, can assert without qualification, "There were no gay men in fifth-century Athens." What does he mean? Surely fifth-century Athenian men — even those sexually interested primarily in other men — did not understand themselves in the same ways as contemporary gays in Greenwich Village or the Castro. Halperin's argument cannot be reduced to this truism. Nevertheless, how individuals in different societies, cultures, and historical periods interpreted and evaluated same-sex desire and behavior, their own and that of their fellows, is part of the issue. Ancient Greeks did not condemn same-sex desire and behavior as such. Indeed, the fact that passionate relations between older and younger men were socially recognized as having legitimate pedagogic functions has been a continuing source of inspiration and self-definition for men drawn to other men. However, there is a serious question as to whether the Athenians categorized sexual desire at all in terms of the gender of the person desired ("object choice" in psychoanalytic terms).[7] The evidence strongly supports the view that they did not distinguish *kinds of persons* by reference to the gender of their preferred sexual objects. So long as adult citizens played the dominant role in sexual interaction (as phallic penetrators), whether they chose to penetrate women or boys was a matter of ethical indifference to the Athenians. This is not to say that sexual behavior as such was ethically neutral. Rather, adult citizens were subject to a highly elaborated model of sexual conduct appropriate to one of their station. This model emphasized the importance of maintaining their status in terms of both the relations they formed and the practices in which they engaged. *Citizens were expected to be on top.*[8] They were permitted to have sexual relations with women, boys, slaves, foreigners — whomever — so long as they took on the role of phallic penetrator.[9]

In *The Uses of Pleasure*, the second volume of his *History of Sexuality*, Michel Foucault elaborates more fully the terms of ancient Athenian sexual ethics: sexual desire and conduct were understood to bear importantly on the capacity of individuals to demonstrate self-control and to exercise the responsibilities of citizens and heads of households. Foucault shows the extent to which the teachings of Greek philosophers and medical writers encouraged an almost ascetic approach to sex well before the advent of Christianity. However, he emphasizes that this ethic was far from universal in its reach: rooted in the social status of citizenship, it was inherently gendered and elitist, projecting specific models of excellence to be emulated by men of honor, rather than codifying abstract rules to be applied generally. For Foucault, sex in ancient Greece did not define the inner truth or identity of individuals. Rather, individuals displayed important personal and social capacities through the deliberate shaping of their sexual conduct and relationships. Sex was understood as an arena of self-making, one aspect of the "aesthetics of existence." Foucault clearly distinguishes this approach from the modern scientific understanding of "sexuality" with its definition of a biologically based, putatively universal normality and its extensive catalogue of perversions defining a variety of flawed human types.

Regarding women, the constraints on their sexual conduct derived from the importance of maintaining their status as the wives or daughters of citizens. Thus, the chastity of women within a household was taken to reflect on the honor of the head of the household.[10] It is important to recognize the extent to which the system regulating gender and sexuality in ancient Athens was pervasively sexist. The celebration of male-male courtship in upper-class circles was itself related to the restrictions on the education and cultivation of women attached to the citizen class. Not only were women denied the privileges of citizenship, but wives and daughters of Athenian citizens were sequestered within the women's quarters of the household, assigned tasks identified with their gender, and rarely permitted even to socialize with men other than relatives. Marriages were arranged for persons of citizen status, and the average disparity in age between husbands and wives was about twenty years. Marital relations were not linked with love or romance. The analysis offered in Gayle Rubin's "The Traffic in Women" may be applied without difficulty to the sex/gender system of ancient Athens.[11] When Aristotle argued later in the fourth century that husbands and wives were in some sense friends, he was apparently breaking new ground.[12]

The institution of "pedagogic pederasty" by which adult citizens courted and formed special relationships with younger men cannot be separated from the subordinate status of women in the culture. Male-male relations were not merely tolerated, they were assigned an important role in the emotional and social development of citizens, who were expected also to marry and establish households. The cultivation of romantic friendships between mature and younger men was seen as an important opportunity for civic education. Such relationships are both dramatized and explicitly discussed in Plato's *Lysis*, *Symposium*, and *Phaedrus*. In exploring the resemblances and differences between ancient pederasty and modern homosexuality, it is critical to recognize that Greek love was inherently asymmetrical and hierarchical. So much so that no single term was available to designate both participants in the relationship: the *erastes* was the lover — the older, higher-status, often wealthier and more powerful, potential phallic penetrator; the *eromenos* was the beloved — the young, beautiful, promising but unformed, potential phallic recipient. In addition to the differences in age and status pertaining to these roles, each was understood to have a distinctive aim in the erotic context. The *erastes'* aim included genital pleasure; the *eromenos* was understood to take no pleasure in being penetrated, but to permit penetration in exchange for some other advantage, ranging from material gifts to affection to education in civic virtue or philosophy.

The opening of Plato's *Charmides*, an early dialogue, provides a provocative glimpse of the conventions of Athenian pederasty at work and the ambiguities surrounding them. The dialogue is narrated by Socrates, who has just returned from the camp at Potidaea after a costly defeat for the Athenian army. (We learn in the *Symposium* that Socrates exhibited considerable courage in the battle, saving the life of his beloved Alcibiades. See the discussion in Chapter Three, section X.) His first stop is a wrestling school, where friends and acquaintances prevail upon him to tell them about the battle. After telling his tale, Socrates inquires about the news at home: "I asked them about things here; what was happening in the field of philosophy; had any of the young men become pre-eminent for wisdom or beauty or both?" (153d)[13] Socrates' interest in philosophy appears linked with his attraction to young men, but he is concerned for their wisdom as well as their beauty. It turns out that there is any easy answer to his question. Young Charmides enters the scene, preceded by "the advance guard and lovers of the young man who is thought to be our most handsome at present." (154a) The entire community seems smitten by the physical beauty of the youth. When he appears, everyone is thrown into disarray. Socrates observes: "All the others appeared to be in love with him, they were so startled and disconcerted. . . . The reaction of the grown men was not so surprising, but I watched the boys and saw that none of them, not even the smallest of them, had eyes for anyone else." (154d) This comment reminds us both that erotic attraction was generally taken to be that of an older for a younger man and that it was not easily contained by the conventions. Charmides' arrival practically causes a riot among the assembled men and boys; they fall all over themselves making room for him.

Socrates' own reactions, as he reports them, further complicate this picture. He mentions that Charmides strikes him as "amazingly tall and handsome" but also that "very nearly all men of that age seem handsome to me." (154c) The young man's admiring cousin Critias does not hesitate to advertise his charms in the most explicit terms. Socrates agrees that Charmides has "an extraordinarily lovely face," but his cousin urges ". . . just let him be persuaded to strip and you won't notice his face at all, his body is so perfectly beautiful." (155d) At this point, Socrates distances himself from an uncritical worship of male beauty; he remarks that Charmides would be "truly irresistible" only so long as he is also "endowed with a fine soul." It is not so easy to strip the soul as the body: "the young man must be of an age to be willing to engage in discussion." (156a) The conversation that follows Socrates' introduction to the young man exhibits the complexity of evaluating the quality of a youth's soul. The subject is *sophrosyne*, the virtue most praised among the Athenian upper-classes. The exchange that follows is familiar to readers of Plato's early dialogues; it proceeds from certainty to confusion as neither young men nor old are able to explain their beliefs in the face of Socrates' relentless interrogation. By the conclusion, one may doubt whether Socrates finds Charmides irresistible; the young man and his cousin playfully suggest that they will have to coerce the older philosopher to undertake the boy's education. Plato's readers would easily recognize Charmides and Critias as members of the Thirty Tyrants who later overthrew the Athenian democracy: all of the by-play about the young man's beauty may well satirize the norms of pedagogic pederasty as superficial and misleading. But Plato does not let us off the hook so easily. Socrates reveals himself as quite vulnerable to the young man's charms:

> That was the moment when I saw what was under his cloak, and I was on fire, and lost my head, and I considered Cydias to be the wisest man in matters of love When speaking of a handsome boy, he said, by way of advice to someone, "Take care not to go as a faun into the presence of a lion and be snatched as a portion of meat." I felt I'd been caught by just such a creature. (155d–e)

This scene testifies to the pervasiveness and power of the attraction of men for youth. Plato displays both the social conventions around male beauty such that an entire community may be agog with admiration, and the impact that a young man may have even on so measured a figure as Socrates. The scene exemplifies the importance for Plato of pederasty as an institution that relates eros to citizenship, virtue, and philosophy; these are themes central to his work. (I return to this subject in Chapter Three.)

These Platonic texts and other sources reveal a current of anxiety surrounding same-sex activities among Athenian citizens. As the comedies of Aristophanes make clear, the adult male citizen who permitted himself to be phallically penetrated by others was a figure of ridicule and contempt, the *kinaidos*.[14] Similarly, Pausanias's speech in Plato's *Symposium* specifically addresses the issue, familiar to young women growing up in America in the 1950s, and perhaps even later, "How far does a good girl go?" Of course, for the Athenians, since daughters were kept in the women's quarters at home, the question was rather more compelling for the sons of citizens, who moved through the city's pervasively male public spaces. The sexual conduct of both boys and girls could bring dishonor on their fathers. A man who sexually violated the child of a citizen committed *hybris* against his father.[15] Indeed, prudent fathers took care that their sons were rarely alone with older men without slaves as chaperones;[16] schools and gymnasia were carefully segregated by age.[17] Women and girls were expected to undergo phallic penetration; passivity in sexual intercourse was regarded as natural for them. Feminine honor within the citizen class was entrusted to husbands and fathers. So also, slaves, foreigners, and other subordinate males were not disgraced by sexual passivity; it was not a violation of their social status, but rather confirmed it. What the sources never quite make clear is whether the sons of citizens were granted a temporary exemption by virtue of youth from the disqualifying effects of phallic penetration.[18] Both the comedies of Aristophanes and the records of Athenian litigation provide evidence of the political power of accusations that a citizen permitted himself to be "used as a woman."[19]

Plato's Pausanias in the *Symposium* argues that whereas the inarticulate Boetians encouraged their boys to submit to anyone interested, and the tyrannical Persians prohibited all erotic relations among males, the Athenians had devised the perfect compromise: they encouraged their citizens to court attractive and promising young men, while urging the younger men to play hard to get. According to Pausanias, the effect of this double standard was to force lovers to prove the seriousness and staying power of their love by creating barriers to its fulfillment.[20] Ambiguity remains as to what happened if the boy concluded that his lover had proved himself. After all, as Pausanias at least never questions, the lover aspires to phallic satisfaction. Sir Kenneth Dover, in part on the basis of his reading of vase paintings, proposed intercrural intercourse as an ingenious solution to this dilemma: the boys offered their lovers sexual release by permitting them to reach a climax between the boys' thighs, thus avoiding anal penetration. In his second edition, Dover has conceded that the evidence on this matter is not so decisive as he once argued. In any event, we may suppose that part of the problem here reflects the tension between official ideology and sexual practice in any culture.[21]

Recognition of these differences in social attitude, and in those that many individuals may be taken to have had towards their own desires and behavior, informs the social constructionist position. Simply stated, Athenians of the fifth century did not understand themselves as defined by their desires for objects of a specific gender or biological sex. What mattered was the political and social status and age of the object of desire, as well as the sexual practices in which the citizen engaged. Halperin concludes that sexual conduct in ancient Athens was an assertion of social status and exercise of power over others rather than the expression of a deep truth about oneself. Indeed he claims that "sexuality" as such was unknown to ancient Athens, if by that we mean an underlying core of personal desire that reveals the "inner" reality of individuals and animates all of their sexual life.[22] Following Foucault, he locates that conception in developments within late-nineteenth-century medicine and psychology, which displaced the church as authoritative interpreter and diagnostician of that truth. Hence, the apparently paradoxical assertion that "homosexuality" has existed for only a little more than one hundred years.

The conception of "sexuality" as an autonomous domain of truth is integrally linked to the conception of "sexual identity." Another way to highlight the difference between ancient Athenian sexual practices and contemporary understandings of homosexuality is to recognize that the Athenians did not consider the person who desired sexual contact primarily with others of his own sex to be a distinctive *kind* of person. The *kinaidos* was a type, but he was defined by his willingness to adopt a phallicly passive role vis-à-vis other adult males, not by the fact that he had sex with males rather than females. Adult men who preferred boys were not singled out so long as they fulfilled their responsibilities as citizens to marry and procreate and so long as they did not engage in sexual practices that violated their status as citizens. Thus, Halperin's denial that there were gay men in ancient Athens reflects the further contention that no one understood himself or was understood by others to be a distinctive kind of person by virtue of his desire to have sex primarily or exclusively with other males.

In this context, controversy about the interpretation of same-sex desires and behavior in ancient Greece is part of an ongoing and increasingly complex contestation as to the meaning of modern homosexuality and the contemporary politics of sexual identity. For the "essentialist," the critical facts are that there were men in that society who experienced same-sex desires, who acted upon those desires, and most importantly, who were not stigmatized for their same-sex desires and activities *as such*. For the social constructionist, the crucial point is that same-sex desire was not taken by either the individual or the society as an important, much less a defining, characteristic of the persons who experienced it. Modern homosexuality identifies a human type unknown to the ancient Greeks, defined for himself as well as for medical and legal authorities and for public opinion by his exclusive or primary desire for sex with members of his own sex. Moreover, in Halperin's work at least, there is an implication that contemporary gay men are further distinguished from ancient Greek pederasts in that their desires are or may be directed at peers in age and social status with whom they may engage in mutual, reciprocal practices and egalitarian relationships.[23] The *kinaidos*, with his exclusive involvement as phallicly passive partner of other adult males, fails to exemplify the versatility and independence of the contemporary gay male.

II. "Greek Love" in the Nineteenth Century

In the late eighteenth and early nineteenth centuries, philosophers, artists, and statesmen increasingly turned to the cultural achievements of pagan antiquity for inspiration and support; ancient institutions and texts became authorities for European cultural and political life. Latin and Greek were established as languages to be learned by aspiring members of the élite. Increased access to representations of the "unspeakable vice" of the Greeks had subversive implications, leading to a cultural celebration of male same-sex desire that contributed to the rise to the first homosexual rights movement. The revival of classical learning had been an important component of the Renaissance in science, politics, and the arts that marked the emergence of early modern Europe from feudal Christendom. Both Greece and Rome continued to be appropriated by Enlightenment arts and thought. Classical models figured in the debates that led to revolution in both North America and France; indeed, revolutionaries on both continents saw themselves as engaged in a Machiavellian "return to principles," cited ancient history and texts in political debate, and had themselves painted in classical garb and pose.[24] During the nineteenth century, classical allusion and rhetoric continued to play an important role in contemporary cultural debate. Athens came to supersede the Roman republic and gain favor over Sparta as a point of reference for political and intellectual forces that saw themselves as progressive — committed to the expansion of democracy, the advance of learning, and the extension of liberty. The ancient polis became a contemporary point of reference for Goethe, Winkelmann, Hamann, Herder, Schiller, Hegel, Nietzsche, on the continent; Jowett, Arnold, Mill, Symonds, Pater, Wilde in England. As the mere listing of these names should indicate, Greek texts and experience could be interpreted in diverse ways; classical studies itself became a site of cultural controversy.

In the last decade, a number of scholars in England and the United States have explored the significance of the appropriation of the Greeks in Victorian Britain.[25] Invocations of ancient Athens figure in the criticisms of conservative currents in politics and culture urged by John Stuart Mill and Matthew Arnold, among others, and the revival of classical learning became a strategy of university reform. In her recent book *Hellenism and Homosexuality at Victorian Oxford*, Linda Dowling has charted these developments in considerable detail.[26] She pays particular attention to the influence of Plato scholar and Master of Balliol College Benjamin Jowett in self-consciously turning the program in *Literae humaniores*, or "Greats," into a preparatory school for future leaders of a progressively styled British Empire. Jowett positioned the texts of Plato at the heart of this curriculum. Indeed, until the 1960s, Jowett's two-volume edition of *The Collected Dialogues of Plato* (1871) remained a standard text at universities throughout the English-speaking world. For Jowett, as for Mill and Arnold, Plato's works provided the defense of an ethical commitment to the free development of critical reason. The method of Socratic enquiry presented a model of critical questioning and robust contestation as an alternative to passive acquiescence in cultural conventions. Vigorous independence of mind was seen as a necessity if England were to avoid cultural stagnation. Although himself a cleric who regarded Plato's work as the greatest of "uninspired" (i.e., non-revealed) literature, Jowett saw the Greek philosopher as an antidote to conformist tendencies at work in the religious and political climate at Oxford in his day.

Dowling shows that these Victorian liberals underestimated the subversive impact of the literature and philosophy that they promoted. In the work of Walter Pater and John Addington Symonds, the contemporary relevance of Plato included a defense of pederasty as a pedagogic and civic institution and an exploration of the aesthetic links between the love of beauty and the love of boys. Although Pater's prose was often obscure in its import, Symonds collaborated with Havelock Ellis on his study of "sexual inversion" and published two works in defense of homosexual rights; the first revealingly entitled *A Problem in Greek Ethics* (1883) followed by *A Problem in Modern Ethics* (1891). Both scholars had been compromised by Oxford scandals involving their connections with younger men.[27] As Dowling demonstrates, the seeds of a Hellenizing defense of same-sex relationships fell upon fertile ground. An earlier, religiously inspired reform led by John Henry Newman had placed the tutorial tie between aspiring student and older male mentor at the heart of the Oxford educational program. Many students came to Oxford from all-male public schools organized into intense hierarchies of older and younger boys. A number of these undergraduates were less cautious than their mentors in spelling out the sexual implications of a commitment to Platonic ethics and education. Oxford experienced a vogue of "boy worship" in the 1870s, and journals appeared devoted to publishing "Uranian" poetry. Outraged prelates preached sermons against these "dangerous" developments.

The connection between the emergence of suspect sexual tendencies among Oxford undergraduates and the central role assigned to Plato within the "Greats" curriculum is exhibited by certain changes that Jowett introduced in his enormously successful and influential translation of *The Collected Dialogues of Plato* as it went through successive editions in the latter decades of the century. Jowett introduced his translation of each dialogue with a concise summary of its arguments and some commentary on its philosophical and literary contents. In the First Edition of 1871, his introduction to the *Symposium* included a brief comment on Greek pederasty only in the context of Alcibiades' admittedly intemperate admission of the power of his love for Socrates. (In Chapter Three, I will offer my own extended reading of the pervasively homoerotic and queer themes in that text.) Jowett devotes two paragraphs to Alcibiades' speech. His own reserve and ambivalence are expressed thus:

> The state of his affections towards Socrates, unintelligible to us and perverted as they appear, is a perfect illustration of the power ascribed to the loves of men in the speech of Pausanias. Indeed, he is confident that the whole company will sympathize with him. . . . The singular part of this confession is the combination of the most degrading passion with the desire of virtue and improvement. . . . The Platonic Socrates (for of the real Socrates this may be doubted . . . [citing Xenophon's memorabilia]) does not appear to regard the greatest evil of Greek life as a matter of abhorrence, but as a subject of irony, and is far from resenting the imputation of such attachments. Nor does Plato feel any repugnance, such as would be felt in modern times, in bringing his great master and hero into connexion with nameless crimes.[28]

Jowett goes on to note that Plato did not share the "modern" recognition of the "glaring" "lack of taste" in the Greek idealization of the beauty of male youth and their failure to be "aroused" by female beauty. However, he remains agnostic regarding the extent to which either Plato or Socrates shared or condemned the prevalent attitude: ". . . for about the opinion of Plato himself, as of Socrates, respecting these male loves we are in the same perplexity which he attributes to his countrymen. . . ." Jowett satisfies himself by marking the wide gulf which separates Christian feeling from "a portion of Hellenic sentiment in the age of Plato."[29]

Compare the celebrative tone of this passage from John Addington Symonds' *Studies of the Greek Poets*, published in 1882: ". . . the chivalry of Hellas found its motive force in friendship rather than in the love of women; and the motive force of all chivalry is a generous soul-exalting, unselfish passion. The fruit which friendship bore among the Greeks was courage in the face of danger, indifference to life when honor was at stake, patriotic ardor, the love of liberty, and lion-hearted courage in battle."[30] Should the reader be tempted to find in this passage a romantic but disembodied enthusiasm for the antique past, consider this person-ification from the second volume of his work: "Like a young man newly come from the wrestling ground, anointed and chapleted, and very calm, the Genius of the Greeks appears before us. . . . The pride and strength of adolescence are his — audacity and endurance, swift passions and exquisite sensibilities, the alter-nations of sublime repose and boyish noise, grace, pliancy, and stubbornness and power. . . . "[31] Later, Symonds praises the ways in which statues of young athletes incarnate the Greek conception of excellence, "the seal and blossom of *sophrysyne*": "Of this sort are the two wrestling boys at Florence, whose strained muscles exhibit the chord of masculine vigor vibrating with tense vitality." What contemporary conclusions does the one-time Oxford don draw from his vision of the glory that was Greece?

> If we in England seek some living echo of this melody of curving lines, we must visit the watery meadows where the boys bathe in early morn-ing, or the playgrounds of our public schools in summer, or the banks of the Isis when the eights are on the water, or the riding schools of sol-diers.[32]

This is pretty strong stuff, especially when one remembers the intense, hierarchi-cal all-male public schools and university colleges where the sons of the British élite were initiated into civilized life through the study of ancient Greek.

By 1892, when Jowett published the Third Edition of his *Plato*, the Master of Balliol found it necessary to supplement his earlier introductory material with a more explicit, detailed, and cautionary address to his readers on the dangers of the Greek vice. In addition to marking the gulf between the sexual mores of Athens in the age of Plato and of Great Britain in the age of Victoria, Jowett goes to some lengths to draw ethical lessons from the dialogues that are consistent with his own vision of a progressive, expanding British Empire characterized by civic virtue and moral rectitude. Nothing in Plato, if properly understood, should bring a blush — or flush — to the cheek of any young person. The treatment of pederasty in the introduction to the *Symposium* has been considerably expanded; page headings announce discussions of "The Greek sentiment of love," "Comparative purity of Greek literature," and "Different aspects of Greek Morals." Jowett appears to have resolved his doubts about the attitudes of Socrates, even the Platonic Socrates, towards the practice. Compare the following with the version above at p. 57, which it replaced:

> The Platonic Socrates (for of the real Socrates this may be doubted; cp. his public rebuke of Critias for his shameful love of Euthydemus in Xenophon . . .) does not regard the greatest evil in Greek life as a thing not to be spoken of; but it has a ridiculous element . . . , and is a subject for irony, no less than for moral reprobation. . . . It is also used as a figure of speech which no one interpreted literally . . . [citations omitted][33]

Jowett's expanded discussion is riddled with contradictions. He provides extensive evidence as to the existence of pederastic institutions in Sparta and Thebes as well as in Athens, to buttress the claim that Plato did not simply make it up. On the other hand, he insists: ". . . Plato never in the least excuses the depraved love of the body . . . , nor is there any Greek writer of mark who condones or approves such connexions. But owing partly to the puzzling nature of the subject . . . , these friendships are spoken of by Plato in a manner different from that customary among ourselves."[34] Indeed! In 1885, the British Parliament had passed the Labouchere Amendment to the Criminal Law Reform Act which prohibited "gross indecency between men" whether in private or in public, regardless of the age and consent of the participants. (Questions about interpreting Plato's *Symposium* raised by Jowett's comments will be addressed at length in Chapter Three.)

Jowett's revisions of 1892 manifest the pressure he felt to contain the subversive sexual implications of his texts, requiring him not only to distance ancient Greek practices from those of Victorian Britain but also to insist that the philosophers Socrates and Plato took a critical distance as well. He devotes two-and-one-half additional paragraphs to wrestling with the morality of pederasty and trying to account for ambiguities regarding it in his texts; the additions comprise almost three pages in an introduction of only sixteen pages *in toto*. Jowett's concerns are also displayed in his revised introduction to Plato's *Phaedrus*. He adds three paragraphs covering almost two pages, with the heading, "Love and marriage." Jowett develops an extended analogy between pederastic love and Victorian marriage. "Partly in jest but also 'with a degree of seriousness,'" he deploys Plato's text for a sermon on the "marriage of true minds" and the necessity of testing true love through conflict and trial. He describes the struggle of two individuals to maintain their ideals and resist temptations leading to marriage and a life long association that may even continue after death, if ". . . the two passed their lives together in the service of God and man . . ." One may wonder how young readers responded to the Master of Balliol's efforts to innoculate them in advance against the Greek vice and to press Plato into service on behalf of Victorian marriage. Certainly more than a few succumbed to the homoerotic lure so evident in the ardor of Symonds' agitated prose.

Oscar Wilde is only the most notorious of a succession of bright young men for whom the glory that was Greece came to include the love of boys. One of the most distinguished products of the Oxford "Greats" curriculum, Wilde had earned a rare "double-first" degree. His own defense of the tradition of pedagogic pederasty, with its somewhat disingenuous emphasis on the spiritual purity of the relation, occurred in the context of his first trial in 1895 on charges of "gross indecency." That trial and the next, which ended in Wilde's conviction, resulted in the disgrace, imprisonment, and early death of Victorian England's most celebrated practitioner of same-sex desire.

Oscar Wilde's flamboyant manner and tragic fate have so much marked subsequent understandings of Victorian homosexuality that it is easy to forget what an idiosyncratic and atypical figure he was. The son of distinguished parents and brilliant undergraduate at Trinity College, Dublin and Magdalen College, Oxford, he already had something of a reputation when he arrived in London in 1878, determined to launch a career as poet and literary figure. Wilde became the public spokesman for a generation of rebels against the constraints of Victorian culture. An over-size and striking figure, he took on a highly stylized manner of speech and extravagant manner of dress to dramatize the "aesthetic" movement's break with tradition. Wilde was among the first modern "celebrities." He lectured widely, and his activities were covered in the press long before his literary works had achieved recognition in their own right. He was a natural attraction for caricaturists and appeared in the papers holding his characteristic sunflower, striking a pose. Known for his quick wit and memorable epigrams, he publicly challenged the authority of established cultural figures like the painter John Ruskin. Wilde was invited to tour the United States where he lectured on new movements in the arts and called on Walt Whitman in Camden.

Despite the provocative persona, in his personal life, Wilde deferred for a period to the conventions of Victorian respectability. In 1884, he married Constance Lloyd who soon bore him two sons. By the end of the 1880s, however, Wilde's associations became increasingly unconventional. In 1886, he met Robert Ross, then seventeen and about to enter Cambridge, who eventually became his lover. Wilde spent more and more of his time away from home in the company of younger men. The publication of *The Picture of Dorian Gray* in 1889 was met with censure and suspicion in the middle class press. However, in the 1890s, Wilde's play "Lady Windermere's Fan" was a big hit in the West End. In the spring of 1895, with "An Ideal Husband" and 'The Importance of Being Earnest" simultaneously enjoying the applause of the London theater audience, Wilde appeared triumphant in his assault on Victorian culture.

By the end of May of that year, after three highly publicized trials, Oscar Wilde had been convicted of the crime of "gross indecency between men" and sentenced to two years imprisonment with hard labor, the maximum. After his release, shunned by family and friends, anathematized by the public that had celebrated him, Wilde went into self-imposed exile in France where he died in

1900 at the age of forty-six. For later generations of men attracted to other men, Wilde's fate became emblematic of the tragedy of homosexual love. However, few have lived so much in the limelight as he. Even then, he found himself in court as a result of his own action in suing the Marquess of Queensberry for libel. Since 1892, Wilde had been very publicly enamored of Lord Alfred Douglas, younger son of the Marquess, then an Oxford undergraduate known as "Bosie." Through Bosie, Wilde became involved with a number of younger men, including servants and "rent boys," who supported themselves through prostitution and occasional blackmail. Queensberry, a flamboyant and somewhat unstable figure, campaigned publicly to end the association between Wilde and his son, finally leaving a card at his club addressed "To Oscar Wilde, posing as a somdomite [sic]." When Wilde sued for libel, Queensberry's attorneys hunted down some of the playwright's less respectable acquaintances as well as employees of hotels and restaurants ready to testify to his excesses. When it became clear that he could not secure a conviction, Wilde's attorneys withdrew the libel charges rather than risk Queensberry's acquittal. However it was too late. The Director of Public Prosecutions authorized charges against Wilde under Labouchère's Amendment, section 11 of the Criminal Law Reform Act of 1885. His first trial, at which Wilde delivered the passionate defense of male love quoted as an epigraph, ended in a hung jury. The second resulted in the conviction that led to his imprisonment, disgrace, and early death.[35]

Even after Wilde's public disgrace, the combination of Platonic texts and intense same-sex community enabled the discovery of passionate desire and the exploration of homoerotic relations. This dynamic is nicely displayed in a passage from E. M. Forster's *Maurice* that I shall quote at length:

> Towards the end of the term they touched upon a yet more delicate subject. They attended the Dean's translation class, and when one of the men was forging quietly ahead Mr. Cornwallis observed in a flat toneless voice: "Omit: a reference to the unspeakable vice of the Greeks." Durham observed afterwards that he ought to lose his fellowship for such hypocrisy.
>
> Maurice laughed.
>
> "I regard it as a point of pure scholarship. The Greeks, or most of them, were that way inclined, and to omit it is to omit the mainstay of Athenian society."
>
> "Is that so?"
>
> "You've read the *Symposium?*"
>
> Maurice had not. . . .
>
> "It's all in there — not meat for babes, of course, but you ought to read it. Read it this vac."
>
> No more was said at the time, but he was free of another subject, and one that he had never mentioned to any living soul. He hadn't

known it could be mentioned, and when Durham did so in the middle of
the sunlit court a breath of liberty touched him.[36]

Set at Cambridge a full generation after Wilde's condemnation, the novel beautifully illustrates the interplay among the intimacies of undergraduate life, the critical questioning of religious and social orthodoxy, and the awakening of same-sex
desire and love. And Plato's texts provide one site where these tendencies meet.
When Maurice later reveals the depth of his feelings for Durham with a passionate embrace, his friend — the knowing interlocutor in the passage above — acknowledges the declaration this way: "'I knew you read the *Symposium* in the vac,'
he said in a low voice."[37]

However, the shadow of Wilde falls darkly over *Maurice* — in the figure of
Ridsley within the novel and in the fact that Forster withheld the work, written in
1913–14, from publication until after his death in 1971. As Alan Sinfield has argued in *The Wilde Century*, the disgraced poet, playwright, and celebrity came to
symbolize the "homosexual" for subsequent generations, involuntarily lending
his flamboyant personal characteristics to the creation of a new social type.[38] As influential as this "camp" image of the male homosexual has since become, we
must not make the mistake of assuming the paradigm was well developed before
Wilde's extraordinary career ended in his public exposure as a "sodomite." In a
sense, Wilde fused in his person distinct types that circulated in nineteenth century Europe: the aesthete, the dandy, the effeminatus, the sexual invert, the boy-
lover, the sodomite. Wilde transformed some of these figures almost beyond
recognition. His consorting with rent boys, blackmailers, and stable boys raised
questions about the sincerity of his invocation of Socrates and the institution of
pedagogic pederasty. On the other hand, despite his writings on socialism and the
visit to Whitman, his aestheticism and dandyism seemed at some distance from
the democratic camaraderie celebrated by his contemporary Edward Carpenter in
defense of male love. There was considerable variety among the models of same-
sex love circulating in nineteenth-century Europe. Each existed within its own
discursive field and cultural context; the links among them and between each of
these and subsequent conceptions of "male homosexuality" are ambiguous and
require detailed investigation. In the next section, I examine the intersection of
two of these in the German context.

III. Hellenism, Sexual Science, and Homosexual Rights

The tensions within the field of cultural representations of same-sex love, even
those which deployed invocations of ancient Greece in its defense, may be further
exhibited by reference to the earliest appearances of a homosexual rights movement in Germany during the late nineteenth century. In 1864, Karl Ulrichs published the first of what became a twelve-volume work that combined a powerful
critique of the legal and social treatment of deviant sexualities with an extended

examination of the phenomena of same-sex love in historical, anthropological, and biological contexts. Ulrichs adopted *Urning* or *Uranian* as his general term for the class of sexual intermediates, characterized by the combination of masculine and feminine biological and psychological qualities. This expression is derived from Pausanias' speech in the *Symposium,* where it distinguishes a "Uranian" or "heavenly" eros from the "pandemic," common or vulgar variety. For Pausanias as for his nineteenth-century followers, this term marks the love of men for boys rather than their love for women. It is justified as a noble pederasty — promoting the development of individual talent, intellectual curiosity, masculine vigor, and public spirit. Intense romantic relationships between younger and older men were justified as an initiation into norms of responsible masculinity. In England not much later, "Uranian" poetry celebrated the beauty of boys.

The Greek orientation of German homosexual activists was carried forward by Magnus Hirschfeld, founder of the first homosexual rights organization "The Scientific-Humanitarian Committee" in 1897; he entitled his first major work *Sokrates und Sappho.* However, both Ulrichs and Hirschfeld joined their appeals to the authority of classical Greece with theoretical formulations of variant sexualities couched in terms of the biology and medicine of their day. Hirschfeld was himself a physician and founder-editor of *Jahrbuch für sexuelle Zwischenstufen* ("The Yearbook of Sexual Intermediates") which engaged Sigmund Freud's careful and critical attention. (See Chapter Four below.) The primary strategy of this first generation of homosexual scholar-activists, like that of today's "essentialist" defenders of lesbian and gay rights, was to use scientific discourse to establish that different sexualities resulted from "natural" variations over which individuals had no control: criminalization of same-sex activities and persecution of their practitioners was denounced as fundamentally unfair. (I shall develop a political critique of this strategy in Chapter Five.) As already suggested above, Ulrichs and Hirschfeld characterized the anomalous natural condition of homosexuals in terms of a confounding of elements separately associated with either male or female sex. The most famous formulation of this "third sex" defined it as the possession of a female brain or soul in a male body, or vice versa. Thus, same-sex object choice was understood to derive from an inversion of male and female characters, such that, for instance, the (heterosexual) female soul housed in a male body directed the male invert towards a male object. These "psychical hermaphrodites" were marked by the "inner androgyny" that Foucault identifies as definitive of the "new species" of homosexual in the passage quoted as an epigraph to this chapter.

In Chapter Four, I develop a reading of Freud's engagement with these "third sex" theories of sexual inversion to further illuminate this historical moment in the articulation of modern concepts of homosexuality. I will show how conventional nineteenth-century medicine, early homosexual rights advocacy, and a seminal work in psychoanalytic theory offered competing conceptions of homosexuality *within* the discourses of science and demonstrate how deeply imbricated *all* these definitions of same-sex desire and identity have been with binary definitions of sexual difference in a heterosexual matrix. As noted above, Ulrichs and Hirschfeld supplemented their scientific arguments with historical appeals to ancient Greece to justify the affirmation and cultivation of biologically based same-sex desires. They adopted an alternative discourse of male same-sex desire from within the humanistic revival of Hellenism that also contributed to cultural definitions of modern homosexuality. Although of continually increasing power and prestige, medicine and science still competed with humanistic studies in the political and cultural life of the nineteenth century. The model of same-sex relations institutionalized in Greek pederasty differs in important respects from the "inner androgyny" defined by the "third sex" theories. With unfortunate implications for the politics of gender, the Greek model ignores lesbianism altogether and constructs male homosexuality in terms of the affirmation of a vigorous masculinity. The hermaphrodite is decisively rejected in favor of the hypermasculine male. Indeed, Freud's appreciation of the institution of pederasty in ancient Greece contributes to the gender asymmetry in his arguments concerning the need to distinguish sexual inversion from sexual-object choice. He insists, with ancient Athens clearly in view, that homosexual object-choice is consistent with the "most complete masculinity" and with extraordinary cultural achievement, while perpetuating stereotypes of lesbians as mannish women. In his regard for the Greeks, Freud was very much a representative of his generation of educated Europeans, albeit more willing than most to address their non-Victorian sexual habits. Nineteenth-century Hellenism, especially in Germany and Great Britain, coexists and competes with sexual science in defining the homosexual as distinctive personage and psychological type.

At the same time that Hirschfeld and his colleagues invoked the "third sex" of "psychical hermaphrodites" to argue for homosexual rights, Adolph Brand, Benedict Friedlander, and other scholars and activists around the journal *Der Eigene* ("The Self-Owner") appealed to the institution of ancient Greek pederasty to defend a model of same-sex relations that centered on the ties between bisexual men and their younger male lovers.[39] These thinkers also exploited a tradition of romantic male friendship and emphasized the links between same-sex love and masculinity, often of a military sort. Far from celebrating the combination of masculine with feminine characters among sexual intermediaries, *Der Eigene* propounded a conception of male homosexuality as a kind of hypermasculinity. Where Hirschfeld and the Scientific-Humanitarian Committee welcomed lesbians and made common cause with feminist politics generally, Brand's organization *Gemeinschaft der Eigenen* ("Community of the Self-Owning"), founded in 1903, explicitly excluded women. Where the former were committed to social democracy, the latter espoused an increasingly individualist and anarchist politics. Occasionally allied in seeking specific law reforms, the two groups had increasingly stormy relations until the Nazi victory in 1933 abruptly ended the German homosexual rights movement. Hirschfeld's Institute for Sex Research was stormed by Nazi students in May 1933 and its extensive library publicly burned. Himself a Jew and already abroad at the time, Hirschfeld never returned to Germany, and died in France in 1935. Brand's house was raided by the Nazis several times, and his papers confiscated. Not Jewish and married as well, Brand ceased his public activities and was permitted to remain unmolested in Nazi Germany. He and his wife were killed during the Allied bombings in 1945.[40]

These moments from the history of sexual science and of the early German homosexual rights movement demonstrate further the extraordinary complexity of the uses of paradigms of same-sex love drawn from the ancient Greeks. (I will explore the difficulties implicit in the image of the hermaphrodite more fully in Chapter Four.) Note here that the rhetoric of Greek love cannot be separated from the multivalent currents of political conflict and gender relations within which it is deployed. In particular, the establishment of pederasty as a civic institution within a polity that systematically excluded women from citizenship authorizes an ideology of male homosexuality that is deeply enmeshed with the defense of gender hierarchy. Thus, *Der Eigene* set itself against contemporary feminism, and Jowett can reconcile Plato's *Symposium* with Christian morality and bourgeois ideology by arguing that the "higher love" praised by Socrates is to be found within Victorian marriage. Remember that pederastic relations were intrinsically hierarchical. For better or for worse, the complex configuration that is the "legacy of Greece" for modern European civilization became an important figure in the emergence of homosexuality as a political and cultural issue in the nineteenth and twentieth centuries. Alongside the discourses of medicine and the human sciences, it offered an alternative language of contestation in defining the ethics of modern sexuality and the politics of sexual identity.

As Eve Kosofsky Sedgwick has argued in persuasive detail, the definition of homosexuality was especially overdetermined by the linkage between patriarchal social forms and emotional bonding among men. The dependence of male domination on the development of an intense male homo*sociality* required vigilant effort to fend off a threatening male homo*sexuality*.[41] Ancient Athenian prohibitions on a citizen's taking the woman's role in sexual intercourse by permitting himself to be anally penetrated demonstrate the extent of anxiety on an analogous front within that activist democracy. Sedgwick has shown these tensions powerfully at work in seminal texts of European modernism. Many of these texts have similarly figured as sources of self-recognition and self-definition for generations of young gay men. What Plato's *Symposium* meant for Forster's *Maurice*, a range of texts has come to mean in the twentieth century. Some of these similarly situate the struggle for sexual self-definition in relation to the texts and figures of ancient Greece: consider Thomas Mann's *Death in Venice*, Herman Hesse's *Magister Ludi*, Andre Gide's *Corydon* and *The Immoralist*, G. Lowes Dickinson's *A Modern Symposium*, Evelyn Waugh's *Brideshead Revisited*, Mary Renault's *The Charioteer*. I do not know whether there are analogous texts for a younger generation coming of age in a climate more receptive to manifestations of same-sex desire, at least within institutions of higher learning where people may still read. Perhaps the wider availability of models of queer identity and desire in the popular culture has undermined the need for and poignant power of such queer classics, both ancient and modern. If so, scenes like that between Maurice and Durham are no longer being enacted. This may not be such a loss. Today, the pair might meet in a course on Lesbian and Gay Studies. Then again, they might find themselves discussing Plato's *Symposium* after all: the interpretation of ancient Greek homosexuality is a major issue in the contemporary controversy between "essentialists" and "social constructionists" as to the status and character of categories of sexual orientation.

So far, this chapter has focused on ancient Greece and its legacies to address historical issues; the next section addresses some of the systematic implications of these examples. Although the emphasis so far has been discursive and grounded in literary texts, the impulse behind historicizing sexuality is to situate both the experience of desire and efforts to theorize it within specific forms of life and political and intellectual institutions. Thus, the concern with sexual science here and in Chapter Four is fueled by its alliance with modes of social control such as courts, clinics, consulting rooms, and schools. Similarly, the revival of Hellenism in the nineteenth century was linked to efforts at social and educational reform and anchored in the intense same-sex experiences of boarding schools, universities, military units, and men's clubs. The importance of thinking about these institutional and political contexts is the subject of the fifth and final section of this chapter.

IV. The Hermeneutics of Sexuality

The emergence of lesbian and gay studies within the academy in the last decade or so has been marked by a debate between "essentialist" and "social constructionist" interpretations of sexual orientation. This controversy has covered a wide range of distinct issues. Many of them cluster around the core question whether the categories of sexual orientation refer to cross-cultural, transhistorical entities that can be defined in "natural," perhaps biological terms, or whether they are largely a function of the distinct historical and cultural forms of life in which they appear. In part, this discussion applies to sexual orientation traditional metaphysical disputes between realists and nominalists as to the status of general terms and concepts. In part, the debate asks whether in the development of sexual orientation in particular, individuals are shaped primarily by "nature," generally interpreted in genetic terms, or by "nurture," understood in terms of early childhood and other social environments. Lesbian and gay theorists also ask whether the field of sexuality permits distinctions parallel to those that feminist theorists have developed between "sex," treated as a matter of biology, and "gender," conceived as a function of culture and social organization.[42] In addition those primarily concerned with the ethical and political ramifications of the debate ask whether an individual's sexual orientation is the determinate outcome of causal factors over which she has no control or whether it is a matter of personal choice.

As Ed Stein has demonstrated skillfully, each of these separate questions engages its own field of conceptual, historical, and empirical issues and distinctions; the relations among these separate enquiries are by no means so clear as appears to many of those writing in the field.[43] Alongside and subtending the issues already mentioned, Stein identifies a further set of questions with important historical, conceptual, and political implications. These turn on the extent to which the categories of sexuality at work in a given culture or historical period may be commensurate with those prevailing in another. Of course, this critical question applies with equal force to the categories that organize sexuality within our own culture. This kind of historically and culturally grounded critical reflection is a pre-condition for considering the further question as to whether any of these categories for conceiving the varieties of sexuality succeed in capturing some cross-cultural, ahistorical "natural" reality.

This section recontextualizes some of these issues in relation to what I call the "hermeneutics of sexuality." At work in the debate between social constructionists and essentialists about sexuality is the "hermeneutic circle" that comes into play whenever we attempt to understand human behavior and social institutions different from those of our own time and culture. Simply put, we cannot interpret others without projecting our own assumptions about human motivation, conduct, society, value, and the like; moreover, the assumptions most difficult to identify and evaluate critically are precisely those so broadly shared and deeply inscribed within our own contexts that we may not be fully conscious of them. This difficulty was first articulated by biblical and historical scholars in the nineteenth century, and efforts to resolve it have informed the development of modern critical scholarship. In this sense, issues about the study of sexuality parallel those found throughout the human sciences.[44] Sexuality generates particular difficulties because its discourses are permeated first by the evaluations of religious morality; later, by the normalizing tendencies of naturalizing discourses in medicine and psychiatry; and, most recently, by reactions against both of these in the movement towards lesbian and gay emancipation. Much of the debate about sexual orientation has arisen in the setting of lesbian and gay scholars' efforts to retrieve and reconstruct a past different from that envisioned by the hegemonic discourses of compulsory heterosexuality. Indeed, one scholar has suggested that the energies at work in the constructionism controversy derive from its underlying character as a political dispute contesting the terms of contemporary lesbian and gay identities and communities:

> . . . it represents a debate about the content and character of gay identity. In other words, it seeks to answer such questions as: In what way do gay people differ from straight? How important are these differences? What implications do these differences hold, and how widely shared are they

among gay people themselves? Ultimately, the constructivist debate seeks to answer a question very different from the ones the participants worry over. It asks, "What does it mean to be gay?"[45]

To which we must add the further question: how much in the way of political work is already being accomplished with the assertion of a unitary "gay identity" or "gay politics"? Or in my own reference to "the hegemonic discourses of compulsory heterosexuality"? One cannot pursue the hermeneutics of sexuality without also engaging its politics.

The distinct critiques of essentialism that figure in lesbian and gay male theorizing complement each other to illuminate the hermeneutics of sexuality. For lesbian and other feminist theorists, essentialism about gender or sexual orientation occludes contemporary differences among women or lesbians that shape both identities and ways of life different from the projections of dominant groups; such theorists have been especially sensitive to the ways in which the experiences of contemporary women are refracted through a range of differences in social positioning. They have challenged the right of any single group to speak for all women or all lesbians, calling attention to the dangers in both politics and theory of generalizing the limited experiences of dominant groups and reinscribing the marginality of others. Within the complex array of modern societies one will find a variety of sexual subcultures marked by gender, nationality, class, race, language, age, or erotic style. In her recent work, *Getting Specific: Post-Modern Lesbian Politics*, Shane Phelan adopts the notion of a *mestiza* consciousness from the work of Chicana lesbian writer Gloria Anzaldua to show the importance of developing models of political identity that avoid the homogenizing assumptions implicit in unitary and exclusive concepts of identity. Phelan finds in *mestiza* consciousness a recognition of the plural, changing, and sometimes conflictual character of individual personal and political identifications. Indeed, the shift from identity to identification already undermines the tendency of essentialist conceptions of identity to reify historical processes and to isolate single strands from complex fabrics of experience.[46] (In Chapter Five, I shall consider further the political dynamics at work in the emergence of naturalized and exclusive identities for marginal social groups by examining the parallel between racial constructions of "Jewishness" and the invention of the homosexual as a new species in nineteenth century Europe.)

The proliferation of feminist theory and artistic work produced by lesbians and women of color sensitive to the multiple intersections of difference in modern societies is now finding its reflection in work by gay men as well.[47] However, the debate about essentialism among gay male theorists has focused on the historical dimension of the problem, asking whether sexual orientation presents universal characteristics common to contemporary and past cultures and social organizations. There is a necessary and recurrent interplay between the interpretation of previous cultures and the understanding of conditions in our own. Quite simply, we cannot answer the question whether Greek pederasty manifests same-sex desire of the same sort as that displayed in contemporary gay life without interrogating both the evidence about ancient Greece and our assumption of a unitary "gay life." To what extent does our picture of the latter depend on evidence or experience that is bound to social class, race, urbanity, or national culture? When Halperin implies that the *kinaidos* lacks the versatility and reciprocity exhibited by contemporary gay men, who is included and who is left out of his characterization of today's scene?

We need to come to terms with both the historical and the contemporary dimensions of essentialism; each debate has something important to contribute to the other. Those concerned with historical questions need to become more self-conscious as to the political assumptions embedded in conceptions of "modern homosexuality" or "lesbian and gay identities" that often lie unexamined in efforts to recuperate the past. I am convinced that the extraordinary range and high quality of recent work in lesbian and gay history works to enrich our capacity to recognize variety and complexity in our own time(s) and place(s). Historical scholarship in recent years has been especially effective in recovering the detailed texture and nuance of everyday sexual life in particular past cultures and subcultures: in works like Randolph Trumbach's "The Birth of a Queen" or George Chauncey's "Christian Brotherhood or Sexual Perversion?" we are introduced to distinctive forms of life, in eighteenth-century London and early twentieth-century Providence, Rhode Island, respectively, each of which was characterized by its own language and taxonomy of sexual types and tendencies quite distinct from each other and from those in currency today.[48] Indeed, the reductionist vocabulary of "gay," "straight," and "bi" seems quite poverty-stricken by contrast. Similarly, work by Lillian Faderman, Martha Vicinus, and Carol Smith-Rosenberg on women's friendships and institutions in the nineteenth century informs and reflects recent political and theoretical debates as to relative roles of sexuality and politics in lesbian self-definition and community formation.[49] The recuperation of past forms of erotic life in all their subtlety and complexity exemplifies the specificity and concreteness needed in analyzing and criticizing contemporary organizations of gender and sexuality.

In fact, Halperin's conception of the contemporary "gay man" as well as Phelan's "post-modern lesbian," and not only those, already mark a shift from the "species" of homosexual that emerged in late-nineteenth-century psychiatry. If they are at some remove from the status distinctions and rigid sex roles of Greek pederasty (and in the latter case, at an almost infinite distance), they are also remote from the "inner androgyny" described by Foucault. Considered as ideal types and forms of life, the contemporary "gay man" and "lesbian" are the heirs of medical definitions of homosexuality, but have been affected and effected as well by a "reverse" discourse of homosexual rights that has interacted for decades with movements for racial and gender equality within contemporary democracies.[50] These possibilities were inherent in the general deployment of sexuality as a form of normalizing power described by Foucault: the construction of homosexuality ". . . made possible a strong advance of social controls into this area of 'perversity'; but it also made possible the formation of a 'reverse' discourse: homosexuality began to speak in its own behalf, to demand that its legitimacy or 'naturality' be acknowledged . . ."[51] These transformations have occurred both as part of a dynamic of lesbian and gay self-understanding and as an effect of the social changes achieved by civil rights movements more generally. The first generation of homosexual rights advocates in Germany participated in the discourses that constructed the new "species." They combined biological determinism with ethical elitism as they argued both the political unfairness of penalizing individuals for an inherent condition over which they have no control and the ethical legitimacy of pursuing same-sex desires idealized by the inventors of Western civilization. Although models of same-sex desire as "interior androgyny" and as "pedagogic pederasty" contributed to the shaping of contemporary queer sensibilities, lesbians and gays committed to gender equality, interpersonal reciprocity, and modern democratic rights cannot embrace them without embarrassment.

V. Democratic Norms and Normalizing Powers

Much more needs to be done in delineating the vicissitudes of homosexual self-definition, community, and politics in the course of the twentieth century. The renascence of activism in the decades since the Stonewall Rebellion has resulted in political and cultural transformations that remain to be charted.[52] Homosexual definition has been subject to a process of meiosis giving rise to a proliferation of practices, identities, communities, and politics — lesbian, gay, queer, transgendered, transsexual, sadomasochistic, fetish, man-boy-loving, and so on. If this appears to be a fragmentation of sexual minorities, it coexists with tendencies that emphasize the intersection of sexuality with gender, race, culture, and social class in the formation of identities and the necessity for a politics of coalition among marginalized groups to effect social change. If Foucault is right about the special significance of sexuality in the shaping of modern politics, then we must try to understand lesbian, gay, and queer politics as a strategic site for the organization of broader social movements within modern democracy. In fact, Stonewall and its aftermath are inconceivable without reference to the Civil Rights Movement of African Americans and their allies and the Women's Movement since the 1960s. Recent decades have seen increasing numbers and kinds of marginalized persons and groups mobilize to assert their claims to equal rights and demand that modern democracies deliver on their promise of equal freedom for all. The proliferation of movements and claims requires a coalitional politics that recognizes multiple forms of difference, common experiences of marginality and exclusion, and a shared commitment to transforming social conditions that perpetuate inequality.

These concerns must be situated within the complex configurations of power in which they arise, not simply that of the movement for lesbian and gay rights and liberation. Foucault and later scholars have emphasized the role of medical science and allied institutions of social control in the invention of the homosexual as a distinctive kind of person. As noted, the very terms that shape contemporary movements of homosexual emancipation contain a legacy of medical and legal discourse designed to discipline and regulate the subjects of late modern societies. Simply reversing the valence of these terms from negative to positive may perpetuate insidious features of domination. Competing descriptions of lesbian and gay life and identity, such as those discussed in the preceding section, have only recently begun to emerge from within lesbian and gay communities. For most of their history, the categories of sexual identification and classification were imposed by diverse social authorities working together to exercise control over individuals: physicians, psychiatrists, social workers, and educators collaborated to define the terms by which behavior was described and evaluated, individuals diagnosed and treated. The transition in the nineteenth century from the theological vocabulary of sin and salvation to the medicalized language of illness and health, marked a sea change that effected the ways in which all sorts of persons were brought to understand themselves and others. Foucault's *History of Sexuality* teaches that the invention of homosexuality was one aspect of the deployment of "sexuality" as a pervasive instrument of control by which professional expertise and social organization combined to produce new forms of subjectivity that internalized social norms. The classification of perversions — together with the socialization of procreation, the sexualization of childhood and the invention of female hysteria — defined a new discourse by which all subjects of industrial societies were to be regulated. The debate about sexual orientation turns on the status and institutions of modern sexuality as such; the politics of lesbian and gay rights and liberation must be situated within the general problematic of modern normalizing power.

Modern democracies are very much shaped by forces other than legal regulation by the state that manifest themselves in a plurality of political and discursive spheres. A distinctive feature of modernity is that it supplements the juridical and repressive model of state action with a pervasive system of social relations that produces new institutional settings, modes of knowledge, and forms of subjectivity.[53] Foucault particularly focuses on the ways in which new instrumentalities for classifying and treating individuals based on the expert diagnosis of an "inner truth" identified with their sexuality work to construct political identities. These innovations in knowledge and social organization — linked with medical practice, pedagogy, social work, criminal justice, etc. — produce forms of subjective self-understanding that both incorporate and transform the new categories. Foucault characterized this pervasive, productive, and multivalent modern power as "normalizing" because of its capacity to shape individuals in ways that enlisted them actively in the perpetuation and enforcement of diffuse social norms. Modern power is intimately established within one's own subjectivity, no longer appearing primarily in the guise of the policeman or judge.

Perhaps the most celebrated and condemned of the new subjectivities is the new "species" of homosexual. As we noted in Chapter One, cultural attitudes towards human behavior in general and sexuality in particular have been dramatically affected by the institutions of psychiatry and psychology and the proliferation of cultural images and attitudes borrowed from these disciplines. Recent history has seen the extension of medical conceptions of health and illness to encompass a wide variety of behavioral and social matters ranging from the use of expertise in the criminal justice system to the pop psychology circulating daily on television talk shows. These tendencies came under increasing intellectual and political attack during the 1960s and 1970s, but the medicalization of sexuality has returned with renewed vigor in the wake of the AIDS epidemic. Lesbians and gays, as well as many feminists, have agreed in their condemnation of the conformist tendencies by which institutional psychiatry in the United States has joined in enforcing social norms of compulsory heterosexuality and gender subordination. Important recent scholarship, however, has shown that early homophile activists welcomed an alliance with mental health professionals only to discover later that the medical model of sexuality is a double-edged sword available to those hostile to lesbian and gay rights as well as to their supporters.

In *Sexual Politics, Sexual Communities: The Making of a Homosexual Minority in the United States, 1940–70*,[54] John D'Emilio retrieves an important chapter in the emergence of a movement for lesbian and gay rights. He stresses the range and diversity of views that informed the thought and action of the homophile movement in the 1950s. One important strand, which came to dominate, emphasized the importance of education and dialogue as weapons against homosexual oppression. For these activists, centered in the Mattachine Society and the Daughters of Bilitis, developing alliances with sympathetic "experts" was an important tactic both in building a self-conscious and politically motivated homosexual minority and in convincing society at large of the injustices of criminalization, police harassment, and general discrimination. Foremost among these experts were members of the mental health professions — psychiatrists, psychologists, and social workers. In the terms of the broader analysis of lesbian and gay rights claims developed in Chapter One, the early homophile movement primarily targeted the criminal law and the abuses of police departments in their efforts for reform. They were concerned about the range of discriminations in employment, housing, and elsewhere, but understood these as effects of criminalization and stigmatization. In pursuit of these goals, they enlisted sympathetic mental health professionals such as Evelyn Hooker, and widely circulated her research which showed that homosexuals were if anything marginally better adjusted than others in society. Educating the middle class was the primary strategy of reform. Remember that in the 1950s a full-blown conception of civil rights for historically oppressed minorities and the use of public demonstrations to dramatize demands for social justice were only just emerging through the efforts of African Americans and their supporters to end segregation.

In the early days of the homophile movement, activism focused on efforts to decriminalize same-sex activity and to undermine through educational work the moral judgments that supported treating homosexuality as criminal or sinful. The categorization of sexual orientation as a psychological phenomenon subject to the clinical judgments of mental health professionals rather than to moralizing public opinion appeared a useful strategy in the struggle for homosexual rights. Thus the homophile movement welcomed alliances with those who urged shifting homosexuality from the discourses of religion, morality, and crime — of right and wrong, good and evil — to the medical discourse of health and illness, function and dysfunction. The impact of the educational campaigns of those days is hard to measure. Although the period was not one of substantive law reform, middle-class attitudes might well have been importantly influenced by this paradigm shift.[55] No doubt the attractiveness of mental health models of sexuality was enhanced by a general tendency among educated people to prefer an apparently secular and scientific approach to ethical questions over one more obviously implicated in sectarian religious traditions. As it turned out, the new language, like the old, was fraught with normativity and readily available for the enforcement of social conformity. Indeed, it was even more insidious because of the diffusion and low visibility of its effects.

With the power of hindsight, we may conclude that the acceptance of a medicalized discourse about homosexuality contributed primarily to a reallocation of institutional roles in enforcing the constraints of compulsory heterosexuality. Rather than displace the coercive moralizing of a criminal law enforced by police, courts, and penal apparatus, the public redefinition of homosexuality as a mental health issue supplemented these gross instrumentalities with subtler forms of social control: a proliferation of therapeutic practices advertised themselves as curing homosexuals, now classified as "sick" by virtue of their erotic dispositions. In effect, as with many ostensibly progressive reforms of the penal law and institutions in the past, the medicalization of homosexuality resulted in encompassing more rather than fewer persons within an extended network of social controls. Mental health professionals worked adjacent to, and in cooperation with, the agencies of the criminal law, which by now include their own "treatment" staffs.[56] In company with other legal reforms directed toward the rehabilitation and treatment of deviant minorities, the pathologizing of homosexuality was used to justify coercive interventions. Whereas the psychologist Evelyn Hooker argued that homosexuals as such were in no greater need for psychotherapy than other groups, the psychiatrists Irving Bieber and Edmund Bergler labeled homosexuality a form of mental illness and announced their own success at effecting cures.[57] Such efforts not simply to punish, but to transform individuals turned out to be even more intrusive than the penal interventions they replaced. In addition, the adoption of the language and ideology of mental health cloaked such interventions in the rhetoric of humanitarian assistance. Compulsory heterosexuality was to be enforced not only in the name of community morality but also with claims to relieve the suffering believed to inhere in the homosexual condition.

This view of the matter circulated widely and was used to enlist concerned parents, families, teachers, counselors, and others in a sustained effort to promote general and individual happiness by curing homosexuals, whether they wanted to change or not. In recent memoirs of coming of age as lesbian or gay in America in the 1950s and 1960s, writers have chronicled the ways in which appeals to the joys of adjustment mobilized homosexuals and their families as well as mental health professionals in this enterprise — at considerable cost to those whose failures to change became an additional source of unhappiness. *Cures* is the revealing and ironic title of Martin Duberman's recent memoir of the period.[58] The characterization of homosexuality as a condition that brought suffering to those so designated traded on the prestige of medical science and gained plausibility from the fact that many homosexuals in this society have indeed experienced considerable unhappiness in connection with our sexual orientations. Whatever impact therapy may have on individuals, treating homosexuality as a medical matter systematically obscures the extent to which this suffering results from social oppression.

The emergence of a renewed movement for lesbian and gay rights and liberation in the wake of the Stonewall Rebellion of 1969 very quickly focused attention on the ways in which medical, psychiatric, and psychological judgments and institutions contributed to the marginalization of lesbian and gay male citizens. Sustained efforts at organization, protest, and education contested the notion that homosexuality as such is a form of mental illness or disorder, which interferes with full functioning, causes suffering, and is amenable to cure. Lesbian and gay activists directed their activities at the American Psychiatric Association and the American Psychological Association to press for reconsideration of the classification of homosexuality as a mental disorder, established officially in *The Diagnostic and Statistical Manual*, then undergoing revision, and embodied in therapeutic attitudes and practices. The appearance of a visible and vocal group of lesbians and gay men demanding to be heard on their own behalf mobilized homosexuals within the professions and catalyzed a debate in which many practitioners and theorists came to question the validity of received opinion. This process of study, debate, and political organization culminated in 1973 with the decision of the American Psychiatric Association to reclassify homosexuality, removing it from the list of mental illnesses and disorders in the manual.[59] The ongoing cultural effects of generations of widespread indoctrination in these views are not so easily countered. However, one predictable effect of the increasing visibility of the variety of lesbian, gay, and queer lives as more and more individuals come out and join together to form queer families and communities is that such stereotypes increasingly will be tested against personal experience and political challenge.

The earlier categorization of homosexuality as a mental illness, and the

74

continuing circulation of conceptions of different sexualities as perverted or immature forms of expression have provided ideological support for the refusal to grant equal citizenship to lesbians and gay men. However, Sigmund Freud himself criticized both the alliance of psychoanalysis with the medical establishment in the United States and the moralizing tendencies of his American followers.[60] Freud's pronouncements on homosexuality or "sexual inversion" are rich with critical potential regarding both popular and psychiatric attitudes towards lesbian and gay rights and liberation. In explicitly political terms, he publicly opposed criminalization of same-sex activities, insisted that homosexuality as such was not an illness, and argued that homosexuals should be considered for psychoanalytic training on the same terms as other candidates.[61] Perhaps the best known, but still too little known, of Freud's texts on the social and clinical status of homosexuality is the 1935 "Letter to an American Mother."[62] It was a private response by Freud to a request from an American woman regarding the advisability of seeking psychoanalytic treatment for her son. In 1951 the anonymous woman chose to release the letter publicly, and it was published in the *American Journal of Psychiatry*.[63] Freud concisely summarizes his views:

> Homosexuality is assuredly no advantage, but it is nothing to be ashamed of, no vice, no degradation, it cannot be classified as an illness; we consider it to be a variation of the sexual function, produced by a certain arrest of sexual development. Many highly respectable individuals of ancient and modern times have been homosexuals, several of the greatest men among them (Plato, Michelangelo, Leonardo da Vinci etc.). It is a great injustice to persecute homosexuality as a crime, and cruelty too.

These comments transcend the terms of liberal tolerance. Freud not only announces it a "great injustice to persecute homosexuality as a crime," but also insists in his own voice that it is "nothing to be ashamed of, no vice, no degradation." His affirmation of the ethical validity of homosexuality depends on two propositions: that some of the greatest figures in history have been homosexual, and that homosexuality is "a variation of the sexual function," not an illness. The statement that homosexuality results from "an arrest of sexual development" does suggest that homosexuals may be sexually immature or worse. (Freud's ambiguities on this point will be explored more fully in Chapter Four.) However, that reservation is immediately followed by invoking the accomplishments of Leonardo, Michelangelo, and Plato. These are particular heroes for Freud: he published monographs on the first two, and identified his own expanded conception of sexuality with the eros of "the divine Plato."

Freud clearly rejects the notion of treating homosexuality as pathology on a medical model: it is "not an illness." That some American psychoanalysts had been vigorous in enacting and defending the inclusion of homosexuality as a mental illness marked a departure from Freud's views. That some of them advanced the promise of "cures" for homosexuality through psychoanalysis as a treatment placed them even farther from the founder of their discipline. To the mother seeking help for her son, Freud went on:

> By asking me if I can help, you mean, I suppose, if I can abolish homosexuality and make normal heterosexuality take its place. The answer is, in a general way, we cannot promise to achieve it. In a certain number of cases we succeed in developing the blighted germs of heterosexual tendencies which are present in every homosexual, in the majority of cases it is no more possible. It is a question of the quality and the age of the individual. The result of the treatment cannot be predicted.

Freud denies that in most cases psychoanalysis can effectively change persons who are homosexual into heterosexuals. In "The Psychogenesis of a Case of Homosexuality in a Woman" he had argued: "one must remember that normal sexuality also depends on restriction in the choice of an object; in general, to undertake to convert a fully developed homosexual into a heterosexual is not much more promising than to do the reverse, although for good practical reasons the latter is never attempted."[64]

Freud does not rule out altogether the potential usefulness of psychoanalysis for his correspondent's homosexual son. His statement here reflects importantly on Freud's general conception of the relation between psychoanalysis and individual happiness: "What analysis can do for your son runs in a different line. If he is unhappy, neurotic, torn by conflicts, inhibited in his social life, analysis may bring him harmony, peace of mind, full efficiency, whether he remains a homosexual or gets changed." The ethic at work here is at some distance from the demands of conventional moralizing. What Freud proposes is an intrapsychic notion of the aims of analysis: psychoanalysis aims at bringing the individual into a more satisfying relation to his own desires. "Whether he remains a homosexual or gets changed" is incidental to this objective. For all of the attention of his American "neo-Freudian" successors to social adjustment and moral conformity, Freud subordinates these concerns to the achievement of a dynamic integration of conflicting desires and demands.[65] Once again, Freud finds himself in the company of "the divine Plato" whose *Republic* proposes a conception of justice as "harmony of soul (*psyche*)." (Plato's analysis of eros is the subject of Chapter Three where the comparison with Freud is pursued further.)

The extent of Freud's disagreements with even his closest colleagues in the founding of psychoanalysis regarding the status of homosexuality is further indicated in a letter to Ernest Jones, which Freud signed together with Otto Rank. After the British psychoanalytic association adopted a policy of refusing to consider homosexuals as candidates for training as psychoanalysts, Jones wrote to Vienna seeking the opinion of his colleagues there. Freud and Rank responded in these terms:

> Your query, dear Ernest, concerning prospective membership of homosexuals has been considered by us and we disagree with you. In effect we cannot exclude such persons without other sufficient reasons, as we cannot agree with their legal prosecution. We feel that a decision in such cases should depend upon a thorough examination of the other qualities of the candidate.[66]

The training of analysts was a critical site for the formation of psychoanalysis in both theory and practice. After the founding generation, candidates were themselves expected to undergo psychoanalysis. Given the complexities of the relationships between analysts and analysands, in which the desires, fantasies, and personal histories of both were implicated, the selection and training of suitable analysts involved complex judgments as to their capacities for sympathetic insight and interpretation and for reflective self-understanding. Freud's insistence that homosexuality as such should not disqualify individuals from consideration indicates the strength of his conviction that homosexuals are capable of the highest human accomplishments.

The juxtaposition of Freud's refusal to disqualify homosexuals for training as analysts with the earlier discussion of the deployment of mental health to enforce social conformity calls attention to an important duality in the legacy of psychoanalysis. At the same time that the techniques of psychotherapy became available to enlist individuals in the project of their own socialization, psychoanalysis held out to an élite the promise of bringing to light the dynamics of their unconscious and the possibility of a deliberate shaping of the vicissitudes of their desires. The vanguard of this élite would be those who themselves trained to become psychoanalysts. For them, the force of social conventions would derive from the role that they played in the history of an individual and the extent to which they could be brought into harmony with inner drives and fantasies. Interestingly, Foucault, who has been so influential in the identification and critique of normalizing power, already marked this ambivalence in *The History of Sexuality: An Introduction*; he refers to the "differentiating role" of the practice: ". . . psychoanalysis gave itself the task of alleviating the effects of repression (for those who were in a position to resort to psychoanalysis) that this prohibition was capable of causing: it allowed individuals to express their incestuous desire in discourse."[67] In this sense, it becomes a primary vehicle in the displacement of sexuality towards a will to truth: "Around it the great requirement of confession that had taken form so long ago assumed the new meaning of an injunction to lift psychical repression. The task of truth was now linked to the challenging of taboos."[68] Although Foucault does not fully develop his insight here, the differentiation to which he calls attention adumbrates the elite and ascetic "aesthetics of existence" that takes center stage in subsequent volumes of his history.[69] The notion that both the ethical quality of an individual life and one's standing as a citizen result from the capacity deliberately to shape one's desires is at the heart of the presentation of eros in Plato's *Symposium*. (In Chapter Six, we will see that Thoreau also links desire with individual ethics and political obligation in insisting on the importance of "resistance to civil authority.")

PART TWO

PSYCHES

CHAPTER THREE

EROS UNBOUND

⌒

A *Queer Reading of Plato's* Symposium[1]

And as for the 'stretching' of the concept of sexuality which has been necessitated by the analysis of children and what are called perverts, anyone who looks down with contempt upon psycho-analysis from a superior vantage point should remember how closely the enlarged sexuality of psycho-analysis coincides with the Eros of the Divine Plato.

—Freud, Preface to the Fourth Edition, *Three Essays on the Theory of Sexuality* (1920)

In this chapter, I develop a reading of Plato's *Symposium* that makes it more fully available for contemporary considerations of the ethics and politics of sexuality. I want to do justice to the same-sex love that provides its context and much of its subject matter and to recognize the enormous attraction of this work for generations of gay readers for whom it has been a source of inspiration and vindication. However, I am troubled by the difficulties inherent in any effort to translate the vision of pedagogic pederasty in the *Symposium* directly into the context of a contemporary politics of sexuality. Despite the genealogical affinities, too much ethical distance separates the institutions of the ancient polis from the actualities and aspirations of modern democracy. Greek pederasty was thoroughly entangled with a deeply sexist and pervasively hierarchical form of life. Contemporary debates between essentialist and social constructionist interpretations of sexuality have focused on the difficulties of translating between these contexts. Equally important, Plato does not simply celebrate the institution of pederasty as he knew it. Rather, he situates eros within a specific dramatic and philosophical setting and embodies it in diverse characters and social types. At the same time, he exhibits the power and pervasiveness of desire as a force at work for both good and ill in the dynamics of self-formation, the intricacies of interpersonal intimacy, and the contestations of democratic politics.

Plato's *Symposium* is a queer text and demands a queer reading. It is marked by exuberant energies and prodigal invention. It presents an excess of images and arguments deployed by a diverse array of complex, sharply etched characters. Their interactions traverse a range that includes virtuoso displays of poetry and rhetoric, agonistic disputation, campy flirtation, angry accusation, and moving self-revelation. Every discourse is deeply embedded in the character of the speaker and the contingent circumstances of the drama: the private party at Agathon's, situated in a turbulent historical context. Eros appears in many guises — sexual, intellectual, political, artistic, metaphysical, religious. Despite the enormous prestige of Socrates' account, it appears beside the extraordinary speeches of Aristophanes and Alcibiades, with their powerful competing visions. Plato's text is unabashed in its representations of erotic passion and playfulness, filled with sexual innuendo and indiscretion. It both displays and satirizes the conventions of Athenian pederasty. The effect is to transfigure the institution along multiple axes, in part generating a tradition of spiritualized friendship memorialized in the term "Platonic love." At the same time, Plato's *Symposium* is charged with homoerotic energy; its arguments and images circulate about that point. Plato's queerness cannot coincide with the contemporary variety. Whereas we are defined by our deviations from a matrix of compulsory heterosexuality, his text defines itself against a background of established upper-class pederasty intimately bound up with a pervasively sexist social system. Plato's text embraces and transfigures the power of eros, subverting the conventions and moving towards the articulation of critical principles. It places questions about sexual difference and desire at the heart of an enquiry into what makes for a good life. The distance between ancient Athenian and modern institutions and the radical character of Platonic reflection enable us to read the *Symposium* even today as an interrogation of the norms and forms by which gender and sexuality are organized.

A powerful tradition among philosophical commentators has treated Plato's *Symposium* as a vehicle for conveying the doctrine about eros contained in Socrates' presentation of Diotima's teaching. The dramatic context and the contents of the other speeches are treated as incidental to this central philosophical task. Some have argued that her eloquent rendition of love as a dynamic ascent from attraction to sensuous particulars towards a vision of the form of beauty itself is a dialectical synthesis of the earlier positions in which the partial truth of each is comprehended in a systematic whole. This reading has generated interesting debate as to the adequacy of the analysis presented there, focusing especially on the question whether Platonic eros can comprehend the love of individuals. My own reading is skeptical of the alleged unity of eros in the *Symposium*, both among the speeches and within Socrates' account. In what follows, I emphasize the loose ends, the unresolved difficulties, the implicit conflicts that Plato's text exhibits.

Plato offers us a complex literary construction in which speeches reveal both general arguments and the specific character of the speaker, where accounts are motivated both by a search for truth and diverse social and personal interests, where the dynamics of desire may lead both to great goods for men and their city and to excess, impiety, and disaster. By retrieving the ambivalent undercurrents that animate the dialogue, I offer a reading that resonates with contemporary understandings of the multiplicity, power, and uncertainty of human drives. Like Freud in more recent times, Plato forces us to attend carefully to the hidden movements of desire, its tendency to generate conflict even as it seeks unity, its embodiment in forms of life that it also threatens to disrupt. The vision of Plato's *Symposium* suggests that the queerness of sexuality derives not simply from its resistance to whatever social norms are historically in place but rather from its figuring of neediness and excess in a dynamic interplay that reveals the human condition as inherently divided and incomplete.

I. The Narrative Frame(s)

Plato's *Symposium* is presented through multiple and overlapping levels of dialogue and narration. The complex literary form contextualizes and qualifies both the dramatic and philosophical content. The subject of desire resists any a priori determination as to the appropriate approach, since the relative importance of feeling and reason is itself at issue. Technically a dialogue between an Athenian named Apollodorus and unnamed others, the *Symposium* is an extended narration of yet another man's account of a dinner party in honor of the tragedian Agathon which Socrates attended some years earlier.[2] The narrator and his interlocutors were just boys at the time of the event, about which Apollodorus later heard from Aristodemus, who had himself been present. Apollodorus claims to have confirmed the story in part with Socrates himself. This "thrice-told tale" is much in demand; only the day before Apollodorus had recounted it to another Athenian.[3] Each narrator emphasizes the fragmentary and selective quality of his recollection; both are portrayed as followers of Socrates who dote on his every word and have eyes and ears for little else.[4] We are invited to consider this account of the dinner party at Agathon's as another installment in an ongoing saga of the words and deeds of Socrates passed on from one enthusiastic admirer or "lover" of Socrates to another over a period of years. These details call attention both to the constructed character of the narrative and to the point of view from which it has been constructed. The speeches in praise of love that form the body of the dialogue are themselves embedded in a speech in praise of Socrates. Understanding the relations among Eros the god,[5] Socrates the man, and erotic love as a phenomenon is a central task in reading Plato's *Symposium*.[6]

Certain idiosyncrasies of Socrates are underlined in Aristodemus's account of the meeting that led to his going to the banquet. Socrates was especially well-dressed for the occasion, had recently bathed, and uncharacteristically wore shoes.

On the way to Agathon's, Socrates fell into a "fit of abstraction" that led him to withdraw from conversation with his friend and to remain immobile on a nearby porch while Aristodemus went on alone to the party to which Socrates had invited him. The banquet had already begun when Socrates arrived. The gathering celebrated the tragedian's victory at the dramatic competition the night before. Indeed, this is the second night of partying; Agathon and his guests have not fully recovered from the preceding night. Only Socrates is unfazed by the earlier excesses. The philosopher is indifferent to drink: by the dialogue's conclusion, he has drunk all the others under the table. Socrates appears untouched by the excess associated with Dionysus. The private party at Agathon's is similarly contrasted with the public festivities of the night before: the celebrants decide to forego excessive drink, to honor Eros rather than the god of tragedy (and wine), and to praise him in speeches rather than plays. Even the flute girls and their music are excluded from this all-male logos-centered gathering.

The physician Eryximachus, emphasizing his professional role, organizes this more sober and orderly structure. Speaking in the name of his special friend Phaedrus, he proposes the praise of Eros as a common topic.[7] He persuades the others to limit their consumption of wine and directs the flute girls to "play for themselves" or for the women in their quarters. The group assembled at Agathon's house comprises a cross-section of upper-class Athenian society. We meet the following: Phaedrus, the lover of speeches, who gives his name to a Platonic dialogue between Socrates and himself devoted to eros and to rhetoric; Pausanias, who is conversant with the ways of life of neighboring societies and with arguments made popular in fifth-century Athens by the Sophists; Eryximachus the physician, who speaks in the language of natural philosophy; and Aristophanes, the comic playwright whose portrayal of Socrates in *The Clouds* is mentioned in Plato's *Apology* as a source of the popular prejudice against him and who lampooned Agathon (as effeminate!) in *Thesmaphoriazousai*. Agathon the young prize-winning tragic poet and Socrates himself complete the roster of speakers who will compete with each other in formal speeches praising the neglected god Eros.

As the narrative proceeds, we note the special relationships between Pausanias and Agathon, Phaedrus and Eryximachus.[8] The praise of eros unfolds against a dramatic background shaped not only by conventional practices of Greek pederasty but also by the participation of two pairs of particular friends. This mutual reflection between the topics of the speeches and the character and situation of the speakers will be brought dramatically home toward the conclusion when the speechmaking is interrupted by the appearance of a drunken Alcibiades, crowned with laurel and accompanied by a crowd. This bright, beautiful, and brave young aristocrat — ward of Pericles and darling of the Athenian democracy — is described by Socrates as his beloved in Plato's *Gorgias* and *Protagoras*.[9] Alcibiades will insist on delivering a speech in praise, not of Eros, but of Socrates, whom he describes paradoxically, given the conventions, as both his lover and beloved.[10] The almost shamelessly specific details of Alcibiades' account of his relation to

Socrates concretely embody the ties between lover and beloved and problematize the relation between philosophical eros and the conventions of Athenian pederasty.

II. Heroic Passions

Phaedrus begins his speech with theogony, a poetic account of the birth of the gods.[11] He argues that Eros is among the most ancient of the gods, appearing immediately after Chaos and Earth, so old that "the parents of love have no place in poetry or legend." (178b) Among the oldest of gods, Love must be a source of the greatest goods. Phaedrus relies on the poets to make his case and does not stop to consider inconsistencies or alternative accounts. The most ancient gods were not necessarily the greatest. The Athenians worshipped a pantheon of Olympian deities that came to power as a result of generations of struggle between divine fathers and sons, culminating in the victory of Zeus. Positioning Eros far back in antiquity, Phaedrus risks the implication that Love is in opposition to the gods of the city. Such a conclusion would be at odds with the general tendency of his rhetoric. Phaedrus's major claim is that the greatness of love lies in its service to the city, instilling a sense of honor that promotes active citizenship and military heroism.[12]

Phaedrus praises eros for its role in inspiring individuals to death-defying acts of martial valor. He offers a vision of eroticized martial masculinity quite alien to most modern conceptions of male homosexuality:[13]

> If only there were a way to start a city or an army made up of lovers and the boys they love! Theirs would be the best possible system of society, for they would hold back from all that is shameful, and seek honor in each other's eyes. Even a few of them, in battle side by side, would conquer the world I'd say. (179a)[14]

Phaedrus's vision of armed eros resonates beyond this text. Plutarch reports just such an "Armed Band of Thebes" founded in 388 BCE and undefeated for almost forty years.[15] There are ironies of Plato's own in this text. In Plato's *Republic*, Socrates argues for the desirability of similarly joining private passion with civic duty. However, that argument differs importantly from Phaedrus' in that the couples are to be arranged by philosopher-rulers and both men and women participate.

Phaedrus's speech proceeds by piling up examples and adjectives. He is an enthusiast, and the objects of his ardor include eros, rhetoric, and myth. However, none of his poetic examples quite works in the way that he proposes. When they do demonstrate the extraordinary power of love, the love in question does not conform to the conventions of Athenian pederasty. Phaedrus mentions three cases in which a great love has transfigured the lover and produced deeds of heroic stature: Alcestis, Achilles, and Orpheus. Alcestis was willing to give her life that

Admetus might live, when his parents and friends all refused. But as a woman and wife to her beloved, Alcestis has no place at Agathon's banquet. Achilles and Patroclus were both warriors and friends in Homer; by the fifth century, they were seen as lovers, at least among upper-class Athenian audiences. However, Phaedrus calls our attention to the fact that Achilles was cast as the younger beloved; his heroic valor on behalf of his lover unsettles standard expectations. Equally important, Achilles did not save Patroclus but rather acted to avenge his death, which had resulted from Achilles' own refusal to fight because of an affront to his honor. Rather than witness to the power of eros, the tale of Patroclus and Achilles is one of anger, stubbornness, wounded pride, confused sacrifice, and furious revenge. Phaedrus's final example is similarly anomalous. Orpheus descended but failed to rescue his wife from the underworld, according to Phaedrus, because of lack of courage; he was punished with death at the hands of women. Hardly the testimony to erotic valor that Phaedrus advertises. None of these examples conforms simply to the pederastic ideal being promoted. Only Alcestis appears straightforwardly heroic in the cause of love, putting the men to shame before this self-congratulatory male audience. Moreover, although Phaedrus's speech claims to celebrate eros, his examples are quite strikingly obsessed with death.

III. Convenient Conventions

Pausanias's speech is thoroughly engaged with the world and its doings. He begins by distinguishing two kinds of love, the heavenly or noble and the earthly or vulgar varieties. While the noble eros is directed only towards boys, the common one includes women as well: "This, of course, is the love felt by the vulgar, who are attached to women no less than to boys, to the body more than to the soul, and to the least intelligent partners, since all they care about is completing the sexual act." (181b) Pausanias links this distinction to the difference between older and younger generations of the gods: the former is the "Uranian eros," attached to Uranian Aphrodite, "the motherless daughter of Uranus." (180d)[16] The other love is attached to Pandemos, or Common Aphrodite, daughter of the Olympian Zeus and Dione. The figure evoked by these pairs is that of the youthful male Eros together with the mature female Aphrodite, sometimes imagined as his mother. In allegorical terms that resonate throughout the dialogue, they signify the connection between love and its proper object, beauty.

Pausanias works his own variations on this theme. He constructs a series of binary oppositions joining on one side pederasty, the archaic gods, the soul, and intelligence; and, on the other love of women, the Olympians, the body, and sex. Pausanias's eloquence covers over some difficulties in his argument which is driven by both erotic and political aims. He adopts the Sophistic distinction between nature and convention, in which nature functioned as the basis for a rational critique of local ethical norms. In keeping with this figural logic, the older generation of gods stands for nature as higher authority than the gods of the city.[17] But

Pausanias wants to have it both ways. He presents himself as a supporter of the customs of Athens, developing an elaborate account of their rationality in erotic matters as compared with neighboring regimes. Where one would expect an appeal to nature, we find instead an elaborate brief for a certain reading of the Athenian law. The appeal to Uranian rather than Olympian authority suggests there may be more distance between Pausanias's attitudes and those of his city than he wishes to admit. The matter is further complicated by the tendency of the Athenians to identify the ancient gods with feminine forces, linked to both maternity and primitive violence; e.g., the Furies in Aeschylus's *Oresteia*. But Pausanias's aim in the speech is to defend a certain form of man-youth relationship.[18] He insists that the love he praises restricts its attention to young men who have reached the age of reason, marked by their cheeks' "showing the first trace of a beard" (181d). Pausanias's pederasty is directed towards the *ephebe* who is poised on the threshold of full citizenship and mature masculinity.[19] He works to contain his eroticism within the confines of respectable civility, suggesting that men attracted to younger boys are slaves to carnal desire, and probably pursue women as well.[20]

Pausanias's point is to defend a specific set of rules, attitudes, and practices which he ascribes to Athens. Although couched in terms of a shared pedagogic commitment to civic virtue, the argument comes dangerously close to reducing the erotic to practical calculation. Although the lover is portrayed by Pausanias as driven to public excess by his passion, there is method to this madness. He actually seeks a promising young man in whom he will invest his feelings and his patronage; his love is a wager on future achievement. Similarly, Pausanias advises the beloved youth — and claims that all Athens does likewise — to hold out until he is sure that the lover is not merely carried away by momentary enthusiasm, but will stay the course. Pausanias's description of pederasty makes it look a lot like the exchange of sexual favors for future patronage cloaked as education in virtue.[21]

The mythological confusions in Pausanias's rhetoric reveal the uncertainty of his own position with regard to Athenian sexual orthodoxy. He, like most of his interlocutors, is an interested party, committed to an aristocratic way of life in which pederasty played an important role. He argues that a young man can pursue no more prudent course in life than to take an older, articulate, successful citizen for a lover — someone very much like himself and his friends. Pausanias rationalizes the conventions of Athenian pederasty as good for the lover, good for the beloved, and good for their city as well. Uranian love is public spirited in its effects, bringing up the young to become good warriors and active citizens. But his political argument applies only to an eros constrained by an aristocratic ethos; the earthly variety is a source of disorder and corruption for both individuals and cities. After all, the conduct Pausanias ascribes to lovers would be called madness in others.[22] Pausanias attempts to establish Phaedrus's city of lovers within Athens. At the same time, his rhetoric justifies Athenian gentlemen in their pursuit of older youth and provides an excuse for these youth to submit to their admirers. The character of special pleading becomes even more evident when we realize that Pausanias never questions the aims of his noble lovers; indeed, he actively promotes the notion that at bottom their erotic aim is sexual satisfaction.

IV. Nature and Technique

While Pausanias spoke, our narrator reports, Aristophanes had been overcome by an attack of hiccoughs — and apparently some uncontrollable laughter as well. Eryximachus offers some professional advice and proceeds to present his own speech while the comic poet struggles to overcome the natural obstacles to his own performance. This bit of business calls attention to the order of the speeches and reminds us of the role of the physical body in conditioning the praise as well as the experience of eros. Both Eryximachus and Aristophanes emphasize the embeddedness of eros in a larger natural order, linked to living bodies as well as to listeners, tales, talkers, and citizens. Eryximachus speaks as the physician and natural philosopher. He takes over Pausanias's distinction between higher and lower, better and worse loves; he transforms eros into a natural principle — or two principles rather — since heavenly eros becomes harmony, and the earthly eros, discord. The poetic physics of Heraclitus and Empedocles hover in the background, but Eryximachus subordinates both eros and nature to technique, to the skills with which men shape the world.[23]

Eryximachus begins by adopting and generalizing Pausanias's distinction between two kinds of love:

> . . . Love does not occur only in the human soul; it is not simply that attraction we feel toward human beauty: it is a significantly broader phenomenon. It certainly occurs within the animal kingdom, and even in the world of plants. In fact, it occurs everywhere in the universe. Love is a deity of the greatest importance: he directs everything that occurs, not only in the human domain, but also in that of the gods. (186b)

Like Pausanias, Eryximachus effects an important revision in the conventional accounts of divine hierarchy. Without mentioning Zeus nor his predecessors, he elevates Eros to the pinnacle of power in the universe. In terms of natural philosophy, Eros has become the *arche* or first principle. Eryximachus builds here on his friend Phaedrus's assertion that Eros is among the oldest of the gods.

However, he also extends Pausanias's argument that there are two quite distinct forms of eros. His language quickly shifts from poetic theology to medical art:

> Consider for a moment the marked difference, the radical dissimilarity, between healthy and diseased constitutions and the fact that dissimilar subject desire and love objects that are themselves dissimilar. Therefore,

the love manifested in health is fundamentally distinct from the love manifested in disease. (186c)

In fact, Eryximachus goes on to claim that love is the subject of medicine par excellence. He argues that medical skill should arbitrate between desire and its objects, marking off the diseased love from the healthy. Eros here slides from desire towards appetite, the medical analogy capitalizing on the links between diet and health. In this generalizing move, Eryximachus postulates harmony as the measure of health and disease. Medicine becomes the art of producing concord among the potentially warring elements of bodily life. (186e)

Eros rules the gods as well as the natural universe, and human technique gives the rule to eros, directing what desires are to be gratified and what denied. Medicine is allied with the arts of physical education, farming, and music: all are defined by their capacity to produce harmony from discord. Eryximachus continually praises the beneficial effects of these arts and their role in distinguishing acceptable from unacceptable pursuits.[24] His elevation of Love to the first principle of nature accomplishes an imperial expansion of the realm of technique. He concludes by annexing the rites of sacrifice and the arts of divination which becomes a branch of the master art of erotics, ". . . the science of the effects of love on justice and piety." (188d)[25] This invocation of piety is rather stunning given the *hybris* of Eryximachus's account. Certain incoherences within Plato's text suggest its limitations. It quickly appears that harmony emerges only from the confrontation of opposites; organic unities are dependent on internal differences. Moreover, passion and pleasure seem always at risk of "slipping into debauchery." To be complete, the account requires a distinct principle by which to measure the difference between healthy and diseased desires.[26] Eryximachus offers none.

The text invites us to entertain some skepticism regarding both the natural philosophy and the medical knowledge on offer in Eryximachus's speech. The principles of healthy and diseased love, harmony and discord, do not appear to do the job he asks of them. Eryximachus offers love as the governing principle of the universe with no mention of sexual difference, heterosexual intercourse, nor of physical reproduction. These are surprising omissions in the speech of a doctor. He perpetuates the terms of noble pederasty, including its denigration of women and of biological reproduction, despite his adoption of the language of natural process. As to the medical skill on offer as the final arbiter of the ethics of erotic life, we find an example of his wisdom early in the *Symposium*. When the men consider how much to drink this evening and Agathon admits he has not recovered from the night before, Eryximachus welcomes the news: "Imagine how weak drinkers like ourselves feel after last night!" Barely pausing for breath, he goes on:

> . . . perhaps it would not be amiss for me to provide you with some accurate information as to the nature of intoxication. If I have learned anything from medicine, it is the following point: inebriation is harmful to

everyone. Personally, therefore, I always refrain from heavy drinking; and I advise others against it — especially people who are suffering the effects of a previous night's excesses. (176d)

In the end, Eryximachus teaches prudent calculation, not unmixed with self-deception, as a means to balanced pleasures. How seriously can we take the temperance lecture of a man with a hangover? The physician advertises his medical technique as a service to Eros, but he has no real disagreements with Pausanias's rhetoric of rationalization.

V. Ontological Lack

Aristophanes' mythopoiesis interrupts the cumulative effect by which the opening three speeches combine literary, political, and naturalizing argument to justify the practices of Athenian pederasty. He is the first speaker who is not identified in the text as having a special relationship with one of the other interlocutors. Aristophanes' singularity at this point stands out in bold relief against the contents of his mythicizing speech, figuring as it does the most intimate connections among human creatures. The break in the sequence is announced with the sneeze by which the playwright rids himself of his hiccoughs. Aristophanes uses the sneeze playfully to express doubts as to Eryximachus's natural philosophy: "Makes me wonder whether the 'orderly sort of Love' in the body calls for the sounds and itchings that constitute a sneeze. . . ." (189a) This reminder of recalcitrant physicality in the wake of the physician's idealizing and ideological picture of bodily processes alerts Eryximachus to the potential of serious disagreement; he warns Aristophanes to speak carefully as he may be called upon to make a formal defense of himself. (189c) The playwright's response emphasizes their differences and links Eryximachus with Pausanias. Aristophanes announces himself as the bearer of a new account of eros: "I shall . . . try to explain his power to you; and you, please pass my teaching on to every one else." (189d)

Aristophanes' teaching has indeed been passed on, albeit finally by Plato's writing. This speech is one of the great moments in Western literature, and has wielded considerable influence on subsequent efforts to picture and theorize the place of love in human experience. It has enjoyed a life beyond its literary context in Plato's *Symposium* and continues to resonate as one of the major alternatives to the views of Socrates in that dialogue. Plato's drama signals as much. As Socrates finishes his later account, Aristophanes is about to take issue with him when the conversation is interrupted. Although Freud invokes "the divine Plato" in support of his "extended concept of sexuality," he engages Aristophanes' speech in the opening section of the *Three Essays* and in *Beyond the Pleasure Principle*.[27] In the former, Freud produces a misreading especially telling in relation to his own objectives in that work: "The popular view of the sexual instinct is beautifully reflected in the poetic fable which tells how the original human beings were cut up into two halves — man and woman — and how these are always striving to unite again in love." He explicitly juxtaposes this view of the organic determinacy of heterosexuality with the fact of homosexual object-choice: "It comes as a great surprise therefore to learn that there are men whose sexual object is a man and not a woman, and women whose sexual object is a woman and not a man."[28] But no reader of Plato's *Symposium* could be surprised by this! In fact, Plato's Aristophanes provides an account of erotic attraction for which heterosexual, male homosexual, and lesbian attachments are equally legitimate variations of an underlying desire to regain a lost primordial unity.

Aristophanes' speech presents a vivid myth of origins. Whereas the earlier speakers opened with genealogies of Eros, the playwright offers anthropogenesis, a story about the emergence of humankind. And it is a story of transgression, punishment, and redemption: "First you must learn what Human Nature was in the beginning and what has happened to it since, because long ago our nature was not what it is now, but very different." (189e) In the beginning, we were creatures possessed of four arms, four legs, two faces, and two sets of genitals. The Ur-humans moved about upright and could proceed rapidly in a circular motion by performing something like cartwheels. This spherical motion resembled that of their parents, the heavenly bodies. At this time, there were three sexes: double-male, double-female, and hermaphrodite. The first were offspring of the sun; the second, the earth; the latter, the moon. Exulting in their powers and possibilities, they mounted an assault on Olympus itself.[29] Unwilling to eliminate the rebellious race and deprive the gods of worship and sacrifice, Zeus resolved to cut them all in half so they went about on a mere two legs, desperately seeking to be reunited with their missing halves. In one stroke, he weakened the creatures and doubled the number of worshippers: "As he cut each one, he commanded Apollo to turn its face and neck towards the wound, so that each person would see that he'd been cut and keep better order." (190E) The navel remains to mark our fallen state as both a reminder and a threat. If we offer further trouble, Zeus will cut again, leaving us to hop about on only one foot.

At first, devoting themselves to seeking their severed halves, the stricken creatures were able to do nothing but mourn their lost connection. Distressed that the race might yet die out, Zeus intervened again. The ur-humans had reproduced directly from the earth, sowing seed that matured into new creatures. Now Zeus, reshaped the contours of our ancestors, organizing the orifices and protuberances as a means of propagation "by the man in the woman." (191c) However, the aim of eros that drives humans to seek each other with such frantic need is not reproduction, but the recovery of a lost original unity. Sexual intercourse and satisfaction adumbrate the restoration of ontological wholeness:

> Suppose two lovers are lying together and Hephaestus stands over them with his mending tools, asking, "What is it you human beings really want from each other? . . . Is it your hearts desire, then — for the two of you to

become parts of the same whole, as near as can be, and never to separate, day or night? (192d)

Aristophanes imagines Hephaestus offering to intervene yet a third time to save an ailing humanity by welding the severed halves into a single being: "Then the two of you would share one life, as long as you lived, because you would be one being, and by the same token, when you died, you would be one and not two in Hades, having died a single death." (192e) The playwright asserts that no lover receiving such an offer would turn it down. He concludes, "'Love' is the name for our pursuit of wholeness, for our desire to be complete." (193a)

Despite the comic details, Aristophanes' vision of desire and its place in human life is a tragic one. Once integral and whole, powerful enough to take on the gods, we have been cut down to size. Our sexual strivings are reminders of the primordial unity we once enjoyed. Desire is a sign pointing toward a lost wholeness that overcomes all separation, even that of the body. Aristophanic lovers long for a single death.[30] But Aristophanes was a comic playwright. This side of utter transcendence and mystical union, success in love is a gift at the gods' disposal. After all, there are no characteristic markers of one's beloved other half. You can never tell who might turn out to be your perfect complement. The best thing to do is to love where you will, attend to your sacrifices, and hope the gods will provide.

As Aristophanes moves from his myth to its lessons, he closes the rhetorical gap between himself and the previous speakers. Love for the other sex among the offspring of the original hermaphrodites is taken as a sign of loose morals and unreliability: adulterers and unfaithful women arise from this lot. Male lovers of the male are praised as the highest sort. Of the descendants of the double-female, he comments only that they have no interest in men, but are oriented towards women: "lesbians come from this class." (191e) Aristophanes reiterates so many of the prejudices of his audience that the critical edge of his tale is somewhat obscured. Implicit in the figure of the severed halves of an original whole is an image of equality and reciprocity between lovers. Aristophanes goes to some length to accommodate his fable to the conventions of pederasty.[31] The result only calls attention to the incongruities: Aristophanes ignores the symmetrical implications of his original tale. He explicitly describes the offspring of the pure male as being drawn first to older men when they are young and to younger men when they mature. Boys who early take pleasure in the company of men will grow up to pursue their own favorites in turn. These are the "manliest" of boys. Aristophanes slyly denies "what some say," that these boys are "shameless," and asserts, "These are the only kind of boys that grow up to be politicians." (192b) At Agathon's banquet, such comments may be welcome at face value, but the irony here is unmistakable.

Curious things happen with biological sex as well as sexual desire on Aristophanes' account. He explicitly characterizes the original humans as coming in three sexes: male, female, and hermaphrodite. But what can sexual difference mean prior to Zeus's punishment in this fable? Sexual reproduction enters the scene only as a result of his second intervention to mitigate the effects of the initial splitting. Previously, humans propagated directly into the ground. We are told that prelapsarian males and females already possessed distinctive genitalia (with androgynes combining both), but these genitals are given no function. It would seem further that there was no sexual activity as such for these creatures: most of their energies went into the rotary motion by which they imitated the perfection of celestial bodies, an image of narcissistic self-sufficiency. Eros appears only with the fall from grace, with divine castration, one might say. Thus, Aristophanes' Ur-humans are credited with sexual difference in the absence of both sexual reproduction and sexual desire. Even the earthy Aristophanes has followed the previous speakers in developing a myth of origins in which sexual intercourse is a consequence rather than a cause, and birth and maternity are left unmentioned. What are we to make of the claim that the Ur-humans themselves were children of the heavenly bodies? For Aristophanes, even the most intensely passionate sexual activity seeks a wholeness beyond the body and its temporality.

For all of the vivid physical imagery, bodies and desires in Aristophanes' speech are transformed into signs of a metaphysical condition. The differences between men and women, between same-sex lovers and differently sexed lovers, diminish when all are recognized as needy beings searching for completion. The objects of desire — male or female, of the same or a different sex — and its aims — pleasure, discharge, companionship, communion — all substitute for a return to primal unity that can be accomplished only through divine intervention. Sexual desires and differences have been translated into a symbolic register of mythological proportion. It is no accident that Freud was drawn to this speech in his own most mythopoetic work, *Beyond the Pleasure Principle*. There he locates the vicissitudes of human desire within a cosmic struggle between the forces of eros, striving towards the creation of ever more encompassing ties with others, and thanatos, the death instinct that blindly seeks return to a state of quiescence prior to the emergence of life. Strikingly, the movement of Aristophanic eros adumbrates the dynamic of Freud's thanatos.[32]

VI. Poetic Production

Agathon, like Aristophanes before him, sets himself apart from the previous speeches, and announces a new beginning. He claims that the others have praised Eros only in terms of the gifts the god has given men, whereas he will be the first to celebrate the god as he is in himself. Rather than recounting the effects of love, Agathon will describe its intrinsic nature. He too begins with the god's genealogy; however, Agathon's theogony systematically inverts the tale with which Phaedrus began. Where Phaedrus insisted on Love's antiquity, Agathon announces him the youngest of the gods; where Phaedrus stressed his strength in battle, Agathon portrays him as a peacemaker; where Phaedrus makes him hard, Agathon shows him soft and delicate; where Phaedrus sees Love as a warrior, Agathon's Eros is a poet.[33] It is easy to recognize in Agathon's picture of the god a portrait of himself. Indeed, after he concludes the speech, the narrator Aristodemus reports: ". . . everyone there burst into applause, so becoming to himself and to the god did they think the young man's speech." (198a) Remember, too, that in *Thesmophoriazousai*, Aristophanes had caricatured the tragedian's effeminacy! But there is more to Plato's art than a parody of the handsome young poet's narcissism. All present agree that Agathon embodies precisely the qualities of youth and beauty so celebrated by the proponents of noble pederasty. The image of himself projected in Agathon's praise of Eros is also a figure of the ideal beloved in the eyes of his fellows.[34]

Young, delicate, supple, the ideal beloved also incarnates the qualities encompassed by *arete*, excellence of character. In Athenian popular morality, such excellence comprised four component virtues: courage, moderation, justice, and wisdom. Agathon follows the conventions in attributing each of these to Eros, although his characterization of these qualities is somewhat idiosyncratic. Justice is identified with peacefulness: ". . . Love is neither the cause nor the victim of any injustice; he does no wrong to gods or men, nor they to him. If anything has an effect on him, it never by violence, for violence never touches love. And the effects he has on others are not forced. . . . " (196c) Although these sentiments appear unexceptionable, it is hard not to wonder whether Agathon envisions a withdrawal from moral agency altogether. After all, how does one insure that he is never to become the victim of injustice or violence?[35] For Agathon, "justice" becomes a kind of complaisance: "And whatever one person agrees on with another, when both are willing, that is right and just."[36] Agathon's treatment of the other excellences is similarly suspect: ". . . he has the biggest share of moderation." This apparently paradoxical assertion is followed by a definition of *sophrosyne* as power over pleasures and pains and its identification with eros on the ground that "no pleasure is more powerful than love." (196d) Not even Ares can resist the force of Eros. Finally, the wisdom of love is identified with its capacity to turn all whom it touches into poets. Eros is identified with poetry, and poetry with creativity more generally. If Eryximachus transforms Love into a master of technique, Agathon subordinates technical knowledge to poetic production and makes Eros poet laureate — instructor of Apollo, the Muses, Hephaestus, Athena, Zeus himself. The youngest and freshest among the gods becomes the teacher of his elders.

The historical Agathon was an innovator in tragedy, and his poetic reversals here celebrate innovation for its own sake. Behind the softness and delicacy may be discerned some sharper edges and harder surfaces; in the supple fluidity of Love, a desperate flight: "He proves my point himself by fleeing old age in headlong flight, fast-moving though it is. . . . Love was born to hate old age and will come nowhere near it. Love always lives with young people and is one of them. . . ." (195b). Agathon here reveals an unsettling underside to the triumphalism of youth: to maintain itself, it must rebel against the order of natural processes, of coming-to-be followed inevitably by passing-away. Eros establishes a new regime in which old age — and ugliness — are permanently banished. Socrates' response suggests that he has not been deaf to the darker themes within this charming song: "Didn't I speak like a prophet a while ago when I said that Agathon would give an amazing speech and that I would be tongue-tied?" (198a) As he continues in this mock-modest vein, he manages to position Agathon in tandem with both Sophistry and archaic female power: "And you see, the speech reminded me of Gorgias, so that I actually experienced what Homer describes: I was afraid that Agathon would end by sending the Gorgian head, awesome at speaking, in a speech against my speech, and this would turn me to stone by striking me dumb." (198c)[37]

Whereas the older tales made explicit that new generations of gods came to power by subduing their elders with force, Agathon would have us believe that Eros the poet will prevail by charming the Olympians into submission. Agathon praises Eros for the surprising capacity of the soft and gentle to master the hard and tough. His portrayal of love glorifies a certain passivity, clearly linked by the Greeks with femininity. In *Thesmophoriazousai*, Aristophanes labels Agathon a *kinaidos*, presents him as effeminate in dress and manner, and organizes the plot around the plausibility of his passing as a woman. But the comic dramatist also portrays the poet's easy deflection of attempts to manipulate him into a potentially dangerous situation. Similarly, throughout the *Symposium*, Plato shows Agathon as young, beautiful, androgynous, and compliant: he even plays at turning over control of his household to the slaves — at least, to plan the meal. At the same time, we are not permitted to forget that this occasion is the second in a row to celebrate his victory at the tragic competition. Agathon has been the object of admiration, first for the entire city, and now for a gathering of its élite; no one challenges his place at center stage until the unexpected arrival of Alcibiades.

Socrates' mention of the Gorgon's head is a provocation: the handsome poet who flees from ugliness in all its forms will not welcome being compared to the dreadful Medusa. In part, the older and famously ugly Socrates extracts revenge for Agathon's restriction of love to the young and beautiful. But the comment also raises a question about erotic power: Socrates implies that the handsome Agathon may turn those who admire him to stone. Perhaps the young Eros disabled Ares by getting him excited. Freud, in a brief note of 1922, suggests that the severed head of Medusa is a figure of castration that represents men's terror in the face of women's genitals; the image of being turned to stone suggests the reassurance that erection provides that one is still intact.[38] But the erect penis is also vulnerable, as the castration of the Hermes statues demonstrates. (See section X below) Freud's insights may not be completely alien to Plato's concerns here. In a society where sexual desire is identified with virile assertion, the ambiguous figure of Agathon calls into question conventional assumptions about who's on top. As we shall see, Alcibiades' account of his own relation to Socrates develops this problematic even further. The image of Medusa suggests that Agathon's narcissistic poetizing conceals the tyrannical wish to make the world into a silent, immobile, and immutable audience, its gaze forever fixed on the poet's countenance. Eternal youth is won at the cost of total stasis. Poetry becomes sculpture — lover and beloved alike locked in a frieze of ardent desire and untouched beauty.

VII. Erotic Intentionality

Socrates, too, begins by announcing his departure from the methods and matter of the earlier speakers. Rather than launching directly into an encomium to eros, he directly engages Agathon on its nature. He moves from badinage about Gorgias and the Gorgon's head toward a more sustained line of questioning that demonstrates a clear critical intent. Socrates insists that he must have misunderstood the evening's project, in that he envisioned not simply heaping up ornamental praises of love, but attempting to tell the truth about the matter. He signals his fresh starting point by challenging all of the genealogical accounts of Love offered so far. Eros is not a god at all, but rather a *daimon*, combining features of the divine and the mortal. Before going on to provide his own genealogy of Eros, Socrates directly questions Agathon. Socrates seeks to establish certain points of agreement on which to build a fuller account. His point is simply stated. Love is intentional in structure: all love is *love of* something, directed towards an object. From this seemingly obvious and innocent contention, Socrates goes on to claim that if love is love of something, it necessarily lacks the thing that it loves.

Socrates appears to find common ground with Aristophanes in emphasizing love's origin in lack. Human loving is a function of our incompleteness: we are not self-sufficient but stand in need of another — or others — for fulfillment. For Socrates, recognition of this need leads to a dynamic of self-overcoming by which lovers continually exceed and transform the conditions of their lives. The dramatic form of the presentation reflects this point. Socrates has interrupted the succession of speeches by engaging Agathon in questions and answers. The exchange exhibits the interaction that Socrates discovers at the heart of all erotic relation: dialogic philosophy succeeds monological rhetoric. With the play of questions and answers, the dichotomy between active speaker and passive listener must give way to an exchange in which each participant must be both active and passive, speaker and auditor, in turn. Such interaction necessarily exceeds the intentions of each. Every move towards another meets responses it cannot completely anticipate. Of course, Agathon is no match for Socrates. Dialogue is no guarantee of equality or mutuality. Hierarchies of intelligence, insight, or rhetorical skill powerfully shape the exchanges, especially between younger and older men. Generations of readers of Plato have complained that too many of Socrates' interlocutors are quickly reduced to the status of yes-men. Agathon is so much caught up with himself that it is hard to imagine much of an engagement. His passivity is not receptivity to the other, but a withdrawal from interaction into protective self-enjoyment.

Plato's text displaces Agathon as interlocutor in favor of a younger Socrates as the philosopher narrates a dialogue between himself and Diotima, the Mantinean priestess, who initiated him into the mysteries of love years before. This shift serves several ends. Socrates lets Agathon off the hook by standing in for his interlocutor and letting his younger self espouse the views he wants to criticize. Similarly, rather than appearing to instruct the tragedian in the ways of love, Socrates positions himself as the student and attributes the wisdom to his (probably fictional) teacher Diotima. However, we must not make too much of the Socratic courtesy on display. Diotima and her teaching bear an uncanny resemblance to the Socrates known to readers of Plato's early dialogues. Of course, that may be because the younger Socrates learned his lessons well. But we cannot discount the range of ventriloquial effects which Plato's audience (and Socrates' within the drama) might be expected to recognize. The dialogue between teacher and student is itself framed and contained by the monologue of the adult Socrates. Within that context, the pattern of identifications established reflects on both the disparities in status, power, and intelligence between teacher and student and the ambiguous representations of sexual difference at work in the latter half of the *Symposium*. Socrates identifies himself with Agathon through the invocation of his own youthful persona; at the same time, he identifies himself with Diotima and her teaching, thus becoming both his own instructor and the instructor of Agathon. Further, the identification of himself with Diotima establishes an additional link between Socrates and the androgynous, even feminized, Agathon. The portrayal of Alcibiades later in the dialogue is also marked by sexual ambiguities that require a revisionary look at the conventions of Athenian pederasty.[39]

Socrates claims knowledge of *ta erotika*, the erotic things, as distinct from the many subjects of which he admits only that he knows his own ignorance.[40] But he attributes the knowledge to Diotima implying that he required instruction about eros. Is eros itself foreign to his nature? What about the fact that this instruction came from a woman? For the second time in a very short period, Socrates has brought a female into this emphatically male gathering. The voice of Diotima was preceded by the head of Medusa: where the latter turned men to stone, the former moved Socrates, at least, to inquire into his beliefs about love. Does Socrates imply that eros is the domain of women in a way that the speeches thus far have obscured? Is there an admission of Socratic ignorance, or at least of Socratic need, here after all? Is eros as the recognition of need the condition of philosophical enquiry? Toward what is it directed?

Starting with Agathon's acknowledgment that all love is love of something, Socrates uses Diotima to construct a sustained argument about the nature and effects of human love. He establishes that eros is relational, directed towards an object that it lacks. Where it appears that one loves that which he already possesses, the true object of desire is the *continued* possession of the beloved. The intentionality of eros is at least two-dimensional — from the lover towards the beloved, and from the present towards the future. The self-enclosed Agathon in particular needs to learn that love is directed toward someone or something *other* and that youth seeks fulfillment in a real future. Socrates underlines his differences with Agathon and the others by concluding that, if love aims at the beautiful, it cannot itself be beautiful; if love aims at the good, it is not itself good. He has arrived at a most unconventional starting point for an encomium, but his interlocutor is in no position to protest: "And Agathon said, 'It turns out, Socrates, I didn't know what I was talking about in that speech.'" (201c)

Socrates' account of Diotima's teaching begins at the point where Agathon became perplexed. How can it be that love is not itself beautiful and good? Is not love a great god? To avoid the unconventional, and perhaps impious, conclusion that Eros may be ugly and bad, Diotima shifts the terms away from such stark contrasts. She rejects the adequacy of binary oppositions. Good/bad, beautiful/ugly, knowledge/ignorance do not exhaustively define the possibilities. There is a vast domain of the intermediate, an "in-between" that cannot be located on either side of such dichotomies. Diotima points from a logic of "either/or" towards a logic of "neither/nor" or of "both/and." This point is dramatically embodied in a context where Socrates is identified with Diotima as both teacher and student, adult and youth, man and woman. In allegorical terms, Diotima indicates a domain of *daimones* neither eternal self-subsistent deities nor mere mortals, but "spiritual" creatures midway between the mortal and the divine. Moreover, the middle way is also the mediating way. For Diotima, eros is the daimonic relation that links the human with the divine.

VIII. Works of Love

Diotima now provides a genealogy of Eros that helps to exhibit his character as a daimon rather than an eternal deity. On a feast day to celebrate the birthday of Aphrodite, among the gods celebrating is Poros (Resource), son of Metis. The mortal Penia (Need) develops a plan to improve her estate. When the drunken Poros goes to sleep in the garden, she lies with him and conceives the child Eros. Eros combines features of both his parents; as Diotima tells us,

> . . . he is always poor, and he's far from being delicate and beautiful . . . instead, he is tough and shriveled and shoeless and homeless, always lying on the dirt without a bed, sleeping at people's doorsteps and in roadsides under the sky, having his mother's nature, always living with need. But on his father's side he is a schemer after the beautiful and the good; he is brave, impetuous, and intense, an awesome hunter, always weaving snares, resourceful in his pursuit of intelligence, a lover of wisdom through all his life, a genius with enchantments, potions, and clever pleadings. (203d)[41]

Diotima identifies eros with almost Protean mobility: ". . . by nature neither mortal nor immortal. But now he springs to life when he gets his way; now he dies — all in the same day. Because he is his father's son, he keeps coming back to life, but then anything he finds his way to always slips away." (203e) The phallic rhythms of excitement and detumescence resonate with cosmic cycles of coming to be and passing away. The insistence on process is carried forward in Diotima's assertion that philosophy, the love of wisdom, is similarly a matter of movement from ignorance towards a knowledge glimpsed but not yet grasped.

A careful reader of this genealogy will have some questions. How is it that Resource earns his name? All the effort in Diotima's tale is undertaken by Penia; Poros just passes out. In the explicit context of sexual seduction, the father is passive; the mother shows herself "brave, impetuous, and intense." What are we to make of the slippage between figures of masculine and feminine, maternity and paternity, activity and passivity, in this tale? If Pausanias could construct a heavenly Aphrodite that knew nothing of the female, has Diotima introduced a mother of eros for whom the male is redundant? Hasn't the priestess of Mantinea hi-jacked the party from the pederasts? How did a woman enter this scene in this first place? Without doubt, Diotima appears as an interruption of the defenses of pederasty mounted by Phaedrus, Pausanias, Eryximachus, Agathon, and even Aristophanes. When Diotima commands center stage, she not only reveals links between sexual desire and biological reproduction that the earlier speakers have obscured, but also defines eros itself as a form of pregnancy.

Love for Diotima is a kind of needy excess. In taking love to be a great god, young Socrates (like Agathon) has identified it with the beloved rather than the lover. The object of love is necessarily beautiful and good, while that which loves — love itself — lacks both beauty and goodness, without being ugly or bad. Love exists in a tension between the object of desire and its absence, perceiving the outlines of what it values without being able to comprehend it. The work of love is to bring the lover into increasingly intimate and productive contact with the object of desire. For Diotima, love is first and foremost a process of dynamic relationality. To love beautiful and good things is to desire that they become one's own. But love does not rest with mere possession: its aim is not only to have, but to become, to make something good of one's own. Pregnancy is the figure for this creative relation to the future, but Diotima refigures it as she proceeds.[42] Sexual desire, intercourse, and reproduction merge metaphorically (slide metonymically?) under the sign of beauty as Diotima generalizes: "All of us are pregnant, Socrates, both in body and in soul, and, as soon as we come to a certain age, we naturally desire to give birth." (206e) Why do lovers desire to make the beautiful and the good their own? To desire to make the good one's own is to desire happiness, *eudaimonia*, living well, flourishing. We do not ask why one wants to be happy. Love then expresses the human aspiration to live well. For Diotima, all men are lovers, just as all men who practice the arts are poets, makers.[43] By defining the good as the object of love, Diotima rejects Aristophanes' view that love seeks to recover an original wholeness.[44] The good and the beautiful point a direction but do not indicate a fixed object. Love aims at making something new; lack is overcome by creativity. Diotima begins with a naturalized model of (hetero-) sexual reproduction common to humans and other animals:

> . . . when a man and a woman come together in order to give birth, this is a godly affair. Pregnancy, reproduction — this is an immortal thing for a mortal animal to do, and it cannot occur in anything that is out of harmony, but ugliness is out of harmony with all that is godly. Beauty, however, is in harmony with the divine. . . . (206d)

The outcome of this train of images and thoughts is to identify the object of love with the fruit of erotic pregnancy. Mortal creatures moved by eros undertake their own renewal by producing new generations.

Eros is the principle that governs the motions of life itself and gives direction to action. It tends to break through boundaries, to transcend its specific object towards an open future. Despite the reference to "men and women coming together in order to give birth," sexual interaction is transfigured into parthenogenesis. The work of love in the world is to bring forth something new. The true object of desire is not one's sexual partner, but one's child.[45] In fact, individual lives are themselves an ongoing process of perpetual perishing and rebirth. Diotima points out that living bodies are not self-subsistent, unchanging entities but result from dynamic interaction with their surroundings; their physical constituents are replaced many times in the course of a life. Similarly, psychic life is a process of transformation and renewal; the love of wisdom is enacted through learning and growth. At the same time that pregnancy is reinterpreted as a capacity of all humans rather than of fertile females who have been inseminated, birth itself is displaced from a single event to an ongoing process and from a biological to a psychological and social context.

This displacement goes through several stages as Diotima continues. The desire to bring to birth in beauty is identified with the desire for honor.[46] Immortality may be achieved through biological offspring or the continuing praise through which the city remembers its distinguished citizens. Thus, Diotima reinterprets the heroic sacrifice of lovers as the quest for personal glory in the ongoing life of a community.[47] Echoing earlier dichotomies between heavenly and earthly love, Diotima distinguishes between pregnancies of the body and of the soul:

> Now, some people are pregnant in body, and for this reason turn more to women and pursue love in that way, providing themselves through childbirth with immortality and remembrance and happiness as they think, for all time to come; while others are pregnant in soul — because there assuredly are those who are even more pregnant in their souls than in their bodies, and these are pregnant with what is fitting for a soul to bear and bring birth. . . . Wisdom and the rest of virtue, which all poets beget, as well as the craftsmen who are said to be creative. But by far the greatest

and most beautiful part of wisdom deals with the proper ordering of cities and households, and that is called moderation and justice. (209a)

Note that the men seeking women are already pregnant themselves. Pregnancy is the cause, not the effect of erotic relationships. The noble young man ripe with excellence seeks out companions with whom to fulfill the potential he carries within. He is drawn to others, first by their physical beauty, but even more by the combination of beauty with public spirit. With a beloved youth, the man finds satisfaction in examining ideas and arguments in pursuit of human excellence. Together, they are inspired to translate their ideas into deeds and works. Women have dropped out of the picture along with the pregnancy of the body.

Pregnant in spirit, young men come together to bring into being the common life of cities — its arguments, investigations, knowledge, arts, and politics; this public life is exemplified in the works of the great poets and lawgivers. These works, and the deeds they celebrate and inspire, win their parents greater renown than any merely human offspring. Diotima's discourse at this point appears to converge with the defenses of noble pederasty offered by the other speakers. Pregnancies of the soul, nourished by friendships between men and youth, expressed in active citizenship and artistic production, belong to the polis. Bodily pregnancies, the intercourse of men and women, the bearing and rearing of human infants, are consigned to a lesser sphere: the household (*oikos*), the private space of women and family. In contrast with earlier speakers, Diotima grants some measure of dignity to this sphere in arguing that biological reproduction gives all life a purchase on immortality. But the introduction of psychic pregnancy and the transposition of erotic striving from the household to the city reasserts the conventional hierarchy.[48]

IX. Higher Mysteries

Erotic excess is not contained within the city walls. The dynamic of overcoming transcends those boundaries as well, bringing men ever closer to the gods. Where Aristophanes sees eros as symptomatic of mortality and a recurrent reminder of the distance between ourselves and the gods, Diotima celebrates eros as mediating between the human and the divine.[49] When Diotima transforms eros from ontological lack to the motive of creative endeavor, she covertly restores to the individual the integrity that Aristophanes displaces to an origin lost beyond one's own ability to recover. On her account, each of us always already possesses the capacity to produce what we lack. Erotic creativity gives rise to what is new and unpredictable. In shifting her conception of the object of desire away from the particular other toward the good and the beautiful, Diotima makes explicit the potential for over-reaching in all of our striving. We love the eternal: our deepest desire is bring to birth an object so full of beauty and goodness that it becomes immortal — we wish to give birth to the gods. Can this really be the teaching of

Diotima about the nature of love? Is this the wisdom into which she initiated Socrates? Is this not *hybris* of the most dangerous sort? Just the kind of ambition that Aristophanes saw as getting our ancestors into trouble? Recall that Aristophanes' criticisms of Socrates in *The Clouds* helped prepare public opinion to condemn him for impiety. After appearing to agree with Aristophanes as to the intimate link between eros and lack, Diotima transforms desire itself into a kind of divine creativity. She proposes an immanent immortality manifest in poetry, politics, and philosophy. Rather than urging pious submission to the gods, Diotima's teaching demands that we bring to fruition the seeds of divinity that each of us bears within.

The ultimate horizon of erotic striving is nothing less than the eternal form of beauty itself. The advent of "the final and highest mystery" marks a break in Diotima's teaching; at this point, she says that Socrates might not be able to follow her in grasping "the purpose of these rites when they are done correctly."(210a)[50] Plato's text offers reasons to separate the "highest mysteries" from the account of spiritual pregnancy that precedes them. Does this interruption mark a real discontinuity in Diotima's account of eros? Importantly, the description of eros as the orderly ascent of the soul through hierarchical stages towards a fixed terminus occurs only after this break. Diotima now describes a continuous progress of eros from an initial encounter with one beautiful person to a culminating vision of the eternal, unchanging form of the beautiful itself. Struck by the beauty of one particular body, the lover is led to see that his attraction is a response to qualities that body shares with all other beautiful bodies. Recognition of this truth effects a profound change in the lover's relation to his first love: ". . . he must think that this wild gaping after just one body is a small thing and despise it." (210b) Diotima does not recommend erotic promiscuity or an aesthetic collecting of beautiful objects. Rather than shifting from one body to many, she argues that the ascent of eros is directed away from bodies altogether. The "ladder of love" is presented as a summary of the prior teaching, from the perspective of its ultimate end.[51] This consummation is ". . . the beautiful itself, absolute, pure, unmixed, not polluted by human flesh or colors or any other great nonsense of mortality. . . ." (211e) What are we to make of a conception of desire for which the attraction to things of beauty leads to a vision that obliterates all particulars? If every object of desire disappears in the beautiful itself, what of the lover? Does he maintain a position of distance from which to behold? Or is this a vision in which the seer himself disappears? How can we evaluate the claim that this vision beyond vision, of a beauty beyond all beautiful things, is the fulfillment rather than simply the end of all loving and all striving?

There is considerable tension within the articulation of Diotima's final vision. On the one hand, she emphasizes the mobility and plasticity of desire, its capacity to attach itself to diverse manifestations of beauty and to range among a number of objects. These vicissitudes of desire suggest a Protean character of the soul transforming itself through a history of erotic attachments. On the other hand, the sudden appearance of a transcendent form of beauty itself as the ultimate goal and organizing impulse behind these transformations seems to foreclose this openness and subordinate it to an orderly procedure of psychic development. The turning away from corporeal realities is a double movement of conversion — from the beauty of particular bodies to the form of beauty that these share, and from the beauty of the particular body to that of the individual soul. Diotima appears to glide quickly from this conception of the individual soul to that of psychic works such as political participation, heroic action, artistic production, and intellectual enquiry. This general recognition of the qualities of beautiful soul leads beyond public life to the activity of the philosopher: ". . . the lover is turned to the great sea of beauty, and, gazing upon this, he gives birth to many gloriously beautiful ideas and theories, in unstinting love of wisdom. . . . " (210d)

This vision appears as an interruption of the lover's experience: ". . . all of a sudden he will catch sight of something wonderfully beautiful in its nature; that, Socrates, is the reason for all his earliest labors." (211a) Somehow, it is both the completion of a series of erotic sublimations and altogether outside and different from that process. Beauty itself is described by Diotima in terms reminiscent of Parmenides' great poem on the One: "First, it always is and neither comes to be nor passes away, neither waxes nor wanes." (211a) This idea can be characterized solely in negative terms: it is not beautiful in one way or another, at one time or another, in relation to one thing or another, for some people but not for others. It cannot be contained in any sensory image or specific idea or form of knowledge. Indeed it cannot even be said to be anywhere in particular nor to be an aspect of anything.[52] This utterly transcendent end is also implicit in the beginning and throughout the intermediate stages of the process. The paradoxical character of these formulations and the insistence on a radical break between erotic striving and consummatory vision actually preserves the identification of eros with excess, openness, and unpredictability. The overriding effect of Diotima's poetry of negative metaphysics must be to separate the ultimate aim of eros from any particular account that may be offered. This insight casts light, and projects shadows, across all of the encomia to love: the difficulties inherent in each speech reflect both the limitations of the individual speaker and the inherent recalcitrance of the subject matter. No account could be adequate to the nature of love, for it must necessarily fail to capture its ultimate horizon. Identifying the form of Beauty itself as the ultimate object of desire works to prevent closure and to maintain a horizon for erotic transcendence.

Diotima's celebration of the life that follows upon such a revelation as the life most worth living, of true happiness and excellence, is as devoid of content as her invocation of beauty itself. We cannot be sure that anyone has achieved such a condition; her earlier caution that Socrates may not be able to follow her into the highest mysteries applies to Plato's readers as well. From what perspective could we evaluate the claims being made? Of a lover who perseveres to win the vision of Beauty itself, Diotima asserts ". . . if any human being could become immortal, it would be he." (212b) There is less — or infinitely more — here than meets the eye. What if humans cannot become immortal? What if it is dangerous even to try? This austere and metaphysical vision receives "loud applause" from the audience at Agathon's banquet, although we are told that "Aristophanes was trying to make himself heard over their cheers in order to make a response to something Socrates has said about his own speech." (212c) We don't get to hear what's on the comic playwright's mind, as "all of a sudden" the orderly succession of speeches is interrupted by the arrival of Alcibiades, who hi-jacks the evening on a course of his own. Aristophanes' attempted intervention follows directly upon Diotima's invitation to Socrates and, through him, to the others, to follow eros along the path to true immortality. Perhaps "all of a sudden" Aristophanes is seized by a vision of humankind hopping about on one foot only.

X. Thus Spake Alcibiades

"All of a sudden," noise, and then a vision. Alcibiades — barely able to stand by himself! Amid the rattling of door, shouts, the shrieks of a flute-girl, Alcibiades appears, half-carried, very drunk, precariously leaning at the door, crowned with a wreath of ivy and violets and ribbons. An image of Dionysus, Alcibiades commands center stage from the moment of his entrance. And he commands the gathering as well, insisting that they join him in drinks and witness his crowning of "the cleverest and best looking man in town." (213a) Aristodemus makes it clear that Agathon's guests fall all over each other making Alcibiades welcome, Agathon making a place for him on the couch, between himself and Socrates. Until now, Alcibiades has not noticed him: "Good lord, what's going on here? It's Socrates! You've trapped me again! You always do this to me — all of a sudden you'll turn up out of nowhere where I least expect you!" (213c) Thus Alcibiades begins an explosion of drunken and extravagant protestations and provocations directed at Socrates. He accuses him of being jealous and possessive while displaying just those qualities himself: ". . . you figured out a way to find a seat next to the most handsome man in the room." (213c) There is no mistaking the intensity and extremity of his own preoccupation with the older man. Alcibiades is all over the map; he pictures Socrates as both jealous lover and unfaithful beloved. The combination of flirtation, jealousy, anger, hurt, and self-hatred in Alcibiades' performance displays aspects of eros that have been treated thus far only at some remove.

The exchange among Alcibiades, Socrates, and Agathon interrupts the relative order that has prevailed during the evening — a departure analogous to Aristophanes' sneeze or Socrates' brief lapse into interrogation of Agathon. Plato's text stages a lover's quarrel in which competing strains of hyperbole and irony interact. The focus of attention is Alcibiades — his drunkenness, his beauty, his excess — but Socrates displays extravagance of his own. After Alcibiades attacks him for finding a place on Agathon's couch, Socrates makes much of his friend's potential for jealous violence: "He yells, he threatens, he can hardly keep from slapping me around." He coyly begs Agathon for protection: ". . . if he gets violent, will you defend me? The fierceness of his passion terrifies me." The exaggeration of Socrates' plea and his almost campy tone command attention. After all, he claims to describe ". . . what it's like to be in love with him. . . ." (213D) Neither Socrates nor Alcibiades quite lives up to the expectations for lover and beloved generated by Diotima's speech. Their behavior confirms Pausanias' claim that lovers act like madmen.[53] However, Alcibiades represents rather more than a Socratic boyfriend brought on to enact and perhaps undermine Socrates' arguments about the effects of eros. The historical Alcibiades was a major, perhaps even tragic, figure in Athenian politics. His appearance in Plato's *Symposium* dramatizes both the power of contingent effects to disrupt an orderly course of affairs and of a turbulent political context to make itself felt in private.

Plato's *Symposium* is filled with echoes of events of 416 BCE. In addition to the almost mythical dimension of Socratic hagiography emphasized by the dramatic frame, the dialogue is saturated with references to the eventual defeat of Athens in the Peloponnesion Wars and the trial and execution of Socrates some years after. Because Agathon's victory at the Lenaian Festival dates the dramatic situation, we can locate the dialogue in relation to several events that were to prove especially fateful for Socrates, his friends, and Athens. In 416, the Athenians organized the Sicilian Expedition the failure of which led to their eventual defeat by Sparta. One of Athens' most talented and attractive leaders, Alcibiades was a darling of the city and was expected to play a leading role in the campaign. However, his promising career was sidetracked by a public scandal as a result of which he was accused of impiety and chose not to return to Athens. Instead, Alcibiades joined Sparta in fighting against his native city. The scandal was caused by the defacement of statues of Hermes that were installed as tutelary deities at buildings throughout the city; they featured large erect penises. One morning in 416, citizens of Athens throughout the city awoke to discover that the statues had been vandalized, the phalluses broken off. Accusations of conspiracy were widespread. Not only Alcibiades, but also Phaedrus and Eryximachus were indicted. They were also charged with profaning the mystery religions by publicly revealing secrets reserved to initiates. Socrates' well-known association with Alcibiades may have contributed to the philosopher's trial and execution for impiety and corrupting the youth in 399. The appearance of Alcibiades at the head of a drunken band carousing in the streets of Athens would surely recall this scandal for Plato's readers. Alcibiades' indiscretions and Socrates' report of his initiation into the mysteries of eros by Diotima reinforce the atmosphere of sexual, political, and religious irregularity. The voice of Aristophanes, defender of Athenian piety, has already been raised in dissent. Alcibiades' vivid presence in this dialogue seems to implicate Socrates in the kind of subversive activity for which the Athenians condemned him.

Alcibiades' speech provides the most detailed and intimate portrait of

Socrates among the many provided in Plato's dialogues. He offers two images of the philosopher's character and supports these with anecdotes drawn from his own experiences with Socrates — in the bedroom and on the battlefield. The portrait is deeply ambivalent, serving as both encomium and indictment. Alcibiades witnesses the coherence of Socrates' personal conduct with the ethical inquiry and exhortation in which he engaged, providing detailed evidence as to the philosopher's remarkable courage and moderation. At the same time, Alcibiades makes angry accusations against Socrates. He denounces him as fundamentally duplicitous and threatens to unmask him in front of his friends: "Should I unleash myself upon him? Should I give him his punishment in front of all of you?" (214e) Alcibiades is far gone in drink and emotionally out of control, his speech full of damning revelations of his own inner turmoil. Yet he insists repeatedly on the truthfulness of his exposure of Socrates, urging the philosopher to interrupt and correct him if he speaks falsely. (215a) Having arrived late, Alcibiades is told that he owes the company a speech praising Eros in exchange for his wine. Alcibiades protests that Socrates is so jealous he may not praise anyone else in his presence, not even a god! For the first and only time, Socrates attempts to intervene: "Hold your tongue!" (214d) Alcibiades has implicitly accused Socrates of impiety, of insisting that he be praised above the gods. He later charges him with *hybris* and deception, with pretending to be a lover when he is not. Alcibiades claims that he is too drunk for calculation, that he simply speaks the truth, as it comes into his head. (214d, 215b, 218a)[54] Although he urges Socrates to object to falsehood, the philosopher does not intervene after his initial silencing gesture. He makes no attempt to rebut Alcibiades' allegations. (215a, 217b)

Alcibiades compares Socrates with two figures redolent of Dionysian sexuality: i.e., Silenus and Marsyas.[55] These images show Socrates to resemble Eros himself as described by Diotima and situate him in the daimonic domain of the erotic :

> Look at him! Isn't he just like a statue of Silenus? You know the kind of statue I mean; you'll find them in any shop in town. It's a Silenus sitting, his flute or his pipes in his hands, and it's hollow. It's split right down the middle, and inside it's full of tiny statues of the gods. Now look at him again! Isn't he also just like the satyr Marsyas? (215b)

This speech is Alcibiades' punishment of Socrates. Like Zeus in Aristophanes' tale, he punishes by splitting his victim in half. Silenus is both an individual and a kind of creature; Marsyas the satyr was of the same type. Satyrs or *sileni* combined the features of men and animals, sometimes sporting the tails or ears of horses, sometimes the hinds of goats. They were rough and hairy, flagrantly virile, often displaying large erections. Followers of Dionysus, they played flutes or pipes to enchant the objects of their considerable lust. Satyr plays were an integral feature of the festivals at which tragedies were performed. An unlikely set of images with which to characterize the philosopher. But surprise and excess are part of the point: "You are impudent, contemptuous and vile (*hubristes*)." (215c) Part of the insult is physical: Socrates, about fifty at the time of Agathon's victory, was the oldest at the banquet, and notoriously ugly.

Alcibiades develops an analogy between Socratic conversation and the music of Marsyas. The satyr's flute music possessed those who listened and prepared them for a revelation of the Dionysian mysteries. (The language of initiation and revelation echoes Diotima's instruction of Socrates.) Socratic music, however, is produced through words alone: ". . . let anyone — man, woman, or child — listen to you or even to a poor account of what you say — and we are all transported, completely possessed." (215d) The juxtaposition of high praise and low insult in Alcibiades' opening salvo is explained by the impact that Socrates' words had upon his own life. Socrates' words set Alcibiades beside himself. He feels intoxicated, his hearts races, tears stream from his eyes, he is driven to frenzy. Listening to him makes Alcibiades intensely dissatisfied, leading him to feel that his political career is a waste, and that he should get his life in order.[56] Although he testifies to the inspirational and emotional power of Socrates' words, he does not witness their efficacy: "So I refuse to listen to him; I stop my ears and tear myself away from him, for, like the Sirens, he could make me stay by his side until I die." (216B) The life that Alcibiades saves by resisting Socratic speech is his life as the favorite of Athenian democracy.[57] In Plato's *Republic*, Socrates sketches a devastating account of the effects of popular adulation on a talented young man; this thinly disguised portrait of Alcibiades shows the tyrannical potential of an unlimited desire for the love of others.

The pathos of Alcibiades' feelings towards Socrates, and towards himself in relation to Socrates, introduces a strong, jarring note into the rhetoric and badinage at Agathon's banquet: "Sometimes, believe me, I think I would be happier if he were dead. And yet I know that if he dies I'll be even more miserable! I can't live with him, and I can't live without him! What *can* I do about him?" (216c) Alcibiades reaches heights of agony in describing the effects of Socrates' music. He presents not only a discourse about eros, but also an enactment of its effects. His speech *shows* us a soul in the grip of eros: the performance is far more ambiguous than the encomia suggest. Plato's picture of Alcibiades may imply that he is so hopelessly tormented that not even the most dedicated and capable lover could change him. Individual character and upbringing set limits to erotic transformation. If so, Socrates cannot be blamed for his failure to reform Alcibiades. Such a view of the limits on the effects of adult love is also implied by the insistence in the *Republic* on the extent to which one is always already shaped by the desires of one's family and community.[58]

The *doubled* character of the *silenus* statues complements Alcibiades' account of Socratic music. The external appearance of the silenus is a mask that conceals another domain entirely. The sileni are ugly, gross, and sensual on the outside, but open up to reveal an interior of beautiful, fine, and ideal images of the gods.[59] The image of the sileni suggests how the ugly and old may yet be a powerful object of desire in a culture devoted to beauty and youth. Although the splitting of the image evokes punishment, the silenus is self-divided. It is marked by inner differentiation rather than fragmentation. This duality is the source of Socratic *hybris*; it is audible in his repeated use of irony. In simplest terms, irony consists in saying something different from what one means: protesting ignorance to disguise one's wisdom, claiming to be in love when one is not. But irony is not simple deception: it is a figure of speech designed to provoke an attentive interlocutor into going beyond apparent and superficial meanings. Presenting himself as an ordinary man seeking the truth in the exchange of opinions, Socrates conceals a wisdom of great beauty; pretending to be a lover in bondage to young men, Socrates offers himself as a beloved ideal who makes them uncertain and ashamed. Socratic irony may enact a self-division that works erotically to lure others into transcending themselves. But its manifestation in the philosopher's speech and character reinforces Alcibiades' accusations of *hybris* and duplicity.

Alcibiades concludes his portrait of Socrates by recounting two experiences in which the philosopher displayed extraordinary moderation and courage. The first appears in Alcibiades' humiliating, funny, and sad tale of his courtship and attempted seduction of the philosopher; the second, in his account of Socrates' heroism on the battlefield. Alcibiades' attempts to consummate the relationship sexually resulted in a succession of frustrations, culminating in a night in bed: "But in spite of all my efforts, this hopelessly arrogant, this unbelievably insolent man — he turned me down! . . . my night with Socrates went no further than if I had spent it with my father or older brother." (219c–d) Socrates' indifference to Alcibiades' proffered charms has made a slave of the *younger* man. In fact, Alcibiades' response to Socrates already inverts the conventions governing lover and beloved: the handsome youth is hot in pursuit of his admirer. He confounds expectations of activity and passivity and reveals a patently sexual aim. Transcending the conventions in a different direction, Socrates calls into question the values of youth, beauty, and sensuality that he appears to embrace. Socratic eros is a mask; underneath the philosopher believes his own efforts to find wisdom are more important than the qualities he pretends to admire in his young friends. Socrates' conduct on the battlefield reveals a similar ambiguity. He saves Alcibiades' life, but disdains the honor he has earned; he performs feats of endurance in harsh weather, but barely appears to notice; he is as fierce and cocky in retreat as in advance. His fellow soldiers admire his accomplishments, but marvel at his strangeness. In both his moderation and his courage, Socrates acts as if his body itself were mere appearance irrelevant to his actual condition. Alcibiades concludes, ". . . as a whole, he is unique; he is like no one else in the past and no one in the present — this is by far the most amazing thing about him. . . . The best you can do is not to compare him to anything human . . ." (221d)

What are we to make of this portrait? How does it reflect on the competing conceptions of eros at work in the dialogue? What does it tell us about the links between love and sexual expression? Alcibiades' tale has been taken to exemplify Socrates' transcendence of sexual desire in ascending Diotima's ladder of love. He is said to look upon the beauty and desires of the body with indifference or contempt, having achieved a more intellectual love. However, the picture of Alcibiades in the dialogue undercuts the effort to base general conclusions on Socrates' behavior toward him. Sex with Alcibiades could be a mistake, without implying that the philosopher renounces all such activity. But then, Socrates himself repeatedly declares that Alcibiades is his beloved. Moreover, after finishing his speech, the young man deflects just this conclusion: ". . . I told you how horribly he treated me — and not only me but also Charmides, Euthydemus, and many others. He has deceived us all. . . ." (222b) The implication seems clear: Socrates did not have sex with the bright young men with whom he spent so much time in flirtatious conversation. Hence the purity of "Platonic love" for future generations. However, there is good reason to resist generalizing Socrates' refusal of erotic engagement. The singularity lies not with Alcibiades but with Socrates. The conclusion towards which the young man builds is the uniqueness of the philosopher among men: he is not to be taken as typical of the human condition. If Alcibiades is right and Socrates' love disguises his status as ideal beloved, the philosopher is a figure for Beauty itself, the ultimate horizon of desire, rather than for Eros. The image of Silenus embodies just this duality. The instrument of Socratic music is speech; our "Socrates" is constructed by many tales and ultimately by Platonic writing. Despite his failed attempt to close with the philosopher sexually, Alcibiades knows that it is his logos that must be penetrated:

> . . . even his ideas and arguments are just like those hollow statues of Silenus. . . . If you are foolish, or simply unfamiliar with him, you'd find it impossible not to laugh at his arguments. But if you see them when they open up like the statues, if you go behind their surface, you'll realize that no other arguments make any sense. They're truly worthy of a god, bursting with figures of virtue inside. (222a)

XI. Comedy and Tragedy

After Alcibiades completes his speech, the evening concludes with a final round of flirtation, interruption, drinking, and conversation. Directing his revelation of Socrates' erotic duplicity at Agathon, Alcibiades provokes another series of exchanges in which he and Socrates compete for Agathon and each other. The threesome on the couch seems unable to settle the priorities and valences of their relations. At this point it is hard to avoid the suggestion that a brief comic allegory is being enacted. *Agathon* means "good" or "noble"; the conflict between Socrates and Alcibiades in part enacts the question whether one's beloved lover or the good occupies the center of attention. The inversions of Diotima's and Alcibiades' speeches permit a reformulation of erotic relations to encompass the reciprocity of "beloved lover" and allow triangulation with an object and aim outside of the pair. But none of this is settled, for "all of a sudden" another group of drunken revelers appears finally to disrupt all remaining semblance of order. Aristodemus reports that amid general carousing, various speakers took their leave; he himself fell asleep. He recalls a final fragment of conversation among Socrates, Agathon, and Aristophanes in which the philosopher argued that the same man ought to be capable of writing both comedy and tragedy. Once again, Aristophanes is sidetracked by the demands of his body and falls asleep before the issue is resolved. Only Socrates remains awake at dawn, and a revived Aristodemus follows him as he goes about the business of another day.

These concluding details support a final effort to contextualize Plato's *Symposium*. Surely the writer envisioned by Socrates' final argument turns out to be his student Plato, author of this queer text that defies the boundaries of genre, traversing not only tragedy and comedy, but philosophy and drama as well. But Plato is not the only writer to have composed Socratic dialogues. My insistence here on the complex queerness of Plato's text is finally reinforced by a brief glance at the conclusion of Xenophon's *Symposium* in which Socrates is shown with different friends at another banquet where Eros becomes the presiding deity and subject of conversation.[60] There the discussion is superseded not by the unanticipated interruption of a drunken lover, but by a display planned in advance by the host. The entertainment culminates with an erotic dance performed by a beautiful young couple, a man and woman. The pair appear to transcend the conventions of public performance and enact deep desires of their own. Xenophon concludes: "When the guests eventually saw them in each other's arms and going off as if to bed, the bachelors swore that they would get married, and the married men mounted their horses and rode away to their own wives with the same end in view."[61]

Plato refuses this neat happy ending. The irony of Socratic speech and character, figured by the "doubleness" of the Silenus mask, is manifest in Plato's writing as well. Neither Socrates' speech nor Plato's text provides a discursive synthesis of the diverse perspectives it enacts. Rather each brings them together in texts marked by exuberance, excess, and conflict — provocations to critical interrogation. In the same vein, we may imagine eros itself as such a complex and mobile relation among bodies and souls, objects and aims, immanence and transcendence. Again and again Plato's *Symposium* displays the power of contingencies of timing, circumstance, or bodily condition to effect both erotic endeavor and social interaction. Socrates' solitary departure at the end underlines his relative independence of such effects and marks his refusal of the role of exemplar: he simply disappears over the horizon on his own way. Where Xenophon's vision of eros culminates with heterosexual intercourse and marriage, Plato refuses such a neat consummation but leaves us instead with the complex task of sorting out for ourselves an evening of dramatic interaction and Socratic singularity.

XII. Eros and Justice

Plato's *Symposium* is not a complete account of eros and its place in human life. One of its major effects is to question the very possibility of such an account. It is a celebration of eros, emphasizing the need we have to connect with each other and the power we gain to transform ourselves and our world. The *Symposium* portrays erotic relations as striving towards the highest realization of human potential, as friend, as citizen, as lover of learning. At the same time, the text dramatizes the risks and ambiguities that accompany this power, its capacity to disrupt the orderly course of affairs and to make men mad with longing and despair. The *Symposium* exhibits the extent to which the influence of eros is itself contingent on individual character and political context. The banquet at Agathon's is a private party among a select group of upper-class men; it abstracts from a range of differences and from the turmoil of public life.[62] But eros does not exist in abstraction, and men do not live for long without some social context. The force of love in bringing us together and moving us towards the future is conditioned by the constraints and possibilities of common life; eros is always already situated within specific cultural and political configurations. The drama of the *Symposium*, especially in the intervention of Alcibiades, shows the extent to which eros is contained by the city and may be distorted by the effects of conflict or ambition. Love and politics meet in concrete contexts where each has the possibility of supporting or disrupting the other. Eros unbound may be the inspiration for great achievement; it may also be the engine of disruption and destruction. A full and satisfying life requires the constraints of justice as well as the needy excesses of love.

Plato's *Republic* supplements the poetic and philosophical evocations of eros in his *Symposium* by sketching the outlines of a *politics* of desire. A critical dimension of its teaching is his insistence that excellence of individual character depends on the organization of education and political culture. Plato's argument that conceptions of justice must be institutionalized in concrete ways of life informs both the construction of the "ideal city" and Socrates' narrative of its inevitable decline. The *Republic* rises to a transcendent image of the good that informs justice in the city and the soul, but dramatizes the deep difficulties of realizing this ideal under the conditions of life in actual cities. The story of the decline of the just city of philosopher-rulers through successive regimes of city and psyche displays the extent to which the individual soul is shaped by conflict within the family, city, and culture in which one is brought up. That effect is enacted through the construction of distinctive forms of desire that animate and shape individual characters. The *Republic* is as much concerned with defining justice in the individual soul as with prescribing a political regime. It teaches that living one's life in harmony with justice will always require translation of the ideal into the historical circumstances in which one lives. The capacity of this vision to continue to inspire readers depends importantly on its formalism. Plato's conception of justice in the soul envisions negotiation among its component elements in an effort to shape a dynamic harmony from conflicting drives and constraints; the idea of justice marks a direction toward which we aspire. The *Symposium* provides an account of the energies that drive that effort. Despite their differences, the *Symposium* and *Republic* agree on the necessity of ordering the materials of one's time, place, and circumstance from a critical perspective that transcends that situation.

Has such a vision anything to contribute to thinking about lesbian and gay politics in this postmetaphysical era? The politics of fixed identities is at odds with some of the deepest ethical, political and metaphysical tendencies of Plato's work. Perhaps surprisingly, I believe that Plato's texts support a queer politics of interrogation, disruption, and contestation of conventional norms. As the *Symposium* witnesses, pressures towards conformity and foreclosure may be generated by any social or sexual orthodoxy, however it configures norms of desire. Queer politics drives toward justice but is suspicious of all claims to know in advance of political struggle what justice requires. It recognizes that the social movements of historically oppressed groups run their own risks of subordinating or marginalizing differences. To the extent that lesbian and gay politics depends on the definition of homosexuals as a specific kind of person defined by an exclusive attraction to others of the same sex, it perpetuates fairly rigid terms of erotic and political identity. The dynamic of needy excess and creative transcendence described in Diotima's speech provides grounds for criticizing any such restriction of one's attention and sympathy. The exclusivity taken to define much modern homosexuality runs counter to the inclusive dynamic of erotic aspiration; a politics based on fixed identities may foreclose the openness to contestation and negotiation required by justice. The indeterminacy of the ultimate horizon of erotic striving rules out any notion that historical hierarchies of masculine and feminine, straight and gay, conformist and queer can define what counts as a good life once and for all for everybody.

Plato's paradigm of excellence aspires to embody the highest form of human possibility; as the arguments of Book Five of the *Republic* emphasize, the opportunities to develop this potential should be equal for all. I believe that Plato concluded from the fate of Socrates that those who aspire to live according to such a vision are always at odds with the world which they find themselves in. Just as the different regimes described in Book Eight of *Republic* pose distinct challenges to those concerned to achieve justice within them, so too modern regimes of class and racial domination, compulsory heterosexuality, and gender hierarchy present their own challenges to contemporary struggles for justice. The obstacles to lesbian, gay, and queer emancipation are both specific and general, recent and perennial. Plato is especially helpful in reminding us of the possibilities and the difficulties that face any person seeking to live a satisfying and meaningful life in any time or place, and of the centrality of eros in that effort. The movement for lesbian and gay rights and liberation also requires historical analysis of the factors at work in the formation of queers as marginal or excluded figures in modern regimes nominally committed to equality and liberty for all. A reading of Sigmund Freud may offer some assistance in that effort. Sharing Plato's insights into the mutual involvement of personal desire and cultural norms, he develops an analysis of the ways in which an inchoate drive is expressed and refracted in a plurality of individual histories and social forms. He too begins with manifestations of same-sex desire but against the very different background of sexual science and bourgeois morality. In the next chapter, by staging Freud's encounter with the proponents of the "third sex" theory of sexual inversion, I trace the contours of an emergent modern homosexuality and reflect on its imbrication with cultural regimes of compulsory heterosexuality.

CHAPTER FOUR

PSYCHOANALYZING THE "THIRD SEX"

✌

Homosexuality, Sexual Difference, and Fantasy[1]

In Chapter Two, I charted the terrain on which the homosexual emerged as a new "species" of humankind in the medical discourse and social organization of late nineteenth-century Europe.[2] That period marked a transition, first indicated by Foucault, from a conception of sodomy as a category of forbidden *acts* defined by secular and religious law to that of the pervert as a *kind of person* defined by medical and psychiatric expertise. The new sciences of sexology and psychoanalysis played an important role in the articulation and criticism of conceptions of sexual deviance circulating in the larger culture and society; the diagnosis of perversion purported to reveal a deep inner truth about the pervert. While the crime or sin of sodomy could be committed by anyone, the acts and desires of the homosexual were treated as *symptoms* of a pathological condition, often figured as "a kind of interior androgyny, a hermaphroditism of the soul."[3] Early proponents of homosexual rights deployed this conception of a "third sex"— a distinct minority defined by an anomalous biological condition over which they had no control — to argue against the maintenance of criminal penalties for same-sex activities and social discrimination against homosexuals. In this chapter, I focus on competing definitions of an emergent homosexuality by staging Sigmund Freud's encounters in his *Three Essays on the Theory of Sexuality* with conventional medical and popular opinion regarding sexual inversion and with the conception of a "third sex" promulgated by pioneering researchers in sexology and early gay rights advocates Magnus Hirschfeld and Karl Ulrichs. Freud systematically engages the latter's conception of homosexuals as "psychic hermaphrodites," whose inherent natural condition is that of "a woman's brain in a man's body" or vice versa. His critique of such theories leads him toward two major insights decisive for psychoanalysis and for defining modern notions of homosexuality: 1) he rejects the adequacy of sexual "inversion" as a definition of (male) homosexuality and distinguishes sexual object choice from sexual identity conceived in terms of gender; and, 2) he generalizes the conception of "psychical hermaphroditism" as a combination of masculine and feminine characteristics to propose a primary, universal bisexuality that precedes the emergence of sexual difference in human development.

Both of these moves contribute to the disarticulation of sexual object-choice from sexual identity, distinguishing forms of desire from conceptions of one's own status as male or female, masculine or feminine. Psychoanalysis opened a domain of critical reflection on sexual desire and sexual identity that was inconsistently pursued by its founder and subsequent psychoanalysts. Both concepts of universal bisexuality and of "same-sex" object choice continue to be defined within a system of binary oppositions between masculine and feminine, same and other. This framework is grounded in neither biology nor psychology; Freud's analysis reveals it to be culturally contingent and mediated by individual history and unconscious fantasy. Although Freud explicitly rejected the adequacy of the model of "psychical hermaphroditism," and Hirschfeld used it to argue for homosexual rights, neither thinker succeeded in freeing himself of cultural assumptions that defined sexual difference in relation to a heterosexual matrix for which each sex/gender is partially constituted by an inherent desire for the other. As Foucault argues, "We must not forget that the psychological, psychiatric, medical category of homosexuality was constituted from the moment it was characterized . . . less by a type of sexual relations than by a certain quality of sexual sensibility, a certain way of inverting the masculine and feminine in oneself."[4] Whatever their intentions, these competing articulations of the concept of homosexuality worked in tandem to ratify stereotypes of effeminate male homosexuals and mannish lesbians. The continuing power of these images reflects the extent to which masculinity remains defined by the choice of feminine sexual object and femininity, by the choice of masculine object.

Freud's *Three Essays on the Theory of Sexuality* is poised on the cusp of an historical transition in the study of sexual variation. Defining the new "species" of homosexual was a controversial matter within the discourses of science, popular opinion, and high culture; Freud is indebted to the efforts of Havelock Ellis and an earlier generation of researchers to establish human sexuality as a legitimate subject of scientific enquiry.[5] Originally published in 1905 and revised periodically through several editions until 1924, the *Three Essays* begin with "'The Sexual Aberrations;" "Deviations in Respect of the Sexual Object" is the very first topic that Freud takes up in the first of the three essays that make up the work. The themes introduced here are reexamined and revised throughout his career. (In systematic terms, his careful discussion in this essay has continuing relevance for the contemporary debate between essentialists and social constructionists discussed in Chapter Two.[6]) Medicine and psychiatry at the turn of the century categorized different sexualities in terms of "sexual inversion" and the "perversions." Freud himself deployed, engaged, and reshaped those categories.[7] Freud did not fail to recognize the radical implications of his analysis. The psychoanalytic theory of the emergence of adult sexuality from a background of repressed infantile sexuality, polymorphous and perverse in its aims and objects, renders all fixed sexual identities problematic and needful of explanation:

> Thus from the point of view of psychoanalysis the exclusive sexual interest felt by men for women is also a problem that needs elucidating and is not a self-evident fact based upon an attraction that is ultimately chemical in nature. A person's final sexual attitude is not decided until after puberty and is the result of a number of factors, not all of which are yet known; some are of a constitutional nature but others are accidental . . . But in general the multiplicity of determining factors is reflected in the variety of manifest sexual attitudes in which they find their issue in mankind. (11–12)

Freud's argument in the *Three Essays* pivots on the insight that human sexuality is not the predetermined outcome of a biological process, but rather the contingent result of vicissitudes of personal interaction that give psychological force to inchoate drives in a context of cultural constraint. Sexual desire is various and changing; sexual identities, provisional and often precarious outcomes of ongoing unconscious conflict produced and sustained by specific forms of life. Freud's text underlines the separation of normative conventions from any natural or biological ground. Psychology charts the dynamic of individual negotiation among conflicting demands from inner drives and social norms. At the same time, Freud often repeats and reflects the judgments of the dominant culture of his time. This tendency is most obvious in his treatment of women in general and of lesbians in particular. In tracking his accounts of "sexual inversion," I hope to recover the critical potential and mark the conservative reiteration within his analysis. Freud's disarticulation of sexual inversion from same-sex object choice among men is accompanied by an uncritical reiteration of images of lesbians as mannish women. Too often, the analysis of universal bisexuality deploys conceptions of masculinity and femininity, activity and passivity, that have been culturally constructed to identify sexual identity and gender role with heterosexual object choice. Indeed, Freud's most radical insight in the *Three Essays*, that heterosexual genital sexuality aimed at biological reproduction is a cultural and psychological product rather than a natural condition, is most in danger of disappearing as he reinstates genital sexuality and heterosexual object-choice as measures of psychological maturity.

Like Plato, Freud reads forms of desire as constructed through complex interaction between erotic potential and the shaping constraints of family and culture. Freud focuses more sharply on the dynamics of conflict, repression and fantasy within individual histories; he does not share Plato's concern with articulating the ethical structures of distinct forms of common life. As a result, he leaves untheorized the culture of gender hierarchy and compulsory heterosexuality within which his subjects are located. But his culture is more nearly our own than those that Plato portrays. Although he lacks the critical distance that informs Socratic reflection and Platonic writing, the tensions and contradictions within Freud's texts illuminate the cultural and psychological contexts of contemporary queer politics.

Theorizing the struggle of sexual minorities for equal citizenship requires the expansion of conventional conceptions of moral autonomy to include freedom in pursuing sexual desires and forming intimate associations. Psychoanalysis offers a powerful framework that recognizes the centrality of desire in defining personal happiness and individual identity and acknowledges the extraordinary multiplicity of its manifestations. Freud's enterprise, troubled and incomplete though it may be, has demonstrated two points crucial to any movement toward full equality for queer citizens: psychoanalysis insists upon *the pervasiveness of sexuality* and *the multiplicity of its forms*. Freud shows with extraordinary subtlety and suppleness the centrality of sexual desire and sexual difference in shaping individual lives and contributing to human accomplishment. At his best, and despite recurrent ambivalence, he emphasizes the diversity and plasticity of the sexual drive, unsettles conventional categories of sexuality, and denaturalizes the norms by which it is governed. From the immanent critique of Freud's theories of female sexuality emerges a third point crucial for the future of queer theory and politics: *the mutual imbrication of sexuality and sexual difference*. Although the asymmetry between Freud's analyses of male and female sexuality shows him reiterating cultural constructions of masculinity and femininity, this very fact underlines the entanglement of sexual desires and identities with the conventions defining gender and sexual development under regimes of compulsory heterosexuality.

I. Types of Inversion

Freud's *Three Essays* provide a veritable palimpsest of his developing understandings of sexuality and its place in human life. His substantial revisions over a period of almost twenty years reflect the results of his ongoing engagement with both clinical materials and systematic theorization. The added footnotes and completely new sections expand and modify the earlier essays, continually recontextualizing them in relation to the emergence of psychoanalysis as a reflective, collaborative discipline. In addition, the *Three Essays* represent a complex argumentative and rhetorical strategy that remains constant throughout the revisions and that bears importantly on the status of homosexuality in Freud's theory of sexuality. The text is divided into three essays: "Sexual Aberrations," "Infantile Sexuality," and "Transformations of Puberty." The first essay begins with a section on "Deviations with Respect to the Sexual Object" of which the first subsection is "Inversion." (The second deals with "Sexually Immature Persons and Animals as Sexual Objects.") Freud's choice of starting point is no accident; he uses the investigation of sexual inversion to effect an expansion and transformation of the very concept of human sexuality.

Freud's taxonomy and analysis complicate the phenomena of sexual diversity to the extent of undermining the conventional medical classifications that provide his starting point. Thus, although he deploys the language of inversion and perversion throughout the *Three Essays*, his initial discussion redefines inversion as deviation (from social norms) with respect to sexual object and perversion as deviation with respect to sexual aim. The object is the person, thing, or idea towards which a drive is directed; the sexual aim, the act that would satisfy the drive. This treatment of inversion undermines the prevalent identification of same-sex object choice with deviation from the subjective identity or gender role assigned to one's biological sex. The popular and medical association of sexual inversion with gender inversion conceived of same-sex desire as a characteristic of mannish women and effeminate men. Homosexual male bodies were understood to contain "souls" or "brains" of (heterosexual) women; lesbian bodies, those of (heterosexual) men. Freud's insistence on a distinction between sexual object choice and sexual identification works to undercut that association while his repeated references to mannish lesbians reinforces it. Similarly, his analysis of sexual perversion as deviation from the normative aim of heterosexual genital intercourse unsettles the very concept of perverted sexual aims even while he continues to deploy it.[8] Widespread sexual practices (kissing, caressing) preliminary to or stopping short of vaginal intercourse are marked as perverted if the pleasures of foreplay be lingered over too long or replace the "end pleasure" of intercourse.[9]

The most radical insight in Freud's *Three Essays* is the de-naturalization of all normativity regarding human sexuality despite his own tendency to reinstate reproductive teleology in models of psychological development. Nonetheless, the analysis of individual psychology in the *Three Essays* distinguishes it from both biological development and cultural convention. Norms cannot be inferred from natural processes or reduced to social rules but rather emerge from complex histories of psychological negotiation between inherent drives and cultural constraints. Freud's analysis drives towards a radical conclusion:

> . . . we have been in the habit of regarding the connection between the sexual instinct and the sexual object as more intimate than it in fact is. Experience of the cases that are considered abnormal has shown us that in them the sexual instinct and the sexual object are merely soldered together. . . . (13–14)

The standard translation here muddles what Freud's German explicitly distinguishes. Sexual "instinct" translates *Triebe* or drive, rather than *Instinkt*. The point is that whereas animal instincts are inherently linked to their objects and aims, human drives are not. Drives undergo historical vicissitudes (*Shicksal*) as a result of which they become attached to objects and oriented towards specific aims. Instincts develop in accordance with a fixed teleology; drives are subject to contingent histories with provisional and often precarious outcomes.

Freud initially describes three main types of sexual inversion; however, taxonomy is just a starting point for his inquiry.[10] He is more interested in locating his types along a spectrum of desire than in constructing hard and fast distinctions among forms of sexuality. He problematizes today's fixed conceptions of homosexuality just as much as the conventions of his own time. Indeed Freud denies the proposition that "homosexuality" defines a single class of psychological phenomena; he rejects it as a diagnostic category for psychoanalysis. Although Freud deploys the generalized language of sexual inversion, he defines its types in terms of object choice: 1) the "absolute invert," similar to today's lesbian or gay man, displays an exclusive sexual interest in objects of the same sex; 2) the "amphigenic invert" or "psychosexual hermaphrodite," similar to the contemporary bisexual, may be attracted to objects of both sexes; and 3) the "contingent invert," similar to today's "opportunistic" homosexual, turns to objects of the same sex as a result of external circumstance, especially when confined in a same-sex environment. (My translation into contemporary categories is licensed by the widespread acceptance of conceiving homosexuality in terms of object choice.) Although it enacts a transition from the "sexual invert" to the modern "homosexual," Freud's text treats the categories as rough approximations to diverse outcomes of individual histories in distinct cultural contexts. The over-all strategy of the *Three Essays* is to establish a continuum of sexual manifestations that result from the persistence throughout one's life of repressed infantile polymorphous perverse desires. Freud consistently reads the varieties of sexual expression — even the most unusual "perversions"— as revealing possibilities inherent in human desire. He questions the adequacy of any conception of fixed sexual identities by insisting that these result from the psychological mediation of inchoate demands originating in the body and of constraints imposed by social organization.

The complexity of Freud's reworking of these notions is reflected in his typology of sexual inversion. The classification of inverts into three kinds is complicated by the introduction of two additional factors that cut across and qualify all three: the individual's subjective attitude towards emergent desires and the timing of their appearance within his history. Freud defines the former as the degree to which the individual affected "accepts his sexual inversion as something in the natural course of things" or to which he rebels against it. The critical question is not whether one's sexual disposition in fact *be* "natural," but rather whether a person accepts or rejects it as such. In his "Letter to an American Mother," (discussed above in Chapter Two,) Freud identifies the individual's attitude towards his sexual dispositions as the crucial issue in determining whether psychoanalysis would be helpful.[11] The second additional factor has to do with the particulars of individual life stories.

Sexual inversion is a temporal phenomenon, it is both the outcome of a history and subject to ongoing vicissitudes. Freud emphasizes the importance of timing along two dimensions: l) the time at which object-choice first becomes

evident, whether early in childhood, at puberty, or even later, and 2) whether it remains constant or alters over time, perhaps vacillating between "inverted" and
"normal" patterns. Subjective attitude and erotic history may be independent of
each other and of the variables defined in the earlier typology. However, Freud
recognizes some overlap: for instance, the "absolute invert" may be most accepting of her situation, which may have appeared early in her life and be least subject
to change. Importantly, Freud recognizes that an individual's memory alone,
shaped as it is by a host of factors, is not the most reliable guide to these questions
of temporality. His observation remains pertinent to the claims of those gay essentialists who argue that homosexuality must be innate since they have desired others of their own sex for as long as they can remember:

> Many writers have insisted with justice that the dates assigned by inverts
> themselves for the appearance of their tendency to inversion are untrust-
> worthy, since they have repressed the evidence of their heterosexual
> feelings from their memory. (3, n.)

Even more important, given Freud's argument about infantile sexuality in the
Three Essays, is the sly implication that heterosexuals have similarly repressed
their own memories of same-sex desires and experience.

II. "Innate" and "Degenerate" Conditions

Freud goes on to criticize the "general view" concerning sexual inversion: that it
is "innate" and "degenerate." Although Freud treats this view largely as popular
opinion, Arnold Davidson has argued persuasively that it expressed the prevalent
opinion of medical authorities in Freud's day.[12] The discussion of these issues in
Three Essays is relevant to two major contemporary questions: whether homosexuality is an essential, genetically determined condition and whether it is a form of
mental illness. Freud defines "degeneracy" as a condition requiring both: 1) the
presence together of "several serious deviations from the norm," and 2) serious
impairment of the individual's capacity for "efficient functioning and survival."
He argues that neither requirement is met by the facts about sexual inversion: it
may appear unaccompanied by other serious deviations from social norms; and "it
is similarly found in people whose efficiency is unimpaired, and who are indeed
distinguished by specially high intellectual development and ethical culture."
(4–5) He concludes that it is of little value to "regard inversion as a sign of degeneracy" if one considers certain historical facts outside the purview of medical practice: that homosexuality was "one might almost say an institution charged with
important functions — among the peoples of antiquity at the height of their civilization" and that it is widespread among "many savage and primitive races,"
while "degeneracy" applies to conditions of advanced civilizations. The reference
to the institution of pederasty among the Greeks reminds us that Freud shared

the legacy of nineteenth century Hellenism discussed in Chapter Two.[13] In a note, Freud welcomes the displacement of the "pathological approach" that sees inversion as "degenerate" by an "anthropological" approach that locates sexual object-choice in complex cultural configurations. (5)

Despite the propensity of subsequent psychoanalytic theorists and institutions to essentialize and pathologize homosexuality, Freud rejects both moves. Although couched in the language of his times, Freud makes two points frequently encountered in the arguments of contemporary theorists: 1) the institutionalization of homosexuality among the ancient Greeks suggests an alternative organization of sexuality within which homosexual attachments, at least between men, were seen as fulfilling positive social functions; and 2) the appearance of homosexuality among "many savage and primitive peoples" attests to both its "naturalness" and to the diversity of culturally-acceptable sexual manifestations.[14] Thus Freud is prepared to invoke historical and anthropological evidence to counter the reduction of sexuality to biological and medical models. He contests both the definition of sexual forms without reference to the cultures in which they appear and the imposition of one's own cultural judgments under the guise of medical expertise. These examples are linked to Freud's more general efforts to theorize the relations between sexuality and social organization. Freud explicitly invokes the conception of eros of "the divine Plato" in defense of his own enlarged conception of sexuality in the Introduction to Fourth Edition of *Three Essays*. In his own anthropological texts and in comments elsewhere that he does not theoretically elaborate, Freud identifies homoerotic ties between men with the cultivation of social solidarity, a connection implicit in the Athenian practice of pederasty and explicitly articulated in Plato's *Symposium*. (See Chapters Two and Three.) Similarly, Freud uses evidence of the ways of life of "savage and primitive races" to develop critical perspectives on contemporary "civilized" sexual arrangements in some of his most speculative anthropological and theoretical texts.[15]

To summarize: Freud deploys historical and anthropological evidence to contest the use of medical judgments to reinforce contemporary social conventions. This move is similar to the efforts of contemporary social constructionists to "denaturalize" conventional sexual terms by attending to different organizations of sexuality in other times and cultures. His specific point as to the inappropriateness of labeling sexual inversion per se as "degenerate" remained salient in the 1973 debates within the American Psychiatric Association as to the classification of homosexuality as a mental illness. Freud argues that, because it has been accepted and approved within some historical and cultural contexts, and because it manifestly coexists with considerable accomplishment within individual lives, homosexuality may be defined as pathological only when it appears linked with *other* deviations from contemporary social norms *and* if it is accompanied by evidence of behavioral or organic dysfunction. It would seem that the American Psychiatric Association in 1973 finally settled on a view quite close to that of the founder of psychoanalysis.[16]

Freud also challenges the common view that treats sexual inversion as innate. His analysis of the contest between explanations of homosexuality in terms of its "innate" or "acquired" character applies to the same tendencies in the debate between contemporary "essentialists" and "social constructionists" about sexual orientation. As Edward Stein has argued in detail, this controversy conflates several distinct conceptual and empirical issues.[17] One of these is the choice between "nature" and "nurture," heredity and environment, as explanations of sexual development. With regard to claims that inversion is innate, Freud acknowledges that this account resembles the reported experiences of individuals in his first category of "absolute inverts"— early and exclusive homosexuals. On the other hand, he argues that such a theory cannot account for the others: those who remain attracted to persons of both sexes, and those who make homosexual object-choices when deprived of outlets with the other sex. He concludes that explanation in terms of innate factors separates out "absolute inverts" as a separate class and abandons any attempt at "universal application." This view amounts to the claim that exclusive homosexuality is innately determined, while other varieties have different etiologies. The result is to isolate one disfavored class as an inherent pathological condition, leaving the broad range of sexual variations unexamined and the course of sexual development unexplained.

Freud's critique of nativist theories does not lead him simply to embrace the contention that all sexual inversion results from experience and social environment. Rather, he argues that although some cases may be explained by reference to "sexual impressions" from their earlier lives or later "external influences," and may be treated through suggestion or psychoanalysis, others subjected to similar impressions or influences do not become sexual inverts. Freud concludes that "constitutional factors" or inherent dispositions play some role in determining sexual orientation. He rejects both single factor theses: that "everyone is born with his sexual instinct attached to a particular sexual object" and that individual sexuality is the result of accidental circumstances and social influence "without the cooperation of something within the subject himself." (7)

Freud proposes a model of dynamic interaction in which inherent desires and dispositions — perhaps constitutional in nature — manifest a generalized drive that is specified through contingent encounters with others in culturally mediated contexts. Such desires, whether fulfilled or frustrated, continue to shape one's sexual life in the form of unconscious wishes and fantasies. Freud spells out a structure and dynamic for these interactions in his theory of the Oedipus complex with its wide ramifications for self-formation. Oedipus appears only briefly and belatedly in the treatment of sexual inversion in *Three Essays* — in a footnote added to the 1910 edition in which the boy's relation to his mother is presented as a decisive factor in the development of some manifestations of male homosexuality. (I will return to the matter of that note later in this chapter.) The general analysis of sexual inversion offered in the *Three Essays* remains salient regardless of that important and contested component of psychoanalytic theory. By treating the question of classification while bracketing etiology, Freud complicates and unsettles both popular and scientific notions of sexual variation. This critical maneuver succeeds regardless of the vicissitudes of Freud's subsequent positive efforts to theorize the genesis of different sexualities.

Although Freud rejects the claim that sexual inversion is innate and degenerate in rigorous, almost austere, scientific terms, his position has important political implications in its historical context. The widespread acceptance of the language of inherent pathology as an explanation of social difference in the nineteenth century legitimized a racist rhetoric that naturalized relations of domination effecting not only homosexuals but also Jews, blacks, and other colonized peoples, as well as women. No less a critic of psychoanalysis than Foucault credits Freud with his opposition to what he calls the "degenerescence" system. Foucault sees this ideological framework as rationalizing a pervasive system of social control:

> Psychiatry, to be sure, but also jurisprudence, legal medicine, agencies of social control, the surveillance of dangerous or endangered children, all functioned for a long time on the basis of "degenerescence" and the heredity-perversion system. An entire social practice, which took the exasperated but coherent form of a state-directed racism, furnished this technology of sex with a formidable power and far-reaching consequences.[18]

For Foucault, this discursive configuration is among the instruments of a distinctively modern normalizing power, discussed in Chapter Two, that produces sexual subjects who internalize negative judgments and police their own efforts to conform.[19] The efficacy of these systems depends on disguising their origins in the politics of domination through strategies of naturalization. Subordinate social status is justified as a reflection of biological inferiority. Freud challenges that identification in the case of sexual inversion. Foucault contends:

> It is all very well to look back from our vantage point and remark upon the normalizing impulse in Freud; one can go on to denounce the role played for many years by the psychoanalytic institution; . . . of all those institutions that set out in the nineteenth century to medicalize sex, it was the one that, up until the decade of the forties, rigorously opposed the political and institutional effects of the perversion-heredity-degenerescence system.[20]

Sander Gilman argues that Freud and the founding generation of psychoanalysts, so many of whom were Jewish, had a particular investment in criticizing the foundations of racism because of its role in rationalizing political anti-Semitism. He also claims that psychoanalysis does not overcome the tendency to naturalize and pathologize social differences, but rather displaces it onto the treatment of sexual difference. (In Chapter Five, I shall consider links between the emergence of the homosexual as a "new species" and the racialized construction of "Jewishness"; in both cases "feminization" is also at work.) However, neither Freud in his critique of sexual inversion as innate and degenerate, nor Foucault in applauding Freud's refusal of the "degenerescence system," nor Hannah Arendt in her treatment of the "Jewish question" recognizes the linkage between racializing essentialisms and the naturalization of gender hierarchy.

III. The "Third Sex" Theory: "Psychical Hermaphroditism" v. Homosexual Object Choice

Thus far the binary opposition between the sexes has been taken as a given. The distinction between male and female, masculine and feminine must be taken as fixed if the "invert" is to be understood as violating its terms in her own case. The involvement of sexual variation with dichotomies of sex and gender remains when sexual inversion is redefined as homosexual object choice. After all, choosing an object of the "same sex" is comprehensible only within a system that distinguishes between one's own sex, figured as the "same," and an "other," figured as "opposite." Early defenders of homosexual rights like Ulrichs and Hirschfeld sought to expand the binary opposition by arguing for both the fact and the legitimacy of a third sex. However, as the formulas of a "female brain in a man's body" and its converse reveal, this "third" is actually a hybrid — defined in terms of elements of the original two. The introduction of a third sex actually perpetuates the primacy of the male-female, masculine-feminine dyad.[21] (This dynamic is repeated in contemporary discussions that conceive bisexuality as the pairing of homosexual with heterosexual object-choices in the same individual.) Bisexuality is sometimes figured as a radical alternative to the opposition between homosexual and heterosexual choices and identities but it reiterates the binary conception of sexual difference. The third-sex theorists of the nineteenth century actively sought to make sexual anomalies acceptable to the legal and political systems of their day. Their analysis of sexual inversion as a mismatch of characters from the heterosexual matrix assimilates its strangeness to variations on old familiar themes. Often their rhetoric echoes patriarchal definitions of masculine and feminine qualities: although they argued that binary opposition between male and female does not exhaust the sexual possibilities, they nonetheless used it to structure their own accounts of different sexualities.

Freud's discussion of these third-sex theories questions the adequacy of the conventional dichotomy:

It is popularly believed that a human being is either a man or a woman. Science, however, knows of cases in which the sexual characters are obscured, and in which it is consequently difficult to determine the sex. This arises in the first instance in the field of anatomy. The genitals of the individuals concerned combine male and female characteristics. (This condition is known as hermaphroditism.) (7)

He argues that some measure of anatomical hermaphroditism may be found among most normally sexed persons and speculates that dimorphic sexuality may have evolved from an earlier unisex condition. Freud proposes that *psychical* hermaphroditism be the combination within a single individual of psychological characteristics associated with the separate sexes. In analyzing hermaphroditism, he emphasizes the continuities among sexual phenomena, while delineating distinct domains within which the polarities of male and female manifest themselves. He insists that hermaphroditism may appear along distinct axes: 1) anatomy (both internal and external); 2) secondary and tertiary sex characteristics; and, 3) psychological qualities. In terms of contemporary discussions, Freud's analysis recognizes a distinction between biological sex and psychosexual or gender identity while at the same time dismantling the alleged unity of biological sex. The over all effect is to contest and pluralize the univocal, "natural" male-female binary opposition that undergirds the dichotomy between inverted and upright forms of sexuality.

Defenders of the theory of a third sex propose that sexual inversion is a form of psychical hermaphroditism. Freud deconstructs this proposal with some care. The explanation of sexual inversion as a form of psychical hermaphroditism requires a close linkage between an individual's deviation as to sexual and gender identities and deviations as to object choice. Freud finds no such linkage. Indeed, he goes to some lengths to show that different manifestations of hermaphroditism do not correlate with each other. Anatomical hermaphroditism may appear alongside a predominance of the secondary and tertiary characteristics of one sex and manifest masculinity or femininity. (I'll come back to the difficulties of defining these psychological factors in due course.) Similarly, an individual may exhibit mixed secondary and tertiary sex characteristics while having no anatomical deviations and a clearly gendered psychology. Crossover between masculinity and femininity may exist independently of any variation in anatomical, secondary, or tertiary sexual characters. Most importantly for theorists trying to explain homosexuals as a third sex, any and all of the above intersexed characteristics may coexist with heterosexual object choice.

Freud's summary of the argument against the third-sex theory of sexual inversion reveals important tensions within his own approach:

Psychical hermaphroditism would gain substance if the inversion of the sexual object were at least accompanied by a parallel change-over of the subject's other mental qualities, instincts and character traits into those marking the opposite sex. But it is only in inverted women that character-inversion of this kind can be looked for with any regularity. In men the most complete mental masculinity can be combined with inversion. If the belief in psychical hermaphroditism is to be persisted in, it will be necessary to add that its manifestations in various spheres show only slight signs of being mutually determined. (8)

The asymmetry between male and female inverts in this formulation reveals that Freud perpetuates socially prevalent attitudes towards gender and sexual identity at the same time that he denaturalizes definitions of sexual normality. This tendency colors his later discussions of lesbianism and his ongoing struggle to analyze female sexuality and femininity. Freud's inability to apply his most radical insights into homosexuality to lesbians is a consequence of his pervasive difficulties in comprehending female sexuality as such. His phallocentrism requires him to read lesbian desire as a symptom of penis envy and of male-identification, foreclosing any effort to imagine the terms of an autonomous feminine desire for other women. These theoretical difficulties are reflected in Freud's case studies: he displays considerable subtlety in dealing with male homosexuality while his few encounters with lesbianism are quite troubled. Freud makes no effort to conceal his admiration for figures like Plato, Michelangelo, and Leonardo. Indeed in his study of the latter, he expresses such enthusiasm for the Renaissance artist, scientist, and inventor that he almost identifies with him; Freud appears to aspire to be the Leonardo of psychology. His studies of "The Wolf-man" and of Schreber's memoirs display extraordinary compassion for these sexually tormented men. On the other hand, Freud does not even recognize the homosexual currents in the emotional life of "Dora" until years later while revising his case study; that case itself is almost a lesson in how *not* to conduct psychoanalysis. Critics in recent years have often focused on his failures in understanding and treating the young woman. However, Freud's own self-criticisms in the original study and in its revisions are already very severe; it is quite remarkable that he chose to pubish it at all.

Freud's most extended encounter with a lesbian occurs in "The Psychogenesis of a Case of Homosexuality in a Woman." (121)[22] Several feminist critics have already developed detailed critiques of this study.[23] Here I want only to note several features that illustrate the asymmetries between male and female homosexuality in Freud's practice. The anonymous subject of this case is an eighteen-year-old woman brought to Freud by parents concerned to end her public infatuation with a woman of suspect reputation some years her senior. She had already attempted suicide after a confrontation in the street between her father and the two women. The sensitivity to individual choice that Freud conveyed in his "Letter to an American Mother" is manifest here as well; he is concerned that the desire for change comes from the parents, not the woman herself. He emphasizes that ". . . the girl was not in any way ill — she did not suffer from anything in herself, nor did she complain of her condition — and that the task to be carried out did not consist in resolving neurotic conflict but in converting one variety of genital organization into another." (137) In his analysis, Freud reiterates many of the arguments about separating object-choice from gender inversion found in *Three Essays*. He finds no visible signs of male character in his patient, although he emphasises that he did not conduct a physical examination. On the other hand, he cannot avoid the tricky terrain of "psychological" masculinity and femininity where cultural stereotypes assert their power. He admits that his patient's "acuteness of comprehension and her lucid objectivity" are "connected with masculinity" only in "conventional rather than scientific terms." (140–41) However, he immediately goes on to assert that "in her behaviour towards her love object she had throughout assumed the masculine part." Freud does not hesitate to conclude: "She had thus not only chosen a feminine love object, but had also developed a masculine attitude towards this object." What Freud gives with one hand, he takes away with the other. He reinstates the identification of same-sex object choice with sexual inversion *for women* as a crucial psychological factor based on cultural definitions of gender-appropriate behavior in pursuing a love affair.

Freud's analysis of the genesis of his patient's desire for other women is similarly effected by his own assumptions about sexual difference. He argues that her earliest pre-occupations with young mothers manifested a desire to become a mother herself, which he treats as an expression of nascent heterosexual desire. However, by her early teens, the interest in the children had given way to erotic interest in the mothers, and the lady of whom her parents so disapproved was not a mother at all, but a *"cocotte"* who lived intimately with another woman and had affairs with men as well. (This woman's bisexuality has a way of disappearing in Freud's analysis.) Freud traces this transition to the birth of her youngest brother, when the young woman was sixteen. At this point Freud sees his patient as decisively turning her attentions from her father to her mother, with the female objects of her interest as mother-substitutes. This turn towards her mother and homosexual attachments results from her taking the birth of her youngest brother as a sign of her father's betrayal; he has given the child that she wishes for herself "to the unconsciously hated rival, her mother." Freud concludes: "Furiously resentful and embittered, she turned away from her father, and from men altogether. . . . She turned into a man and took her mother in place of her father as love object." (144–45)

Not only does Freud in this analysis perpetuate a reading of his patient's object choice as a consequence of her masculine identification, but also he regards the latter as itself a consequence of the disappointment of her heterosexual desire for her father. This bright and attractive young woman becomes a masculine lover of women as a protest against her father's refusal to return her love. In his later writing about female sexuality, Freud comes to recognize that a girl's attraction towards her father cannot be taken as somehow natural or original, but emerges against the background of a pre-Oedipal attachment to her mother. He sees nothing of this homosexual background in *Psychogenesis*, but rather insists on the derivative character of his patient's attraction to her mother and other women.

Freud so strongly identifies himself with the father in this case that he breaks off his treatment at an early stage. He sees his patient as transferring her anger at her father's betrayal to her analyst, to the extent of producing dreams designed to deceive him with their apparent revelation of heterosexual desires. Rather than working through this material, Freud recommends that the young woman find a female analyst if she wishes to continue her treatment. In *Dora*, it was the patient who broke off treatment as a result of the complexities of transference. It is hard not to read this decision as expressing some anger on Freud's part: ". . . she intended to deceive me just as she deceived her father. . . . But I still believe that . . . the dreams partly expressed the wish to win my favor; they were also an attempt to gain my interest and good opinion — perhaps in order to disappoint me all the more thoroughly later."(152) Freud forestalls this outcome by ending the treatment. Why has he so completely identified with the father and his wish to convert the young woman from lesbianism? Freud has already warned the reader of the difficulty of such a conversion; indeed, he has suggested that it is not an appropriate aim of psychoanalysis except when the patient herself wishes it.

The issue is not so much his patient's desire for women, but her "masculine protest" her refusal to accept a subordinate role because she has been born a female. Freud reads her lesbianism, her suicide attempt, her coolness in treating his interpretations as mere interesting possibilities, all as expressions of her "attitude of revenge and defiance against the father." (150) Freud cannot resist taking sides in this struggle. He deploys the tools of analysis on behalf of an explicitly political reading: "A spirited girl, always ready to fight, she was not at all prepared to be second to her slightly older brother; after inspecting his genital organs she had developed a pronounced envy of the penis. . . . She was in fact a feminist; she felt it to be unjust that girls should not enjoy the same freedom as boys, and rebelled against the lot of woman in general." (156) What is shocking here is the ease with which Freud conflates the biological, psychological, and social domains that he is at such pains to distinguish in the *Three Essays*. Why should the refusal to accept restrictions on her freedom be reduced to envy of the penis? Why should the presence or absence of that organ determine social status and personal power? Why must Freud ally himself so strongly with the conventional order rather than with the rebellious young woman? Can it really be reduced to the fact that *he* was born with a penis?

The trouble with Freud's analysis has more to do with his understanding of sexual difference than of homosexuality as such. Although both psychoanalysts and feminist critics have revised and criticized Freud's accounts of femininity and female sexuality, his analysis of lesbianism may be compromised beyond hope of recuperation. Outside the context of evaluating Freud, the question remains how deeply entangled concepts of homosexuality as object choice rather than sexual or gender inversion remain with a heterosexual matrix that defines each sex in terms of its desire for the other. The profound difficulties within Freud's version of psychoanalysis may themselves be symptomatic of the depth and power of patriarchy and compulsory heterosexuality in a culture that we continue to inhabit.

Freud transforms the conception of psychical hermaphroditism into that of universal bisexuality. His quarrel with the third-sex theory of inversion is that it restricts the recognition of mixed sexual characters to a statistically infrequent and normatively deviant group of inverts. Freud rejects this "minoritizing view" (in Eve Kosofsky Sedgwick's formulation), which defines homosexuals as a distinct group set off from the majority of the population, to introduce a "universalizing" analysis, which sees same-sex desire as a possibility for all. For psychoanalysis, each individual negotiates, consciously and unconsciously, a complex history of masculine and feminine subject positions and hetero- and homosexual object choices. The balance of *Three Essays* explores the implications of universal bisexuality in infancy for redefining the sexual drive and the vicissitudes of development. Although his theory of universal bisexuality unsettles binary oppositions of sexual identity and difference, Freud remains inconsistent in applying it to lesbianism, female sexuality, and femininity.

IV. Universal Bisexuality and Sexual Difference

Psycho-analytic research is most decidedly opposed to any attempt at separating off homosexuals from the rest of mankind as a group of a special character. By studying sexual excitations other than those that are manifestly displayed, it has found that all human beings are capable of making a homosexual object-choice and have in fact made one in their unconscious. (11)

The transformation of psychical hermaphroditism from an hypothesis based on a biological anomaly into a universal bisexuality at work throughout the varieties of individual development proceeds in tandem with the generalization of hermaphroditism in its other forms: ". . . it appears that a certain degree of anatomical hermaphroditism appears normally." The universalizing move extends to the second type of hermaphroditism as well: ". . . in general the secondary and tertiary sexual characters of one sex occur very frequently in the opposite one. They are indication of hermaphroditism, but are not attended by any change of sexual object in the direction of inversion." Again, the choice of sexual object is distinct from possession of characteristics of both sexes, though, Freud's primary concern is with "*psychical* hermaphroditism." In a footnote in the first edition, Freud finds universal bisexuality implicit in the work of the third-sex theorists:

. . . the majority of authors who derive inversion from bisexuality bring forward that factor not only in the case of inverts, but also for all those who have grown up to be normal, and that, as a logical consequence, they regard inversion as a result of a disturbance in development. (8)

Freud cites favorably an article quoting Hirschfeld's claim that "there are masculine and feminine elements in every human being." Freud also refers to the work in sexology of Chevalier, Krafft-Ebing, and Herman. In 1910, he added: "Fliess (1906) subsequently claimed the idea of bisexuality (in the sense of *duality of sex*) as his own." (Freud's italics) Remember that "bisexuality" in this context refers to male/female duality rather than to variation between homosexual and heterosexual object-choice.

The laconic reference to Fliess and the originality of the idea of bisexuality condenses the long, complex history of Freud's collaboration with Fliess, which was ending bitterly as he wrote his *Three Essays*. That history helps explain the relegation to footnotes of the most explicit references to universal bisexuality despite its pervasiveness as a critical theme within the theory of *Three Essays*. Fliess had accused Freud of conveying Fliess's concept of bisexuality to Otto Weininger, who then published it as his own in *Sex and Character*.[24] Weininger was a brilliant young Jew and homosexual whose work is a classic of anti-Semitic and homophobic discourse. After publishing it in 1903 at the age of twenty-three, the tortured young man dramatically killed himself within the year — at the Beethoven House in Vienna. The book was something of a *succès de scandale*, widely read and translated into many languages. In it, Weininger deploys the concept of bisexuality to analyze sexual desire and promulgates an almost metaphysical view of sexual difference. (I'll return to Weininger below and consider linkages among homosexuality, Jewishness, and femininity at length in Chapter Five.)

In a letter to Fliess of July 20, 1904, Freud acknowledges only that the matter had been considered with his patient Swoboda, a friend of Weininger's, ". . . who had learned about bisexuality (which comes up for discussion in every treatment) from me. . . . he did not learn from me any more than what comes up in treatment — that a strong homosexual current is found in every neurotic." In this context of concern about originality and attribution, Freud mentions his own project:

> At present I am finishing "Three Essays on the Theory of Sexuality," in which I avoid the topic of bisexuality as far as possible. At two places I cannot do so: in the explanation of sexual inversion — there I go as far as the literature permits (Krafft-Ebing and predecessors, Kiernan, Chevalier, and the others); furthermore, when I mention the homosexual current in neurotics.[25]

Less than one week later, Fliess writes defining the idea the ownership of which was at issue: ". . . the idea of persistent and inevitable bisexuality of all living beings (not merely the predisposition to bisexuality). . . . the idea that the living substance is both feminine and masculine in all living beings. . . ."[26] On July 27, Freud further defends his associations with Swoboda and Weininger, whose manuscript he now admits to having examined. At the same time, he acknowledges his own indebtedness to the third-sex theorists, implicitly challenging Fliess's claim to complete originality:

... at that time, I was already familiar with the references in the literature in which the idea of bisexuality is used to explain inversion. You must admit that a resourceful mind can on its own easily take the step from the bisexual disposition of some individuals to extending it to all of them, though this step is your *novum*.[27]

Although Freud displays a caution required by the delicacy of his relations with Fliess at this time, he takes the step described above in his own analysis of sexuality and its vicissitudes in the *Three Essays*. Freud closes the section entitled "Bisexuality" with this summary:

Nevertheless, two things emerge from our discussions. ... a bisexual disposition is somehow concerned in inversion, although we do not know in what that disposition consists, beyond anatomical structure. And, secondly, we have to deal with disturbances that effect the sexual instinct in the course of its development. (8–9)

Despite the containment of an explicit discussion of bisexuality to this subsection, Freud's treatment of the perversions and infantile sexuality exposes the implications of *universal* bisexuality for understanding human sexuality in general.

Freud's moves beyond Fliess, to incorporate universal bisexuality into a conception of the polymorphous perverse character of infantile sexuality. By situating infantile bisexuality and perversity in a developmental context, the *Three Essays* provide an ambiguous legacy for psychoanalysis: on the one hand, the conception of a succession of specific stages lends itself to a normalizing teleology that identifies maturity with genital heterosexuality aimed at reproduction; on the other hand, Freud uses the model of historical vicissitudes to emphasize the contingency of this outcome from interactions among inherent drives, familial patterns, and cultural constraints. Infantile sexuality — and with it the bisexual and polymorphous character of the sexual drive — plays a continuing role in adult life through the mediation of unconscious fantasies. Perhaps the deepest impulse of the *Three Essays* is articulated in the language of a footnote added in 1915:

... psychoanalysis considers that a choice of an object independently of its sex — freedom to range equally over male and female objects — as it is found in childhood, in primitive states of society and early periods of history, is the original basis from which, as result of restriction in one direction or another, both the normal and the inverted types develop. Thus from the point of view of psychoanalysis the exclusive sexual interest felt by men for women is also a problem that needs elucidating. ... (11–12)

Much of Freud's later work can be understood as unpacking the implications condensed in this passage.

In the *Three Essays* Freud vacillates between developmental and historical accounts of the stages of libidinal organization, but both tendencies preserve the
stability of a binary opposition of the sexes. Although Freud recognizes that sexual difference itself is a contingent cultural outcome of the developmental histories of boys and girls, too often he treats masculinity and femininity as natural
universals. Here, too, an important counter-current surfaces periodically in the
text. In a footnote to "The Differentiation Between Men and Women," added in
1915, Freud writes: "It is essential to understand clearly that the concepts of 'masculine' and 'feminine,' whose meaning seems so unambiguous to ordinary people,
are among the most confused that occur in science." He distinguishes "at least"
three senses, referring to a psychological distinction between activity and passivity, to a biological sense, and to a sociological one. Freud acknowledges: "The first
of these three meanings is the essential one and the most serviceable in psychoanalysis. When, for instance, libido was described in the text above as being 'masculine', the word was used in this sense, for an instinct is always active even when
it has a passive aim in view." (85) This comment is both important and deeply
problematic. Especially when we notice that in explaining the "biological" meaning, Freud restricts it to the presence of spermatozoa or ova and the functions related to them. In the next sentence, however, he asserts that "as a rule" activity is
linked with "biological masculinity," although some species depart from this
norm by assigning these characteristics to the female. Freud's analysis of the "sociological" component further complicates his view:

> [it] . . . receives its connotation from the observation of actually existing
> masculine and feminine individuals. Such observation shows that in hu-
> man beings pure masculinity or femininity is not to be found either in a
> psychological or a biological sense. Every individual on the contrary dis-
> plays a mixture of the character-traits belonging to his own and to the op-
> posite sex; and he shows a combination of activity and passivity whether
> or not these last character-traits tally with his biological ones. (86)

Just as he vacillates between teleological and historical models of development,
Freud both disarticulates and deploys the connection between biological characteristics and psychological qualities, slipping from spermatozoa to generalized
"activity." In his discussion of the "sociological" sense, for which no individual is
purely masculine or feminine, he reasserts the centrality of universal bisexuality.
But "bisexuality" as a concept presupposes the availability of independent
definitions of sexual difference. When Freud gets specific, masculinity and femininity are defined by a heterosexual cultural matrix.

The ambivalent potential of bisexuality to emancipate or more deeply to entrench desire within the heterosexual matrix of sexual difference is dramatically
revealed in the use to which Otto Weininger put the idea in *Sex and Character*.
Weininger argues that each person includes both masculine and feminine

elements within himself, but identifies the former with all that is great and glorious and the latter with all that is low and corrupt in human life. He does not identify his sexual polarities with biological features, but rather develops a Platonizing conception of sexual difference as defining basic elements within the human psyche. His formulations are driven by intense personal feeling, but they resonate with the history of Western misogyny, linking the masculine with spirit, intellect, creativity, and ethical control, and the feminine with body, emotion, materiality, and sexual excess. Although each individual combines both aspects, Weininger insists that some human types, not just biological females, are characterized by disproportionate feminine influence — most notably Jewish men and male homosexuals. (I return to this theme in Chapter Five.) In terms of sexual attraction, Weininger supplements the conception of sexual polarity with that of complementarity. He actually proposes a quantitative measure of each component and argues that couples work by providing between them the full complement of each sex. Thus, an effeminate man (say, 70% f; 30% m) would be attracted by, and find fulfillment with, a masculine woman (70% m; 30% f, in the ideal case). Weininger's concept of bisexuality is independent of object-choice; each polarity is figured as heterosexual in its desires.

In fact, his analysis works oddly to disembody sexual desire, displacing its object into the metaphysical domain of the complete pair with its full complement of masculine and feminine. Havelock Ellis was also fascinated by couples comprised of feminine men and masculine women. Ellis himself married a lesbian whose story he disguises as a case study in his *Studies in the Psychology of Sex*. The affinity between Weininger's view and Aristophanes' speech in Plato's *Symposium*, discussed in Chapter Three, is also striking. Although Weininger does not allow for the double-male and double-female creatures in that myth of origins, he shares Aristophanes' vision of desire as aiming at ontological wholeness lodged in the couple. Weininger's relegation of male homosexuals to an abject status is a function not only of his self-hatred, but also of his pervasive misogyny; oddly enough, in Aristophanes' speech, denigration of the feminine was coupled with praise of pederasty as hypermasculine.

Freud avoids Weininger's manifest Platonizing of sexual difference, but his identification of activity with masculinity and femininity with passivity risks a similar essentialism. He claims both that libido is distinctively masculine and that it is universally present in humans as the sexual drive.[28] Effectively, in characterizing libido as male, he masculinizes sexual agency itself. This identification further problematizes the "feminine" component in universal bisexuality. As feminist critics of Freud have argued at least since Beauvoir, he reduces femininity to an opaque and undefined "otherness" seen from a decidedly masculine perspective.[29] As we saw in "The Case of Homosexuality in a Woman," Freud imagines active desire as masculine, the female lover of women as motivated by envy of the penis, engaged in a feminist protest. A full account of the active/passive dichotomy would require sustained attention not only to his account of sexual difference but also to his discussion of ambivalence in the "perversions," especially sadomasochism. Freud sees sadism as an outgrowth of the active tendencies of the sexual drive, while masochism is secondary, the effect of aggressive drives turned against their subject in the absence of a suitable object. Freud emphasizes the active/masculine character of libido, but also works to undercut that identification by insisting on the dynamic of ambivalence and on the activity of the drive even when directed towards passive aims:

> . . . certain among the impulses to perversion occur regularly as pairs of opposites. . . . We should be rather inclined to connect the simultaneous presence of these opposites with the opposing masculinity and femininity which are combined in bisexuality — a contrast which often has to be replaced in psychoanalysis with that between activity and passivity. (26, see also 65)

The circle here appears complete. The ambivalent coexistence of impulses toward both sadistic aggression and masochistic submission within the individual is explained in terms of her primary bisexuality, combining masculine and feminine qualities. These qualities are redefined by psychoanalysis in terms of psychological activity and passivity, although here too there is ambiguity, since "an instinct is always active even when it has a passive end in view." But Freud perpetuates the historical association of these with the sexual binary. Although he acknowledges that definitions of masculinity and femininity are cultural conventions, he insists on maintaining a "psychological link" between masculinity and activity, femininity and passivity. (As we have seen in Chapters Two and Three, these associations have a long cultural history, both in the sex/gender system of ancient Greece and in "the divine Plato's" celebration of eros in his *Symposium*.) Despite his general tendency to separate analytically notions that have been conventionally and historically joined, Freud reinstates this pair as the key to sexual difference in the psychological domain. I do not hope to disentangle all of these strands here. The multiple and pervasive ambiguities suggest a need to theorize more fully the extent to which the formula "universal bisexuality" condenses a dynamic of ambivalence. Equally important, the inconsistencies around sexual difference may rise to the level of systematic aporia that require a rethinking of the most fundamental terms. What is the status of conceptions of sexual difference that cannot be reduced to biology, but appear compromised as general analytic categories by the specificity of their cultural and personal manifestations? At best, we must conclude that, in the *Three Essays*, the connections among the psychoanalytic, biological, and sociological senses of masculine and feminine are "merely soldered together," leaving serious questions about the coherence of a concept of bisexuality that appears to depend on just such connections.

Freud's version of universal bisexuality derives from his engagements with, and transformations of, Fliess's biological speculations, "third-sex" theories of sexual inversion as a form of "psychical hermaphroditism," and an emergent discourse of homosexuality conceived as same-sex object choice. As we have seen, each of these frameworks contains its own mode of unstable connection with a binary system of sexual difference within a heterosexual matrix. Masculinity and femininity are defined by a set of specific, often complementary characteristics clustering around desire for the other as proper object. Within each theory, the explanation of sexual variation depends upon a system of sex and gender that articulates conceptions of "same" and "other" through linked concepts of biological sex, gender role, sexual identity, and heterosexual object-choice. Freud's formulation of universal bisexuality re-aligns the terms and redistributes the connections among them, but it also brings to the surface increasingly complex underlying difficulties. Judith Butler defines the trouble in these terms:

> The conceptualization of bisexuality in terms of dispositions, feminine and masculine, which have heterosexual aims as their intentional correlates, suggests that for Freud *bisexuality is the coincidence of two heterosexual desires within a single psyche.* . . . [W]ithin Freud's thesis of primary bisexuality, there is no homosexuality, and only opposites attract. (Italics in original)[30]

Can we theorize different sexualities without depending on a heterosexual matrix that necessarily codes variation in object-choice as transgressing norms of sexual and gender identity? It remains a task for sexual social theory to determine whether Freud's troubles with desire and sexual difference are symptomatic of any attempt to think through the varieties of sexuality within a context of compulsory heterosexuality. The scene becomes even murkier as we recognize that, for Freud, bisexuality figures not only the subject of desire, but its object as well.

V. Fantasy and the Object of Desire

Despite these difficulties, in the *Three Essays,* Freud deploys the concept of universal bisexuality richly to complicate our understanding of different sexualities and their normative contexts. The implications for conceiving the dynamics of sexual desire were already apparent to Freud in a letter to Fliess from 1899: ". . . But bisexuality! You are certainly right about it. I am accustoming myself to regarding every sexual act as a process in which four individuals are involved."[31] Each erotic pairing must be seen as involving *four* partners: one may experience one's own desire as both masculine and feminine, and as directed towards an individual object itself imagined as both masculine and feminine, regardless of the biological sex of either subject or object. This expansion of the concept of universal bisexuality to include the object of desire reflects a refinement in the theory of sexual inversion. In notes added in 1915 and 1920 Freud endorses the distinction between inversion in the subject and inversion in the object elaborated in the work of his colleague Sandor Ferenczi:

> He rightly protests that, because they have in common the symptom of inversion, a large number of conditions, which are very different from one another and which are of unequal importance both in organic and psychical respects, have been thrown together under the name of 'homo-sexuality' (or to follow him in giving it a better name, 'homo-erotism'). He insists that a sharp distinction should at least be made between two types: 'subject homo-erotics', who feel and behave like women, and 'object homo-erotics', who are completely masculine and who have merely exchanged a female for a male object. (13)

Freud points out that Ferenczi recognizes "subject homo-erotics" as "true sexual intermediates in Hirschfeld's sense of the word," but diagnoses "object homo-erotics" as obsessional neurotics who may resist their inclinations and be subject to change through psychoanalysis. Freud's own position once again emphasizes both the continuity and plurality of sexual manifestations: "While granting the existence of these two types, we may add that there are many people in whom a certain quantity of subject homo-erotism is found in combination with a portion of object homo-erotism." (13)

Contemporary readers will have noticed the gendered character of Freud's exposition of Ferenczi's views. (The emphasis on masculinity continues in his interpretation of Greek pederasty discussed below.) As noted earlier, Freud explicitly perpetuates the identification of same-sex object choice with inversion of sexual identity in women:

> The position in the case of women is less ambiguous; for among them the active inverts exhibit masculine characteristics, both physical and mental, with peculiar frequency and look for femininity in their sexual objects — though here again a closer knowledge of the facts might reveal greater variety. (11)

Indeed! One fact that will require explanation is the existence of feminine (and female) sexual objects who are prepared to respond to the attentions of masculine female inverts. Perhaps the lack of a historical institution like pederasty with its provision for age-specific variations from gender roles helps to obscure this issue for Freud. However, his insistence on a sexual difference within inversion is at one with his analyses of lesbianism as a form of feminist protest. Freud's insistence on the difference between male and female homosexuality directly results from his phallocentric accounts of sexual difference and sexual agency.

Consider his treatment of the "Sexual Object of Inverts." Freud problematizes the object of desire, in part developing his comment to Fliess imagining four characters in every erotic pairing. The issue turns on the imbrication of sexual inversion with the binaries of sex and gender defined by the heterosexual matrix. Once again Freud opens the door to a radical destabilizing of the heterosexual matrix but does not walk through. According to Freud, the proponents of psychical hermaphroditism assume that the invert simply desires the (heterosexual) object appropriate to the biological sex other than his own. Thus, a male invert is like a (heterosexual) woman in taking a male sexual object. Freud concedes that there are male inverts whose desires may be described in this way. However, he insists that male sexual inversion also appears in a distinctly different mode: "There can be no doubt that a large proportion of male inverts retain the mental quality of masculinity, that they possess relatively few of the secondary characters of the opposite sex and that what they look for in their sexual object are in fact feminine mental traits. . . ."(10) The evidence does not come from the consulting room, but from ancient history: "It is clear that in Greece, where the most masculine men were numbered among the inverts, what excited a man's love was not the masculine character of a boy, but his physical resemblance to a woman as well as his feminine mental qualities. . . ." Freud's description of the beloved boy's feminine mental qualities reiterates culturally specific codes of gender: ". . . his shyness, his modesty, and his need for instruction and assistance." He finds further support in the fact that classical pederasty defined the beloved in terms of his youth. As the boy matured and began to take on the appearance and character of an adult man, he ceased to be an appropriate object for pursuit and himself became a lover of boys. Plato's dialogues include some playful exchanges as to the precise age or qualities that transform a young man from desirable beloved to a desiring lover in his own right. (Indeed, as noted in Chapter Two, this asymmetry in homoerotic relations was reflected linguistically: no single term like our own "lover" applied to both partners in an affair; rather, the Greeks distinguished the older, active *erastes* from the younger, passive *eromenos*.)

Freud uses these historical facts to draw radical conclusions about the object of desire:

In this instance, therefore, as in many others, the sexual object is not someone of the same sex but someone who combines the character of both sexes; there is, as it were, a compromise between an impulse that seeks for a man and one that seeks for a woman, while it remains a paramount condition that the object's body (i.e., genitals) shall be masculine. (10)

Here Freud's recognition that one anyone may desire in both masculine and feminine modes and that one's desire may easily be directed to both men and women leads to the insight that the character of the sexual object itself is sexually ambiguous. One may well be attracted to feminine characteristics combined with male genitals (and, by implication, the reverse). Far from resisting the complications for more conventional views that set in here, Freud appears to welcome them; in 1915, he completed the paragraph partially quoted above this way: "Thus the sexual object is a kind of reflection of the subject's own bisexual nature."

The figure of the hermaphrodite makes a surprising reappearance as Freud conjures a beautiful boy from ancient Athens equipped with all the feminine graces but redeemed from the female by the presence of a penis. Note the slippage in the formulation that ". . . it remains a paramount condition that the object's body (i.e., genitals) shall be masculine." Freud's effort to defend the masculinity of ancient pederasts feminizes the beloved boy, but the effort runs aground as he goes on to associate the youth with his body and identifies the body with its genitals; ultimately the focus is the penis. However, we may also imagine the attractions of a beloved young person, masculine in character and intellect, but equipped with a vagina.[32] As we shall see, something like this is at work in the "Case of Homosexuality in a Woman." Male homosexual desire is plausible for Freud because he can imagine the penis as both instrument and object of desire. Indeed male heterosexual desire is thinkable only as the result of a prior identification with the father and his penis. As Judith Butler has argued with great power, this "masculine disposition" must be understood as the effect, not only of cultural taboos on incest with the mother, but also of a prior prohibition on homosexual desire. Identification with the father is constructed upon the boy's loss of his father as object of love.[33] Freud does not enter the vertiginous maze of desires and identifications that his theory requires. As these examples should make clear, the sexual ambiguities at issue here are heavily laden with the hermeneutic baggage of personal and cultural fantasy. Consider that list of "feminine" qualities exhibited by Athenian boys: ". . . shyness, . . . modesty, and. . . need for instruction and assistance." (10) Recall the "masculine" acuteness and objectivity displayed by Freud's lesbian patient.[34] Beneath the particulars, one may discern echoes of the fundamental contrast between activity and passivity that Freud identifies at the heart of the psychoanalytic concept of sexual difference. The identification of this pair with masculinity and femininity is not justified, except within the terms of cultural constructions that Freud often views as arbitrary but insistent pressures to be negotiated by historically emergent subjectivities.

Freud does not pursue his suggestion that the object of desire "may be a reflection of the subject's own bisexual nature." However, the idea that objects of desire are not simply persons in the world but constructions based on the subject's history of desires and identifications as mediated by unconscious fantasies is quite radical.[35] It forces us to reconsider yet again the simple division of desire into that directed towards "the same" or "the other" "sex." Both the binary oppositon between male and female, masculine and feminine, and the identification of one's sex with the presence or absence of certain genital organs are problematized by Freud's proposal that the object of desire may be a compromise formation between "an impulse that seeks for a man and an impulse that seeks for a woman."

Rather than a matter of fact about a biological organism, the object of desire is composed of "character[s] of both sexes." Freud implies an analogy between the organization of adult sexual drives from "component drives" originally identified with the polymorphous perverse impulses of childhood and the construction of objects of desire from traits that have become associated with masculinity and femininity. The sources here are not merely the conventions of one's culture, but memories and fantasies unconsciously maintained from early in the individual's life and invested with her own specific history of desire, satisfaction, and frustration.

The "sex" of the object of desire condenses a complex story of previous aims, objects, and identifications; at the same time, it reflects a similarly constructed subjective sexual identity. Both the subject of desire and its object are permeated with conscious and unconscious fantasy — precarious and provisional outcomes of the ongoing vicissitudes of an inchoate drive as it bumps up against others in the world. The ambivalence that characterizes sexual subjectivity for Freud converges with the ambiguities that shape the object of desire to render sexual difference itself largely a matter of personal and cultural fantasy. For Freud, these fantasies are most often projected by the subject on the others that mattered most early in life, usually the members of her family, especially the figures of father and mother.

The hermaphrodite, introduced early in the *Three Essays* as a biological anomaly but made to do increasing work as a figure of universal bisexuality with distinct psychological and social dimensions, finally appears as a fantasmatic creature around which masculine and feminine traits are made to circulate and coalesce. This figure reappears strategically in Freud's ongoing engagements with homosexuality and with sexual difference. Consider poor Schreber, who imagines himself to be growing breasts prior to being transformed into a woman, or the vulture in Leonardo's memory of childhood, associated with Egyptian deities possessed of both breasts and penis.[36] Freud will eventually argue that baby boy and baby girl both start out their lives as one sex — male — the girl believing herself possessed of a penis in the form of her clitoris. Freud's attempts to understand female sexuality eventually led him to discover a pre-Oedipal "phallic mother," to imagine a time before the onset of "castration anxiety" and "penis envy" when boy and girl alike believe their mother to be possessed of a penis. The path from universal bisexuality to the hermaphrodite as fantasmatic subject and object of desire results in profoundly unsettling consequences for sexual difference as Freud figures the mother-infant relationship as a homosexual tie between two males.

These speculative possibilities are directly reflected in Freud's interpretations of case material. Let us return briefly to the "Case of Homosexuality in a Woman." I have already discussed Freud's interpretation of his patient's choice of female love objects as substitutes for her mother and of the turn toward her mother as an effect of disappointment at her father's betrayal fueled by her desire for revenge against him. However, in presenting the attachment to "her latest love, the 'Lady,'" that led to the crisis with her father, her suicide attempt, and referral to the analyst, Freud briefly touches on another aspect of that connection: "On account of her slender figure, regular beauty, and off-hand manner, the lady reminded her of her own brother, a little older than herself. Her latest choice corresponded, therefore, not only with her feminine but also with her masculine ideal; it combined gratification of the homosexual tendency with that of the heterosexual one." (143) Freud concludes this comment by reminding his readers of the complexity of the nature and origins of sexual inversion and "the extensive influence of the bisexuality of mankind." He develops the latter theme only in relation to his patient. However, this is the only reminder in the case study of a fact about the beloved woman mentioned earlier on: ". . . she lived with a married woman as her friend, having intimate relations with her, while at the same time she carried on promiscuous affairs with a number of men." (133)

Freud pursues the ambiguity of the young woman's sexual object in one direction only: as a reminder of her brother, the lady satisfies her "masculine ideal." Why should the brother incarnate that ideal? All that we learn of the brother is that Freud's patient refused to accept subordination to him for no better reason than that he had a penis, and she didn't. With regard to that one fact, the lady did not resemble her brother. Is that all the masculine ideal amounts to? Possession of a penis? The lady is bisexual in the contemporary sense as well as Freud's: she had sex with both women and men. Is it the fact of her relation to other women that makes her so attractive to Freud's patient? Is that what the masculine ideal comprises? How can Freud assume that his patient's association of her beloved with her brother results in heterosexual desire? He has insisted in his analysis of this very relationship that the young woman "had throughout assumed the masculine part." In that case, perhaps the relationship is better understood as a homosexual relation between two men. Perhaps the lady has become a substitute for the lost father, or engaged her lover's latent memories of a pre-Oedipal attachment to her mother. There is no simple answer to these questions. They can only be resolved through the work of analysis; neither masculine nor feminine traits and subject positions refer simply to anatomy. Once Freud recognizes the role of fantasy in determining sexual difference, relations of identity and difference become provisional and unstable, mobilized by the unconscious dynamics of desire.

This reading of the intersections of desire and identification in the context of fantasmatic constructions of sexual difference similarly complicates the account of male homosexuality Freud develops in *Leonardo da Vinci and a Memory of his Childhood*. In a study notable for its author's sympathy and admiration for his subject, Freud nonetheless proposes an interpretation of one form of male homosexuality that has circulated widely in the culture. The argument is that Leonardo's desires for younger men were a result of an intense identification with his mother coupled with a narcissistic desire for his own younger self as an object of desire. It is not so very far from this view, however subtly elaborated, to the stereotype of gay men as pretty boys hung up on their powerful mothers. This view does appear in *Three Essays*, although relegated to a footnote added in 1910, the year Freud published the study of Leonardo. Before concluding this reading, I want to explore briefly that theory in light of the ambiguous character of both subjects and objects of desire and the role of fantasy in constructing sexual difference.

In the note, which I will quote at length, Freud claims that although it has not developed "a complete explanation of the origin of inversion," psychoanalytic research has "discovered the psychical mechanism of its development":

> In all the cases we have examined we have established the fact that the future inverts, in the earliest years of their childhood, pass through a phase of very intense but short-lived fixation to a woman (usually their mother), and that, after leaving this behind, they identify themselves with a woman and take *themselves* as their sexual object. That is to say, they proceed from a narcissistic basis, and look for a young man who resembles themselves and whom *they* may love as their mother loved them. . . . [A]lleged inverts have been by no means insusceptible to the charms of women, but have continually transposed the excitation aroused by women on to a male object. They have thus repeated all through their lives the mechanism by which their inversion arose. Their compulsive longing for men has turned out to be determined by their ceaseless flight from women. (11)

The account offered above, and developed more fully in the *Leonardo* essay, looks quite different from the cultural cliche when we recognize that the "woman" or "mother" in this account as well as the male homosexual's "self" are constructions rather than simply recognizable persons in the world.[37] Equally important, the markers of sexual difference, "penis" and "breasts" in this account, cannot be reduced to bodily organs but must also be understood as creations of fantasy, both personal and cultural.

Judith Butler's analysis in *Gender Trouble* of the melancholic character of gender identification sheds light on Freud's analysis. The boy's loss of his mother results in an identification through which he is consoled by incorporation of the beloved object. As Butler powerfully argues, this incorporation is a fantasmatic construction. Similarly, in Freud's account of this mode of homosexual object-choice, the self that one narcissistically seeks to adore, as one identifies with the beloved and feared mother, is itself a condensation of past vicissitudes of identification and desire. Neither the identification with the mother nor the taking of one's "own" sex as an object reflects the playing out of inner dispositions; they result from the impact of cultural prohibitions within an individual history. As Butler writes, they are neither unitary nor fixed:

> The alternative perspective on identification that emerges from psycho-analytic theory suggests that multiple and coexisting identifications produce conflicts, convergences, and innovative dissonances within

gender configurations which contest the fixity of masculine and feminine placements with respect to the paternal law.[38]

She goes on to argue that the strategy of incorporation as a response to loss that consolidates gender identity is itself a fantasy: ". . . the incorporation of an identification is a fantasy of literalization or a *literalizing fantasy.*"(Italics in original)[39] The literalizing inscribes the fantasy on the body itself, disguising the dynamics of gender identification as biological sex.

Penis and breast are not simply body parts but figures that condense ambiguities of both sexual subject and object and conflicts among sexual aims. In *Leonardo*, after associating the artist's memory/fantasy of being beaten about the mouth with the tail of a bird associated with anatomically hermaphroditic Egyptian deities, Freud explicates the ways in which that tail functions as both penis and breast. The tail stands for the penis as object of homoerotic desire but also as the longed-for maternal breast. Freud adopts this fantasy of young Leonardo as his own image of the original aim of desire in the *Three Essays*: "No one who has seen a baby sinking back satiated from the breast and falling asleep with flushed cheeks and a blissful smile can escape the reflection that this picture persists as a prototype of sexual satisfaction in later life." (48) Later, Freud writes: "There are thus good reasons why a child sucking at his mother's breast has become a prototype of every relation of love. The finding of an object is in fact a refinding of it." (88) However, Leonardo's identification of himself with his mother transforms the maternal breast into the penis that he offers to the younger men who come to stand in for his infantile self.

As a clue to the sexuality of Leonardo, figures of both infant and bird fantasmatically combine — or vacillate between — signifying masculine and feminine subject positions and objects of desire. Notice too how conventional conceptions of activity and passivity are confounded by the alternation between breast feeding and fellatio. Finally, the meaning of these fantasies, like the sexuality in question, remains open and undecidable. Even more important for the emergence of individual sexual identities, the notions of masculine and feminine which shape the desiring subject and its ambivalent relations to ambiguously sexed objects are themselves imaginary and fantasmatic constructions on a cultural scale.[40]

VI. Psychoanalysis and Queer Theory

I am drawn to the inclusiveness of "queer" rather than "lesbian and gay" politics. It seeks to embrace lesbians, gay men, bisexuals, transvestites, transsexuals, sadomasochists, boy-lovers, and any other "others" who find themselves marginalized and abjected by the normalizing force of modern sexuality. A movement based on narrowly defined "lesbian and gay" identities risks further marginalizing those who elude its terms. "Queer" unsettles conventional modes of organizing sex and gender and alerts us to the risk of reinscribing patterns of exclusion as we seek to achieve equality for some, more "respectable," sexual minorities. Adding "lesbian" and "gay" to "heterosexual" in the repertoire of acceptable identities in our society would be a real but limited accomplishment in the struggle for full equality. The use of "queer" strikes a cautionary note about the risks of any politics based on fixed normative identities. "Queer theory" emphasizes the variety and weirdness of all sexualities: the formation and multiplicity of "heterosexual" identities and desires require theorizing as much as the formation of diverse and allegedly deviant sexualities. At its best, queer theory contests the adequacy of dividing the world into straight and gay, hetero- and homosexual, challenging the dependence of these binaries on equally rigid, powerful, and problematic oppositions between male and female, masculine and feminine.[41]

Here psychoanalysis may be an important ally with a continuing role in the work of clarifying and contesting our conceptions of sexual desires and identities. The legacy of Freud's persistent and troubled efforts to theorize same-sex desire continues to inform contemporary queer theory, often through critical engagements with his texts that expand both psychoanalytic and queer perspectives.[42] Psychoanalysis articulates dimensions of sexuality that must figure in our ongoing efforts to comprehend and transform its social manifestations. Freud's analysis in his *Three Essays* of the variety of phenomena encompassed by notions of sexual inversion and perversion radically extends the varieties of human sexuality beyond the restrictive and familiar terms of homosexuality and heterosexuality. He consistently emphasizes the continuities between normal and deviant sexuality and seeks to explain the emergence of the former from a context of infantile sexuality that is itself polymorphous and perverse. Freud rejects the restriction of human sexuality to a biologically based teleology in which the object and aims of the sexual drive are taken to be fixed and determinate, culminating in genital heterosexual intercourse aimed at reproduction. Instead, he offers a model of adult sexuality as the product of complex and contingent interactions among individual desires, familial relationships, and cultural contexts. He transforms the minoritizing notion of a "third sex" as an explanation of homosexuality into a concept of universal bisexuality from which adult sexualities develop and which plays a continuing role in the unconscious lives of all. In doing so, he introduces a complex psychological dynamic that can be reduced to neither biology nor culture. Refusing the reduction of sexuality to biology, he recognizes that sexual difference is deeply implicated in cultural forms and social structures that organize individual histories and shape sexual identities. Finally, he uncovers an irreducible dimension of fantasy at work in the vicissitudes of sexual desire, difference, and identification.

Sexual identities — whether homosexual, heterosexual, or other — emerge against a background of primary bisexuality. Infantile sexuality combines features that are culturally defined as masculine or feminine; its aims are polymorphous and perverse. All human beings have the potential for both homosexual and heterosexual object choices, occupy both male and female subject positions, and have desires directed towards a variety of non-genital aims. Indeed the conception of polymorphous perverse infantile sexuality envisions a field of erotic possibility and a range of sexual manifestations broader than the more differentiated "universal bisexuality." The concept of bisexuality depends on a framework of sexual difference shaped by regimes of compulsory heterosexuality; however, Freud's analysis of sexual development unsettles culturally constructed oppositions between male and female, masculine and feminine, active and passive, heterosexual and homosexual. Nonetheless, these binaries shape individual subjectivities through conflicting historical ties of desire and identification within the family that exercise continuing power in adulthood through their resonance in the unconscious.

As Judith Butler has shown, psychoanalytic theory opens a door to the understanding of sexual identities as produced through cultural prohibitions of incest and homosexuality that dispose individuals to adopt positions within a heterosexual matrix of gender definition. Freud lays the groundwork for a critical analysis; but he also exhibits compulsory heterosexuality at work in the inconsistency of his applications. In *Three Essays*, he insists that inversion of object choice is compatible with "full masculinity,"[43] but perpetuates cultural stereotypes of female homosexuals as masculine. This difference between Freud's treatment of male and of female homosexuality points up a continuing asymmetry. This discrepancy is an aspect of Freud's treatment of female sexuality generally. Freud seems unable to imagine the terms of autonomous female desire outside a phallic economy. His phallocentrism resonates both in his treatment of femininity (the centrality of castration and penis envy) and in his understanding of the specifics of male homosexual development and desire. These analyses inadvertently demonstrate the profound reach of patriarchy and compulsory heterosexuality, and the extent to which the construction of sexual difference is marked by conflict and contradiction. Freud's eventual formulation of a "negative" Oedipus complex, as a corollary of primary bisexuality, shows every infant to be shaped by conflicting ties of both identification and desire with adults of both sexes. Freud recognizes a current of ambivalence running through the vicissitudes of both desire and identification. In the pre-Oedipal "phallic" mother, believed by the infant to possess both male and female sexual characteristics, Freud reveals the depth of ambiguity that underlies the vicissitudes of sexual definition.

Freud's "developmental" model emphasizes the precariousness and contingency of the stages through which identities take shape. Rejecting the model of a determinate teleology that programs organic development, he insists that the attitudes of the individual subject towards her desires is a major factor in achieving psychological maturity and mental health. Genital heterosexuality results from a series of complex negotiations; it may result in as much personal unhappiness as deviations from the social norm, especially for women.[44] "Normal" sexuality is achieved through both an organization of "component" drives into genital primacy and the selection of heterosexual objects outside the family. Sexuality comprises a history of libidinal investments in distinct body parts that provide sexual pleasure and excitation in diverse and shifting modes. There is nothing inevitable about the succession of phases from oral through anal to phallic (only to be eclipsed by latency until the emergence of "true" genital sexuality with puberty). No stage disappears entirely; rather, each may play some role in later stages and return to prominence as "regression" or neurotic symptoms later in life. The precariousness of heterosexual outcomes helps explain the force with which their "naturalness" comes to be defended.

Freud's analysis of paranoia provides a starting point for theorizing the virulence and prevalence of homophobia in modern societies. He is emphatic in asserting an intimate link between clinical paranoia and the repression of homosexual desires. In several essays and case studies, he identifies the mechanism by which unacceptable love becomes hate and is projected onto the object of desire as a justification for hating him in return.[45] If Judith Butler is right in seeing the prohibition of homosexuality as prior to that of incest in setting the stage for the Oedipus complex, the production of homophobia is a predictable accompaniment of adult heterosexual identities. Given Freud's conception of the universality of homosexual desire, widespread feelings of hatred, fear, and disgust directed against open and suspected homosexuals appear to derive from the same mechanism of repression and projection that he identifies in paranoia.[46] The implications of this analysis for understanding homophobia are quite strong. "Paranoia" is not just another form of repression accompanied by discomfort and repugnance, it is marked by hallucination and delusion. Socially, homophobia is not simply a form of moral disapproval sustained by Lord Devlin's "feelings of indignation, offense, and disgust," it is psychotic.[47] Freud further suggests a link between sublimated homosexual desires and the emergence of heightened social and ethical feelings, elucidating an intimate connection between male homosexual desire and the bonds of citizenship.

This close analytic association among same-sex desire, homophobia and homosexuality informs Eve Kosofsky Sedgwick's analyses of the distinctive forms and tensions characterizing modern male "homosociality." She situates the analysis of male homosexuality in the political context of patriarchal domination where close ties among men work to maintain their collective power over women, but attain an intensity fraught with sexual tension. For Sedgwick, this results in a perilous conjunction between a necessary homosociality and a threatening homo-*sexuality* that is kept at a distance by virulent homophobia.[48]

Freud's founding of psychoanalysis, resonant as it is with contradictory impulses towards critique and conservatism, reflective self-understanding and objective science, provides one of the few instances available to us as moderns of a sustained effort to generate both a theory of the human and a practice of reflection. Here, too, Freud's project has deep affinities with Plato's efforts to realize the Socratic injunction to know oneself. The various shifts in Freud's conceptions of the methods of psychoanalysis and the continuing debates regarding both analytic technique and therapeutic aspiration point towards the extraordinary difficulty of realizing these ambitions. Much of the literature contesting and defending the methodology of Freud's work as a contribution to natural science or to medical therapy overlooks its importance as inventing a new reflective practice. (In their different ways, Ricoeur, Habermas, and Foucault have seen this.)[49] One continuing strand in Freud's engagement with this project has been his recognition of Socratic *maieusis* or midwifery: no analyst, however powerful his insight, can substitute for the patient in achieving an understanding of herself.

Despite its frequent violation in practice (including Freud's own), psychoanalysis emerged from a decision to listen to individuals whose voices often went unheard and to subject the analyst to a real encounter. The achievement of insight is further complicated by the extent to which the mental lives of both analyst and analysand remain opaque to themselves. The phenomenon of transference demonstrates both the difficulties that face a practice that combines dialogue and self-reflection and the need to engage both desire and the unconscious in the work of analysis. The centrality of the intersubjective in forming the self requires social practices that go beyond introspection, however self-critical; the power of the unconscious requires techniques that go beyond rational dialogue, however probing. The interventions of feminist and queer theorists in psychoanalysis insist on the political dimension of reflective practices that engage the vicissitudes of desire and the resistance of the unconscious. The insistence that women and queers may collectively address and influence the deliberations of psychoanalysis may unsettle it institutionally but remains true to its most radical innovations. Theorizing sexuality is inherently contestatory work along several axes — personal, political, and philosophical.

The moment of Freud's recognition of the imposed character of organization vis-à-vis the sexual drive has exercised a powerful attraction for thinkers who see in it a utopian moment denied in Freud's later, more pessimistic reflections on the relation between civilization and the drives. Emphasizing the contingent and conventional character of all restraints, they have seized the emancipatory potential inherent in a fragmentary and polymorphous desire.[50] Other queer theorists have challenged Freud's deployment of narcissism in the explication of homosexuality. Feminist and lesbian theorists have been unrelenting in their engagement with Freud's account of sexual difference; their critique and revisions have delineated the deep implication of patriarchy and compulsory heterosexuality in processes of self-formation in our culture. These works include efforts not only to criticize the structures currently in place but also to envision sexual difference and desire outside the heterosexual matrix. The engagement between psychoanalysis and queer theory requires us to shift focus from the vicissitudes of desire within the psyche to the politics of modern democracy as a site of utopian hope and ongoing contestation. In Chapter Five, I rework Hannah Arendt's analysis of the "Jewish question" to illuminate the interplay of civic equality and social difference in the politics of sexuality.

PART THREE

POLITICS

CHAPTER FIVE

REFIGURING THE JEWISH QUESTION

⤤

Hannah Arendt, Political Equality,

and Social Difference[1]

In this chapter, I attempt to recuperate Hannah Arendt's vision of democratic politics to theorize the reach of a movement for lesbian and gay rights and liberation. Arendt is almost unique among philosophers of the twentieth century — and perhaps any century — in placing democracy and politics at the center of her thought. Her unrelenting effort "to think politically and to see historically" led her to situate aspirations toward freedom and equality within specific contexts that conditioned the efforts of individuals and groups to shape their common lives. Her own experiences as a German-Jew reinforced her sense of the contingency and urgency of political matters, while her training and temperament led her to question all intellectual orthodoxies. For Arendt, the moral pluralism that Rawls enumerates among the conditions of justice is not simply a response to social complexity, it is a reflection of the plurality and agency inherent in the human condition. She understands the effort to reconcile commitments to political equality with the recognition of social differences as a problematic central to modern democracy. Similarly, her experience of Nazi anti-Semitism led her to reject attempts to characterize social differences in terms of inherent natural conditions as a denial of political equality and a foreclosure of democratic contestation. Arendt sees the political sphere as an arena of self-making in which diverse individuals and groups interact to create themselves and to shape their common world. In applying Arendt's vision of democracy to contemporary queer politics, I shall emphasize her conception of equal citizenship as the capacity to act in concert with others, her insistence on the ability to establish a private household as a precondition of political participation, and her critique of naturalizing essentialisms as a limitation on political agency. Arendt's conception of the institutional status of citizenship as a guarantee of human rights helps to focus the range of issues raised by a movement for lesbian and gay emancipation. Her insistence that rights can be secured only through equal membership within a political society suggests that she would support the claims of lesbian and gay citizens to protection against social retaliation for the exercise of political rights.[2] Her claim that freedom to participate in the public sphere presupposes a capacity to establish private households lends support to the argument that equal citizenship requires the recognition of rights to marry or otherwise establish legally recognized domestic partnerships. The great power of Arendt's analysis of the problematic history of modern democracy is to direct our attention to the broader historical and cultural matrix within which rights-claims and political differences are debated and decided.

Born to an assimilated German-Jewish family in Königsberg in 1906, Arendt studied philosophy with Martin Heidegger, Edmund Husserl, and Karl Jaspers. She offers not only a body of work rich in insight for exploring the conditions and possibilities of our political life, but also an exemplary life for those concerned that their thinking engage the world. Just launched on a promising career in academic philosophy when Hitler came to power in 1933, Arendt emigrated to France and devoted herself to working with the Jewish Agency helping young Jews escape Europe to settle in Palestine. Leaving France in 1940, she came to the United States and devoted herself to political and cultural work among the refugee Jewish community and within the context of Jewish community life and Zionist politics. Finding herself often in opposition, as an independent and critical voice, she nevertheless engaged herself fully in the struggles of her day. Eventually she became editor-in-chief of Schocken publishers and did the work that eventuated in *The Origins of Totalitarianism*, which remains the single most impressive attempt to come to grips with the full implications of twentieth-century European history. Only later in life, when she was already a formidable presence in the intellectual world, did she return to academics, for many years only on part-time and visiting bases. She was the first woman appointed as a full professor at Princeton and among the first at Berkeley and the University of Chicago. She never ceased to write and speak to the ongoing political crises of her day. She did not set out to devote herself to political thought, much less to specifically Jewish causes and the ramifications of the Jewish question. The contingencies of her life and of twentieth-century history brought these issues to the fore in the most compelling way, and she responded with a fullness of moral passion and intellectual engagement exhibited by few. Her life and work comprise an unrelenting effort to take up "the burden of our times" with a commitment always "to think what we do" animated by an undying "love of the world."

I. Plurality, Democracy, and Political Agency

Arendt's theoretical writings link democratic politics to fundamental aspects of the human situation, most importantly, the irreducible fact of plurality and the distinctiveness of our capacity to act. Crucial to her vision is a conception of active citizenship and robust public life; like the reformers of nineteenth-century Europe and Freud before her, she found inspiration in the Athenian polis. In that context she articulats the sharp division between the household and its proper activities, necessary to sustain life, and the city in which common action aims at a glory transcending self-preservation. She reminds her readers that the ancient Greeks regarded courage as an eminently political virtue. Echoing the praise of public life by Diotima in Plato's *Symposium*, Arendt emphasizes the quest for glory and immortality as the motivating force in the active life. However, she does not follow Diotima in finding eros at the heart of it all. Rather, she appears to contain the erotic within the domain of the household, along with other activities rooted in the urgencies of the body. The starkness of this boundary between private and public appears to exclude not only a wide range of concerns but also large numbers of persons from public life. Arendt acknowledges that the freedom of citizens to act in the polis was utterly dependent on the labor of others — women, slaves, artisans, resident aliens — who provided for life's necessities. Although her view of the polis is to some extent mythical and idealized, she does not conceal the flaws in its foundation that make it unacceptable as a form of political life today. She seeks rather to retrieve from her historical narrative an image of democratic citizenship and public life increasingly hard to discern among the institutions and practices of modernity.

Despite her turn to the ancient polis, Arendt believed that the continuity of tradition was irretrievably disrupted, broken, and shattered by events for which it had somehow also prepared the way. Precisely this gap "between past and future" enables us to examine the fragments of tradition in the light of current historical circumstances and perhaps find some material with which to construct anew.[3] Her effort to redeem some moments from the fatally troubled political and philosophical history of the modern West leads her to write about the great democratic revolutions of the eighteenth century,[4] the French Resistance,[5] the revolts in Hungary and East Berlin,[6] the Civil Rights and anti-Vietnam War movements in the United States, and the student movement in Europe and the United States in the 1960s.[7] In these studies, she displays greater sympathy for the egalitarian aspirations of modern democracy than is manifest in *The Human Condition*. The historical specificity of these works requires us to recontextualize the division between private and public formulated in that book. In this chapter, I use Arendt's analysis of the Jewish question in modern Europe, which she saw as intertwined with the fate of the nation-state, to investigate fundamental dilemmas of sexual minorities within modern democracy, especially the tensions between aspirations to political equality and the facts of social difference.

Often the demands of historically oppressed groups for democratic citizenship are framed in terms of the affirmation and embrace of previously marginalized identities. Although my focus here is on the movement for lesbian and gay rights, and on queer politics more generally, these concerns necessarily intersect with those of the women's movement and of racial, religious, and national minorities. Some features of Arendt's conception of politics that at first blush seem inimical to the concerns of the oppressed have great potential for shedding light on the particular turns that social movements have taken in our time. Although Arendt articulates the aspirations of historically excluded groups for full participation in the shaping of a common life, she also interrogates assumptions of "identity politics" that threaten to foreclose democratic contestation by reiterating historical tendencies to reification and marginalization. Arendt's rejection of the social question is in part a critique of the intrusion of private interest into the public domain; she sees a danger that appeals to social equality may justify a regime of administrative manipulation that limits political struggle and the capacity to act. Arendt argues that politics at its best is not simply a means for negotiating interests and aims, but a space within which individuals and groups shape themselves through interaction with others in a common world. Action occurs in concert with others to whom one appears, with each participant both agent and spectator. For Arendt, politics is always potentially about self-making and the search for recognition. The articulation and negotiation of interests is secondary to the mutual determinations through which individuals and groups enact their identities and determine who they will become. This process is necessarily interpersonal, unpredictable, and open-ended.

Arendt is pre-eminently the philosopher of plurality: for her, to be human simply *is* to be in the world with others. Our existence consists in appearing at a distinct location that opens out to others who view us from perspectives of their own. This multiplicity of perspectives constitutes the world. It cannot be apprehended from any single, correct point of view, nor can it exist independently of the overlapping but distinct perspectives that comprise it. This plurality which today many name "difference" is inherent in the very possibility of sharing a world. The speech and actions through which individuals and groups express themselves comprise the only answers to the question, "Who are we?" Identities are not inherent and fixed, but constructed and revised through ongoing interaction. Arendt consistently emphasizes that politics becomes possible only through recognition of human plurality and the open-ended character of action.

She joins Foucault in rejecting a juridical model of power which reduces action to the choice between command or obedience to sovereign authority. Her analysis of conditions in Europe between the world wars leads her to be skeptical of abstract conceptions of human rights that are not anchored in concrete historical institutions with the power to protect actual individuals. In particular, the institution charged with protecting individual rights has been the nation-state, which she see as torn between its particularistic national legacies and universalist aspiration to democratic equality. Arendt analyzes the problematic of modern democracy as turning on the need to distinguish political equality from social - homogeneity. She praises the founders of the American republic for inventing constitutional structures based on a variety of countervailing powers and interdependent authorities rather than investing all power in a unitary sovereign. Similarly, in "On Violence," she analyzes political power itself as derived from the assent of diverse citizens with differing opinions. In "Civil Disobedience," she rejects the idea that law need command unquestioned obedience of democratic citizens; she proposes instead that civil disobedience is a legitimate expression of political dissent from majoritarian opinions and policies. Arendt rejects the notion that a common good or public interest is the ultimate rationale for political action. Political action and deliberation are ends in themselves through which plurality is manifested. Public spaces provide a crucible within which diverse aims may be proposed, interrogated, and contested; they cannot themselves be subordinated to instrumental analysis.

Arendt's commitment to plurality informs her conception of agency. Although she emphasizes the capacity of individuals to begin something new when they intervene in the public sphere, she rejects any conception of a sovereign self or unitary subject underlying the capacity to act. In a Nietzschean vein, she sees the deed itself as that through which a doer comes to be. The very structure of *The Human Condition* with its distinctions and divisions among public, private, and social domains (and among labor, work, and action as distinct activities), defines individuals and their worlds as intrinsically multiple and diverse, shifting in their emphases and orientation. Similarly, when she returns to the realm of "inner life" in her final work, *The Life of the Mind*, she organizes her inquiry around a plurality of mental capacities: thinking, willing, and judging. Arendt embraces the diversity of our intellectual experience and attempts to chart the terrain and its difficulties. Rather than constructing some abiding structure or underlying unity, she discovers self division and difference as pervasive themes in historical attempts to figure the experiences of thinking and willing. In this work she draws on the Socratic conception of thought as a conversation of the soul with itself, a view that Plato developed in his own reading of the soul as divided and dynamic. Although Arendt had little sympathy for Freud, her agonistic conception of self-making in relation to others has affinities with his insistence on the intersubjective and conflictual contexts of psychic formation.

Both the character of human interaction and the specific conditions of the world that contains and constrains it are contingent, historical configurations. The plural contexts of action, political and mundane, are themselves the residue of past actions within a variety of public spaces. These contingent outcomes both limit and create opportunities for further action. So long as the world persists and is inhabited by humans with a capacity to begin something new through their actions, we cannot determine in advance the character and outcome of political life. Arendt is unrelenting in her critique of the ways that modern "society" reduces politics to administration and normalizes unpredictable action as routine behavior. The satisfaction of human needs is organized by experts rather than by persons acting together in concert to determine their shared aims and transform the conditions of their lives. Modernity, in its attempt to solve "social questions" results in the triumph of bureaucracy — "the rule of no one" — in which the capacity to act is submerged by continuing pressures to conformity, to predictable behavior. (Arendt's critique of "the social" owes much to Max Weber and coincides interestingly with Foucault's analysis of modern normalizing powers.) For Arendt, the socialization of life is as hostile to the domain of privacy as it is to the possibility of political action. The substitution of intimacy and inwardness for the substantial place of the household, with all its exigencies, results in even greater human fragility and worldlessness. Although she does not attend to the special roles of medicine and social science in regulating behavior, Arendt comes very close to Foucault in recognizing how distinctively modern regimes of power deploy subjectivity itself as an instrument of social control. For Arendt, modern times have been and continue to be so perilous for human possibilities, precisely because there is no fixed, unchanging essence or human nature. Our condition as a plurality of beings in the world is radically contingent and conditioned by historical circumstances that shape and constrain the abilitiy to exercise our capacities. Who we become results from our shared efforts to shape ourselves from the contingent materials of our natural condition, common history, and situation in the world.

II. Private and Public — Personal and Political

It is perhaps especially appropriate to begin this reading of Hannah Arendt's understanding of the connections between the personal and the political with passages from a letter she wrote to her friend and mentor Karl Jaspers on January 26, 1946, shortly after they had resumed a relationship that had been interrupted by the war. In the course of catching him up on the conditions of her life in America, Arendt makes a number of comments bearing on her attitude towards the "Jewish question" and more generally, on the connections among the personal, political, and intellectual dimensions of her life. Matter-of-factly, she reports: "I continue to use my old name. That's quite common here in America when a woman works, and I have gladly adopted this custom out of conservatism (and also because I wanted my name to identify me as a Jew)."[8] In another letter later that year, she declared: "Politically, I will always speak only in the name of the Jews when circumstances force me to give my nationality."[9] The decision to retain her "own name" is a political one; it is a way of identifying herself as a Jew under historical circumstances when being a Jew had become a fateful and dangerous condition. Arendt is neither revealing some deep truth about her personal identity nor making a declaration of religious faith. Retaining her "Jewish name" is a sign of affiliation and solidarity with a people who have suffered mightily the burdens of twentieth-century European history.

However, this political gesture is necessitated by an additional fact (to that of her birth in a Jewish family) — she has married a non-Jew. Both of these facts of her life, putatively "private" in the extreme, are taken by Hannah Arendt to have important political and social consequences: "If I had wanted to become respectable, I would either have had to give up my interest in Jewish affairs or not marry a non-Jewish man, either option equally inhuman and in a sense crazy. . . ." (29) Arendt's political and intellectual engagement with "Jewish affairs" lasted nearly a lifetime. Moreover, her analysis of the anomic consequences of Jewish attempts at assimilation in nineteenth-century Europe focuses importantly on the displacement of the strains of unequal political status onto private life, especially in the context of "mixed marriages." The question of "respectability" echoes Arendt's later critique of the tyranny of the social. Equally important, her rejection of respectability aligns her with the "conscious pariah," a term that she adopted from the French-Jewish thinker Bernard Lazare.[10] For Arendt, Jews in nineteenth-century Europe who were in a position to assimilate to Gentile society were forced to choose between a parvenu conformism to standards of behavior by which they were always found wanting and an abject status outside of society as members of a pariah people. In both cases, the individual was reduced to a function of her social status. The "conscious pariah" refuses this choice and insists on thinking for herself.

In this letter to Jaspers, Arendt alludes with some irony to her sense of the importance of remaining outside of society for preserving one's integrity: "As you see, I haven't become respectable in any way. I'm more than ever of the opinion that a decent human existence is possible today only on the fringes of society where one then runs the risk of starving or being stoned to death. . . ."(29) The importance of maintaining a thoughtful independence of social convention is a central theme in Arendt's work right up to her thesis on "the banality of evil" in *Eichmann in Jerusalem* and her portrayal of thinking as a dialogue of the soul with itself in *The Life of the Mind*. The connection between this withdrawal into conversation with oneself and "a decent human existence" is made explicit in the latter work: "When everybody is swept away unthinkingly by what everybody else does and believes in, those who think are drawn out of hiding because their refusal to join in is conspicuous and thereby becomes a kind of action." [11]

Remarks in this letter illuminate the relationship between Arendt's intellectual work and her political commitments. She defines her writing and thought in these terms: "My literary existence, as opposed to my existence as a member of society, has two major roots: First, thanks to my husband, I have learned to think politically and see historically; and, second, I have refused to abandon the Jewish question as the focal point of my historical and political thinking. . . ."(31) In describing her current work to her former teacher Jaspers, she invokes her husband as mentor; he was Heinrich Blucher, for many years professor of philosophy at Bard College. Her thinking is itself dependent upon the conversations of friendship and intimacy, perhaps even on the sharing of a household. The juncture of the private domain of thought with the public world of writing becomes a site of tension in her friendship with Jaspers as she explains her ambivalence about contributing work to a new German journal as he has urged her to do:

. . . it is not an easy thing for me to contribute to a German journal. . . . It seems to me that none of us can return (writing is surely a form of return) merely because people again seem prepared to recognize Jews as Germans or something else. We can return only if we are welcome as Jews. That would mean that I would gladly write something if I can write as a Jew on some aspect of the Jewish question. (31–32)

As these passages from her letter to Jaspers should indicate, the "Jewish question" had a complex resonance in the intellectual, political, and personal aspects of Arendt's life. Indeed, one of the most fascinating aspects of her correspondence with Jaspers is the interplay among their sustained, reflective exchanges on the politics of the twentieth century; their ongoing dialogue about the complexities of Jewish, German, and German-Jewish identities; and, the unfolding of a rich and rewarding friendship that came to include two couples, each comprised of a non-Jewish German man and a German-Jewish woman.

From the outset of her engagement with the Jewish Question in *Rahel Varnhagen*, Arendt insisted that the great mistake of European Jewry and its friends was to treat as a social question what was inherently a political question about equal citizenship. Arendt's concern for the pressures on personal lives generated by the strains of legal emancipation and social assimilation focused particularly on marriage and the family. Restrictions on intermarriage and the stigma attached to "mixed marriages" by both Gentile and Jewish communities were important factors in maintaining Jewish difference and subordination. Arendt addressed the political significance of restrictions on marriage in other contexts as well: already in the 1950s, she identified the anti-miscegenation laws in the southern United States as a major component enforcing racial inequality.[12] She was similarly critical of religious restrictions on marriage in the State of Israel.[13] If we think with Arendt against Arendt on the issue of the relation between private households and the public arena of citizenship, we see that the capacity to establish and maintain a household affects both the personal and the political domains.[14] Drawing the boundaries between private and public and ensuring that all democratic citizens have a place in both is an issue not of normal politics, but of the politics of founding celebrated in her work of the 1960s.[15] The construction of domesticity on egalitarian terms becomes a crucial piece of the unfinished business of democratic revolution. Might Arendt's recognition of the mutual penetration of the personal and the political adumbrate a politics of gender and sexuality?

Lesbians, gays, and other sexual nonconformists remain outside the circle of those whom the American democracy must at least claim to include. This is not simply a matter of social acceptance or moral disapproval. As we saw in Chapter One, the Supreme Court in *Bowers v. Hardwick* denied to homosexuals fundamental rights of privacy guaranteed for all other citizens. Although that case involved the refusal to overturn the Georgia sodomy law, it effectively ratified a pervasive system of legal and political disabilities for queer citizens. Lesbians and gays are constructed as second class citizens in the contemporary United States. Homosexual activities, even between consenting adults in private, are criminal offenses in one-half the states; in only nine states are lesbian and gay citizens protected against retaliation by employers and others for the exercise of political freedom in their efforts to attain full equality; homosexual citizens are not permitted to exercise a primary public duty by serving openly in the military on the same terms as other citizens; same-sex couples and queer families are denied legal recognition throughout the nation.[16] In *Romer v. Evans*, the Supreme Court recognized that the decision of a popular majority in Colorado to ban civil rights protections for lesbians and gays amounted to an effort to consign homosexuals to second-class citizenship. Just as the social enforcement of a segregated way of life once promoted white supremacy in the South, the denial of legitimacy to the lives of queer citizens has become an important element in maintaining a heterosexist culture throughout the United States. Arendt's analysis of the Jewish question leads us to be profoundly suspicious of the displacement of political equality onto the social domain and the characterization as "private" of the denial of fundamental rights to an unpopular minority.

In what follows, I pursue the analogy between the treatment of Jews in nineteenth-century Europe and of homosexuals in the contemporary United States more fully. In section three, I probe Arendt's analysis of anti-Semitism and of the ambiguous situation of assimilated Jews in gentile society to shed light on two central phenomena of lesbian and gay life: homophobia and the closet. In section four, I use Arendt's reading of Proust to show how the racial construction of Jews and homosexuals as "natural" essential identities in the nineteenth century worked to foreclose the individual and collective agency of both groups. In the concluding section, I turn to recent work by Sander Gilman on "Jewishness" to attend more fully to the interpenetration of race with sexuality and gender within scientific discourse.

III. The "Jewish Question"

At least as old as Proust, the analogy between the "Jewish question" and the situation of homosexuals has been deployed quite recently by Larry Kramer in *Reports from the Holocaust*[17] and Eve Kosofsky Sedgwick in *Epistemology of the Closet*.[18] Kramer explicitly invokes Arendt's analysis of anti-Semitism from *The Origins of Totalitarianism* and her critique of Jewish leadership during the Final Solution from *Eichmann in Jerusalem*.[19] He uses Arendt to establish an analogy between anti-Semitism and contemporary homophobia and to criticize leaders within the gay community for their responses to the AIDS epidemic. His argument focuses almost exclusively on Arendt's contention that modern European Jews were made vulnerable to anti-Semitism because some enjoyed highly visible wealth without the responsibilities of political power. Kramer compares this situation with that of contemporary gay men whom he casts as conspicuous consumers in the pursuit of their own pleasures. Kramer's picture of lesbian and gay realities is distorted and inaccurate, although it may capture a widespread perception. As for Arendt's *Eichmann* book, Kramer's reading misses her nuance and continually crosses the line from identifying the complexities of agency in totalitarian contexts to simply blaming the victims. Kramer uses the comparison of gays with Jews to support his own aggressive intervention in the AIDS crisis relying on the hyperbolic and misleading analogy between the epidemic and the Nazi attempt at genocide.[20] But there is more to the analogy between anti-Semitism and homophobia, Jewish history and lesbian/gay existence, than Kramer's example suggests.

Eve Kosofsky Sedgwick's *The Epistemology of the Closet*, opens with a reading of the story of Queen Esther, (as refracted by Racine's play and Proust's allusions), as a coming out story in which Esther's concealment of her Judaism from king and court figures as a metaphor of the closet.[21] For Sedgwick, the comparison between homosexuals and Jews turns on the possibility of concealment, of passing, and is reinforced in Racine by his figuring of the Jews as "an unclean people" and "an abomination against nature." The closet is central to Sedgwick's interpretation of the emergence of homosexuality in the nineteenth century in contrast with a pervasively homosocial order where close ties among men perpetuated male domination. She argues that homophobia protected homosocial men from the dangerous proximity of an expressed and threatening homo-*sexuality*. Homosexuals were marked as abject, marginal "Others," yet were invested with powers of invisibility and disguise. According to Sedgwick, the "minority politics" of the story of Esther and its conservative treatment of gender suggests a complex relationship between gender as a universal category and homosexuality as a minority identity that does not easily permit the establishment of priority. Rather, Sedgwick marks a vacillation, within both homophobic and emancipatory discourses, between "minoritizing" views of homosexuality that define a distinct group with a common identity and "universalizing" views that link homosexuality to tendencies shared by all human beings. That vacillation, which is also enacted in the differences between Freud and the third sex theories of early homosexual rights activists,[22] may be read as expressing in general theoretical terms an analogy with the social dilemmas of assimilation and difference generated by Jewish emancipation.

Hannah Arendt's own engagement with the Jewish question was in large part a response to the contingent historical developments that made the issue a central concern in twentieth-century European politics, with life-or-death implications for those affected. In an interview in 1964, Arendt reflected on her turn away from scholarship after 1933:

> I realized what I then expressed time and again in the sentence: If one is attacked as a Jew one must defend oneself as a Jew. Not as a German, not as a world-citizen, not as an upholder of the rights of Man, or whatever. . . . belonging to Judaism had become my own problem, and my own problem was political. Purely political![23]

These attitudes are fully developed in Arendt's unrelenting investigation of the question of what it has meant to be a Jew in modern Europe: "It has been one of the most unfortunate facts in the history of the Jewish people that only its enemies, and almost never its friends, understood that the Jewish question was a political one" (56).[24] Arendt insists that one can understand this tragic history only by focusing on both the actions of those with power and the responses of Jews themselves to the conditions they faced. She rejects the claim that anti-semitism is necessarily an eternal, recurrent theme in the history of the West, and she dismisses more general scapegoat theories, because neither attends to the specificities of historical circumstance and political agency among Jews.

Treating the Jewish question as a social issue resulted in a double movement by which Jews were characterized in psychological rather than religious or national terms and Jewish difference was attributed to inherent racial characteristics. Arendt argues that the racial construction of Jewishness combined with the refusal of European Jewish communities to engage in collective political action to increase their vulnerability to the forces of anti-Semitism within modern totalitarianism. The modern nonpolitical and, increasingly, nonreligious and non-national understanding of Judaism displaced the burdens of inequality onto personal and family life. Ultimately, she claims, Judaism was transformed into "Jewishness": the effects of a common history and collective political status were attributed to individual Jews as immutable racial characteristics. This tendency was reinforced by the chauvinism with which some secularized Jews continued to cultivate a sense of "chosenness" despite the eclipse of their traditional faith. "Jewishness" became part of the self-understanding of individual Jews: "And the more the fact of Jewish birth lost its religious, national, and socioeconomic significance, the more obsessive Jewishness became; Jews were obsessed by it as one may be by a physical defect or advantage, and addicted to it as one may be to a vice." (84) By the time genocidal anti-Semites came to power, many throughout society were prepared to accept the characterization of "Jewishness" as an essential trait that could not be changed, but only accepted or eliminated.

Arendt sees the specifics of the Jewish question as deeply implicated in the transition to modernity and the emergence of the nation-state in Western Europe. Throughout the middle ages, the political and social rights and privileges of Jews, like those of other groups, were defined by their collective status in relation to a web of interlocking historical and legal relationships. Because they were not members of Christendom, the Jews were always outside the boundaries of traditionally defined classes and communities. Periodically exiled from various parts of Europe, Jewish families became extended across conventional boundaries and maintained ties that made them useful as sources of both funds and information. As powerful princes worked to consolidate territory and to centralize administration in national states, Jewish financial support became for them an alternative to feudal ties. Jewish status and privilege became closely linked with consolidating national monarchies, without Jews themselves playing a *political* role in these transformations. Jews were increasingly dependent on nation-states without becoming part of the nation. Because of their relative powerlessness, Arendt argues that Jewish communities became an easy target for those forces that opposed the end of feudalism and the consolidation of nation-states. The extended Jewish family figured importantly in the perception of Jews as having no loyalty to local communities. Resentment of this alien and self-enclosed entity within the body politic was heightened by the visibility of a small number of banking families that financed the new order.[25] When modern racial ideologies appeared with the "pan–" movements in Germany and eastern Europe, this widespread conception of Jewish existence, together with the Biblical notions of chosenness adopted by these movements, made anti-Semitism a political issue.[26] For Arendt, the history of the Jews as a people outside the nation-state but implicated in its development positioned them as models for movements eager to ground politics in ties of "blood" rather than citizenship and as targets for these same movements whose real adversary was the nation-state.

Just as Jews came to represent the modern democratic nation-state in the eyes of its discontents, so too homosexuals may bear the weight of a range of dissatisfactions with liberal society, especially as homosexuality is taken to threaten traditional institutions of religious or family life. The prominence of anti-gay images and rhetoric in the political campaigns of social conservatives in recent United States elections employs lesbians and gays as dramatic figures embodying a whole range of distinctively modern threats to the hegemony of religiously based "family values." Many of these political movements are actually opposed to the liberal state as such with its promise of equal freedom for all — including women and racial and religious as well as sexual minorities.

The French Revolution and the Napoleonic Wars made legal equality and Jewish emancipation an issue throughout Europe. This situation reflected a more general incoherence within nation-states that established legal and political equality against the background of increasingly stratified class societies. Arendt argues that Jewish emancipation had different ramifications for distinct classes within Jewish society as well. Access to non-Jewish society was available to "exceptional" Jews willing to separate from the "Jew in general" and the collective life of the Jewish people. Wealthy or educated Jews faced a choice between remaining in solidarity with a people stigmatized as pariahs, and embracing the status of parvenus in a larger society that condemned their fellow Jews. Often, these "exceptions" joined in condemning some segment of the Jewish people — the poor or immigrants from Eastern Europe — in the same terms applied by the larger society to all Jews. The conditions of their assimilation were highly ambiguous. Although expected to forego identification with the Jewish community, these few were admitted to high society *as Jews*, recognized as interesting precisely because of their questionable origins: "under no circumstances were they allowed simply to disappear among their neighbors." (65) This description of the situation of assimilated Jews bears an uncanny resemblance to that of homosexuals whose lives are structured by the closet. The contradiction between public persona and personal existence falsifies both domains; trying "to be a Jew at home and a man in the streets" generated intolerable strains. Homosexuals in the closet are analogous to the parvenus, while out gays become pariahs. Arendt's "conscious pariah" adopts the stance of today's ironic but engaged and self-affirming queer.

The interaction of "exceptional" Jews, non-Jewish society, and the political environment of the nation-state led to the construction of "Jewishness" as a *racial* category: "Instead of being defined by nationality or religion, Jews were being transformed into a social group whose members shared certain psychological attributes and reactions, the sum total of which was supposed to constitute 'Jewishness.'" (66) This increasingly sharp focus of the Jewish question on the most private and intimate details of individual life among assimilated Jews produced a recognizable "Jewish type" that exercised an ambiguous fascination for a society increasingly plagued by boredom: "Jews became people with whom one hoped to while away some time. The less one thought of them as equals, the more attractive and entertaining they became." (67) For Arendt, "Jewishness" was itself an effect of complex political, social, and psychological interactions: "As long as defamed peoples and classes exist, parvenu- and pariah-qualities will be produced anew by each generation with incomparable monotony, in Jewish society and everywhere else." (66) However, the interplay between political equality and social difference led to the eventual "racialization" of marginal groups in the course of the nineteenth century. Those qualities that defined some groups as social exotics were "naturalized," in popular opinion and in scientific discourse, to become identified with inherent biological or racial conditions that individuals could not escape. Foucault labels this tendency the "degenerescence system."[27] This historical social, political and ideological configuration gave rise to both "Jewishness" and "homosexuality" in late nineteenth-century Europe.[28]

Hannah Arendt's analysis of the impact of anti-Semitism on newly-emancipated, assimilating Jews in European society in the nineteenth century resonates richly with Sedgwick's work on the dynamics of the closet in organizing the discourses of homophobia; lesbians and gays are consigned to a regime of silence and discretion, subjected to a knowing social gaze that defines us as both radically "other" and perfectly transparent. Arendt's portrayal of the peculiar combination of attraction and repulsion that fueled the exoticization of Jews and homosexuals in fin de siècle France evokes a sense of uncanny repetition in a world where clean-cut lesbians hold hands on *Newsweek* covers, queer *ménages à trois* stage lovers' quarrels on the Oprah Winfrey show, and supermarket tabloids detail the last days of the actor Raymond Burr — "Perry Mason," "Ironside" — with his longtime male lover. All of this at the same time that same sex activities remain criminal in half the states, only nine states protect homosexual citizens against discrimination and nowhere in the U. S. may same-sex lovers establish socially and legally recognized households. Arendt's lesson from the history of nineteenth-century anti-Semitism: celebrity is no substitute for political equality.

IV. "Accursed Race," "New Species"

JACK: Yes, but you said yourself that a severe chill was not hereditary.

ALGERNON: It usen't to be, I know — but I daresay it is now. Science is always making wonderful improvements in things.

— Oscar Wilde, *The Importance of Being Earnest* (1895)

Hannah Arendt introduces the comparison between Jews and homosexuals in *The Origins of Totalitarianism* with a reading of Proust: "There is no better witness, indeed, of this period when society had emancipated itself completely from public concerns, and when politics itself was becoming a part of social life." (80) Proust dramatized the "racial" conceptions of "Jewishness" and "homosexuality" that emerged from complex negotiations between demands for conformity and assertions of difference:

> Proust's "innate disposition" is nothing but this personal, private obsession. . . . Proust mistook it for "racial predestination," because he saw and depicted only its social aspect and individual reconsiderations. . . . Both [Jews and homosexuals] felt either superior or inferior, but in any case proudly different from other normal beings; both believed their difference to be a natural fact acquired by birth; both were constantly justifying *not what they did, but what they were*; and both, finally, always wavered between such apologetic attitudes and sudden, provocative claims that they were an elite. [emphasis added] (84)

Arendt uses Proust to portray the interplay between political and social factors that transformed Jews and homosexuals into exotic specimens. She situates this exoticization of Jews and homosexuals within the triumph of bourgeois society: "The victory of bourgeois values over the citizen's sense of responsibility meant the decomposition of political issues into their dazzling, fascinating reflections in society." (80) Groups associated with transgression offered a locus of fascination and a promise of passion. This shift did not reflect a new tolerance for acts and conditions previously linked to crime or sin. Rather, crime itself had become attractive and was savored by a society grown sated with respectability. Here, what Eve Kosofsky Sedgwick, in her essay on Proust, calls the "spectacle of the closet" is identified as the social condition of both assimilated Jews and closeted homosexuals.[29] Each is distinguished by his "open secret":[30]

> This in turn resulted in the typically equivocal situation in which the new members could not confess their identity openly, and yet could not hide it either. . . . only one's Jewishness (or homosexuality) had opened

the doors of the exclusive salons, while at the same time they made one's position extremely insecure. (82)

Arendt's characterization of this effect on Jews resonates with the ambiguities of the closet: "In this equivocal situation, Jewishness was for the individual Jew at once a physical stain and a mysterious personal privilege, both inherent in a 'racial predestination.'"(82)

Arendt's treatment of the Jewish question converges with Michel Foucault's account of the formation in the nineteenth century of "perverted" sexual identities as biologically grounded and medically defined conditions. As described in Chapter Two, nineteenth-century discourse was marked by a shift from a universalizing interdiction of sexual acts, potentially criminal or sinful but within the capacity of *any* ordinary person, to the minoritizing construction of "perverted" sexual identities in a medical classification for which behavior became "symptomatic," that is, revelatory of an inner truth about fundamentally *different kinds* of persons. This discursive shift also marked a transition from controlling individual behavior primarily through religious and juridical prohibitions directed at one's conduct toward the effort to produce "normal" individuals through newly dominant medical, pedagogic, and therapeutic professions and practices. For Foucault, this transition marked the emergence of a new species: "Homosexuality appeared as one of the forms of sexuality when it was transposed from the practice of sodomy onto a kind of interior androgyny, a hermaphroditism of the soul. The sodomite had been a temporary aberration; the homosexual was now a species."[31]

Arendt's analysis of the comparison between Jews and homosexuals supports Foucault's emphasis on the contingent historical and fundamentally political character of the construction of sexual identities. According to Arendt, the complex and ambivalent shift, "from crime to vice," in social attitude towards Jews and homosexuals put each in a precarious position: "Human wickedness, if accepted by society, is changed from an act of will into an inherent, psychological quality which man cannot choose or reject but which is imposed upon him from without and which rules him as compulsively as the drug rules the addict."(80) For Proust, the transformation of criminal action into an inherent vicious behavior results in a denial of human dignity, as moral responsibility is displaced by the language of racial predisposition or medical pathology. Arendt describes his insight in these terms:

"Punishment is the right of the criminal," of which he is deprived if (in the words of Proust) judges assume and are more inclined to pardon murder in inverts and treason in Jews for reasons derived from . . . "racial predestination." It is an attraction to murder and treason which hides behind such perverted tolerance, for in a moment it can switch to a decision to liquidate not only all actual criminals but all who are "racially" predestined to commit certain crimes. (80–81)

For Arendt, this insight foreshadows the grim reality of the concentration camps, where Nazi racial ideology led to the incarceration and eventual murder of "racially" defined groups independent of any actions of individuals, and where convicted criminals, punished for specific violations, benefited from legal status denied to the innocent.[32] Jews and homosexuals were finally undone by this revaluation of the stigmas by which they had been historically defined, the sins or crimes of rejecting Christ and Christendom or of practicing sodomy. Jews were still suspected of harboring a tendency to treason; homosexuals were still seen as threatening religious and family values with their transgressive desires. These associations with treason and illicit passion, which made them exotics, were reified as immutable qualities by nineteenth-century racial ideology: "Jews had been able to escape from Judaism into conversion; from Jewishness there was no escape. A crime moreover, is met with punishment; a vice can only be exterminated." (87)

Arendt uses Proust's text to focus on the construction of Jews and of homosexuals in racial terms that perpetuated historical stigmas. I want to develop this analogy further by reading some passages from the section of Proust's *Cities of the Plain* called "the accursed race"(*la race maudite*). The narrator Marcel has been spying on a serendipitous assignation between M. de Charlus, a middle-aged aristocratic queen, and Jupien, a retired tailor. His observation of the flirtation and subsequent sexual encounter between the two leads to an extended meditation on homosexuals and their place in the world.[33] The narrator describes his "discovery" of the Baron's homosexuality:

> Although in the person of M. de Charlus another creature was coupled, as the horse in the centaur, which made him different from other men, although this creature was one with the Baron, I had never perceived it. Now the abstraction had become materialized, the creature at last discerned had lost its power of remaining invisible, and the transformation of M. de Charlus into a new person was so complete. . . . (636)

Critical to this transformation is a shift in the narrator's view of the Baron's *sex*: "I now understood, moreover, why earlier, when I had seen him coming away from Mme. de Villeparisis's, I had managed to arrive at the conclusion that M. de Charlus looked like a woman: he was one!" This moment in Proust powerfully illuminates several of Foucault's insights into the emergence of the homosexual as a new species. The narrator has witnessed an act of sodomy; what he describes is a "transformation" of the Baron into "a new person." Here is Foucault's description of the emergent homosexual:

> Nothing that went into his total composition was unaffected by his sexuality. It was everywhere present in him: at the root of all his actions because it was their insidious and indefinitely active principle; written

immodestly on his face and body because it was a secret that always gave itself away. It was consubstantial with him, less as a habitual sin than as a singular nature. . . . a certain way of inverting the masculine and feminine in oneself.[34]

M. de Charlus is not only exotic, he is monstrous in the narrator's eyes. His strangeness is somewhat clarified by uncovering his inner femininity, identified as the truth that explains the Baron's earlier ambiguity: he really was a woman all along. However, in Proust's text, there is a further turn in this dialectic of concealment and revelation. After all, Marcel discovers the Baron's "inner truth" only as a result of a fairly complicated effort to spy and eavesdrop on the two men. The elaborate account of M. de Charlus' dalliance with Jupien and of the revelation of the Baron's nature also exposes its narrator as a voyeur.

Arendt does not comment on this complex erotic dynamic nor on its feminization of the homosexual. However, sexual ambiguity and gender inversion are central to Proust's portrayal of the "race" of homosexuals.[35] We are again in the presence of the "third sex," defined most famously as a "female brain in a male's body."[36] (Recall the discussion of Freud's engagement with this theory in Chapter Four.) The new medical conception of homosexuality combined an earlier notion of gender inversion with inversion of the sexual object. Proust joins that figure with the rhetoric of Greek pederasty as he defines the Baron's inner femininity in terms of (hetero)sexual object choice:[37]

He belonged to the race of beings, less paradoxical than they appear, whose ideal is manly precisely because their temperament is feminine, and who in ordinary life resemble other men in appearance only; there where each of us carries, inscribed in those eyes through which he beholds everything in the universe, a human form engraved on the surface of the pupil, for them it is not that of a nymph but that of an ephebe. A race upon which a curse is laid and which must live in falsehood and perjury. . . . (636)

The Baron is not figured as one of Freud's "completely masculine" pederasts, but the (hetero)sexual object that attracts his female psyche is an ephebe, trembling on the verge of manhood, the most desirable beloved for Athenian gentlemen.[38] This passage further illustrates the ambiguity that pervades this entire section as a result of the problematic position of its narrator.[39] Figuring homosexuality in terms of the forms inscribed in the gaze of desire serves to remind the reader of the narrator's own intensely interested observation of the encounter between two men. His ambiguous rhetoric joins the discourse of racial science with Greek and Biblical myth and the language of medical pathology: ". . . what they have been calling their love . . . springs not from an ideal of beauty which they have chosen but from an incurable disease." (639) Later, "psychical hermaphroditism," femininity and the primitive are joined in a phantasmagoria of evolutionary biology: "In this respect the race of inverts . . . might be traced back further still . . . to that initial hermaphroditism of which certain rudiments of male organs in the anatomy of women and of female organs in that of men seem still to preserve the trace." (653)[40] This deployment of the languages of science and pathology works to provide some cover for the voyeurism of the narrator. His construction of himself as the disinterested observer is already at work earlier in the section where he describes himself passing time as a "botanist" studying the sex life of flowers when he happens to witness the encounter of the Baron and Jupien. Ruminations on the erotic language of flowers are threaded throughout Marcel's portrayal of the mores of the "accursed race," positioning the narrator in a stance of scientific detachment that preserves the distance between an acceptable homosociality and a pathological homosexuality, between the narrator's "disinterested" gaze and the amorous glances exchanged by the men on whom he spies.[41]

Soon after, Proust introduces "the dark comparison" between the race of homosexuals and the Jews. Jews and homosexuals, as members of stigmatized groups, internalize the social gaze that abjects them. They come to reject each other and to identify themselves with their deep desires for those with power, Christians or "normal" men, "shunning one another, seeking out those who are most directly their opposite, who do not want their company, forgiving their rebuffs, enraptured by their condescension. . . ." (638) Both combine the parvenu's anxious search for acceptance by others with the self-hatred that divides him from others of his kind. Here Proust moves from an essentialist to an historical conception of both homosexual and Jewish identity, noting the tendency of each to claim Socrates and Jesus as forebears, ". . . without reflecting that there were no abnormal people when homosexuality was the norm, no anti-Christians before Christ, that the opprobrium alone makes the crime because it has allowed to survive only those who remained obdurate to every warning, to every example, to every punishment, by virtue of an innate disposition. . . ." (639) The paradox is inescapable: this "innate disposition" results in "Jewishness" or "homosexuality" only under social conditions of Christian orthodoxy or compulsory heterosexuality.

Insistent in his use of metaphors of race to portray their condition, Proust likens homosexuals not only to Jews, but to blacks as well, suggesting that this accounts for the persistence among them of dangerous desires that distinguish them from "the other race" among which they live:

Perhaps, to form a picture of these, we ought to think, if not of the wild animals that never became domesticated, of the lion cubs, allegedly tamed, which are still lions at heart, then at least, of the negroes whom the comfortable existence of the white man renders desperately unhappy and who prefer the risks of life in the wild and its incomprehensible joys. (647)

Proust pervasively associates the trope of race with references to "primitive" nature (including animals and plants), to the "feminine," and to the discourses of science and medicine. At once, male homosexuality is identified with femininity and figured as a threatening animality. (We are not far from the rhetoric by which gays in the military are imagined as both lacking in the manliness to be good soldiers and posing a predatory threat to their fellows in the showers.)

But the rhetoric of science does not completely displace politics. Proust presents a playful variation on the Biblical account of the origins of "the accursed race" in Sodom and Gomorrah. It appears that the angels charged with destruction of the cities of the plain, not being themselves sodomites, were easily fooled by the disguises and deceptions perpetrated by those sinful folk: "they allowed all the shameless Sodomites to escape. . . . With the result that they engendered a numerous progeny. . . . established themselves throughout the entire world. . . . " (655) The narrator rejects one "political solution" to the Sodomite diaspora:

> I have thought it as well to utter here a provisional warning against the lamentable error of proposing (just as people have encouraged a Zionist movement) to create a Sodomist movement and to rebuild Sodom. For no sooner had they arrived there than the Sodomites would leave the town so as not to have the appearance of belonging to it, would take wives, would keep mistresses in other cities where they would find, incidentally, every diversion that appealed to them. (655–56)

Proust has inverted the relations between the hidden race and that larger society in which they live. It appears that not all deception is laid at the door of that minority of sexual intermediates who harbor souls with desires at odds with those proper to their biological sex. It would seem that the boundary between these "psychical hermaphrodites" and the "other race" that dominates society is not so easy to draw. Indeed, diversity and fluidity of desires and sexual identities may be the real open secret of Proust's world. In recognizing that the descendants of Sodom would continue their diaspora even after the rebuilding of their city, the narrator notes that ". . . everything would go on very much as it does to-day in London, Berlin, Rome, Petrograd or Paris." (656) Once again like the Jews of Europe in the nineteenth century, contemporary sodomites are denizens of its major cities. In fact, they may be no different from their fellows after all.

Proust's text exhibits and problematizes the rhetoric of race in figuring both Jews and homosexuals. But Arendt's reading occludes Proust's attention to the dynamic of feminization and the role of scientific and medical discourse in racializing Jewishness and homosexuality. Proust shows the extent to which at the turn of the twentieth century, racial characterization employed the language of science and pervasively linked difference to the "feminine" and the "primitive." Perhaps these insights were more available to him because of his own interest in the discourses of sexology and the specificities of homosexual existence. Taken together,

Arendt and Proust provide a complex genealogy of the production of "natural" identities as an attempt to stabilize an order disturbed by tensions between equality and difference. By marking as inherent qualities the effects of shared historical circumstance, racialized identities served to naturalize and internalize the subordination of marginal groups, subjecting them to continuing social control as distinct, transparent, and permanent minorities. The construction of Jewishness and homosexuality as essential identities in the nineteenth century worked to foreclose the individual and collective agency of both, limiting their capacity to determine what they were and who they might become. Arendt and Proust alert us to the disempowering effects of accepting naturalized definitions of sexuality and race that are in fact produced and maintained by a history of political oppression and social abjection.

V. The Politics of Sexuality

In this section, I supplement Hannah Arendt's analysis to emphasize the role of science in the racial construction of "Jewishness" and recognize the historical imbrication of race with gender and sexuality. The comparative genealogy of Jewishness and homosexuality becomes even more salient for contemporary queer politics when we note the important role that science and medicine played in paving the way for political anti-Semitism. This discourse racially constructed "the Jew," especially the male, as a feminized and sexually primitive figure. In several recent books, the historian of medicine Sander Gilman has articulated the intimate linkages among race, gender, and sexuality in nineteenth-century science.[42] His account complements rather than contradicts Arendt's interpretation of the historical interactions through which Judaism as a religious, national, or collective socioeconomic status became "Jewishness" understood as an innate psychological attribute of individuals. Gilman argues that racial conceptions of Jewish identity were pervasive in Europe during this period although the details varied. Even Jewish physicians and scientists worked within the prevailing paradigm, although they sought to alleviate its more negative consequences, especially those bearing on their own capacity to achieve "objective" knowledge.

Although the focus of Gilman's inquiry is the construction of a "Jewish body," such a concept was always fraught with implications for the intellectual, psychological, and, especially, sexual status of Jews. The "Jewish body" was defined in terms of a diverse collection of qualities and dispositions, most carrying a negative valence within nineteenth-century European culture and society. These characteristics included distinctively marked languages and linguistic competence, skin and hair color and texture, facial structure and characteristics, general physical appearance and capacity, propensity to mental illness and physical disease, tendencies to sexual excess and perversion. With the passing of a political and social system explicitly grounded in Christianity, the intimate if problematic link between Judaism and the dominant religion was severed: "Jewishness" as a racial type was contrasted not with the Christian faith but with the "Aryan race." Gilman contends that all of the components of "Jewishness" presumed the Jewish male as their object; at the same time, the "Jew's body" was feminized and linked to a threatening sexuality. The practice of ritual circumcision with its resultant genital marking of Jewish men played a central role in medical research on Jews, in the culture of anti-Semitism, and in debates within Jewish communities. Lamarckian theories about the inheritance of acquired characteristics licensed the identification of circumcision as a "racial" marker of the male Jew despite the fact that it was a result of ritual practice. This stereotype, together with the association of Jews with a propensity for mental illness and syphilis, combined to mark Jews as infectious agents of sexual corruption within the body politic. That tendency was "explained" in terms of the Jewish practice of endogamy, which was conflated with incest. The Jewish family became the site of a pathological difference that bred elements threatening to the mental, physical, and sexual health of "normal families." Thus, anti-Semitism as a political movement and social attitude gained credence from the racial science of the day: "racial models of the Jew . . . are found not only in the 'crackpot' pamphlet literature of the time; they were present in virtually all discussions of pathology published from 1880 to 1930. It is in the 'serious' medical literature. . . [that] these ideas of Jewish difference appear. . . ."[43]

Gilman amply demonstrates the affinities between the racial rhetoric of "Jewishness" and that associated with constructions of homosexuality as a third sex. Homosexual men were similarly feminized; and lesbians characterized as masculine women. Moreover, closer examination of the figures deployed regarding Jews reveals a whole cluster of family resemblances. Like homosexuals, Jews were understood in terms of biologically based inherent characteristics, and yet thought to be capable of a dissembling invisibility (like the Baron de Charlus). They shared: access to a "hidden language" understood only by others of their kind; possession of a distinctive pattern of speech which involuntarily revealed their "inner nature"; propensities to mental illness and physical disease, especially those linked with sexuality; identification with urban living and with the ills of urban civilization; perception as sources of danger to normal families; incapacity to discharge the (manly) duties of citizens, especially military service; and a tendency to debilitating self-hatred. Jewish physicians themselves accepted many of these characterizations, while emphasizing the role of historical oppression in creating such conditions. Defenders of homosexual rights advanced the immutable, biological basis of that condition as an argument against criminal penalties and discrimination. The medicalized discourse of race was treated by both homosexual rights advocates and Jewish activists as a given with potentially emancipatory implications, while anti-Semites used it in their campaigns against Jewish civil rights, and medical authorities worked to develop techniques for the control or cure of "sexual perverts."

In *Freud, Race, and Gender*,[44] Gilman argues at some length that Freud's rejection of biological explanations of psychological and social phenomena as "innate and degenerate" conditions reflects the universalizing aspirations of a generation of Jewish doctors working to overcome the racial construction of Jewishness prevalent in their profession. He contends that the founding generation of psychoanalysis displaced their own anxieties about this move onto women. While they rejected the "degenerescence system" in other respects, they continued to regard sexual difference as grounded in an inherent natural condition. Thus, they racially constructed femininity in a manner that they refused for Jewishness and male homosexuality. Gilman's work on the medical discourse of race combines with Arendt's more political treatment of racism to show that the production of inherent naturalized identities is very much the result of historical deployments of power. Once produced, these constructions can be pressed into service equally by progressive or reactionary forces. Gilman's material also demonstrates the need to integrate interpretations of race and sexuality with an analysis of the rhetoric of feminization, the ideology of gender, and the political status of women.

At this point, we may step back to examine the distinctive contributions of Hannah Arendt and of other theorists to our understanding of this complex genealogy of race and sexuality. First, Arendt's analysis of the Jewish question is emphatic in attending to its contingent historical character. There is no master discipline or Archimedean point from which to grasp the significance of questions regarding the status of Jews in modern nation-states. Rather Arendt developed and revised a series of historical narratives — from *Rahel Varnhagen* to *Origins* to *Eichmann* — interpreting the specific configurations of political, social, and ideological factors that gave shape to modern anti-Semitism and the vicissitudes of Jewish history in Europe. Her understanding that racial categories of collective behavior of whatever sort emerge from complex interactions among various groups under specific political conditions underlies the historical discussion. Arendt sees that the particular character of racial thought derives from both the ideological stereotypes of dominant groups and the diverse responses of those so labeled. She reminds us that analyses that deny all agency to oppressed groups reiterate racist reductions of collective activity to the behavioral outcomes of inherent natural conditions. She insists that the distinctively political dimension of human life is the capacity to initiate actions in concert with others, through which we share in defining who we are to become. Any attempt to define persons in terms of inherent essential qualities, with reference not to "what they did, but what they were" (84), whether in the service of racist oppression, scientific explanation and control, or emancipatory identity politics, risks a radical distortion of the human condition.

Arendt practices a historical specificity that interrogates the claims of all general theories of human action by locating them in relation to the concrete exigencies of particular circumstance. In that spirit, her rigid theoretical dichotomy between private and public is undermined by her own sensitive and nuanced portrayal of the interpenetration of the two in the history of Jewish persecution and emancipation. Similarly, Gilman's discussion of "Jewishness" in nineteenth-century medicine and racial science suggests that Arendt's account of anti-Semitism and modern Jewish existence must be developed further to include the dynamic of feminization and the role of scientific discourse in its articulation and institutionalization. Arendt was perhaps too uncritical in separating "pseudo-scientific" propaganda from the practices of established science. Her genealogy of race must be supplemented by Foucault's emphasis on the appearance in modernity of new forms of disciplinary power deploying expert knowledge and related techniques of social control. This kind of historical analysis, which Gilman has performed for the Jewish question and which has informed much work in lesbian and gay studies,[45] complements and extends the kind of concrete political reflection practiced by Arendt, specifically with reference to totalitarianism. Foucault presses that sort of reflection into practice, tracing the pervasive reach and institutional manifestation of normalizing practices that shape an individual's very sense of self and produce the subjectivities they control.[46] He is especially acute in seeing that discourses of sexuality inform a range of pedagogic and therapeutic practices through which individuals are brought to understand themselves as bearers of an inner truth marked as a biologically grounded "sexual identity." His analysis of sexuality as a mode of social control calls for a politics that contests the definition of the sexual identities it seeks to mobilize.

Neither Arendt nor Foucault theorizes the role of gender in modern society and politics. Arendt's analysis of anti-Semitism proposes in part that the attribution of inherent biological differences to minority groups is an attempt to reintroduce in naturalized terms social differences that have been banished from modern democratic political discourse. But she does not seem to recognize that the single most pervasive "natural" difference recognized in modern societies is the one between men and women. Racializing ideologies must be linked to the politics of sexual difference, especially given the extent to which racial groups and sexual minorities have been subordinated through strategies of "feminization." Already involved in racial accounts of "Jewishness," gender is pervasively at work in the construction of "sexual identities." (As I argued in Chapter Four, it is almost impossible to disentangle the homosexuality from fantasmatic constructions of sex and gender within a binary matrix that maintains compulsory heterosexuality and the subordination of women.) A politics of sexuality must be conceived in tandem with a politics of sexual difference that directly confronts and analyzes the identification of femininity as a primary figure of abjection in Western culture.[47] Why did Hannah Arendt fail (refuse?) to think the place of gender in politics? I will not hazard a full explanation of her silence, but it is certainly linked to the exclusions that are effected by her rigid containment of household and social matters in *The Human Condition*. It may be that Arendt accepted uncritically a naturalized and essentialist view of gender at odds with the entire spirit of her critique of race thinking and racism. Arendt's hostility towards Freud and psychoanalysis may be in play here as well. In part motivated by a rejection of the scientific claims of

173

psychoanalysis, Arendt also expressed a deep discomfort with the project of theorizing the intimacies of personal life. She clearly preferred the indirection of literature. Only in the early *Rahel* does she engage with an individual life in all of its messiness; she even wrote about Rahel's dreams. It is no surprise that she later distanced herself from this book and rejected its "psychology." But under the conditions of modernity, as Arendt's own rich treatment of the Jewish question reveals, one cannot understand politics and history without reference to the dynamics of family life from which subjects emerge and to the social and ideological matrices within which they develop. Gilman's account of "Jewishness" in medical discourse and Foucault's narrative of the emergence of "sexuality" as a mode of social control provide additional incentive, in contexts relevant to Arendt's work, for a more radical thinking of the politics of the personal, with a sharp focus on the question of gender.

If Arendt's own thinking must be tested and reformulated to confront gender, so too, the question of sexual difference must be reworked by Arendt's political and historical thinking. As we saw in Chapter Two, some feminists and queer theorists have rejected essentialist accounts of gender and sexuality as occluding identities and ways of life different from the projections of dominant groups. These critics have been especially sensitive to the ways that race, social class, culture, religion, ethnicity, and nationality refract the experiences of contemporary women, challenging the right of any single group to speak for all women, or all lesbians, or all women of color.[48] This critique displays a deep affinity with Arendt's practice regarding the Jewish question, her insistence on the differences among Jewish notables and masses, rich and poor, Western and East Europeans, financiers and intellectuals, parvenus and pariahs. Arendt's genealogy of anti-Semitism and Jewish existence passes through the prisms of religion, nationality, political status, and social class. The demand to see historically and to think politically mandates rejection of a master category that holds the key to understanding historical contingency and political difference. Among contemporary theorists of gender and sexuality, Judith Butler has expressed this imperative with special cogency:

> To prescribe an exclusive identification for a multiply constituted subject, as every subject is, is to enforce a reduction and a paralysis, and some feminist positions, including my own, have problematically prioritized gender as the identificatory site of political mobilization at the expenses of race or sexuality or class or geopolitical positioning/displacement. And here it is not simply a matter of honoring the subject as a plurality of identifications, for these identifications are invariably imbricated in one another, the vehicle for one another. . . .[49]

Arendt's genealogy of Jewishness and Foucault's genealogy of homosexuality combine to suggest that essentialized collective identities are best understood as the products of complex political and social interactions. Butler's deployment of psychoanalysis demonstrates a similar dynamic at work in the formation of personal identities from individual histories within the intersubjective contexts of early life. These identities are shaped by excluding those aspects of existence that threaten the self's unity and by treating them as an abject other against which one comes to define oneself. Butler sees this dynamic at work in the construction of shared political identities as well — in the processes that mark designated groups as marginal and in the emancipatory movements that work to resignify their marginality and transform their social status.

The politics of sexuality and the emancipation of sexual minorities must avoid the hazards of a politics of "exclusive identification." Arendt and Proust on the Jewish question, Proust and Foucault on homosexuality, Butler on the dynamic of identification more generally, these perspectives converge to emphasize that personal and collective identities are enmeshed with the socio-economic, political, juridical and moral imperatives governing any particular culture and historical period. As Arendt recognized in her correspondence with Jaspers, personal life is situated deeply in political contexts, the private implicated in the public. In modernity, "identity" functions as a highly ambiguous sign, alternately and sometimes simultaneously indicating personal and political processes and outcomes. This is no accident. Personal and group identities emerge from a setting of interacting, sometimes conflicting, affiliations and desires. Self-formation is an inherently political process: identities are formed by negotiating a plurality of forces and relations, affirming some, excluding others, to reach provisional settlements, themselves subject to repudiation, revision, and transformation. The materials available for self-making are themselves conditioned by particular cultures and their histories; they include specific configurations of race, gender, sexuality, class, religion, and nationality. The identities of both individuals and communities are contingent, provisional, and often precarious accomplishments; they are established by defining the boundaries of individuals and groups. They divide the world into self and other, friends and enemies, neighbors and strangers, citizens and aliens, allies and adversaries. Hegemonic entities like the nation state and minority communities like the Jews in Europe each re-enact these founding gestures and interact in reinforcing or contesting their borders. If nineteenth-century bourgeois society defined normality for assimilating Jews, these "exceptions" secured their inclusion by projecting stereotypes used to mark all Jews onto a segment of the population — East Europeans or the poor. Similarly, just as dominant institutions enforce compulsory heterosexuality by pathologizing homosexuality, contemporary lesbian and gay movements have themselves sometimes pathologized or marginalized other sexual nonconformists such as transvestites, transsexuals, sadomasochists, pedophiles, or bisexuals.[50]

The genealogies in this essay demonstrate how essential naturalized identities were ascribed to subordinate groups by dominant social attitudes supported by established science in the racial and sexual politics of the nineteenth century. The efficacy of this move depended in part on obscuring its political origins by invoking the alleged neutrality of science and indifference of nature. Contemporary "essentialist" defenses of homosexuality as an inherent natural condition that is biologically determined, over which individuals have no control, and for which they ought not to be penalized, may reiterate that history.[51] Capitalizing on an analogy with race made attractive by the promise of constitutional equality, these essentialist defenders of lesbian and gay rights do not account for the history of racial oppression that necessitated the development of such remedial doctrines in the first place. They are not alert to the historical and political fact that essentialism is a double-edged sword. There is nothing essentially progressive or emancipatory about the essentialist maneuver, as Arendt persuasively demonstrates. Her account provides a much needed cautionary note, reminding us that the most insidious effects of racial thinking resulted from its acceptance even by those it marked as inferior. The point is reiterated by Judith Butler: such "exclusive identifications," accomplished through their own constitutive negations and disavowals, may lead to reduction and paralysis. For both Arendt and Butler, the politics of naturalized identities is at odds with democratic commitments to plurality and public debate.

The production of marginalized sexual subjects is linked with a diversity of other normalizing practices that produce and maintain inequalities throughout late modern societies. Not simply "lesbians and gays," but particular communities and individuals characterized by class, race, nationality, and religion as well as gender and sexuality make up the complex, pluralized cultures in which we live. There is no single factor or comprehensive theory by which to rank the contending political and psychic forces. However, as a pervasive dimension of modern normalizing power, sexuality provides a promising and much needed strategic site for political organization. Informed by the genealogy of its historical production, a democratic politics of sexuality must forego the temptations of exclusive identification and forge alliances for common action from intersecting and multiple identifications and communities. The crucial task is to secure the public space and shared purpose necessary for action without inscribing new exclusions and foreclosing future agencies. This democratic politics of sexuality requires an ongoing willingness to contest boundaries of community, redefine coalitions for concerted action, and reconfigure relationships between personal and political identities. Such a politics has profound implications for the ethics of self-formation as well as for modern democratic practice. In the next chapter, I will offer a reading of Henry David Thoreau that examines further the mutual relations of democratic contestation and deliberate self-making. Thoreau's insistence that deliberate living in a democratic polity may require "resistance to civil authority" provides a broader context for articulating the links between citizenship and the politics of desire.

CHAPTER SIX

QUEER CITIZENSHIP

><

Thoreau's "Civil Disobedience" and the Ethics of Self-making[1]

for Don Gifford

Henry David Thoreau's "Civil Disobedience" proposes a radical conception of democratic citizenship in which the individual's political situation poses both hazards and opportunities for constructing a meaningful life. He systematically subordinates political and legal obligations to an ethic of self-making, but recognizes the citizen's involvement with the public policies of modern democracies. Political conflict complicates the project of living deliberately, of striving towards integrity and justice. Resistance to civil authority becomes an essential component of self-making; however, Thoreau situates the struggle for justice within the individual's negotiation of her own conflicting desires. Like Socrates, Thoreau interrogates the conventions of his society and insists on the centrality of living in agreement with oneself. Like Arendt, he sees agonistic contestation as central to democracy and political action as an arena of self-formation. Like Plato and Freud, he recognizes desire as the motivating force in ethical life. Like Foucault, he rejects a juridical model of power in favor of a conception of the productive capacities of an "aesthetic of existence." Reading "Civil Disobedience" together with *Walden* yields a democratic ethos that sees resistance not as a matter of subjection to higher law but rather as the deliberate shaping of oneself in relation to one's desires, friends, and community. Thoreau's texts are "queer" in their insistence on the centrality of nonconformity to democratic politics and on the idiosyncrasy, conflict, and recalcitrance of desire in the ethics of self-making.

Thoreau's writings have had extraordinary influence on the emancipatory politics of the twentieth century. Gandhi credited it with providing important support for his own doctrine of *Satyagraha*. He translated portions of the essay as early as 1907 for publication in South Africa in his journal *Indian Opinion* and later sponsored its distribution in pamphlet form.[2] Later, Martin Luther King, Jr.

studied Thoreau's work at Morehouse College, and cited Thoreau along with Gandhi, Tolstoy, Jesus, and Socrates, as a source of his own form of nonviolent civil disobedience. Indeed, he claimed that his college reading of Thoreau helped him to see that the Montgomery bus boycott was not simply an economic pressure tactic but at bottom a refusal to cooperate with the evil of racial segregation.[3] In the last few years, advocates of lesbian and gay rights and liberation have also invoked Thoreau in support of recourse to various tactics of direct action. Richard Mohr has argued that maintaining the moral integrity of lesbians and gays requires resort to civil disobedience where conformity to the requirements of law would violate basic dignity.[4] ACT UP, Queer Nation, and other militant lesbian-gay-queer organizations have included civil disobedience among a variety of tactics to publicize their claims in the wake of the AIDS epidemic. In "From Thoreau to Queer Nation," Henry Abelove argues that the thought and example of the Concord writer shed light on both the "action" as a distinctive political gesture developed by Queer Nation and its celebration of "nationhood."[5] In "Thoreau's Bottom," Michael Warner has explored Thoreau's texts, especially the *Journals*, to uncover his engagement with the erotic economies of sameness and difference, self and other, at a time prior to the emergence of an official discourse of homo- or heterosexuality.[6] Warner explicates Thoreau's "unflagging emphasis on the subjective principle of modernity" in the context of political philosophy as well as providing a penetrating reading of the complex erotics of his texts.[7] Thus, Thoreau's radical political stance has been invoked on behalf of the cause of lesbian and gay emancipation at the same time that his texts have been liberated with queer readings. The "queering" of Thoreau involves rather more than an effort to add to the list of eminent practitioners of same-sex desire. Not his personal practices, but the unrelenting insistence of his texts on interrogating conventional social arrangements and their complex figuring of desire as a motive in self-making make Thoreau available for contemporary queer politics and theory.

As Don Gifford, author of *The Farther Shore*, pointed out in unpublished lectures delivered at the height of the activist Sixties, there is an anomaly in the adoption of "Civil Disobedience" as a primer for democratic social movements: Thoreau's essay describes a persistent dilemma that confronts the individual in the context of all collective action. Gifford argued that ". . . the essay is disturbing and unsettling, puzzling and ambiguous, and that is why so many who quote the essay . . . have the impulse to transform the questions into answers, to treat the essay, in Gandhi's phrase, as a 'grammar of action,' instead of as a *grammar of questions*."[8] Thoreau's own uneasy relationship with contemporary abolitionists points up the extent to which he is an unlikely sponsor of mass political actions, no matter how sympathetic he might have been to their objectives. Originally titled "Resistance to Civil Government," the essay alternates importantly between urging the individual to withdraw from the collective contexts in which one is immersed and recognizing that such withdrawal is necessarily a tactical retreat to be followed by return to the exigencies of action. The argument of his essay is framed by the founding doctrines of American democracy: individual rights, equality, and the consent of the governed. It moves through a radicalization of these assumptions towards affirming the sovereignty of "the majority of one." The democratic individual is necessarily engaged to some extent in the business of politics, situated in a network of overlapping social and natural relations.[9] However, she is also capable of transcending these relationships in the direction of an authentic realization of her own ultimate possibilities. The duty of resistance to civil government arises insofar as the political context makes it impossible to "mind one's own business," to live one's life fully and deliberately without becoming complicit with injustice. In this reading of Thoreau, I hope to reawaken the questioning inherent in the multiple gestures of resistance that comprise his teaching on civil disobedience. I follow Abelove and Warner in emphasizing the queerness of these texts, especially when situating the politics of "Civil Disobedience" in relation to the vision of the "double self" embodied in *Walden*. Thoreau's essay serves to problematize the concept of political action and of the subject that engages in it. In the process, his argument unsettles the very distinctions by which it proceeds — between conscience and expediency, spectator and agent, individual integrity and collective consequences. Thoreau's texts enact a complex effort at self-overcoming in which striving to live by higher laws is inextricably entangled with impulses towards aggression and sensual satisfaction. In political terms, Thoreau embodies a model of "queer citizenship" that combines the rejection of social conformity with the founding of a new polity of individuals seeking sovereignty in shaping their own desires and bound to their fellows by ties of affection, friendship, and mutual respect.

I. "Resistance to Civil Government"

The story of Thoreau's refusal to pay his poll tax because of his opposition to slavery and the Mexican War, and of the night he spent in Concord jail as a result is the stuff of legend in activist communities. However, Thoreau's ironic and deflationary portrayal of his own conduct reveals his sense of the essentially problematic character of political action. The episode is recounted quite late in the essay; its presentation, hardly heroic. It is a commonplace that Thoreau's actions in refusing to pay his tax and spending a night in jail were politically without visible effect; his account of the events invites the suspicion that a comedy of sorts was enacted in Concord that day. Rather, as Gifford points out, the effective locus of action is the lecture Thoreau delivered at the Concord Lyceum and the essay he subsequently published in 1849 in a volume with the surprising and evocative title *Aesthetic Papers*, edited by Elizabeth Peabody:

> The real answer is not in the gestures described or in the argument contained in the essay; the real answer is the essay itself: the essay is the dramatic gesture which transforms a minor squabble about the payment of a

179

poll tax and a larger squabble about a concluded war into effective individual dissent.[10]

(When Thoreau delivered the lecture in February, 1848, the Mexican War was practically settled.) Thoreau's was a modest voice in the advocacy of civil disobedience as a form of resistance to slavery. Wendell Philips led the Abolitionist call for resistance to illegitimate authority, denouncing the United States Constitution itself as "a covenant with death."[11] Advocacy of civil disobedience in the name of a higher law was characteristic of the anti-slavery movements of the eighteenth and nineteenth centuries; even Thoreau's radical individualism and pervasive anti-institutionalism had roots in Quaker teachings of the "inner light" that informed some branches of abolitionism.[12] Perry Miller has traced some of these themes back through Jonathan Edwards to the anti-nomianism of Anne Hutchinson and to earlier Quaker incursions in Puritan New England.[13] Finally, Thoreau got the specific idea of refusing to pay his poll tax from his Concord neighbor Bronson Alcott, who had already refused for some years, but who had permitted himself to be deprived of even one night in jail when friends paid the tax on his behalf. What, in the face of these facts, accounts for the continuing influence of Thoreau's essay and for its ability to move us today? I believe that its very ambiguity is an important source of its power. Thoreau defines the contours of the modern self, divided between a heightened feeling of personal responsibility for social wrong and a sense of impotence over against the machinery of a complex society. This "double self" is not just spectator of the world, but is engaged to act within it, at once responsible for living deliberately and responsive to the claims of the world. It is moved by the aspiration to act in accordance with higher principles, but is also stirred by primitive appetites and aggressive impulses. Rather than offering a theoretical solution of these dilemmas, Thoreau constructs narratives in which the individual negotiates deep conflicts by alternating experimentally between action in the world and withdrawal into a judging consciousness.

Thoreau's essay both deploys and radicalizes the rhetoric of the American democracy: "I heartily accept the motto, — 'That government is best which governs least'; and I should like to see it acted up to more rapidly and systematically." (224)[14] This Jeffersonian creed, which figures also in Emerson's "Politics," is immediately under pressure from an insistent "I" to become "That government is best which governs not at all," undercut a bit by ". . . when men are prepared for it, that will be the kind of government which they will have." (224) Thoreau here separates himself from the "no-government" men, while leaving open the possibility that at some point, "no government" may indeed be the best. At the same time, he implicitly raises the question, "What kind of government might command the respect of the author of 'Resistance to Civil Government?'" If making known one's views of the matter is a step toward obtaining such government, the essay itself must be analyzed as a civic act.

Thoreau develops his critique in terms of a distinction between expediency and conscience that limits government strictly to enabling individuals to pursue their separate and concerted activities. Even the principle of majority rule is derived from an prudent acknowledgment of the superior force of greater numbers. The majority has no claim to superior judgment of right and wrong:

> Can there not be a government in which majorities do not virtually decide right and wrong, but conscience? — in which majorities decide only those questions to which the rule of expediency is applicable? Must the citizen even for a moment, or in the least degree, resign his conscience to the legislator? Why has every man a conscience then? (225)

Thoreau not only limits government to the domain of expediency but also denigrates the ethical force of positive law: "I think that we should be men first and subjects afterwards. It is not desirable to cultivate a respect for the law so much as for the right. The only obligation which I have a right to assume is to do at any time what I think right." (225) Undue respect for law at the expense of conscience makes one a machine in the service of the state, ". . . a mere shadow and reminiscence of humanity, a man laid out alive and standing . . . buried under arms with funereal accompaniments. . . ." (226) However, right requires more than a rejection of society and withdrawal from political life. Conscience may call us to a higher service: "A very few, as heroes, patriots, martyrs, reformers in the great sense, and men, serve the State with their consciences also, and so necessarily resist it for the most part. . . ." (226) The duty of resistance is both a form of civic virtue and an assertion of individual *life*. The paradox here is that to serve one's fellow men fully, with one's entire self, is to risk becoming an enemy to one's government: "I cannot for an instant recognize that political organization as *my* government which is the slave's government also." (227) Thoreau presents resistance not only as an individual moral necessity but also as a service to the state. However, the state served by conscientious action is not identified with existing institutions, but rather is constructed by individual acts of resistance. Potentially civil disobedience is the founding of a new republic.

In the United States, especially, "all men recognize the right of revolution. . . ." (227) With Locke and Jefferson behind him, Thoreau's general claim is not so radical. What heightens the rhetoric is his assertion of its pertinence to contemporary circumstances. He denies legitimacy to the governments of his day because they authorize slavery and they conduct an aggressive war in Mexico: ". . . when a sixth of the population of a nation which has undertaken to be the refuge of liberty are slaves, and a whole country is unjustly overrun . . . I think it is not too soon for honest men to rebel and revolutionize." (227) The deliberation that determines one's duty is not a calculation of expediency, but a demand of conscience: "If I have unjustly wrested a plank from a drowning man, I must restore it to him though I drown myself." (227) Thoreau's radicalism here consists in the claim that duty to one's fellows may require a person to take actions that threaten political communities that actually exist: "This people must cease to hold slaves, and to make war on Mexico, though it cost them their existence as a people." (228) Thoreau's relation to the nation, to America, is quite complex in these passages. I think Abelove is correct in recognizing a collective dimension to his thought that cuts against and modifies his radical individualism. But "nation" does not quite capture the figure of aspiration that Thoreau evokes; nationality carries with it implications of determination by race, culture, and ethnicity that are quite foreign to Thoreau. He clearly distinguishes between the government and the people it claims to represent, but also between popular opinion and historical aspiration. The political action he calls for is not violent revolution. The "existence of a people" in a democratic polity derives from the consent of the governed. The government that supports slavery and wages unjust war must forfeit the consent of individuals of conscience. Thoreau urges his fellow citizens to refuse to cooperate with those who perpetuate slavery: "I quarrel not with far-off foes, but with those who, near at home, cooperate with, and do the bidding of those far away. . . ." (228)

For Thoreau, those who fail to act under these circumstances are themselves enslaved. Contrary to later theorists who find civil disobedience justified only after lawful methods of protest have been exhausted, Thoreau urges resistance through lawbreaking as both an assertion of one's freedom to refuse evil and as a call to one's fellow citizens to join the effort.[15] Civil disobedience for Thoreau is essentially an appeal from the government to the people and from the opinion of the majority to the conscience of the individuals who comprise that majority. He rejects political means like voting as ". . . a sort of gaming, like chequers or backgammon, with a slight moral tinge to it, a playing with right and wrong, with moral questions. . . ." (228) Trusting to ordinary politics divests moral matters of their inherent urgency: "The character of voters is not staked. I cast my vote, perchance, as I think right; but I am not vitally concerned that that right should prevail. I am willing to leave it to the majority." (229) Matters of expediency may be left to government and to the rule of the majority; matters of conscience are of vital concern to individuals and may not be delegated to others. Rather, Thoreau insists: "Cast your whole vote, not a slip of paper merely, but your whole influence." (233)

The community addressed by appeals to higher principle is not the government or the nation or popular opinion; Thoreau's invocation of traditional political rhetoric constructs an *ideal* of America identified with historical aspirations towards liberty and equality. He calls the nation to live up to its own professed standards. The assertion of the claims of conscience at the expense of political institutions, of "the existence of a people," is an attempt to found a new community of conscience, of those who ". . . serve the state with their consciences also. . . ." Thoreau links personal integrity with political action by situating the self within the historical context of American democracy. Ironically, the very importance that Thoreau attaches to personal authenticity leads him to recognize the citizens' responsibility for social injustice:

> It is not a man's duty . . . to devote himself to the eradication of any, even the most enormous wrong; he may still properly have other concerns to engage him; but it is his duty, at least, to wash his hands of it, and, if he gives it no thought longer, not to give it practically his support. If I devote myself to other pursuits and contemplations, I must first see, at least, that I do not pursue them sitting upon another man's shoulders. I must get off him first, that he may pursue his contemplations too. (229–30)

The argument moves quickly from the apparent ease and indifference of "washing one's hands" to the rather more difficult task of "getting off another's shoulders."

Thoreau shows us ourselves, in apparent innocence, comfortably enjoying the protections of a system of government founded upon the exclusion and exploitation of others. The principle of justice at work here is demonstrably egalitarian: Thoreau will not consider whether those on whose shoulders we pursue our contemplations are properly employed as caryatids. Indeed, he insists that they have a right to pursue contemplations of their own. To recognize one's complicity in the exploitation of others requires a person of conscience to resist the inertia by which well-meaning citizens become party to injustice and to withdraw support from the system. Thoreau advances no new arguments against slavery or the aggressive war in Mexico; he does not even trouble to rehearse the old ones. Rather he is concerned to show those who share his moral ideals just what their beliefs demand of them:

> Action from principle, — the perception and the performance of right, — changes things and relations: it is essentially revolutionary and does not consist wholly with anything which was. It not only divides states and churches, it divides families; aye, it divides the individual, separating the diabolical in him from the divine. (230–31)

Critically, Thoreau places obligation to principle above one's ties to institutions like government, church — even family. Equally important, he recognizes that individuals are likely to feel divided within themselves when faced with demands for conscientious action. Authentic resistance results from inner struggle. The active refusal to cooperate with social wrong is also a gesture of self-overcoming. Taking a stand has revolutionary implications, compelling one's neighbors and government representatives to reassess their own moral positions. The acts of one "honest man" may occasion a transformation of social attitudes. Thoreau makes a political argument that injustice is perpetuated as much by indifference as by deliberate malevolence and an ethical argument that conscientious resistance is an end in itself: "For it matters not how small the beginning may seem to be: what is once well done is done forever." (233)

The most wholehearted acts of resistance may land one in prison. That is part of the point. Thoreau does not emphasize the importance of the civil disobedient's acceptance of his punishment as a sign of his fidelity to the law, of his acceptance of the general legitimacy of the system. That argument, which has been important for contemporary theorists, is alien to Thoreau's spirit. He joins the abolitionists in denying legitimacy to a Constitution fatally compromised by its tolerance of slavery. For Thoreau, acceptance of punishment by the conscientious serves to *delegitimate* the government that is forced to lock up its most ethically engaged citizens. The fact of his imprisonment gives the resister a considerable moral and rhetorical advantage: "Under a government which imprisons any unjustly, the true place for a just man is also a prison. . . . how much more eloquently and effectively he can combat injustice who has experienced a little in his own person." (233) Thoreau's great appeal to Gandhi and King lies here. The challenge posed by nonviolent resistance to the moral authority of the state turns on the willingness of civil disobedients to risk themselves wholly in making their case and to endure suffering for their beliefs. However, Thoreau's specific concern is not with the victims of injustice. The teaching of "Civil Disobedience" is directed at those otherwise comfortable citizens who become aware of injustice perpetrated in their names. Free citizens concerned for justice should voluntarily go to prison to challenge fellow citizens and public officials to change their course: "It is there that the fugitive slave, and the Mexican prisoner on parole, and the Indian come to plead the wrongs of his race should find them. . . ." (233)

The genius and radicalism of Gandhi and King translated Thoreau's politics of conscience into a program of resistance for the oppressed, for those whom the state has excluded from its community of consent. Thoreau's text was available for this purpose because of its central focus on agency and its recognition of the mutual interaction between social situation and self-definition. Gandhi and King inspired their supporters with a sense of political agency grounded in the shared experience of surviving oppression. In terms defined by the distinct but complementary arguments of Rawls and Arendt, they moved from conscientious refusal as an individual moral imperative to civil disobedience as a collective, political act.[16] Lesbians and gays in contemporary America find themselves in an ambiguous situation in relation to political power: given the intersections of sexuality with social class, gender, race, and ethnicity, some lesbians and gay men, especially, enjoy positions of comparative wealth and privilege, while others are among the least advantaged in a complexly-layered society. This disparity is enhanced by the ability of many to benefit from social imputations of heterosexuality to those who do not actively deny it. Closeted middle-class white gay men may well enjoy the -

prerogatives of full citizenship denied to their less advantaged fellows. The appropriation of Thoreau's conception of resistance for theorizing queer politics serves a dual function: it reminds us of the capacity of even the worst off to effect their circumstances and of the duty of those better off to recognize their involvement in the fates of all who are excluded or marginalized by contemporary regimes.

Collective political action may generate problems for conscientious participants quite similar to those raised by the involvement of citizens in the acts of the democratic state. Social movements based on a single status or exclusive identification risk cutting off individuals from the multiple roles and relationships that define modern subjects and limiting their responsiveness to oppressed people outside their own group. Further, the demands of solidarity with the victims of injustice, or with one's own group as it asserts its common claims, may be in conflict with the ideal of deliberate choice by each "majority of one." Organized activity on behalf of even the most worthy causes imposes its own restraints on individual discretion. Thus, Thoreau could write of his fellow advocate of civil disobedience, the abolitionist Wendell Philips: he ". . . does himself an injustice when he reminds us of the American (Anti-slavery) Society which he represents; really he stands alone."[17] Thoreau approaches anarchism in his insistence on the moral autonomy of citizens of free societies, but "Civil Disobedience" is not addressed to the victims of oppression as they combat the injustices they suffer. As his essays of the 1850s reveal, he was especially sensitive to the urgency of fighting slavery: his celebrations of John Brown reveal his conviction that extremes of injustice call for extreme responses that complicate the moral position of the conscientious agent concerned to change the world.

Thoreau's account of his own confrontation with the state and its representatives appears as something of an anticlimax: "I have paid no poll-tax for six years. I was put into jail once on this account, for one night. . . ." (236) He portrays the state as revealing the moral weakness of its position by resorting to incarceration, confining his body when it could not persuade his soul. His thought remained free, and freely divested the state of its last vestige of authority: "I saw that the State was half-witted, that it was timid as a lone woman with her silver spoons, and that it did not know its friends from its foes. . . ." (236) Thoreau presents himself as remaining a friend to the State, calling it to its own highest aspirations. The caricature of the state is rather gentle; there is something of Chanticleer crowing in the portrayal of his own resistance: "It is not armed with superior wit or honesty, but with superior physical strength. I was not born to be forced. I will breathe after my own fashion. Let us see who is the strongest. What force has a multitude? They only can force me who obey a higher law than I." (236) Compare his earlier question: "Why does it (the state) always crucify Christ, and excommunicate Copernicus and Luther, and pronounce Washington and Franklin rebels?" The strain on his rhetoric reveals a profound reluctance on Thoreau's part to confront the realities of state power and the graver threats underlying its authority to lock him up.

One night in the Concord jail was a small price for the moral and rhetorical advantage it provided Thoreau; however, his posturing disappears when he comes later to write about the forcible return of Anthony Burns to enslavement in Virginia or the condemnation of John Brown to death by hanging. The confrontation of those men with the state's full repressive force raises the question of power in its starkest form. Radical political action may be met by state violence and require armed resistance if it is to succeed.[18] But the militant activist risks compromising his own moral position. Thoreau's night in jail resembles comedy more than it does these tragedies:

> When I came out of prison . . . a change had to my eyes come over the scene, — the town, and State and country — greater than any than mere time could effect. I saw more distinctly the State in which I lived. I saw to what extent the people among whom I lived . . . were a distinct race from me by their prejudices and superstitions, as the Chinamen and Malays are; that, in their sacrifices to humanity, they ran no risks, not even to their property. . . . (238)

The experience of punishment at the hands of the state is instructive in refiguring his relationships with the State and with the people. His commitments to humanity estrange him from his neighbors and from the nation. But there is profound ambiguity in this vision. Leading a party of these same neighbors in a huckleberry party on the afternoon of his release, he discovers ". . . the State was nowhere to be seen." (239) Although he never abandons the pressure on himself "to trace the effects of my allegiance," Thoreau systematically undercuts the heroic stance: ". . . I quietly declare war with the State, after my fashion, though I will still make what use and get what advantage of her as I can, as is usual in such cases." (239)

The ironic detachment[19] that informs Thoreau's presentation of his own acts of resistance may in part explain what Emerson characterized as simple lack of ambition: ". . . instead of engineering for all America, he was the captain of a huckleberry-party."[20] But Thoreau anticipates such complaints; his refusal of conventional ambition results from his relegation of the state to instrumental status: "I am not responsible for the successful working of the machinery of society. I am not the son of the engineer." (236–37) These comments echo his earlier insistence that government is a matter of expediency. However, maintaining this position puts him at risk of becoming a powerless onlooker like those "patrons of virtue" he earlier skewered: "They hesitate, and they regret, and sometimes they petition; but they do nothing in earnest and with effect. They will wait, well disposed, for others to remedy the evil, that they may no longer have it to regret." (228) This problem is not easy to resolve. In part, it is a matter of perspective: one man's earnest engagement may appear to another as no more than regret. On the other hand, results matter. It takes some effort to stop riding on the backs of others in complex societies founded on exclusion and exploitation. Thoreau cannot avoid the subjective implications of a conception of conscience that depends so completely on the intensity of individual commitment. To ask for effectiveness as well as commitment is to open the panoply of questions concerning the calculation of results that Thoreau seeks to avoid. All political action occurs within at least two distinct forums, of the individual conscience and of political consequence. To be both earnest and effective may not be possible; the results of one's actions lie outside individual control. The matter cannot be settled in principle, but only through a dynamic interaction between the individual and her world. Hence, the irony and paradox in Thoreau's oscillation between apparent contraries exemplifies the kind of thinking that our situation requires. The individual is situated in the midst of shifting perspectives and relations through which she must experimentally make her way. At the very least, she is both active participant engaged in a social and natural context and critical spectator capable of withdrawing to judge both herself and others. Perhaps unexpectedly, the essay on "Civil Disobedience" moves through these oppositions towards reconciliation. In the final paragraph, Thoreau reasserts the continuity of his views with the individualism inherent in democracy and emphasizes his hope for a transcendence of the forms of common life we know. The establishment of a society based on justice and respect for the individual is seen as preparation for ". . . a still more perfect and glorious State, which also I have imagined, but not yet anywhere seen." (243) Thoreau appears to envision a new American founding, a community of sovereign individuals. The invocation of this imaginary horizon gives support to Abelove's insistence on a collective dimension to Thoreau's vision, but it cannot be identified with any nation. It is a glimpse of utopia, nowhere in the world, manifesting itself in heroic acts and ennobling friendships. The "still more perfect and glorious state" expresses our aspiration towards a community of free and equal persons.

II. Problematics of Political Action

One may catch a glimpse of the community ". . . imagined, but not yet anywhere seen" in the rare but moving acts of those "who serve the State with their conscience's also." The efficacy of action according to principle depends on its capacity to change how others see the world and to stir them to action of their own. Thoreau's rhetoric of resistance identifies a "double movement" by which the individual recognizes the extent to which she is implicated in the wrongs of her society and actively dissociates herself from them by refusing to cooperate. However, the movement of withdrawal from society is necessarily temporary and incomplete. To some extent, withdrawal may salve the individual conscience, but resistance aspires "to get off the shoulders" of the oppressed as well. Not only the earnestness of the actor, but also the effectiveness of the action contributes to its moral worth. This is the problematic of political action: civil disobedience originates in individual conscience, but seeks to have a social impact even as it rejects the normal workings of politics. Resistance must define its own objectives, primarily to awaken one's fellow citizens to the wrongs in which they collaborate and inspire them to undertake their own gestures of conscientious refusal. Thoreau does not permit us simply to wash our hands of society; having acted, one initiates further consequences for which there is additional responsibility. We cannot elude our history. For Thoreau, there is no action, no living, without risk. Like Hannah Arendt, he believes that through our actions we determine what we are and who we may become. Thoreau's ethics are both contextual and transcendent, alternating between historical situation and inner awareness. However, he offers no certain foundation in "higher laws" and insists that all calculation of political consequences is a gamble with integrity.

As the crisis of the United States in the 1850s became more acute, Thoreau's essays more urgently, almost desperately, probe the limits of political action and the responsibilities of the "double self." Importantly, most of them originated as public lectures, delivered at the Concord Lyceum and elsewhere. They are crystallizations of political speech, addressing specific historical circumstances.[21] "Slavery in Massachusetts" was provoked by the furor in Massachusetts over the use of state courts and agencies to enforce the Fugitive Slave Law by returning Anthony Burns to his "master" in Virginia. This event caused considerable public protest bringing slavery home to Massachusetts. Thoreau deplores the role of his local government in maintaining and enforcing slavery in the South. He rejects the alibi that state officials did only what the law required. For Thoreau, that is precisely the problem: "What is wanted is men, not of policy, but of probity — who recognize a higher law than the Constitution, or the decision of the majority." (G257)[22] To those who resist this demand, he admonishes: "I would remind my countrymen that they are to be men first, and Americans only at a late and convenient hour." (G256) Once again humanity overrides nationality in defining both moral obligation and political identity. However, Thoreau denies himself recourse to transcendent, universal principles, secured by reason or religious authority. He appeals directly to the experience of his fellow citizens and conjures the claims of a more ambitious patriotism:

> The effect of a good government is to make life more valuable, — of a bad one, to make it less valuable. . . . [B]ut suppose that the value of life itself should be diminished. How can we make a less demand on man and nature, how live more economically in respect of virtue and all noble qualities, than we do? I have lived for the last month . . . with the sense of having suffered a vast and indefinite loss. I did not know at first what ailed me. At last it occurred to me that what I had lost was a country. (G259)

The disappointment evoked by these last sentences has its source deep in the collective aspiration of Americans to build a "city upon a hill," to create a community of conscience as well as convenience. The energy and urgency of Thoreau's appeal is drawn from the shared expectation that "our community" is better than that. The perpetual risk of democratic politics is that government will exceed its mandate of expediency and morally compromise the citizenry instead. The acts of officials may become matters of personal urgency for the citizens, because they act in our names: ". . . the State has fatally interfered with my lawful business. It has not only interrupted me in my passage through Court Street on errands of trade, but it has interrupted me and every man on his inward and upward path . . ." (G260)

The enforcement of slavery in the courts and on the streets of Massachusetts is a direct threat to the individual's moral stature: "If we would save our lives, we must fight for them." (G260) The politics of the Fugitive Slave Law constitute a moral crisis for all conscientious Americans: "Who can be serene in a country where both the rulers and the ruled are without principle? The remembrance of my country spoils my walk. My thoughts are murder to the State, and involuntarily go plotting against her." (G260) The force of this essay is to bring home the wrong of slavery to Thoreau and his fellow citizens of Massachusetts. To see oneself as complicit in injustice requires a conscientious citizen not only to express a dissenting opinion but to take action as well. The tone of frustration and bitterness that pervades the essay results in part from Thoreau's inability to propose any resolution of the problem. Even in more narrowly literary terms, the conclusion is unsatisfactory. Thoreau offers this reformulation of Kant's categorical imperative: "Behave so that the odor of your actions may enhance the general sweetness of the atmosphere. . . ." (G261) He goes on to develop this trope into a reflection on slavery and the stench of death. The preciosity of the figure calls attention to its desperation. Thoreau has forcefully rejected an ethic based on the calculation of political consequences as a kind of gambling with morality. He cannot count on Divine Providence to guarantee the "higher law," and he has satirized the narcissistic "regret" of those who stand by and witness the triumph of injustice. The attempt at an aesthetic resolution of these difficulties in this essay fails not only figuratively but historically. Thoreau remains silent about the efforts of his fellow citizens to save Anthony Burns through direct action. In fact, his friend Thomas Wentworth Higginson and a group of sympathetic Bostonians mounted an armed attack on the courthouse to rescue Burns. They were turned back, and a deputy marshal was killed in the episode. The major consequence of this action was that President Pierce sent federal troops to Boston to ensure that state authorities enforce the Fugitive Slave Law.[23] Despite his evasions, Thoreau is too sensitive to the stakes here to let himself off easily. What is to be done when one's thoughts have become "murder to the State?"

Thoreau confronts the challenge of direct action most explicitly in his essays on John Brown. Delivered originally as a lecture in Concord on October 30, 1859, and subsequently in Boston on November 1 and Worcester on November 3, "A Plea for Capt. John Brown" was published in a collection of anti-slavery essays, *Echoes of Harper's Ferry*, in 1860. John Brown presents both a challenge and an opportunity. The challenge derives from the appeal of direct action to overcome the sense of impotence and personal loss charted in "Slavery in Massachusetts." For Thoreau Brown was a man who acted in accord with "higher law," with his own convictions of what is right. He becomes one of the few persons whom Thoreau acknowledges to command moral authority. But his acts were bloody. The raid on Harper's Ferry was necessarily violent and almost certainly futile. Even Brown's admirers saw madness in this undertaking. In the background were difficult questions about Brown's role in the massacre of five pro-slavery settlers at Pottowatomie, Kansas in 1856 in retaliation for the killing of free-soilers in Lawrence.[24] Nevertheless Thoreau, with his distrust of both normal politics and the abstraction of universal principle, saw in Brown an opportunity to portray exemplary action. In figuring someone other than himself as the hero of these essays, Thoreau avoids the irony and deflation at work in "Civil Disobedience." Instead, he runs the risk of idealization. Thoreau's rhetorical strategy is to self-consciously display that process at work. John Brown's capacity for militant actions rather than speeches and gestures was linked to shedding the blood of innocents. Thoreau's essays exhibit a deeper irony as he contains the violence by transforming Brown from a man of action into the practitioner of a higher rhetoric. Brown's life becomes "a trope for parable-makers."

Thoreau praises John Brown as revolutionary, humanist, transcendentalist, truth-teller, and martyr. He is a representative of America at its best, the heir of both Puritan and Revolutionary founders. In these essays, Brown's aggressive actions become vehicles of moral instruction and inspiration. As revolutionary, Brown is even "firmer and higher principled" than the fighters at Concord Bridge: "They could bravely face their country's foes, but he had the courage to face his country herself when she was in the wrong." (G212) Thoreau contrasts Brown's lack of formal education with his "public practice of Humanity" in the conduct of his life: "Such were *his humanities* and not any study of grammar. He would have left a Greek accent slanted the wrong way and righted up a falling man." (G272-73, emphasis in original)[25] Thoreau goes on to praise Brown as ". . . a transcendentalist above all, a man of deeds and principles. . . . Not yielding to a whim or transient impulse, but carrying out the purpose of a life." (G274) Strikingly, in an essay composed before the trial, Thoreau emphasizes Brown's qualities as a speaker:

> . . . he did not overstate anything, but spoke within bounds. I remember particularly, how, in his speech here, he referred to what his family suffered in Kansas without giving the least vent to his pent-up fire. It was a volcano with an ordinary chimney-flue. . . . He was not in the least a

rhetorician, was not talking to Buncombe or his constituents anywhere, but to tell the simple truth and communicate his own resolution: therefore, he appeared incomparably strong. . . . (G274)

In an inversion at least as old as Plato's *Apology of Socrates*, the simple truth-teller becomes the practitioner of a consummate rhetoric: "It was like the speeches of Cromwell compared with those of an ordinary king." (G274) Thus, the heroism of John Brown comes to consist in his effectiveness in communicating the demands of conscience to his fellows.

Brown's life itself becomes an exercise in the rhetoric of resistance. Like the heroes of old, he depends on the appearance of a bard to immortalize his example. Thoreau was educated in the Greek classics just as were the Europeans of his day; he draws on the links among heroism, poetry, and immortality found in Homer and exploited by Diotima in Plato's *Symposium* and by Hannah Arendt in her conception of action in the public sphere. Thoreau explicitly compares Brown's virtue with the physical courage displayed in the charge at Balaclava:

> . . . the steady and for the most part successful charge of this man, for some years, against the legions of slavery, in obedience to an infinitely higher command, is much more memorable than that, as an intelligent and conscientious man is superior to a machine. Do you think that will go unsung? (G278)

Brown's conduct meets the prophetic demand of "Civil Disobedience" and "Slavery in Massachusetts" for citizens strong enough to represent the highest aspirations of their countrymen through resistance to their government. Thoreau's John Brown is the hero of a distinctly American epic:

> He did not recognize unjust human laws, but resisted them as he was bid. For once we are lifted out of the trivialness and dust of politics into the region of truth and manhood. No man in America has ever stood up so persistently and effectively for the dignity of human nature, knowing himself for a man, and the equal of any and all governments. In that sense, he was the most American of us all. (G282)

Brown in his individuality exemplifies the paradoxical aspiration of the American democracy to nourish citizens strong enough to say "no" to their country in its errancy and to found a community of conscience.

To see Brown as representative of America's higher destiny is to redefine the terms of our political order: "We talk about *representative* government: but what monster of government is that where the noblest faculties of the mind and the *whole* heart are not represented." (G285) Militant resistance evokes a higher

politics. But the persistent emphasis on Brown's *rhetoric* reveals Thoreau's ambivalence in celebrating acts whose militancy includes violence against the innocent. In this passage, the apotheosis of Brown is also his disarmament:

> No, he was not our representative in any sense. He was too fair a speci-
> men of man to represent the like of us. Who then *were* his con-
> stituents? . . . Truth is his inspirer, and earnestness the polisher of his
> sentences. He could afford to lose his Sharp's rifles, while he retained his
> faculty of speech, a Sharp's rifle of infinitely surer and larger range.
> (G284)

Thoreau does not simply ignore the issue of violence but rather seeks to displace
it onto the state power that maintains slavery: "We preserve the so-called 'peace'
of our community by deeds of petty violence everyday. . . . We are hoping only to
live safely on the outskirts of this provisional army. So we defend ourselves and
our roosts, and maintain slavery." (G288–89) The problem of violence is further
deflected by emphasizing Brown's courage in risking his own death for the sake of
his principles. Indeed, Thoreau renders Brown's resoluteness as the rare, authentic human death: ". . . in order to die you must first have lived. . . . Only a half-
dozen or so have died since the world began." (G289–90) Echoing an earlier
undertaking of death for the salvation of others, Thoreau sees the passion of John
Brown as teaching us to reevaluate our own relations to death and to life:

> These men, in teaching us how to die, have at the same time taught us
> how to live. If this man's acts and words do not create a revival, it will be
> the severest possible satire on the acts and words that do. It is the best
> news that America has ever had. (G290)

Brown is not only the Puritan prophet and true American revolutionary, but
Thoreau's account of his life is to become the new gospel for a people nourished
on the Book. The intensity of Thoreau's identification with his hero suggests an
erotic dimension underlying the moral argumentation. In this context, the disarm-
ing of Brown — insistence on the loss of those Sharp's rifles — is also a castration
that enables the sublimation of the writer's desire.

The hagiographic tendencies of "A Plea for Capt. John Brown" culminate in
"The Last Days of John Brown," which Thoreau prepared as a speech for deliv-
ery at memorial services for Brown on July 7, 1860 and published in *The Liberator*
of July 27, 1860. Here, Brown's martyrdom is likened not only to the passion of Jesus but also to the execution of Socrates. Thoreau's language recalls the concluding words of Plato's *Phaedo*: "Our thoughts could not revert to any greater or wiser
or better man with whom to contrast him, for he, then and there was above them
all. The man this country was about to hang appeared the greatest and best of
them all." (D170–71)[26] The execution of Brown administers the kind of shock that
may force a complacent society to take stock of itself and recognize the difference

between conventional and genuine piety. Thoreau transforms Brown's hanging into an instant symbol:

The North, I mean the *living* North, was suddenly all transcendental. It went behind the human law, it went behind the apparent failure, and recognized eternal justice and glory. Commonly, men live according to a formula, and are satisfied if the order of law is observed, but in this instance, they to some extent returned to original perceptions, and there was a slight revival of the old religion. They saw what they called order was confusion, what they deemed justice, injustice, and that the best was deemed the worst. This attitude suggested a more intelligent and generous spirit than that which actuated our forefathers, and the possibility . . . of a revolution on behalf of another and an oppressed people. (D178)

The events are taken as a text with a vital message for those who read it correctly. That message is both a revival of the old religion, and an inspiration to complete and fulfill the promise of the American Revolution. The death of John Brown announces what Nietzsche called a "transvaluation of values." His teaching calls us to set an inverted world right side up.

In his martyrdom, Brown becomes a successful emancipator: "He has liberated many thousands of slaves, both North and South. They seem to have known nothing about living or dying for a principle." (D174) Again, as in the earlier essay, Brown's directness and composure in the face of death are presented as a rhetorical teaching: "The art of composition is as simple as the discharge of a bullet from a rifle, and its masterpieces imply an infinitely greater force behind them." (D175) By figuring his words as rifle shots, Thoreau effaces the real guns used by Brown and his followers. Brown's death is almost welcomed as the expiation that transforms violence into spirit, life lost into a text that figures the truth:

. . . he was not to be pardoned or rescued by men. That would have been to disarm him, to restore to him a material weapon, a Sharp's rifle, when he had taken up the sword of the spirit, — the sword with which he has really won his greatest and most memorable victories. (D176)

The abandonment of Sharp's rifle for "sword of the spirit" sublimates the aggression while preserving the phallic power. The confrontation with death that was taken in the "Plea" as a warrant for the authenticity of his life now becomes the means of his immortality. The "good news" is complete as Thoreau announces the transition from passion to resurrection:

Of all men who were said to be my contemporaries, it seemed to me that John Brown was the only one who *had not died*. . . . I meet him at every turn. He is more alive than ever he was. . . . He is no longer working in secret. He works in public, and in the clearest light that shines in this land. (D176–77)

By the end of the 1850s, Thoreau's frustration in finding political action that was both earnest and effective led him to transform John Brown's militancy into a text calling men to change themselves and the world. When war finally came, Thoreau was appalled by its horrors.

III. The "Double Self" and the Aesthetics of Existence

Thoreau's political teaching is distinctive in its insistence on individual transcendence of the terms of ordinary politics. Resistance is inscribed in texts; reading them, students are challenged to become seers.[27] Vision requires revision; a heightened conscience seeks expression through actions that are essays in self-transformation. The social world in which we are immersed provides the context for self-making. But the self is not only expressive; it seeks to meet others on a higher ground than the daily grind of politics, to find them as neighbors and as friends, in ideals of mutuality and reciprocity. Thoreau calls for the founding of a new order in which equals meet and interact without sacrificing the integrity of their personal quests. Indeed, he projects a conception of friendship in which sovereign selves are seen as agonistically engaged in stimulating each other to renewed efforts at self-making.[28] Thoreau's contempt for the calculations of expediency leads him often to minimize the importance of ordinary politics for the business of deliberate living. He does not celebrate civic virtue as necessary for human fulfillment, yet his vision of the social context of our lives leads him to urge militancy rather than quietism or conformity. We are implicated in the doings of democratic society; its wrongs diminish each of us. The duty of resistance to civil authority is derived from the individual's division between immersion in a social world and aspiration toward ethical integrity. Community appears as both the immediate context of personal striving and the far horizon of higher principle: it is both conventional and ideal.

Henry Abelove reminds us that Thoreau's *Walden* was not immediately received as a contribution to an emerging American canon, but was seen rather as an odd and subversive effort. Its author was frequently labeled "eccentric," as a "sport," as having "an odd twist in his brains." One reviewer recommended it "to all fops, male and female both." Further, the text's teaching was denounced as "selfish," a solitary experiment, "casting off all ties of family." The absence of any reference to female companionship was treated as a rejection of the values of civilized life.[29] Rejecting the efforts of later readers to provide a more domestic Thoreau, Abelove recuperates the teaching of *Walden* for contemporary queer politics, especially those of Queer Nation. He interprets Queer Nation's conception of "actions" rather than demonstrations, protests, or other forms of dissent in terms of their performative dimension. Rather than simply expressing dissident political opinions, Queer Nation stakes a claim for marginalized people to a central political role by acting as if "the society I live in is mine."[30] Abelove stresses the collective character of this effort as a justification of the language of nationalism, but notes that Thoreau refuses to identify the nation with the State. He argues that the work of *Walden* is to invoke a revitalized commitment to the nation as a replacement for conventional emphases on domesticity and family as dominant sites of community.[31] In the reading that follows, I embrace the queering of Thoreau but argue that nationalism, even in its queer form, is foreign to him — and for good reason. Thoreau consistently rejects the narrowing of sympathy based on conventional distinctions. Abelove's concluding identification of "Queer Nation" with "America" smacks too much of the exceptionalism that insists on a unique spiritual or political role for the United States in world history. I turn instead to Thoreau's celebration of friendship as an ideal reciprocity between equals and to his figuring of America as an imaginary community of aspiration to explicate the collective dimension of his thought. Abelove is surely right in seeing performativity as central to *Walden*; Thoreau envisions acting in accordance with principle not only as a means of self-making but also as the founding of a ". . . still more perfect and glorious State, which also I have imagined, but not yet anywhere seen."[32] In doing so he provides a model of queer citizenship that joins the individual pursuit of moral integrity with the creation of a community of friends.[33]

The eccentricity of the author of *Walden* was widely noted by critics responding to its publication: Thoreau's queerness is well attested even in Ralph Waldo Emerson's tribute published after Thoreau's death.[34] As Abelove observes, Emerson works to reconcile his Concord friend with the attitudes and expectations of his audience, but he does not disguise the fundamental opposition between Thoreau's thinking and conventional opinion. Thoreau's queerness was at the heart of his character. It cannot be reduced to sexual desire, conduct, or fantasy, but rather defines an adversary stance towards prevalent systems of belief and a personal position outside dominant social institutions:

> He interrogated every custom, and wished to settle all his practice on an ideal foundation. He was a protestant *à la outrance*, and few lives contain so many renunciations. He was bred to no profession; he never married; he lived alone; he never went to church; he never voted; he refused to pay a tax to the state; he ate no flesh, he drank no wine, he never knew the use of tobacco; and though a naturalist, he used neither trap nor gun.[35]

Having established the distance between Thoreau and his own society, Emerson goes on to argue that his idiosyncrasies concealed a serious commitment of faith and a higher patriotism. Although there is some truth in this reading, Emerson's portrait conflicts with the writer's self-presentation in *Walden*. Paradoxically, he exaggerates Thoreau's uniqueness to make him more acceptable to conventional readers in the end. Emerson asserts: "He had no temptations to fight against, — no appetites, no passions, no taste for elegant trifles."[36] Not only is this claimed contravened by many details in *Walden*, but it actually works to make Thoreau less demanding, less threatening. After all, a man without temptations is in no position to lay down the law to ordinary mortals who face them daily. Emerson's praise effectively undermines Thoreau's status as an exemplary writer whose work challenges its readers to change their lives. Emerson tends to reduce Thoreau's commitments to a special case:

> . . . it required rare decision to refuse all the accustomed paths and keep his solitary freedom at the cost of disappointing the natural expectations of his family and friends: all the more difficult that he had a perfect probity, was exact in securing his own independence, and in holding every man to a like duty. But Thoreau never faltered. He was a born protestant.[37]

Emerson's prose vacillates between regarding Thoreau's course in life as the result of a deliberate decision based on the exercise of independent thought — with implications that should discomfit all those who admire his work — and reducing it to an effect of his inherent condition. "A born protestant," who never falters, a man with "no temptations to fight," is so different from the rest of us as to pose no threat to settled habit. (This ambiguous encomium resonates oddly with Alcibiades' insistence on the utter uniqueness of Socrates in Plato's *Symposium*; it is praise that works to diminish its subject's exemplary status.) But Emerson concedes that Thoreau treated his fellows as subject to the same harsh standards as himself: ". . . his first instinct on hearing a proposition was to controvert it, so impatient was he of the limitations of our daily thought. This habit, of course, is a little chilling to the social affections; . . . it mars conversation. Hence, no equal companion stood in affectionate relations with one so pure and guileless."[38]

Emerson never quite deprives his friend of agency: he recognizes the distinctiveness of Thoreau's embrace of individual deliberation and utopian aspiration. Importantly, Emerson figures this independence as lying outside marriage and the family: "He chose, wisely no doubt for himself, to be the bachelor of thought and Nature."[39] Emerson repeatedly stresses Thoreau's difference and isolation although he recognizes a certain stubbornness in political matters, as when Thoreau persisted in lecturing on John Brown despite pressure from abolitionists to delay. He does not account for the Concord writer's commitment to public speaking and writing, a concern with affecting the thoughts of others and changing social conditions that exceeds the need for personal expression. Emerson's most astute observations of his friend lead us back to a close reading of Thoreau's texts: "I must add the cardinal fact, that there was excellent wisdom in him, proper to a rare class of men, which showed him the material world as means and as symbol. . . . This was the muse and genius that ruled his opinions, conversation, studies, work, and course of life. This made him a searching judge of men."[40]

In place of calculations of political expediency or the appeal to divine or rational law, Thoreau proposes an essentially *aesthetic* standard for judging human actions. The magnitude and intensity of such a project is the subject of *Walden*. I can do no more than indicate how its complex picture of human individuality bears on Thoreau's politics. As with Kierkegaard, Nietzsche, and Heidegger, the emphasis on individual vision in Thoreau's conception of agency raises questions as to what extremes may be justified in the name of self-formation. Thoreau's explicitly political essays contain little in the way of general argument to provide reassurance on this score. Rather, they employ rhetorical devices to contain the more explosive implications of the sovereignty of individual choice: irony in "Civil Disobedience," self-conscious mythmaking in the John Brown essays. Thoreau inscribes actions in texts that transform them from political program to personal problematic. His essays are maieutic in their efforts — which include paradox and provocation — to elicit reflection and self-examination in the attentive reader. The political aim of Thoreau's writing is to awaken a slumbering polity to the demands of deliberate living. His engagement with the issues of his time places him squarely on the side of liberty, equality, and justice. His circumstance and judgment have insulated his work from the anxiety generated by the cases of Nietzsche and Heidegger. However, the politics of the twentieth century force us to scrutinize with care any view that emphasizes self-making without noticing the risk that self-assertion may impose unjustified costs on others. Further, Thoreau's rejection of conventional norms and invocation of aesthetic judgment may leave him without resources in the face of moral extremes. In what follows, I want to show that Thoreau's writing evinces a deep awareness of the moral ambiguities of self-formation. Indeed, a major pressure on his literary effort is the need to portray the dynamics by which the individual negotiates her way between self-abnegation and self-aggrandizement. Thoreau adopts and transforms the contemporary rhetoric of "higher law" as a guide to conscientious action; at the same time, he rejects any recourse to legalism or rationalism. At the heart of Thoreau's portrayal of individuality in *Walden* is the "double self" divided between community and solitude, action and reflection, goodness and wildness. The dynamic of ambivalence so important for Freud in mapping the vicissitudes of desire is very much at work as Thoreau charts the interplay between aggressive impulses to annihilate the other and aspirations towards community and reciprocal recognition.

In *Walden*, the section called "Higher Laws" presents some of the most difficult puzzles in that deeply puzzling text. The chapter begins with the narrator's observation of a woodchuck, which occasions ". . . a strange thrill of savage delight, and [I] was strangely tempted to seize and devour him raw, not that I was hungry then, except for that wildness which he represented." (139–40) Thoreau embraces this impulse as integral to himself, although it co-exists with competing desires that point in an opposite direction: ". . . I found in myself, and still find, an instinct toward a higher, or, as it is named, spiritual life, as do most men, and another toward a primitive rank and savage one, and I reverence them both. I love the wild not less than the good." (140) These divided desires reveal fundamental ambiguities in one's relation to nature and to one's fellow creatures. We are not only travelers, spectators, and students of nature, but hunters, fishermen, and woodchoppers. Thoreau rejects the easy moralizing that urges an unequivocal embrace of spirituality and rejection of all carnal desire and exploitative activity; at the same time, he celebrates purity as an ideal. In fact the movement of this passage enacts an ascent that resonates powerfully with Diotima's "ladder of love" in the *Symposium*.[41] Where Diotima explicitly begins with a man's erotic attraction to a beautiful youth, Thoreau begins with the aggressive impulse to shoot and kill animal life and the appetite to devour meat. The Sharp's rifles and swords that figured the problematic of violence in the John Brown essays become hunting rifles and fishing rods in *Walden*'s reflections on boys' growing up. Thoreau affirms a sublimation of savage desire by which hunters and fishermen in their youth grow up to become naturalists and poets:

> . . . when some of my friends ask me anxiously about their boys, whether they should let them hunt, I have answered, yes, — remembering that it was one of the best parts of my education, — *make* them hunters, though sportsmen only at first, if possible, mighty hunters at last, so that they shall not find game large enough for them in this or any vegetable wilderness, — hunters as well as fishers of men. (141)

This ascent does not completely break with its ambiguous origins: "There is unquestionably this instinct in me which belongs to the lower orders of creation; yet with every year I am less a fisherman though without more humanity or even wisdom: at present I am no fisherman at all. But I see that if I were to live in a wilderness I should again be tempted to become a fisher and hunter in earnest." (142) Thoreau portrays a struggle towards purity, but he conveys a Nietzschean sense that the only chastity worth winning results from victory over one's own contrary desires. It is not just a matter of forbearance, but of recognizing and overcoming the wildness within.

This aspect of the "double self" recalls both classical and Christian notions of humanity as divided between the animal and the divine: "We are conscious of an animal in us, which awakens in proportion as our higher nature slumbers. . . . It is reptile and sensual, and perhaps cannot be wholly expelled, like the worms which, even in life and health, occupy our bodies." (146) These snakes and worms recall Biblical accounts of the Fall as well as phallic imagery of rifles and fishing rods. Intimations of carnal desire and primitive aggression condition our striving toward purity: "I fear that we are such gods or demigods only as fauns and satyrs, the divine allied to beasts, the creatures of appetite, and that to some extent, our very life is our disgrace. . . ." (146) These demigods are Diotima's daimons; the fauns and satyrs figured Socrates' ironic speech and character in Alcibiades'

198

encomium. As in the *Symposium*, these images are used to reflect fundamental dualities in human nature.[42] Purity cannot be attained simply by turning our backs on our animal nature. Thoreau does not propose ignoring the urgencies of bodily life but working to wrest a significant form from these very materials: "We are all sculptors and painters, and our material is our own flesh and blood and bones." (147) Through our bodies we find ourselves immersed in a social and natural world, subject to internal pressures from desire as well as conscience. The dynamic interaction between inner urges and natural circumstance repeats the relation between conscientious action and social context that informs the political essays. The trajectory of sublimated appetite and aggression in "Higher Principles" describes a struggle that motivates the aspiration to individual integrity and egalitarian community. Thoreau writes in keen awareness of the pervasive atmosphere of desire that surrounds all striving: "All sensuality is one, though it takes many forms; all purity is one. It is the same whether a man eat, or drink, or cohabit, or sleep sensually. They are but one appetite. . . ." (147) Although his vision is chaste and austere, he recognizes its deeply problematic character: "What is chastity? How shall a man know if he is chaste? He shall not know it. We have heard of this virtue, but we know not what it is." (147)

The familiar dualisms of mind and body, spirit and flesh, individual and society, provide important dimensions of the experiment in deliberate living reported in *Walden*. In a critical passage, Thoreau brings them together in a vision for which "doubleness" becomes definitive of the human condition:

> With thinking we may be beside ourselves in a sane sense. By a conscious effort of the mind we can stand aloof from actions and their consequences, and all things, good and bad, go by us like a torrent. We are not wholly involved in nature. . . . I only know myself as a human entity; the scene, so to speak, of thoughts and affections; and am sensible of a certain doubleness by which I can stand as remote from myself as from another. . . . [a] spectator sharing no experience, but taking note of it. . . . (90–91)

This rich description evokes a plethora of modern portrayals of the alienation of self-consciousness. For Thoreau, the project of living deliberately becomes aesthetic in a dual sense: the self becomes a theater in which both actor and spectator are engaged. Each of us is charged both as an artist, making the most we can of the materials of life, and as a judge evaluating the results of that ongoing effort. Though Thoreau sees the spectator in us as characterized by impersonality — "It is no more I than it is you" — it does not have access to a Kantian domain of transcendental reason. In viewing one's life, it beholds "a kind of fiction, a work of the imagination only." (91) We cannot avoid, in the important questions of life, the need to risk judgment without outside support. Thoreau recasts Kant's categorical imperative in terms that aestheticize morality and foreground the divisions between actor/artist and spectator/judge: "To affect the quality of the day, that is the highest of arts. Every man is tasked to make his life, even in its details, worthy of the contemplation of his most elevated and critical hour." (61)[43] Morality cannot be reduced to law or convention, reason or calculation. The ambiguities in Thoreau's essays reflect the pervasive ambiguity of our situation in the world. The emphasis on self-division may be threatening in ways that are not completely contained by Thoreau's rhetoric. Some formulations generate anxiety even as they seek to reassure: "With thinking we may be beside ourselves in a sane sense." We are not without resource, but life itself becomes an exercise in both acting and judging. Thoreau explicitly links the division of the self against itself with the proximity of other, similarly-divided creatures: "This doubleness may easily make us poor neighbors and friends sometimes." (91)

IV. Agonistic Friendship and the Dynamics of Desire

In discussing friendship, Thoreau offers a portrayal of social relations rather different from the expedient mutual assistance pacts of the "Civil Disobedience": "I think that I love society as much as most, and am ready enough to fasten myself like a bloodsucker for the time to any full-blooded man that comes my way." (94) This remarkable sentence opens the section of *Walden* called "Visitors" that occurs somewhat earlier in the text than "Higher Laws." Of considerable interest in its own right, especially for a queer reading of Thoreau, this passage also provides a complex erotic context for the later section. Both Abelove and Warner call attention to the portrait of Thoreau's friendship with a French-Canadian woodcutter that appears in "Visitors." They stress the homoerotic feeling that animates the writer's admiration for the man's embodiment of primitive nature and moral simplicity. Not without some education, the woodcutter had been taught by a parish priest to pronounce the characters of the Greek alphabet. Thoreau reads to him from Homer's *Iliad*, translating the scene in which Achilles chastises Patroclus for weeping "like a woman." Abelove reads the staging of this scene as a seduction in which both the woodcutter and the reader figure as the objects of Thoreau's desire. Recall that Achilles and Patroclus were treated as lovers in Phaedrus's speech in the *Symposium*[44] and the subversive implications of invocations of Greek friendship in the nineteenth-century Hellenism.[45] In a complementary vein, Warner shows that the images of murky depths and bottomless ponds that pervade *Walden* are sustained by an erotics of anal penetration; Thoreau finds that Walden Pond, said to be unfathomable, is easily plumbed. These metaphors surface in Thoreau's description of the woodchopper as well: "He suggested that there might be men of genius in the lowest grades of life . . . who are as bottomless even as Walden Pond was thought to be, though they may be dark and muddy." (101) Alongside the anal eroticism charted by Warner run fantasies of oral incorporation, beginning with Thoreau's identification of himself in the section's opening as a "blood-

sucker" ready to attach himself to "any full-blooded man that comes my way."
The first man that appears in the text is the wood-chopper accompanied by a
proliferation of images of oral incorporation in which the positions of eater and
eaten appear to slide out of control. The wood-cutter is introduced in the narrative as one ". . . who had made his last supper on a woodchuck that his dog had
caught." (97) Among his qualities later catalogued: "He was a great consumer of
meat. . . . " Not only a great eater, he is a mighty hunter as well, and his dog is especially good at catching woodchucks. He loved to talk, and Thoreau celebrates
his simplicity and good sense as well as his capacity to form his own opinions,
however inexpert their articulation. His activities in the woods are a source of joy
as well as livelihood:

> Looking round upon the trees he would exclaim, — "By George, I can
> enjoy myself well enough here chopping; I want no better sport." Some-
> times, when at leisure, he amused himself all day in the woods with a
> pocket pistol, firing salutes to himself at regular intervals when he
> walked. (98)

Thoreau pictures his friend as a primitive, a child, an animal: "In him the animal
man chiefly was developed." (98) But the writer equips him with all the indicia of
aggressive masculinity — a pistol, an ax, even a dog that retrieves woodchucks for
dinner. The woodchopper not only eats woodchucks, he is figured as one himself:
"He was so genuine and unsophisticated that no introduction would serve to introduce him, more than if you introduced a woodchuck to your neighbor." (99)
Thoreau's association of the woodchopper and the woodchuck is intense; it slides
metonymically into an identification of the two. When we reach the later section
on "Higher Laws," we find Thoreau himself admitting his own deep desire to fall
upon a woodchuck that has crossed his path and devour it raw, not for the food,
but for "the wildness in it." The identification of the woodchuck with the woodcutter in Thoreau's fantasies discloses an erotic context for the ensuing discussion
of hunting, fishing, and eating meat that brings it closer to Diotima's ladder of
love than it may have seemed. The sublimation that Thoreau envisions begins
not with a simple animal appetite for food but with an erotic desire for oral incorporation of the other, especially a man marked by his wildness.

Thoreau's celebration of friendship is tinged by some anxiety as to its carnal
origins. Blaming conventions of social life and ordinary politics for coarsening and
trivializing our interactions, Thoreau adumbrates forms of friendship in which the
highest in each may reach out to the other. Such community is as hard to achieve
as any deliberate living, and Thoreau imagines intimate conversation across a
pathos of distance. The sublimation of instinct in "Higher Laws" is paralleled by
an insistence in "Visitors" on a physical distance that separates the bodies of men
as it enables closer spiritual contact:

. . . if we speak reservedly and thoughtfully, we want to be farther apart, that all animal heat and moisture may have a chance to evaporate. If we would enjoy the most intimate society with that in each of us which is without, or above, being spoken to, we must not only be silent, but commonly so far apart bodily that we cannot hear each other's voice in any case. Referred to this standard, speech is for the convenience of those who are hard of hearing; but there are many fine things that we cannot say if we have to shout. (94–95)

The woodcutter is introduced shortly after this passage. It is hard to resist thinking of his visits with Thoreau when rereading the sentence that concludes the passage above: "As the conversation began to assume a loftier and grander tone, we gradually shoved our chairs farther apart till they touched the wall in opposite corners, and then commonly there was not room enough." (95) Given the thematics of incorporation in this text, we might imagine Thoreau somewhat frantically moving his chair farther away lest he give in to a deep desire to eat the man up alive.

The combination of fantasies and fears about oral incorporation with the celebration of friendship between men appears also in the essay on "Friendship" that Thoreau included in *A Week on the Concord and Merrimack Rivers*. This essay is complex and subtle in the changes it wrings on its central themes as it proceeds. Rather than attempt a full reading, I want only to note several moments in the text that reflect on the themes of this chapter. The most striking resonance occurs in Thoreau's account of the exemplary friendship between the Indian Wawatam and the fur trader Henry:

The stern imperturbable warrior, after fasting, solitude, and mortification of body comes to the white man's lodge, and affirms that he is the white brother whom he saw in his dream and adopts him henceforth. He buries the hatchet as it regards his friend, and they hunt and feast and make maple-sugar together.[46]

Thoreau evokes a pastoral picture of friendship across the distance between white man and native American: the writer and woodchopper have been displaced by the fur trader and warrior, but "wildness" remains an element in their bonding. Even more dramatically, it appears that their union is founded on the warrior's forbearance from a literal act of oral incorporation: "If Wawatam would taste the 'white man's milk' with his tribe, or take his bowl of human broth made of the trader's fellow-countrymen, he first finds a place of safety for his Friend, whom he has rescued from a similar fate."[47] This extraordinary statement is followed by a staging of the fur trader's leave-taking and the Indian's blessing ". . . after a long winter of undisturbed and happy intercourse in the family of the chieftain in the wilderness, hunting and fishing. . . ."[48] The repression of cannibalistic appetites by the warrior cements the friendship and licenses the pair to share the joys of an otherwise uninhibited wilderness life. Thoreau is a bit distanced from this tale as he recounts it from the fur trader's memoirs, but his selection of it as an exemplary fable of male friendship reveals his affinity for these currents, whether fact or fantasy. He is aware of the distance between the friendship he celebrates and the conventions of his own society. Indeed, he figures his ideal in terms of a contrast between the "heathen" and the Christian:

> Friendship is not so kind as is imagined; it has not much human blood in it, but consists with a certain disregard for men and their erections, the Christian duties and humanities, while it purifies the air like electricity. There may be the sternest tragedy in the relation of two who are more than usually innocent and true to their highest instincts. We may call it an essentially heathenish intercourse, free and irresponsible in its nature. . . .[49]

This paragraph concludes with Thoreau imagining that the effect of the conversion of "the Friend" from heathen superstition and mythology to the "newer testament" of Christianity would be the reduction of friendship to charity. Thoreau goes on to argue that friendship is not limited to couples, but rather may be extended to a third and beyond. He allows himself a utopian moment in which noble friendship extends towards one's own society and beyond to foreign nations: ". . . for though its foundations are private, it is in effect, a public affair and a public advantage, and the Friend, more than the father of a family, deserves well of the state."[50]

Throughout the essay, Thoreau positions himself outside the framework of marriage and the family. Early on, while acknowledging a natural compatibility between men and women, he implies that it is grounded in inequality: men seek women for conversation because they are so willing to listen. He insists that true friendship occurs only in relations between equals: "Yet Friendship is no respecter of sex; and perhaps it is more rare between the sexes, than between two of the same sex. . . . A hero's love is more delicate than a woman's."[51] Later, in describing his unwillingness to respond to the demands for more open expressions of friendship from a woman of his acquaintance, he declares himself ". . . a religious heathen at least, — a good Greek."[52] It is hard to separate the misogyny in this passage from its recognition of the effects of gender inequality on the possibilities of reciprocity: "For a companion I require one who will make an equal demand on me of my own genius. . . . I value and trust those who love and praise my aspiration rather than my performance."[53] Although these invocations of the Friend come close to narcissism in figuring a mirror of the self, Thoreau's economy of sameness and difference does not track subsequent formulations within a heterosexual matrix. Why should the differences between men and women be more fundamental than those between white man and Indian, civilized and savage, writer and woodcutter?[54]

Thoreau proposes a model of egalitarian friendship freely undertaken by sovereign individuals as an ideal with implications for public life; he rejects the exclusivity that accompanies couples, families, neighborhoods, nations.[55] As Warner observes, "Thoreau practically embodies the principle of 'voluntary association' that puts the self at the center of civil society. . . ."[56] His essays and narratives include concrete evocations of such relationships as well as complex explorations of deliberate individual life. However, his embodiments of friendship are pervaded by fantasy. He sometimes acknowledges its elusive, fantasmatic character: "There is on earth no institution which friendship has established; it is not taught by any religion; no scripture contains its maxims. It has no temple, not even a solitary column. There goes a rumor that the earth is inhabited, but the ship-wrecked mariner has not seen a foot-print on the shore."[57] At the same time, Thoreau holds on to the idea of friendship as a vision moving us towards more complex lives: "All men are dreaming of it, and its drama, which is always a tragedy, is enacted daily. . . . O, my friend, may it come to pass, once, that when you are my Friend I may be yours."[58] Critically, for Thoreau friendship figures not only reciprocal recognition, but also a shared orientation towards the highest and best in life. In this respect, too, his essays echo Diotima's teaching: "My Friend is that one whom I can associate with my choicest thought."[59]

Sublimation is not just an ascent of the self towards higher forms of expression; it is also a movement between men that establishes the distance necessary for a higher intimacy. This double movement culminates is a transformation of the interpersonal domain. However, the endpoint is not narcissistic mirroring or self-reflection — or contemplation of a transcendent idea — but rather writing. The conversation that Thoreau ultimately recommends is not simply that of the "soul with itself," but of the reader with his texts. Not speech, but writing, is the vehicle of the most profound communication: ". . . the noblest written words are commonly as far behind or above the fleeting spoken language as the firmament with the stars is behind the clouds. . . ." (69) Whereas the orator is bound by his occasion and the conversationalist by his interlocutor, the writer addresses himself to the thinker in all of us, to any who would make the effort to understand. The written work both symbolizes the fullest life, and establishes a community among those seeking to achieve it: "A written word . . . is something at once more intimate and more universal than any other work of art. It is the work of art nearest to life itself. It may be translated into every language, and not only be read, but actually breathed from all human lips. . . ." (69)

Thoreau's writing "prescribes no rules to strong and valiant natures," but rather seeks to show us a text in which we may read ourselves. In *Walden*, the cycles of the day and of the year frame his experiment. Living itself is characterized by rhythms of withdrawal and return, ascent and descent. Our double nature can be negotiated only through the active and attentive exploration of its polarities. Thoreau insists that the search for foundations, for a ground from which to undertake our enterprise, leads us deep within ourselves and to the most distant horizons: "Why has man rooted himself thus firmly in the earth, but that he may rise in the same proportion into the heavens above?" (117) We pursue the business of living within the contexts of our bodies, our neighborhoods, our society, our natural environment; they provide both the setting and the material of our self-making. This project is enacted in time. At its heart is the paradox of our "doubleness" and the rhythms by which we repeatedly seek to make a divided self whole. Both the demand for conscientious action and the longing for mutual friendship interrupt these natural cycles. They provide encounters with real difference that force us to pause and take stock. These moments provide a glimpse of the "farther shore" of our striving. In *Walden*, immediately before recounting the episode of his arrest and imprisonment that figures in "Civil Disobedience," Thoreau indicates the ultimate horizon of his political and moral vision:

> Every man has to learn the points of the compass again as often as he awakes, whether from sleep or any abstraction. Not till we are lost, in other words, not till we have lost the world, do we begin to find ourselves, and realize where we are and the infinite extent of our relations. (115)

The necessary interruption of the process of deliberate living calls into question the sovereignty of the double self and reminds us of its situatedness in a complex of social and natural relations and of its longing for a "still more perfect and glorious state" and for the noble friendships that will spur it to continued striving.

Thoreau's recognition of the facts of interdependence and the ideal of companionship returns us to questions about the importance of desire and intimate relations in the ethics of self-making. His own resolute independence of the conventional institutions through which his fellow citizens pursue these needs requires us to contest the adequacy of marriage, family, and nations to our highest aspirations toward friendship and community. In the contemporary United States, lesbians, gays, and other queers are excluded from full participation in these institutions. Our marginalization has led to the invention of alternative forms of intimate association in the interstices of the dominant society. At the same time, many long for legal and social recognition of the "families we choose." In the final chapter, I will interrogate the demand for lesbian and gay marriage in the contexts of principles of liberty and equality, the vicissitudes of self-making, and the contestation of modern democracy.

CHAPTER SEVEN

INTIMACY AND EQUALITY

><

The Question of Lesbian and
Gay Marriage[1]

for Ed Stein

"Intimacy and Equality," like "Sexual Justice" juxtaposes terms that do not sit
easily together within liberal political discourse; the sense of incongruity is
heightened by the proximity to "lesbian and gay marriage." If not oxymorons,
these phrases suggest a conflation of categories of private and public, at the very
least, a blurring of boundaries that many modern thinkers have been concerned
to delineate clearly and protect. *Sexual Justice* has contested the ways in which
these boundaries have been drawn in relation to controversies over lesbian and
gay rights. In one sense, this book explores the ramifications for queer politics of
the feminist insight that the personal is the political, a juxtaposition that requires
revision of both terms. In this concluding chapter, I bring previous arguments
about democratic norms, erotic self-formation, and contestatory politics to bear on
the specific issue of lesbian and gay marriage. I proceed along two tracks: an interrogation of recent claims by proponents of lesbian and gay rights to a right to
marry or otherwise establish legally recognized domestic partnerships (and to
bear and raise children)[2] and a revisiting of the constitutional right of privacy as a
resource for movements of homosexual liberation. A primary objective of this
chapter is to emphasize the extent to which even the most intimate associations
between individuals are situated within a matrix of social relations and legal
arrangements that both constrain and support them. Given the critical importance of interpersonal relationships as a site of self-making and a dimension of
human fulfillment, full equality for lesbian and gay citizens requires access to the
legal and social recognition of our intimate associations. These, like public associations, provide the social context in which we frame, enact, and revise our conceptions of the good life and form our personal and political identities. The
demand for recognition of lesbian and gay personal relationships has appeared,

and could appear, only within the context of a political and social movement by which queer citizens have rejected the confines of the closet and emerged to insist on full democratic equality. Democratic citizenship implies the freedom to join with others in shaping diverse institutions of erotic life. I will conclude this chapter by examining a form of life at some remove from lesbian and gay marriage, the gay male sex club.

I begin with the growing demand by lesbian and gay citizens for a right to marry or otherwise establish legally and socially recognized domestic partnerships. Marriage provides one of the few intrumentalities in modern society by which individuals may join together to form associations that impose obligations on third parties. The decision to establish institutions to sustain shared lives and to have one's intimate commitments socially recognized expresses human needs for affiliation and domesticity. The desire for intimate human connection runs very deep and across differing modes of sexuality; social recognition and legal support are required to maintain the always precarious associations through which such connections are realized. No doubt under the anomic conditions of modernity, couples and families are under enormous strain. These fragile relations are often made to bear the full weight of individual needs for community. Claims for the recognition of lesbian and gay families have emerged from the background of an increasingly visible queer community within which such social choices become feasible. The personal and political overcoming of the closet has provided the social and historical conditions for reconstructing lesbian and gay intimate associations. Whether these aspirations may best be fulfilled through securing access on equal terms to the already troubled institution of marriage or through the creation of new forms of socially recognized intimate relations and family life remains an open question. Indeed, I will conclude by defending the importance of maintaining a plurality of ethical institutions for the diverse and concerted pursuit of erotic life.

Much of this chapter reexamines the history and controversy around the constitutional right of privacy discussed in Chapter One. I argue that constitutional privacy rights remain an important source of ethical and political justification for movements of homosexual emancipation, especially as refigured in terms of the "freedom of intimate association" invoked by Justice Blackmun in his dissenting opinion in *Bowers v. Hardwick*.[3] Blackmun claims that the right of privacy protects sexual activity between free and equal citizens as part of their ongoing efforts to define themselves in close relation to others and to construct shared institutions for the conduct of life. My own defense of privacy rights is sensitive to the sustained critique of the very conception of privacy-based arguments by some feminist thinkers and shares their concerns about the invocation of privacy rights to defend the traditional nuclear family as a site of gender subordination.[4] Despite the historical force of these objections, the concept of privacy as freedom of intimate association has continuing importance in both feminist and queer politics, so long as such rights are defined in close connection with democratic conceptions of equality and the claims of each citizen to control important decisions affecting her life. In its brief history, the constitutional right of privacy has been the site of vacillating and sometimes inconsistent efforts by the Supreme Court both to promote the nuclear family as a locus of social value and to protect individual autonomy in crucial areas of personal life. The conflict between these aims surfaces most dramatically in the decisions and ensuing controversies regarding a woman's right to abortion. In this context, the insistence by the Court in *Hardwick* on reiterating the connection between privacy and family rights must be seen as a retrograde moment in the struggle over women's sexual and reproductive freedom as well as a setback in the effort to obtain lesbian and gay equality.

I. Why Lesbian and Gay Marriage?

In recent years there has emerged an increasing insistence on the legal and social recognition of lesbian and gay relationships and community institutions. The emphasis on lesbian and gay associations and families sets the stage for a more complex conception of the relations among sexuality, citizenship, and domesticity than that implied by arguments for decriminalization or for protection against discrimination. Although these claims appeal to fundamental conceptions of political equality, they go beyond anti-discrimination arguments by asserting positive dimensions of lesbian and gay citizenship. This development emphasizes human interdependence and situates individual efforts to lead a satisfying life within the context of personal, familial, and civic relations and responsibilities. Moreover, the rights at issue pertain not only to individuals, but also to couples, families, and voluntary associations. The personal contexts from which such claims emerge matter enormously to the people affected; they are at the heart of the efforts of many to find happiness and meaning in their lives. The state functions in relation to these issues not only as a civic shield protecting queer citizens against retaliation for the exercise of fundamental political freedoms, but more positively as an agency of empowerment in the pursuit of full lives. Political and legal decisions in this area have a direct and forceful impact on the intimacies of personal life. They include matters affecting the entire span of the life cycle — from determining the custody of children of lesbian and gay parents to the safer-sex education of queer students in public schools to the rights of partners in caring for sick or dying lovers. Ultimately at stake is acceptance of the moral legitimacy and ethical validity of the shared ways of life of lesbian and gay citizens.[5]

Resistance to these claims is almost certainly increased by the perception that the traditional family is already in trouble and may not be able to tolerate any additional strain. These issues provide a focal point for comprehending the resistance to lesbian and gay rights generally: lesbians and gays are constructed as posing a threat to "family values" already under siege in contemporary society. For many conservatives, queer families are simply the last straw. And yet, the seriousness with which lesbians and gays urge their capacities to share in the responsibilities of family life (and military service) also provides a perhaps surprising locus for potential reconciliation with the defenders of traditional community norms.[6] The arguments of Andrew Sullivan discussed in Chapter One exhibit this tendency. Shifting ground from sexual freedom to the recognition of lesbian and gay partnerships and families asserts a commonality with the professed aspirations of the heterosexual majority and undercuts the construction of queers as sexual subversives — so much so that some queer theorists fear that lesbian and gay marriage may mark the cultural triumph of compulsory heterosexuality. Feminist critics remind us of the historical role of marriage in maintaining the subordination of women.[7] Regarding these feminist objections to lesbian and gay marriage, an important counterargument has emerged urging that the *prohibition* of same-sex marriage works as an important factor in maintaining gender hierarchy by denying women any form of legitimate intimacy other than heterosexual marriage. In *Baehr v. Lewin*,[8] the Supreme Court of the State of Hawaii determined that state laws that restrict marriage to members of different sexes must be subjected to the highest level of scrutiny under their state's constitution, since they potentially violate its ban on sex discrimination. The claim advanced there, which has been developed by several legal scholars,[9] is that the prohibition of same-sex marriages serves to maintain the subordination of women in much the same way that laws against interracial marriage upheld white supremacy in the southern United States until the Supreme Court ruled them unconstitutional in 1967 in the well-named case of *Loving v. Virginia*.[10] A serious case has been advanced that permitting same-sex marriages is itself an important step towards gender equality. Whether lesbian and gay families conform to the normalizing regimes of compulsory heterosexuality or act to subvert and challenge its gendered forms remains an open and controversial question. (I shall return to it in sections IV and V below.)

What are we to make of the attention given to these issues in recent years? Especially when we remember that same-sex activities remain crimes in half the states and that only nine states provide lesbian and gay citizens basic protections against discrimination. Certainly, for those affected, the status of marriage or domestic partnership brings concrete financial and material benefits. In addition, legal recognition of a couple's status may gain acceptance for them in the eyes of the community, their families, and even themselves. The conjunction of material and symbolic gains associated with marital or partnership status requires some untangling here to clarify the political and ethical issues involved.[11] Let me reiterate: the institution of marriage provides a distinctive opportunity for individuals to create by their own decision a new association that institutionalizes mutual obligations and imposes duties on third parties. Both legally and socially, spouses are entitled to consideration not available to those not so recognized. Coverage under employee-benefit plans is only one of the most obvious of these entitlements, which range from shared invitations to social events to rights under a lease or rent-control law to access to hospital rooms and nursing homes and participation in life-or-death decisions concerning one's partner. Generally, two persons may adopt a child together only if they are married to each other. Partners eager to share responsibility for bringing up the children produced during the recent and ongoing lesbian "baby boom" regularly encounter the legal stumbling blocks resulting from their nonmarital status. Similarly, gay male couples are often denied the opportunity to bring up children as foster and adoptive parents because of their nonmarital status. The experience of many gay men during the AIDS epidemic has forcefully and painfully brought home the extent to which involvement in the fate of another may be reserved to spouses and members of a "natural family." In modern democracies, access to the status of marriage remains an important mode of personal empowerment.

Perhaps even more importantly, the assertion of lesbian and gay demands for recognition of the forms of our shared lives, with particular emphasis on intimacy and family, signals the emergence of queer politics from a defensive fight for mere survival towards an effort to secure the social conditions of human flourishing on equal terms with other citizens. Lesbians and gays have been able to survive at all on the margins of society only through the creation of informal networks of sustenance and support. Individuals have struggled to maintain intimate personal ties against considerable odds, and they have been supported in their efforts by relations of friendship and community. In fact, queer social life has become the site of processes redefining kinship in modern society with implications for all sorts of folks whose needs are not met by prevailing models.[12] As communitarian thinkers have especially emphasized, human life is a social enterprise. Humans are born needy and dependent; our emergence as individuals results from interaction with others in the contexts of family and community. Our needs for recognition by and exchange with others are transformed as we mature, but we do not outgrow a fundamentally social condition. In liberal societies, the claims of community depend on individual choices to create and sustain common institutions. By turning to marriage, partnership, and family rights, the movement for lesbian and gay rights and liberation affirms deeply felt human desires to establish intimate relationships as part of the ongoing conduct of life, culminating for many in the desire to bear and raise children of their own or otherwise share in the care of others.

II. Privacy Rights, Sexual Freedom, and Family Values

In this section I return to the constitutional right of privacy discussed in Chapter One to focus on the role of judicial constructions of marriage and the family in the articulation of individual rights. I find a dual structure at work. On the one hand, the identification of privacy rights with participation in marriage and the family is taken as the strongest possible indication that such rights have been historically acknowledged in the American political tradition and are entitled to enforcement by the U. S. Supreme Court. In tension with this linkage of personal rights to membership in marriage and family is the dynamic of constitutional equality by which, once acknowledged as fundamental, privacy rights have been extended to include all persons recognized as citizens, regardless of their family or marital status. Of course, this egalitarianism came to an abrupt halt with the denial of privacy rights to homosexual citizens in *Bowers v. Hardwick*. Nevertheless, in the area of reproductive rights, the initial construction of constitutional barriers against the intrusion of the state into marital privacy has been transformed into a conception of the individual citizen as herself bearing rights not only against the state but also against competing claims of a spouse, parent, or other family member. These tensions within the privacy jurisprudence are explosively manifest in the ongoing conflict about a woman's right to abortion. However, even without reference to the problematic status of the fetus, the earlier privacy cases already reveal an unstable relationship between a conception of rights belonging to the autonomous individual and one derived from marital status or family membership.[13]

Recall that the constitutional right of privacy enunciated in *Griswold v. Connecticut* and subsequent cases has become increasingly problematic in relation to the recent jurisprudence and politics of the Supreme Court.[14] For those convinced of the importance of privacy rights within modern democracies, it is a sad fact that its most coherent and theoretically impressive defense is found in Justice Blackmun's *dissenting* opinion in *Bowers v. Hardwick*.[15] When the Supreme Court refused to invalidate Georgia's consensual sodomy law as a violation of constitutionally based privacy rights (at least insofar as the law applied to homosexuals), the hopes of many lesbian and gay citizens for constitutional vindication of our claims to equal citizenship were dashed. However, the arguments of Justice Blackmun's dissent have a political and ethical validity that transcends their failure to carry the day in the decision of that case. Oddly enough, the failure of a majority of the Court to recognize the power of queer citizens' claims to constitutional equality has energized rather than defeated the lesbian and gay political movement, shifting attention from the federal courts to state courts and legislatures as well as to the court of public opinion. The denial of fundamental privacy rights to homosexual citizens foregrounds the importance of defending such rights politically and points toward an alliance between minorities concerned with sexual freedom and feminists committed to women's reproductive rights. Although the right of privacy does not deliver all that is required to secure equal protection for poor and younger women, it remains a lynch pin in constitutional arguments for the right to choose.

The constitutional right of privacy formulated in *Griswold* comes into play when a litigant seeks to have federal courts invalidate state legislation as an infringement of personal rights under the Due Process Clause of the Fourteenth Amendment. Justice Douglas, who wrote the opinion of the Court in *Griswold*, found privacy rights to be grounded in general principles or values that underlie the specific provisions of the Bill of Rights. His task of justification was somewhat complicated by the prior history of constitutional adjudication that often set liberal proponents of an expansive reading of individual rights based on a literal interpretation of the specific provisions of the Bill of Rights against conservative jurists willing to impose on the states only those constraints found to be deeply embedded in the traditions of American political practice. No literal textual authority exists for the right of privacy.[16] In *Griswold*, Douglas identifies privacy as the fundamental value underlying the First, Third, Fourth, and Fifth Amendments which include such specifics as the prohibition of unreasonable searches and seizures, the protection against compulsory self-incrimination, the guarantee of free exercise of religion, and the proscription against quartering soldiers in people's homes. In his concurring opinion, Justice Goldberg emphasizes the Ninth Amendment declaration that the "enumeration of certain rights" in the Constitution should not be construed as to "disparage other rights which are retained by the People." This language buttresses Douglas's insistence that the specific provisions of the Bill of Rights indicate general areas for constitutional protection rather than restricting the reach of personal rights to their literal application. Thus, the Court in *Griswold* holds that among the unenumerated rights retained by the People under the United States Constitution is the right of privacy implicit in many of its specific provisions. In applying this principle, the Court finds that the Connecticut statute's application to married couples decisive: "This law . . . operates directly on an intimate relation of husband and wife and their physician's role in one aspect of that relationship."[17] (As we shall see below, the conservative Justice Harlan relied on this fact to reach a similar conclusion from quite different premises). Douglas proceeds from this characterization to list other fundamental rights previously recognized by the Court despite their not being enumerated in specific provisions of the Constitution.[18] Importantly, he focuses on rights of *association*: the right of parents to send their children to a school of their choice[19] and of students to study foreign languages.[20] These cases, which emphasize the integrity of the family and protect parental decision making against state control linked those rights to the *public* terms of First Amendment freedoms:

> The right of freedom of speech and press includes not only the right to utter or print, but the right to distribute, the right to receive, the right to read . . . and freedom of inquiry, freedom of thought, and freedom to teach . . . indeed the freedom of the entire university community. . . . Without these peripheral rights the specific rights would be less secure.[21]

Douglas forcefully argues that privacy rights are derived from fundamental rights of political association: "In *N.A.A.C.P. v. Alabama*[22]. . . we protected the '*freedom to associate and privacy in one's associations*' [emphasis added] noting that freedom of association was a peripheral First Amendment right."[23] In *N.A.A.C.P. v. Button*,[24] according to Douglas, the Court emphasized that forms of association protected under the First Amendment were not only political, but any which contributed to the "social, legal, or economic benefit" of their members. Implicit in Douglas's analysis is the redefinition of privacy from a negative right to be left alone to a positive capacity to form voluntary associations with others.

This formulation places the right of privacy close to the center of the scheme of individual rights protected by the Constitution and charged with enforcement by the Supreme Court.[25] By insisting on its continuity with more obviously public modes of association, Douglas identifies the right of privacy as a critical component of democratic freedom rather than as a naturalized, pre-political right linked to traditional family structures. Nonetheless, the agreement of seven justices from diverse constitutional perspectives on the result in *Griswold* depends importantly on the Connecticut law's intrusion into the marital relationship. The statute forbade without qualification the use of contraceptives: "Would we allow the police to search the sacred precincts of marital bedrooms for telltale signs of the use of contraceptives? The very idea is repulsive to the notions of privacy surrounding the marriage relationship" writes Douglas for the Court.[26] Given that his argument has already invoked the specific Fourth Amendment prohibition of "unreasonable searches and seizures," one must question the limitation of privacy to "marital bedrooms," now figured as "sacred precincts." After all the Fourth Amendment provides, in part: "The right of the people to be secure in their persons, houses, papers, and effects, against unreasonable searches and seizures, shall not be violated. . . ." It would appear that the privacy of the bedroom of any person's, married or single — and not just of her bedroom, is to be respected and protected. In the crunch, Douglas is unwilling to forego the rhetorical and political advantages of that "marital bedroom." Yet, in defining the constitutional status of marriage, he adumbrates the destabilizing tendencies implicit in the *Griswold* decision:

> We deal with a right of privacy older than the Bill of Rights. . . . Marriage is a coming together for better or for worse, hopefully enduring, and intimate to the degree of being sacred. It is an association that promotes a way of life, not causes; a harmony in living, not political faiths; a bilateral loyalty, not commercial or social projects. Yet it is an association for as noble a purpose as any involved in our prior decisions.[27]

On the one hand, Douglas risks making privacy rights dependent on marital status; on the other hand, he explicates the constitutional status of marriage itself by analogy with rights of political association that pertain to individual persons as citizens. That the Fourteenth Amendment requires equality in the treatment of citizens or legal persons has had important consequences in the brief and troubled history of the constitutional right of privacy.

The most important single precursor to the *Griswold* decision was Justice Harlan's dissenting opinion in *Poe v. Ullman*[28] in which the Court had declined to rule on the Connecticut contraception law. The conservative jurist concludes that the law violates constitutional standards from arguments quite different from Douglas's. The language of that dissent, which Harlan himself quotes in his concurring opinion in *Griswold*, is quite revealing of the conflicting notions of privacy that are partially obscured by the fact of a seven-justice majority in that case. He argues: ". . . a statute making it a criminal offense for married couples to use contraceptives is an intolerable and unjustifiable invasion of privacy in the conduct of the most intimate concerns of an individual's personal life." However, Harlan insists that he "would not suggest that adultery, homosexuality, fornication, and incest are immune from criminal inquiry, however privately practiced," but

> the intimacy of husband and wife is necessarily an essential and accepted feature of the institution of marriage, an institution which the state not only must allow, but which always and in every age it has fostered and protected. It is one thing when the State exerts its power either to forbid extra-marital sexuality altogether, or to say who may marry, but it is quite another when, having acknowledged a marriage and the intimacies inherent in it, it undertakes to regulate by means of the criminal law the details of that intimacy.[29]

Justice Harlan could not have been clearer that the privacy he is concerned to protect as "inherent in the concept of ordered liberty" is derived from an individual's status within the legally defined and socially sanctioned institution of marriage. Moreover, Harlan is at some pains to exclude from the right of privacy any conception of individual sexual freedom outside of marriage. Indeed, in Harlan's view, the state's interest in the promotion of marriage provides justification for a wide range of restrictions on individual sexual conduct. Perhaps most importantly for present purposes, he recognizes the extent to which marriage itself is a legal and social construction: it is after all the State that "may forbid extra-marital sexuality altogether" and that determines "who may marry." The traditionalist, almost statist, terms of Harlan's analysis contrast sharply with Douglas' assimilation of marriage to associational freedom in *Griswold*.

By 1972, the Supreme Court was required to address the ambiguities and tensions inherent in *Griswold* as a result of legislative actions taken in direct response to that decision. In *Eisenstadt v. Baird*, the Court ruled on the constitutionality of a Massachusetts law, similar to that of Connecticut, that had been amended in light of the earlier ruling to prohibit the distribution of contraceptive material *except* in the case of registered physicians and pharmacists providing the materials to married persons.[30] For the Massachusetts legislature, the privacy rights enunciated in *Griswold* were identified with the relations of marital partners and their healthcare providers. Not so for the Supreme Court. In an eight-to-one decision, the Court, by Justice Brennan, announced that "viewed as a prohibition on contraception per se," the statute ". . . violates the rights of single persons under the Equal Protection Clause. . . . whatever the rights of the individual to access to contraceptives may be, the rights must be the same for married and unmarried alike."[31] In terms of the contrast between Harlan's traditionalist analysis and Douglas's associational analysis of marriage, the Court comes out squarely on the side of the latter:

. . . the marital couple is not an independent entity with a mind and heart of its own, but an association of two individuals each with a separate intellectual and emotional make-up. If the right of privacy means anything, it is the right of the *individual*, married or single, to be free from unwarranted intrusion into matters so fundamentally affecting a person as the decision whether to bear or beget a child. . . . [emphasis in original][32]

So much for the exclusiveness of "the sacred precincts of marital bedrooms."[33] This decision squarely identifies privacy as an individual right. The marital bedroom has become "a room of one's own," and the emphasis shifts decisively from protection of the institutional integrity of the family to respect for individual autonomy in making certain kinds of decisions.

The logic of these developments within the jurisprudence of privacy rights culminated in 1973 with the Court's decision in *Roe v. Wade*.[34] The critical point for this analysis is that the Court relied on *Griswold* and its progeny to ground the assertion of the fundamental right of a woman to make such important decisions as whether to end or continue her pregnancy: "The right of privacy . . . is broad enough to encompass a woman's decision whether or not to terminate her pregnancy. . . . All of these factors the woman and her responsible physician will consider in consultation."[35] Under circumstances fraught with implications for marriage and the family, no mention is made of these institutions and the state's interest in preserving and maintaining them.[36] The woman's physician is given a consulting role; her husband, if any, does not appear. Even with the erosion of the rights articulated in *Roe* by subsequent decisions of the Court, the majority in the most recent abortion case, *Casey v. Planned Parenthood*,[37] overturned the provision of the Pennsylvania law that required a woman to notify her spouse of a decision to have an abortion. Moreover, in justifying that decision, the Court explicitly refers to the danger that the spousal notification requirement might actually place women at risk of physical harm through battery by angry husbands. Privacy rights are effectively deployed in *Casey* to defend a woman's decisional autonomy from being subordinated to her marital status. The Supreme Court's privacy doctrine has traveled a considerable distance from the family-centered traditionalism of Justice Harlan's dissent in *Poe v. Ullman*, which had been so important in preparing the way for *Griswold*. Protection of the traditional family unit has been superseded by the defense of individual autonomy rights, and autonomy is linked to freedom of association. It is no accident that the privacy cases have concerned matters like contraception and abortion: the right of privacy expresses in normative constitutional terms the disarticulation of sexuality from reproductive imperatives that results from the widespread circulation of contraceptive technologies. Still, the Supreme Court has refused to formulate a constitutional right of sexual freedom, especially as it effects homosexual citizens. At the same time, the decision in *Bowers v. Hardwick* must be read in part as a protest against constitutional support for a woman's right to choose.

III. "The Alleged Right to Commit Homosexual Sodomy"

By 1986, many constitutional scholars agreed with civil libertarians and advocates of lesbian and gay rights that a challenge to state laws that criminalize acts of sodomy performed in private by consenting adults would state a powerful claim within the developed logic of the privacy cases. Then, by the narrowest possible majority, the Supreme Court decided *Bowers v. Hardwick*.[38] Writing for the Court, Justice White went beyond rejection of that claim to characterize the very assertion of a "constitutional right to commit homosexual sodomy" as "facetious." By now a great deal of ink has been spilled analyzing and criticizing the decision of this case.[39] Very few scholars have defended White's reasoning, even among those who support the outcome. My specific concern in this section is to track the interplay of conceptions of individual liberty and of marital or familial integrity in the logic and rhetoric deployed to justify the Court's decision. I shall then return to Justice Blackmun's dissent. My aim is to consider the implications of these competing analyses of the right of privacy for thinking about lesbian and gay family rights.

The decision in *Hardwick* looms over all subsequent efforts to theorize and litigate lesbian and gay rights in the U.S. constitutional context. Although a clear setback in the struggle for lesbian and gay emancipation in the courts, it has worked to mobilize queer organizing efforts that may have become complacent in the belief that the Supreme Court would soon vindicate basic rights to sexual freedom. Since that was not to be, the movement for lesbian and gay rights has gone on to articulate its goals in broader and more political terms. Political protest and personal coming out have been reinterpreted in terms of the assertion of individual and communal pride as both an intrinsic good and an instrument for transforming social attitudes. Although of undoubted legal authority — and thus a stumbling block on the road to constitutional vindication — *Bowers v. Hardwick* has not been accorded the kind of moral authority Americans sometimes bestow on the Supreme Court (most clearly in the matter of racial justice since *Brown v. Board of Education*).

Some of the reasons for this may be found in the text and history of the decision itself. Although also addressing a highly controversial issue in a deeply divided polity, the Court in *Brown* spoke with one voice: the decision was unanimous and was articulated in a single opinion. Even *Roe v. Wade* was decided by a seven-to-two majority, although often this fact has been obscured by subsequent political struggles over abortion rights. *Hardwick* could not be a closer case. Recently disclosed information reveals even more fully the contingency of the outcome. In the papers of late Supreme Court Justice Thurgood Marshall, now available in the Library of Congress, one learns that the original vote on the court when the case was conferenced was five-to-four in favor of *upholding* the Court of Appeals decision and *overturning* the Georgia sodomy law. On April 8, 1986, Justice Lewis Powell circulated a memorandum to his colleagues explaining that, although he continued to entertain reservations as to the penalties in the Georgia law, which prescribed imprisonment for up to twenty years, he was changing his vote on the bottom-line question as to the statute's constitutionality. As a result, Justice White was assigned to write the opinion of the Court rather than a dissenting opinion, and Justice Blackmun's analysis became a dissent rather than the law of the land. And that's not the end of it. In a press conference at the National Press Club in October 1992 after his retirement and in subsequent interviews, Powell acknowledged that he *now* believes he voted the wrong way in *Bowers v. Hardwick.*[40]

The Supreme Court's decision was precipitated by a series of events in August 1982 culminating in the arrest of Michael Hardwick for violating the Georgia sodomy law with another adult male in the privacy of his bedroom.[41] Although the District Attorney stated that he did not intend to prosecute Hardwick based on the evidence then available, Hardwick went to federal court to enjoin any prosecution under the sodomy law as unconstitutional. The District Court dismissed his action, but the Court of Appeals for the Eleventh Circuit reversed that judgment, with a divided court holding that the statute violated Hardwick's fundamental rights because "his homosexual activity is a private and intimate association that is beyond the reach of state regulation by reason of the Ninth Amendment and the Due Process Clause of the Fourteenth Amendment."[42] The Supreme Court reversed the Court of Appeals, holding that the constitutional right of privacy did not extend to "a right to commit homosexual sodomy." The terms of White's argument are quite important. First, the restriction of the Court's attention to *homosexual* sodomy. The Georgia statute defines the crime of sodomy as follows: "(a) A person commits the offense of sodomy when he performs or submits to any sexual act involving the sex organs of one person and the mouth or anus of another. . . ." The Georgia sodomy law applies to *everybody* — male, female, married, single, heterosexual, homosexual. There are state laws that forbid sodomitical acts only between members of the same sex. *Georgia's law is not one of them.* As Justice Blackmun points out in his dissent, the Court refuses to consider the explicit language of the statute, but effectively rewrites it to avoid considering the constitutionality of its application to heterosexual men and women including married couples:

> . . . [the] Court's almost obsessive focus on homosexual activity is particularly hard to justify in light of the broad language. . . . the Georgia legislature has not proceeded on the assumption that homosexuals are so different from other citizens that their lives may be controlled in a way that would not be tolerated if it limited the choices of those other citizens.[43]

In fact, the Georgia sodomy law by its terms intrudes as fully into the "sacred precincts of marital bedrooms" as did the Connecticut contraception law invalidated in *Griswold*. The *Eisenstadt* holding implies that exempting married couples from such a law would have violated the equal protection rights of the unmarried. The Court's refusal to consider the Georgia law's application to heterosexual sodomy itself discriminates between homosexuals and heterosexuals in violation of the principle of equal protection of the laws that it is charged to enforce against the states under the Fourteenth Amendment. Indeed, in his dissenting opinion in *Hardwick*, Justice Stevens argues that the Georgia law as applied to heterosexuals is unconstitutional and that any attempt to apply it solely to homosexuals is unjustifiable and violates equal protection constraints.

Having restricted the reach of the Georgia statute contrary to its plain language, White goes on to re-interpret the line of cases comprising the jurisprudence of constitutional privacy rights. Discussing a list of cases, including *Griswold, Eisenstadt, Roe,* and five others, he describes them as "dealing with": "child rearing and education," "family relationships," "procreation," "marriage," "contraception," and "abortion." Without further ado, the Court concludes:

> Accepting the decisions in these cases and the above description of them, we think it evident that none of the rights announced in those cases bears any resemblance to the claimed constitutional right of homosexuals to engage in sodomy that is asserted in this case. No connection between family, marriage, or procreation on the one hand and homosexual activity on the other has been demonstrated. [Moreover,] any claim that these cases nevertheless stand for the proposition that any kind of private sexual conduct between consenting adults is insulated against constitutional proscription in unsupportable.[44]

This argument returns to Harlan's analysis in *Poe v. Ullman* with its emphasis on legal and social commitments to preserving the integrity of marriage and the traditional family. But that paradigm is inadequate to the insistence on equality which decided *Eisenstadt* and to the concern for individual autonomy made explicit in *Roe*.[45] White engages in considerable intellectual gymnastics to secure the privacy cases within his domestic circle. Few commentators have found his efforts persuasive.[46]

One point stands out: in White's opinion, there is no *conceivable* link between homosexual activity and procreation, marriage, or the family. The result is that, cast out of the "sacred precincts" of the traditional family circle, homosexuals find themselves stripped of privacy rights altogether. By its silence regarding the reach of the Georgia law and its "almost obsessive concern with homosexual activity,"[47] the Court has implied that heterosexuals may well be protected against the intrusion of the state's criminal law, because of the putative link between heterosexuality as such and "marriage, procreation and the family." (It is hard to follow the strange logic of negation by which abortion and contraception are "connected" to procreation and the family but nonprocreative homosexual activity is not.) One result of this judicial legerdemain is that the same physical acts may be permitted to heterosexuals and prohibited to homosexuals, making the criminality of the acts dependent on the sexual orientation of the person charged. Yet at the same time, homosexuals as a class are defined by a propensity to commit the self-same "criminal" acts permitted to heterosexuals. The circle of argument here is rather narrow, and certainly vicious.[48] Indeed, White revealingly overstates his case when writing that ". . . the proposition that any kind of private sexual conduct between consenting adults is constitutionally insulated from state proscription is unsupportable."[49] I suppose he means "*every* kind of private sexual conduct," since on his own account of previous cases private heterosexual conduct (even among the unmarried, with or without contraception) is so insulated. Interestingly, in an earlier draft of the opinion to be found in the Thurgood Marshall papers, the sentence just quoted reads: ". . . any claim that these cases nevertheless stand for the proposition that any kind of private sexual conduct is *not* insulated against constitutional proscription is unsupportable." The rhetoric of White's opinion is excessive throughout, starting with the assertion that Michael Hardwick's claim to constitutional protection, supported by the Court of Appeals and almost endorsed by a majority of the Supreme Court, "must be facetious."[50]

In the tendentious revision of the privacy jurisprudence quoted above, the language itself shows evidence of the strain. White claims to "accept" these decisions, at least under the descriptions he offers in *Hardwick*. Nonetheless, as discussed in Chapter One, *Bowers v. Hardwick* has unsettled the jurisprudence of the constitutional right of privacy. Certainly, the effort in White's opinion to recuperate the traditionalism and family values at work in Harlan's conception of privacy rights comports with the efforts of a number of justices to overturn *Roe v. Wade*. It is no accident that White dissented in *Roe* and that Blackmun is its author. Those concerned for the right of privacy and for women's reproductive rights may be to that extent relieved by the re-affirmation of the *Roe* decision in *Casey*; by White's subsequent retirement; and by his replacement with Justice Ruth Bader Ginsberg.

IV. Intimate Associations and Equal Citizenship

The argument of this chapter had been fully developed and presented in a variety of settings when Justice Harry Blackmun announced his retirement from the Supreme Court. Revisions were in process when President Clinton nominated Judge Stephen Breyer to succeed to his place. Breyer was confirmed quickly and easily by the Senate. It is not hyperbolic to see Blackmun's retirement as signaling finally the end of an era. Somewhat ironically, his departure leaves the Supreme Court without a veteran spokesman for the legacy of the Warren Court that had actively defined its role as the defender of individual and minority rights. The irony, of course, derives from the fact that Harry Blackmun was not a member of the Court when Chief Justice Earl Warren presided, but was appointed later — by Richard Nixon. At the time of his appointment and for several years thereafter, he appeared indistinguishable from his Minnesota colleague and friend Warren Burger, whom Nixon had appointed Chief Justice. For some time, journalists referred to them as the "Minnesota twins." (Burger wrote a concurring opinion in *Bowers v. Hardwick* that almost makes White's opinion for the Court look moderate.)[51] However, the fact is that Justice Blackmun's tenure on the Court saw his emergence as a great spokesman for human rights — in his *Roe v. Wade* opinion, his *Hardwick* dissent, and his belated but passionate dissents on the death penalty. His moral and political transformation should caution us against too quickly judging the merits of the successor generation. In the context of this chapter, it is worth noting that Justice Breyer served as law clerk to Justice Goldberg during the term *Griswold* was decided. (Recall that Goldberg wrote an eloquent concurring opinion drawing on the Ninth Amendment as authority for the Court's duty to enforce rights other than those explicitly enumerated in the Bill of Rights.) The Ninth Amendment has since become an important component of arguments supporting the contention that the Framers had an expansive conception of the rights of the people, which the language of the Constitution was intended not to foreclose. The most important of these currently contested, unenumerated rights may well be privacy.

The most comprehensive argument in support of the constitutional right of privacy appears in Blackmun's dissent in *Bowers v. Hardwick*. In Chapter One, I argued that Blackmun not only summarizes and justifies the privacy jurisprudence in relation to doctrines of fundamental rights, but also sketches the terms of a "constitutional morality" in which concepts of liberty, equality, and moral pluralism are articulated.[52] For Blackmun, at issue is the right of individuals to pursue happiness and to define and revise their personal identities through freely chosen intimate associations with others. This moral and legal principle lies at the heart of the scheme of constitutional protections of individual rights. Moreover, by emphasizing the place of "intimate association" within a broader context of political neutrality and moral pluralism, Blackmun lays the groundwork for incorporating substantive ethical concerns into a liberal concern for the right and for human rights. In this section, I explore the implications of Blackmun's treatment of the relation between individual freedom and the social construction of domestic institutions. My reading of Blackmun's opinion takes it as the expression of seminal philosophical arguments that transcend the legal and institutional context of its writing. In constitutional terms, it has no legal authority, although one may hope that it will come to join the dissents of the "great dissenter," the nineteenth-century Justice Harlan, whose "premature" dissenting opinions on racial justice were eventually vindicated by the decisions of a later generation of Justices. The most famous of these was in *Plessy v. Ferguson*, which established the constitutionality of segregation with the "separate but equal doctrine," finally rejected in *Brown v. Board of Education*. The Supreme Court in *Romer v. Evans*, began its opinion with a quotation from that dissent condemning the Court's endorsement of second-class citizenship for blacks in the South. Is it too much to hope that in overruling the Colorado constitutional amendment restricting the rights of lesbian and gay citizens the Supreme Court was also signalling its disapproval of the outcome in *Bowers v. Harwick*?[53] However, my primary concern here is not legal but philosophical — to spell out the ethical and political implications of the "freedom of intimate association" on which Blackmun grounds the constitutional right of privacy. Returning to the question of marriage, I argue that privacy rights require analysis in close connection with constitutional norms of equality that affect both gender hierarchy and the citizenship of sexual minorities.

In his *Hardwick* dissent, Blackmun summarizes the constitutional jurisprudence of privacy rights protecting both certain decisions that are taken to belong primarily to the individuals affected and certain places that are insulated against social and legal intrusions. In responding to the Court's limitation of these protections to marriage and the family, Blackmun warns against "closing our eyes to the basic reasons why certain rights associated with the family have been accorded shelter under the Fourteenth Amendment's Due Process Clause."[54] Blackmun concludes that these institutions are constitutionally protected less because of any calculus of social benefits than "because they form so central a part of an *individual's* life." (My italics.) He focuses on the ethical concerns underlying claims to fundamental rights. Blackmun rejects the definition of "the alleged right to commit homosexual sodomy" as a configuration of body parts and situates sexual activity within emotional and interpersonal relationships. In terms of recent identity politics, Blackmun sees the intersubjective domain of intimacy as a site for the construction of personal identities that require expression through association with others.[55] Critically, he denaturalizes family values by interpreting them as various ways in which people come together to build shared lives:

> . . . a necessary corollary of giving individuals freedom to choose how to conduct their lives is acceptance of the fact that different persons will make different choices. [The] fact that different individuals define themselves in a significant way through their intimate sexual relationships with others suggests, in a Nation as diverse as ours, that there may be many "right" ways of conducting those relationships, and that much of the richness of a relationship will come from the freedom an individual has to choose the form and nature of these intensely personal bonds. . . . the Court really has refused to recognize . . . the fundamental interest all individuals have in controlling the nature of their intimate associations with others.[56]

This argument concentrates a number of important insights into both sexual freedom and the character of domestic institutions. For Justice Blackmun, individual freedom must be socially situated and expressed through affiliation with others.

The individual is not defined in abstraction, but comes to define herself through a history of relationships and affiliations. A society that truly values individual freedom must eventually recognize a diversity of shared forms of life, especially in the context of intimate association. Freedom of choice is a necessary component in legitimizing institutions within democratic societies, but decisions require embodiment in social practices and institutions if individuals are to flourish.[57] Blackmun's analysis resonates with the insights of Plato and Freud in acknowledging the multiplicity of human desires and their interaction with political and cultural contexts in the shaping of personal aspirations and identities.

Blackmun's point — central to any understanding of modern intimacy — is that consensual relations among adults are both expressions of the voluntary choices of individual participants and necessary elements in the construction of intersubjectively-constituted personal identities. Freedom in the choice of partners and modes of relationship is one component of the good of intimate association that produces socially-recognized shared forms of life. Intimate associations often find expression in sexual activity. Blackmun suggests that a plurality of forms of intimate association is itself a good in a nation so large and diverse as the United States.[58] Individual freedom of association requires a diversity of forms of social life. Thus, variations of personal and sexual expression have an irreducibly political dimension requiring the social recognition of "experiments in living." Moreover, the existence of different sexualities with their own modes of intimacy is itself an aspect of democratic freedom. Although Blackmun focuses on the *intimate* dimension of freedom of association in elaborating his conception of constitutional privacy rights, he situates intimacy within a plurality of voluntary associations. This argument echoes Thoreau and Arendt in locating the ethics of self-making in the context of democratic contestation and political action. In contemporary lesbian and gay life, it is crucial that queer couples and families emerge in relation to a proliferation of social institutions — from student groups to professional associations to AIDS mobilizations to bars, bath houses, and sex clubs. Although these latter may seem anomalous in the context of constitutional morality, we cannot ignore their historical and ongoing role in the sexual and social lives of gay men especially. Increasingly in major urban centers in recent years, lesbians have joined together to establish similar institutions. With the advent of the AIDS epidemic, gay male centers of sexual activity have become sites of "safer-sex" education and political mobilization. All of these institutions provide the context from which more continuous forms of sexual intimacy, friendship, and family emerge.[59] The critical importance of intimacy as a constituent in most persons' conceptions of themselves and their aims in life leads to its protection as a fundamental right: "[It] is precisely because the issue raised in this case touches the heart of what makes individuals what they are that we should be especially sensitive to the rights of those whose choices upset the majority."[60]

Finally, Blackmun's analysis of freedom of intimate association allows us to reframe the question of marriage and the family within the privacy jurisprudence.

The freedom of intimate association requires not only a negative right to be left alone, but also a positive capacity to create intimate spaces and social support for personal choices that establish and maintain personal relationships and identities.[61] These intimate spaces are often figured as "home." Domesticity is the metaphorical and actual space of intimacy: the privacy cases demonstrate the dependence of such a sphere on its recognition by legal and social authorities. These decisions have constructed a domain of intimacy through which mutual personal decisions are not only insulated against interference from government or society but also given a place in the world. In part, this construction results from recognition of tradition and established social practice; in part, it requires the Court to apply fundamental principles of liberty and equality to domains previously governed by majoritarian morality. Blackmun's analysis points toward the need to recognize a plurality of intimate associations through which individuals may pursue their goals and within which they may establish their homes and together shape their personal identities.

Within the normative framework of democratic constitutionalism, the recognition of intimate associations requires their conformity to ideals of freedom and reciprocity. In the earlier privacy cases, traditional marriage and family arrangements were emphasized without acknowledging that they may conflict with overriding concerns for individual autonomy and civic equality. These intimate associations are entitled to constitutional protection as fundamental rights only when they comport with the requirements of equal liberty for all. Justice Blackmun's argument for a constitutional right of privacy grounded in a positive freedom of intimate association recognizes deep human needs for intimacy and the extent to which even the most personal relations require social and legal support.

But why marriage? To what extent may the valorization of marriage implicit in demands for lesbian and gay equality of access conflict with feminist theory and the aspirations of the women's movement to overcome gender subordination and the institutionalized abuse of women? Feminists have eloquently and persuasively demonstrated the ways in which the institution of marriage has historically reinforced male privilege and maintained the subjection of women. Recent scholarship has demonstrated that many of the recent reforms in divorce law, sometimes in the name of gender equality, have also functioned to disadvantage women both economically and socially.[62] In ongoing relationships, marital privacy has been invoked to shield abusive men and perpetuate the vulnerability of women to sexual and physical violence.

The decision of the Supreme Court of the State of Hawaii in *Baehr v. Lewin*, mentioned in section I, has called attention to a different feminist analysis of same-sex marriage. In deciding that the denial of marital status to same-sex couples must be scrutinized in light of state constitutional prohibitions on sex discrimination, that court has given legal authority and political impetus to an argument advanced by a number of scholars in recent years.[63] Before concluding my own analysis, I want to consider the argument about gender equality and heterosexual marriage as formulated by Cass Sunstein.[64] He develops an analogy between miscegenation laws that banned interracial marriage and the denial of marital status to same-sex couples. In terms of constitutional equality, both cases present instances of formal legal equality established against a background of social hierarchy. Bans on miscegenation applied equally to whites and blacks; the restrictions on same-sex marriage equally effect women who want to marry women and men who want to marry men.

How then is the denial of marital status to same-sex couples a case of sex discrimination? In *Loving v. Virginia*, the Supreme Court held that the prohibition of interracial marriages was part of a system that maintained white supremacy. Sunstein argues that limiting the institution of marriage to couples that include both a woman and a man works to maintain a caste system based on gender. Drawing on feminist legal and social analysis,[65] he argues that gender hierarchy is supported by a definition of roles in which "compulsory heterosexuality," in Adrienne Rich's phrase, is deployed to subordinate women to the men they love and marry. For women to refuse their place in this heterosexual matrix is to be cast out of central social institutions and to be denied social status and benefits.[66] Heterosexual marriage has perpetuated a gendered division of labor within the household and social distinctions between private and public spheres that maintain women's subordination. Sunstein concludes that constitutional norms of sex equality require access to marriage for same-sex couples as part of an assault on the gender caste system. If Sunstein's view is correct, the establishment of lesbian and gay marriages should have transformative, or at least subversive, effects on the organization of gender relations.

This argument is not easily evaluated in part because it requires complex historical judgments and predictions concerning the effects of legal and social innovation. At one level, the institution of same-sex marriages and households must pose a challenge and provide alternatives to the gendered divisions of labor still prevalent in so many places. Of course, lesbians and gay men may replicate these patterns through the assumption of gender-stereotyped roles. But the evident disarticulation between social role and biological sex within same-sex couples subverts assumptions about the naturalness of gender. Moreover, to the extent that gender remains at work, even in same-sex relationships, it is hard to see why securing recognition of lesbian and gay marriage will increase its power. Blackmun's dissent points toward the desirability of legal and social recognition for a diversity of forms of intimate association and family life. Such an emphasis should lead to the articulation of legal forms of intimate association outside the marital paradigm of a monogamous pair joined for life. However, focusing on a "right to marry" that has been denied to lesbian and gay citizens has distinct proximal advantages. As directed toward a status currently available to heterosexual citizens, marriage claims can be formulated in terms of the denial of constitutionally protected "equal protection of the laws." The argument that this exclusion is a form of sex discrimination in particular strengthens that case given the currently unprotected status of homosexuals as a class under constitutional law. If Blackmun provides ethical grounds for recognizing fundamental rights of intimate association, then political ideals of equal citizenship and legal norms of "equal protection" complete the case for recognizing lesbian and gay marriage — in terms of constitutional morality if not of positive law. The ethical and social question remains: whether the identification of rights to intimate association with access to marriage might foreclose the diversity of forms of life that Blackmun so eloquently evokes.

I have several concerns about the argument for lesbian and gay marriage based on gender equality. First, this legal strategy must not be permitted to obscure the specificity of lesbian and gay oppression nor subordinate the claims of queer citizens to tactical moves in the struggle for gender equality. The equality of the sexes and equal citizenship for sexual minorities are related but distinct goals. In the United States today, pervasive legal disabilities define homosexuals as second-class citizens.[67] Recall the following: frequent criminalization of private sexual conduct; denial of constitutional privacy rights well established for heterosexual citizens; failure to protect lesbian and gay citizens from retaliation for the exercise of political freedom; stigmatization of efforts to attain constitutional equality as "special rights"; the imposition of a special code of silence on homosexuals in the armed forces. The second-class citizenship of homosexuals in the contemporary United States conflicts fundamentally with the egalitarian aspirations of modern democracy. As Arendt's analysis implies, the capacity to establish a household of one's own has been a historical condition for the exercise of active citizenship in the public sphere. The assertion of a right to marry derives ethical and political force through its appeal to ideals of equal citizenship. In terms of other social inequalities tied to class and income, marital status makes available "off the rack" a package of rights otherwise available only through expensive "custom-made" legal arrangements. While continuing to hope for and celebrate a plurality of "experiments in living," I am reluctant to accept a situation where lesbian and gay couples must find alternatives to marriage whether they wish to or not, whether they can afford it or not. Thus, the demand for state recognition of same-sex marriage or domestic partnership appears as a necessary corollary of equal citizenship in the domestic sphere. Although some advocates worry that success on this front would result in the assimilation of a distinct lesbian and gay ethos and to the imitation of heterosexist models, this objection strikes me as both understating and exaggerating the importance of formal legal rights. It underestimates the practical consequences of legal recognition as a form of empowerment by which individuals may create institutions that third parties must acknowledge. On the other hand, it overstates the extent to which such recognition deprives individuals of the capacity to shape and revise the institutions they voluntarily create. To the extent that opposition to lesbian and gay domesticity invokes an image of sexual outlaws inventing radically alternative forms of life, it underestimates the extent to which even our most intimate activities are implicated in forms of social life, even through their interdiction. After all, outlaws, especially, are defined by the law.

IV. Same-Sex Marriage as Civil Disobedience

Civil disobedience has been a crucial instrument for effecting social and political change in the struggles of minorities towards democratic equality throughout the world during the twentieth century. As I argued in Chapter Six, at the same time that leaders of oppressed groups like Gandhi and King acknowledged Thoreau's influence on their own strategies and theories, they radically transformed his conception as they adapted it to the needs of large numbers of people excluded from power, rather than the smaller number of citizens who dissent from the policies of their governments. Lesbian and gay citizens of modern democracies are in an anomalous position here: formally enjoying equal citizenship, we are nonetheless subject to pervasive legal disabilities and vulnerable to social and economic retaliation for the exercise of civil rights. Henry Abelove has argued for the importance of civil disobedience as a tactic for queer politics, while Richard Mohr has urged its necessity as a vindication of the dignity of lesbian and gay citizens in the face of oppressive laws.[68] In this section I will consider same-sex marriage as itself a mode of civil disobedience in the struggle for lesbian and gay rights and liberation. This argument has both political and theoretical dimensions, as it forces us to reconsider the role of civil disobedience in relation to the rights and duties of democratic citizenship. It also provides the occasion to bring the thinkers considered in previous chapters to bear on one specific issue in lesbian, gay, and queer politics.

While Thoreau is the writer most closely identified with theories of civil disobedience, it is an explicit theme in the work of John Rawls and Hannah Arendt, as well as implicit in Plato's dramatization of the trial and death of Socrates. Martin Luther King, Jr. invokes Socrates as well as Jesus in his defense of the moral genealogy of the civil rights movement in his "Letter From a Birmingham Jail." Rawls and Arendt wrote during the late 1960s and early 1970s, by which time not only African Americans and their supporters but also opponents of the Vietnam War and students opposed to the policies of their universities had made widespread use of the practice. Civil disobedience was no longer a fringe phenomenon but focused questions central to the politics of modern democracy. In arguing that same-sex marriage should be seen as a form of civil disobedience, I begin with Thoreau's conception of the ethics of individual self-making, which converges with Socrates' arguments in the *Apology* and *Crito*. Then I shall turn by way of some distinctions in Rawls and Arendt to her more political reading of civil disobedience as inherent in the American spirit of voluntary association and democratic contestation.

In what sense is same-sex marriage a form of civil disobedience? "Civil disobedience" generally refers to the deliberate breaking of a law to protest its injustice. Such lawbreaking is distinguished from crime and militant resistance in that it is undertaken in public; the civil disobedient foregoes violence and accepts the legal penalties for his infraction. Thoreau's refusal to pay his poll tax to protest the injustices of slavery and the Mexican War is a case in point. However, there are variations that require some attention. When African Americans and their white supporters "sat in" together at segregated lunch counters or bus terminals in the South during the 1960s, the injustice of segregation that they protested was itself instantiated in the law that they broke. This is "direct" disobedience. Often, however, as in Thoreau's case, the injustice being protested may be pervasive and at some distance from laws governing the ordinary citizen. Thus, Thoreau and the Abolitionists refused to pay taxes otherwise legitimate because these taxes contributed to support slavery in the South or the war in Mexico. This is "indirect" disobedience. During the 1960s, except for cases of draft resistance, many protests were of this form; tax resistance or demonstrations designed to disrupt traffic were justified because they publicized less ordinary and more objectionable government activities.

The legal status of same-sex marriage is somewhat anomalous in this context. No state permits same-sex couples to marry. However, marriage itself is a status that may be conveyed only by authorized agencies of the state. Demands for lesbian and gay marriage do not treat the state solely as an instrument of coercion that may interfere with individual liberty, but rather as a positive agency of empowerment. Quite simply, one cannot confer on oneself and one's partner the legal status of marriage; neither can a religious or political functionary acting without statutory authority. Marital status is a positive legal creation. On the other hand, to go through the motions of marriage in a public commitment ceremony is not a crime; it simply fails to secure the legal effects of marriage. Public same-sex commitment ceremonies may be effective means of calling attention to the exclusion of lesbians and gays, as their performance at political demonstrations in recent years reveals. Unless the occasion includes other acts in violation of law, they are not technically instances of civil disobedience. Cases where same-sex couples have staged sit-ins at marriage license bureaus that refuse to issue licenses to them present a clear example of indirect civil disobedience. The legal and ethical situation is somewhat different in those states where sodomy remains a crime. Here different difficulties arise: in jurisdictions where sodomy is a crime, many same-sex couples break the law whenever they have sex. (Despite frequent assertions to the contrary, this is not *necessarily* true. These laws often prohibit specific practices rather than same-sex activity as such. Same-sex partners may well engage in practices other than those specified. Consider that neither mutual masturbation nor fisting violates the Georgia sodomy law. The sexual imagination of intimate partners may well outrun a legislature's repressive fantasies.)

However, private lawbreaking — even where one refuses to acknowledge the legitimacy of the law broken — is not yet civil disobedience. There is an explicitly public dimension of civil disobedience that is directed towards one's fellow citizens to convince them of the injustice being protested. Celebrating same-sex commitment ceremonies where many same-sex practices are forbidden partly overcomes this deficiency. While not technically breaking any law, the couple implicitly announces its willingness to do so and contests the justice of these criminal laws. But the demand for lesbian and gay marriage goes beyond opposition to criminal penalties. On the analogy of "smoke-ins" to protest marijuana laws, one can imagine a public celebration of forbidden practices to protest the overreach of the criminal law. However, this form of civil disobedience may conflict with individuals' understanding of the role of sexual intimacy in their partnerships. At the very least, it fails to capture important aspects of the relations between those who wish to marry. I do not intend to discuss further possible tactics of civil disobedience to protest the injustice of denying recognition to lesbian and gay couples; rather, I explore the ramifications of different conceptions of civil disobedience for thinking about same-sex marriage and queer politics.

Thoreau situates civil disobedience firmly in relation to the ethics of self-making for democratic citizens. He emphasizes the extent to which the individual is implicated in the policies of her government whether she likes it or not. Relegating most politics to the domain of expediency, Thoreau does not celebrate civic activism as an aspect of personal fulfillment. He approachs the question more negatively. Resistance to civil authority becomes necessary in a polity based on the consent of the governed when the government threatens or perpetrates acts that the individual regards as unjust. In a democracy, silence results in complicity; integrity requires that one actively dissociate oneself from injustice or bear some responsibility. Thoreau urges that it is not enough publicly to wash one's hands of the matter; the democratic citizen concerned for her integrity must refuse to benefit from the effects of political inequality or social exploitation. Thoreau wrestled with the dilemmas posed by his insistence that one seek some measure of effectiveness as well as the earnest expression of one's disagreement. He cautions against reinstating an unthinking conformity to political correctness in the context of social movements, however just their aims.

Thoreau's focus on conscientious dissent and deliberate self-making in face of the collective pressures of democracy lends support to a politics of contestation and an ethical imperative of coming out for lesbians and gays in heterosexist regimes. The public declaration and celebration of one's interpersonal commitments may well result from an individual need to refuse complicity in a regime of silence and to openly work out the realization of one's desires. On the other hand, it is easy to imagine Thoreau cringing at the prospect of a same-sex commitment ceremony involving hundreds of couples on the grounds of the Washington Monument as part of a March for Lesbian and Gay Rights and Liberation. Not only his aversion to collective politics of all sorts, but also his rejection of marital and familial institutions comes into play here. Thoreau's celebration of agonistic friendship is highly ambivalent; his evocations of this image are highly idealized and fraught with a sense of impossibility. The imaginary community of sovereign individuals remains always just over the horizon, unlikely to manifest itself more than momentarily, even for a polity of two. Thoreau's teaching on resistance is a necessary reminder of the risks posed by democratic politics to individual integrity, but it remains a cautionary tale rather than an incitement to constructive political action.

Plato's account of the trial and death of Socrates results in a similarly limited conception of the ethical dimensions of political action. Indeed, Plato's *Crito* has been read by many over the centuries as an unequivocal defense of the citizen's obligation to obey the law, as least within democratic regimes.[69] However, this interpretation is based on rather too hasty an examination of Socrates' arguments and the dramatic and historical context of his choice. Moreover, it fails to account at all for an important statement in Plato's *Apology of Socrates* that the philosopher would be bound to disobey any order of the court that prohibited him from continuing his life of public inquiry. Let me try briefly to summarize his position before applying it to the circumstances at hand. In offering Socrates an opportunity to escape prison and avoid the death sentence to which he has been condemned, his old friend Crito accuses him of making light of his obligations to friends and family. Socrates insists that he can only undertake such an action if it comports with the principles on which he has insisted throughout his life. Foremost among these is the ethical axiom that it is better to suffer than to commit a wrong. The argument turns on the issue whether, having been unjustly condemned by the city's lawful institutions, he would be wrong to break the law by escaping. Famously, Socrates concludes that it would be unjust and remains to meet his death. The arguments that lead to this conclusion are worth rehearsing.

Socrates argues that to break the law would be an instance of breaking his word, of failing to keep a promise that he has made. The promise in question is his tacit undertaking to abide by the laws of Athens. He finds this promise implied by his remaining in Athens after reaching the age of maturity when he would have been free to leave the city without penalty. Moreover, he finds it especially telling in his own case that he left the city only in its military service. Socrates made no efforts to change the laws, but avoided political participation. He concludes that he had no quarrel with Athens prior to his conviction for impiety and corrupting the youth. Even at his trial, he did not challenge the laws under which he was tried, but rather insisted that he had not committed the offenses charged. Socrates supplements his ethical argument with more specific prudential and contextual factors such as his advanced age and the difficulties he would face in finding another city where he could continue with his life of enquiry.

Throughout, Socrates appeals to the importance of remaining consistent with the views he has defended, the decisions he has made, and the kind of life that he has led. Socrates' commitment to respect the laws of Athens is not an instance of universal principle, but a consequence of his own personal history and beliefs. To the extent that Socrates' obligation derives from a general argument about consent, the political character of the regime becomes very important. Socrates implies consent not simply from the fact of continued residence in the city, but from specific provisions of Athenian law that made his continuing to live there a matter of free choice. He specifically mentions that the law would not have imposed penalties on him for leaving and taking his property with him. In addition, his agreement is predicated on the fact that he never tried to change the laws in a system where as a citizen in the democracy he might have chosen to do so. His own refusal of active political participation expresses his acquiescence in the laws of city. Socrates' sense of obligation results from both his own personal choices and from the conditions of citizenship in the Athenian democracy. If he had not enjoyed the status of citizenship (as about eighty percent of those living in Athens did not) or if citizenship did not bring the freedom to emigrate without penalty and to participate in making and changing the laws, these arguments would not apply.

The ethical axiom on which his decision depends is not itself defended in the *Crito*, but taken as a cardinal personal belief: at issue is Socrates' committment to the principle he has long defended. In the *Gorgias*, Socrates' arguments in support of the view that it is better to suffer than commit a wrong turn on an individual's living in agreement with himself: "I think it's better to have my lyre or a chorus that I might lead out of tune and dissonant, and have the vast majority of men disagree with me and contradict me, than to be out of harmony with myself, to contradict myself, though I'm only one person."[70] Similarly, in the *Apology*, when Socrates tells his fellows citizens that he could not obey an order to give up his practice of questioning others in public, he invokes his personal belief: "The unexamined life is not worth living." Socrates' obligation to obey the laws of his city derives from the necessity of remaining true to himself, keeping his promises, and acting consistently with his beliefs. Concern for his integrity could lead him either to obey or to violate the law. In either case, he acts for reasons of his own. His sense of moral agency is so strong that it overrides the consequences he may be asked to pay: for him, it is always the better choice to accept suffering rather than to act against one's principles. However, he threatens to break any law or command that would require him to abandon the life of enquiry. The right is not defined by the law: disobedience may be justified when it is necessary to avoid wrongdoing, to remain consistent with one's own commitments. As with Thoreau, Socrates subordinates political consequences to ethical integrity: action in the public sphere is mandated only when necessary to avoid responsibility for injustice. Although Socratic arguments by no means foreclose civil disobedience in the context of lesbian and gay politics, they go far to limit its reach. At the same time, Socrates' insistence on the importance of seeking the truth by publicly examining one's opinions and those of others suggests that the silence of the closet would be anathema to him. That queer old citizen-soldier would surely object to the legitimacy of any such policy as "Don't ask, don't tell!"

A broader conception of the uses of civil disobedience is provided by John Rawls and Hannah Arendt writing and thinking in the wake of the anti-war,

Civil Rights, and Student Movements of the 1960s. Their theorizing of civil disobedience is indebted to the redeployment of Socrates and Thoreau on behalf of oppressed social groups in the thought and practice of Gandhi and Martin Luther King, Jr. I will begin with Rawls's articulation of a useful theoretical distinction and then turn to Arendt's figuring of civil disobedience as integral to American democracy. Rawls distinguishes between "civil disobedience" and "conscientious refusal." The latter occurs when an individual is directly confronted by a law or command that requires her to do something that violates her fundamental principles, whether these be political, ethical, or religious. As the term suggests, "conscientious refusal" is primarily negative in form and focuses on the moral status of the agent who is required to submit to the law or command. Thoreau's refusal to pay the poll tax or Socrates' threat to disobey any command to desist from his investigations are actions of this sort, as is coming out by a member of the United States armed forces required to remain silent by the current policies governing lesbians and gays in the military. By contrast, Rawls defines civil disobedience as ". . . a public, nonviolent conscientious yet political act contrary to law usually done with the aim of bringing about a change in the law or policies of the government."[71] The key term here is "political." Rawls sees acts of civil disobedience as a form of address to one's fellow citizens. Not only does civil disobedience aim at effecting political change, it also appeals to the general sense of justice within a community: ". . . it is an act guided and justified by political principles, that is, by the principles of justice which regulate the constitution and social institutions generally."[72] Although the acts undertaken may be justified by an individual's moral and religious principles as well, their political appeal is to principles shared by the majority of the community and the dissenting minority. Rawls finds civil disobedience especially appropriate as an assertion by minority groups confronting systematic violation of the liberties of equal citizenship "more or less deliberate over an extended period of time in the face of normal political opposition."[73] In terms developed in Chapter One, Rawls justifies civil disobedience as a vehicle for the vindication of "constitutional morality" by minorities whose claims to equal citizenship have been ignored by courts and legislatures. Lesbian and gay citizens of the United States have been in precisely these circumstances since the Supreme Court's decision in *Bowers v. Hardwick*. For Rawls, the political dimension of civil disobedience lies in its aim to change public policies, its address to democratic majorities, and its appeal to the principles of historical communities.

Writing at about the same time, Hannah Arendt develops an analysis of civil disobedience that situates it even more profoundly at the heart of democratic contestation. Although she too distinguishes the conscientious objection of a Socrates or Thoreau from the emancipatory movements of oppressed minorities, her conception of the political is much broader than Rawls's. She identifies it in the character of civil disobedience as a concerted action by which minorities express dissident opinions and bring into being new forms of voluntary association. For

Arendt, civil disobedience is the action of a group, rather than an individual, expressing shared opinions and convictions that differ from the majority within a democratic polity. Like Rawls, she sees it is as a fundamentally nonviolent and public means that seeks to bring about change. Like Thoreau, Arendt sees the practice of civil disobedience as expressing something basic to the "spirit" of American democracy; it is a reaffirmation of the consent of the governed as the source of legitimacy. For Arendt, the consent underlying modern democracy is manifest in agreement *among* the citizens to sustain common institutions. This "horizontal" social contract she distinguishes from a "vertical" agreement like that between the citizen and the personified laws in Plato's *Crito*, or between ruler and ruled. Here she agrees with Foucault in rejecting a juridical model of political authority. Where Socrates' argument turns on a tacit consent to abide by the laws that is sustained by the ethical obligation to keep one's promises, Arendt sees consent of the government as reflecting the positive dependence of democracy on the support of its citizens. In that sense, the underlying importance of assent is affirmed through concerted manifestations of active dissent in democratic contestation. Arendt links her conception of active consent to John Calhoun's doctrine of "concurrent majorities" and to Alexis de Tocqueville's observation about the crucial role of voluntary associations in American democracy: "Consent and the right to dissent became the inspiring and organizing principles of action that taught the inhabitants of this continent the 'art of associating together,' . . . the peculiar strength of the American political system."[74] It is crucial for Arendt that this conception of consent presupposes and maintains a plurality of agents who are not absorbed into an overarching unity of "the people," nor subjected to a common sovereign power. In her essay, "On Violence," Arendt argues that power itself is produced by the concerted actions of citizens and sustained by their ongoing consent to democratic institutions.[75] In *On Revolution*, she praises the founders of the American polity for rejecting the European conception of a sovereign authority and inventing a federal model of diverse and interacting communities and agencies.[76]

Plurality as a dimension of the human condition is reflected and respected by democracy as a political practice. Arendt goes so far in her defense of a multiplicity of groups and opinions within the public sphere as to propose the institutionalization of dissent and disobedience. Although she stops just short of endorsing the apparent paradox of a constitutional amendment that recognizes the right of minorities to disobey the law, she sees the capacity to do so as a component of fundamental political freedom. She recognizes an affinity between contesting minorities of opinion and pressure groups. Despite her aversion to a politics based on economic and social interest, she endorses both as manifestations of the spirit of voluntary association. Arendt's argument here converges with Blackmun's insistence that freedom of association, and a plurality of forms of intimate association, is a direct corollary of personal and political liberty. Like the Supreme Court Justice in his *Hardwick* dissent, she embraces social diversity as a consequence of political equality. Both see associational freedom as most needful for nonconforming minorities. Importantly, Arendt recognizes that civil disobedience may be required precisely at those historical moments when the Supreme Court fails to vindicate fundamental rights:

> The establishment of civil disobedience among our political institutions might be the best possible remedy for the failure of judicial review. . . . These minorities of opinion would thus be able to establish themselves as a power that is not only 'seen from afar' during demonstrations and other dramatizations of their viewpoint, but is always present and to be reckoned with in the daily business of government.[77]

This argument is particularly salient for lesbians and gays after *Bowers v. Hardwick*. Arendt's interpretation of civil disobedience as the concerted articulation of opinions held by groups dissenting from established majorities is also useful in the context of the contemporary politics of sexuality. She emphasizes that the stakes for civil disobedients cannot be reduced to pleading "special interests," nor are they the expression of naturally grounded essential identities. Rather, dissenting groups act to vindicate basic rights of democratic citizenship and express unpopular convictions or opinions. As I have argued throughout this book, the movement for lesbian and gay rights emerges from a commitment to vindicate the ethical legitimacy of nonconforming desires and forms of life. The demand for same-sex marriages with its recognition of the pervasive influence of legal status on personal life becomes a form of *political* dissent in Arendt's sense precisely by making minorities visible in relation to the "daily business of government."

As I revise this chapter, same-sex marriage has become an issue in the 1996 Presidential campaign. During the Iowa caucus campaign, the Christian Coalition sponsored a meeting at which candidates were asked to respond to the Christian "social agenda." Patrick Buchanan — who surprised commentators with a very strong second-place showing — held center stage at this meeting in a speech denouncing lesbian and gay marriage. His argument was simple and clear: to recognize same-sex partnerships as "marriages" was to accord "homosexual lifestyles" a legitimacy equivalent to that accorded others in the society. This Buchanan refuses to do. However, he is correct in his assessment of the stakes in this debate. Since that time, both candidates Clinton and Dole have announced their opposition to same-sex marriage. They both support a bill introduced into the 84th Congress to counteract in advance any decision by the Hawaii Supreme Court leading to the acceptance of same-sex marriage in that state. The bill would deny any federal legal status to such unions and support state efforts to do likewise in face of constitutional requirements that states give "full faith and credit" to the acts of others states. This proposal is called "The Defense of Marriage Act"! Whatever lesbian and gay controversialists may make of same-sex marriage, politicians of the right and center do not take it to be a vindication of traditional family values.

Unlike arguments for decriminalization or protection against discrimination, the case for lesbian and gay marriage is ethical and political through and through. At bottom the demand for legal recognition of same-sex partnerships is a demand to acknowledge the validity of lesbian and gay forms of life. To the extent that lesbian and gay citizens are prepared to assert this claim, and occasionally to break the law publicly in doing so, we are challenging the moral consensus that supports compulsory hetrosexuality. The belief that traditional values sustained by the nuclear family define the sole ethical arrangement of one's intimate associations is being challenged in a number of areas. The vigorous assertion of the values implicit in "families we choose" is a contribution to this ongoing democratic contestation of the organization of personal life. Moreover, as Arendt recognizes, concerted acts of civil disobedience not only express an opinion but work actively to transform the political practices of a society by introducing new forms of association. In this sense, they are examples of what Foucault calls "productive power."

No one can deny that marriage is already a troubled institution in modern liberal societies. The rate of divorce, the number of single-parent households with children, the increasing incidence of single-person or unmarried-combination living arrangements, the number of children growing up with connections to multiple families through remarriage, all these realities emphasize the extent to which the model of a nuclear family composed of husband, wife, and the children they conceive and raise together is already a fiction. The need to rethink the legal arrangements by which we secure our common lives and the rearing of our children seems obvious. I find it hard to believe that pressure for lesbian and gay marital and parental rights will actually operate to entrench further and to legitimate more fully these institutions as we know them.

One of the merits of focusing on queer families as a political issue is its small-scale and associational character. In fact, lesbians and gays are "marrying," sharing commitment ceremonies, bearing and raising children, establishing households and families, in unprecedented numbers.[78] All they seek from the state is the additional empowerment that derives from legal recognition. This shifting pattern of homosexual intimacy is itself the product of decades of concerted activities through which more and more queer citizens have rejected the closet to create a movement of personal and political transformation. The proliferation of queer couples and families may help to redefine the social and legal conditions available to sustain intimate and domestic relationships more generally. In the meantime, the energies mobilized around the demands for recognition of lesbian and gay families already extend the discourse of "family values" beyond the terms of conservative lament and the scapegoating of single mothers. Lesbian and gay marriages, domestic partnerships, the reconceiving of family institutions as modes of intimate association among free and equal citizens, all are efforts to appropriate, extend, and transform the available possibilities.

V. Productive Power and Forms of Erotic Life

Modern democracies are very much shaped by forces other than state power that are manifest in a plurality of political and discursive spheres. As Foucault has powerfully argued in a number of influential works, a distinctive feature of modernity is that it supplements the juridical and repressive model of state action with a pervasive system of social relations that exercises power through the production of institutions, modes of knowledge, forms of subjectivity.[79] In *The History of Sexuality: An Introduction*, Foucault particularly focuses on the ways in which developments in late-nineteenth-century science and medicine generated new instrumentalities for classifying and treating individuals based on the expert diagnosis of an "inner truth" identified with their sexuality. However, he insists that these discursive innovations brought with them a counter discourse. Modern power generates its own sites of subversion and resistance. These innovations in knowledge and social organization — linked with medical practice, pedagogy, social work, criminal justice, etc. — produce forms of subjective self-understanding that both incorporate and transform the new categories.[80] Foucault characterizes this pervasive and multivalent modern power as "productive" because of its capacity to shape individuals in ways that enlist them actively in the perpetuation and enforcement of diffuse social norms. Power is intimately established within one's own subjectivity and intimate relations, no longer appearing primarily in the guise of the policeman or the judge. In the later volumes of his *History*, Foucault emphasizes the extent to which socially situated subjects may undertake deliberately to fashion their own "aesthetics of existence." Like Thoreau, he celebrates the capacity of individuals to reshape the conditions of their lives. Like Arendt, he recognizes the extent to which the pervasiveness of power creates the potential of democratic contestation.

I have argued that same-sex marriage offers such a site of deliberate and democratic transformation of social norms. I want to conclude by defending the ethical significance of quite different institutions in which nonconforming forms of erotic life have been organized — gay male bathhouses and sex clubs. The conjunction of political and medical authorities in responding to the AIDS epidemic provides a telling manifestation of what Foucault calls "biopower." Power is exercised not only by the diffuse activities of psychiatrists, psychologists, educators, and social workers, but also by medical doctors, all authorized by the rhetoric and institutions of "public health." Medical expertise is deployed by state agencies to define and enforce public policy regarding intimate sexual behavior. However, the alliance of political and medical authorities in this case clashes with another distinctively modern institution, the urban market economy, in which sexual satisfaction has come to figure as yet another commodity. The intersection of these divergent modes of modern power has created fissures within which individuals and communities have found space to exercise their own agency. In recent years, the official policies towards AIDS education and prevention in New York City and

San Francisco present opposing models of the use of state power to effect changes in individual behavior.

New York State Public Health officials have defined as "unsafe conduct" both anal and oral intercourse, with or without a condom. State and city officials are authorized under Public Health laws to fine and close down businesses that permit any such activities on the premises. Periodically agents of the health authorities visit movie houses, bookstores, and social clubs where sexual activity occurs and take court action against locations where unsafe sex has been found to occur. Sites of recreational sex open and close intermittently; efforts to organize these places for ongoing safer sex education are desultory, since anything other than mutual masturbation violates the health codes. In many cases, sexual activity is driven from gay sex-affirmative settings with a commitment to AIDS prevention to more fly-by-night operations and to public parks and restrooms. Gay men interested in pursuing an active sex life outside of long standing relationships often find themselves very much on their own, with little support in negotiating safer-sex with unknown partners they are unlikely to see again. I realize, of course, that many American citizens may find this state of affairs a desirable fate for a morally questionable style of life. But how many of them would seriously propose the death penalty for such unconventional behavior? As with efforts to prevent explicit AIDS education in schools, that is the predictable effect of these policies: more people are likely to contract HIV as a result of their adoption. In the instance of public health policies about safer sex in recreational settings, the additional victims will be gay men. The model of power at work in New York City is juridical. The law defines prohibited behavior, sanctions violators by closing their more congenial gathering places, and the devil take the hindmost. If you don't conform, you are out in the cold. Like it or not, gay men committed to nonconforming sexual mores are outside the law, despite the fact that some years ago New York's highest court overturned the sodomy law as a violation of the State Constitution. The New York State Health Code strikes at individuals by depriving them of communal settings in which to construct voluntarily an alternative and *safe* form of casual sexual interaction.

The situation in San Francisco is somewhat different. Early in the epidemic, city officials decided to close the bathhouses, a policy that was subject to heated public debate and about which the gay community was deeply divided. More recently, however, a variety of gay institutions have sprung up dedicated to providing congenial environments for the pursuit of casual but safer sex among consenting adults. These clubs are organized among themselves and have adopted common policies regarding lighting, sanitation, and the provision of safer-sex guidelines and condoms. Each club has its own rules for sexual conduct within the common parameters insisting on the use of condoms in anal intercourse; some permit only mutual masturbation, others permit more individual discretion, all insist that members and visitors comply with guidelines that each place posts. Although many safer-sex clubs actually employ monitors to enforce the rules, most function on the basis of voluntary compliance. The existence of some diversity in defining acceptable practices permits individuals to choose the setting that most closely conforms to their own assessment of acceptable risks. Within each club, these voluntary decisions give rise to a shared ethos of sexual conduct that is mutually enforced by the participants. The result is that those gay men for whom sexual activities in a group setting are an important part of erotic life are able to enjoy interactions with kindred spirits who also share a commitment to safer-sex practices. Each individual confronts the need to think through his own preferences and make a deliberate decision as to which constraints he will accept in the interests of his own health and that of his partners. The effect of this collaboration among public health officials, private businesses, and members of the gay community is to create a social environment in which erotic desires and prudential interests mutually support each other. Sexually active individuals voluntarily join to create the conditions of a celebrative but safer sexual subjectivity. Here is normalizing power at its most effective, but transformed by the agency of effected individuals. No doubt about it, these policies, institutions, and individual attitudes generate a highly normative context for sexual activity; however, the very dependence of the scheme on diffuse and pervasive support among the participants results in a form of life expressive of the most general commitments and erotic investments of those who participate.[81]

Clearly, normalizing power is available for deployment in multiple directions on behalf of a plurality of individual and shared interests. In modern democracies, ideals of moral autonomy and ethical community are realized through equal citizenship and freedom of association. Sexual citizenship is manifest in erotic self-making and a variety of institutions of intimate association; these range from same-sex partnerships and queer families to sex clubs and bathhouses. The proliferation of voluntary associations and the intensification of community among lesbians and gay men in face of the AIDS epidemic, together with an increased willingness to confront hostile majorities when life itself is at stake, have created and sustained a democratic politics of desire. One immediate effect has been to increase the possibilities for a shared, deliberate affirmation of the varieties of queer sexuality and identity.

NOTES

Introduction: Democracy, Difference, and Desire

1 The decision in *Romer v. Evans*, —U.S.— (1996), No. 94–1039, was announced on May 20, 1996. Selections from the opinions appear in The *New York Times*, May 21, 1996. The quotations in the text are taken from a complete copy of the opinion that the author obtained through the internet. That text is not paginated.

2. See Benjamin Constant, *Political Writings*, ed., tr., B. Fontana (Cambridge, UK: Cambridge University Press, 1988), pp. 306–328.

3 See especially, Gayle Rubin, "Thinking Sex" in Abelove, Biale, and Halperin, *The Lesbian/Gay Studies Reader* (NY: Routledge, 1993), pp. 3–44.

Chapter One: Theorizing Lesbian and Gay Rights

1. This chapter is a revised and expanded version of "Autonomy, Equality, and Community: The Question of Lesbian and Gay Rights" in *Praxis International*, 11:2, July 1991. Reprinted by permission of the publisher. Sections VI and VIII are completely new. Earlier versions were presented to the Society for Lesbian and Gay Philosophy at the meetings of the American Philosophical Association in New Orleans in April, 1990; the Fourth Annual Conference on Lesbian and Gay Studies at Harvard in October, 1990; the Society for Systematic Philosophy at the American Philosophical Association in Boston in December, 1990; the Columbia University Seminar on Homosexualities in March, 1991; as well as in lectures at Williams College and the Massachusetts Institute of Technology. I am grateful to all of those whose oral and written responses have helped me to clarify my arguments, including: Robert Anderson, Seyla Benhabib, Robert Berman, Judith Butler, Ron Caldwell, Claudia Card, Wayne Dynes, Frank Farrell, Ellen Haring, Michael Koessel, Peter Lipton, Richard Mohr, Hart Murphy, Michael Sherman, Rosemarie Tong, Randolph Trumbach, Richard Winfield. Special thanks to Edward Stein who first encouraged me to undertake this work and who has continued as a careful critic and generous friend. Thanks to Judith Butler, Bonnie Honig, Tamsin Lorraine, Sean O'Connell, Paul Robinson, Charles Shepardson, Ed Stein and David Stern for comments on drafts from which Section VI was taken. Section VIII was written in response to questions raised by an anonymous reader for Routledge; Ed Stein commented on an earlier draft.

2. The references to "lesbian and gay rights" throughout this paper are not intended to elide historical differences in the treatment of the two nor to settle contested political issues by rhetorical fiat. However, as I hope the text will make clear, the range of issues defined by my second and third categories of claims apply in common to both gay men and lesbians. Exclusive attention to decriminalization, a

primary concern of gay men, sometimes serves to disguise the extent to which the legal status of homosexuality has pervasive effects on both gay men and lesbians.

3. 106 S. Ct. 2841 (1986).

4. Cf., e.g., *People v. Onofre*, 51 N.Y. 2d 476 (1981).

5. See, e.g., Richard Posner, *Sex and Reason* (Cambridge: Harvard University Press, 1992); Andrew Sullivan, *Virtually Normal* (New York: Alfred A. Knopf, 1995).

6. Sullivan, *op.cit.*

7. "Developments in the Law — Sexual Orientation and the Law," 62 *Harv. L. Rev.* 617–36, Jan. '89.

8. Richard Mohr, *Gays/Justice* (NewYork: Columbia University Press, 1990), especially Chapters 5–7.

9. *Romer v. Evans* — U.S. — (1996).

10. *Baehr v. Levin* 852 P2d 44 (Hawaii 1993).

11. These issues are treated more fully in Chapter Seven below.

12. See n.3.

13. *Griswald v. Conn.* 388 U.S.479 (1965).

14. 394 U.S.557 (1969).

15. 405 U.S.438 (1972).

16. 410 U.S.113 (1973).

17. 277 U.S.438 (1928).

18. The philosophical issues posed by natural rights theories will be considered more fully in Section 5, IV and V below.

19. See especially, *The Federalist*, #84.

20. C. R. Sunstein, Sexual orientation and the Constitution: a note on the relation between due process and equal protection, 55 U. Chi. L. Rev 1161-79, Fall '88. Sunstein argues importantly that whereas the due process clause looks back upon the history and traditions of the nation, the equal protection clause addresses its universalist aspirations.

21. See Karst, The Freedom of Intimate Association, 89 Yale L. J. 624 (1980).

22. The major contributions by the initial participants who have given their names to the controversy are: Patrick Devlin, *The Enforcement of Morals* (London: Oxford University Press, 1965) and H. L. A. Hart, *Law, Liberty, and Morality* (Stanford: Stanford University Press, 1963), and "Immorality and Treason," reprinted in R. Dworkin, *The Philosophy of Law* (London: Oxford University Press, 1977). This exchange has generated an extensive literature that will not be treated here.

23. See especially, Ronald Dworkin, *Taking Rights Seriously* (Cambridge: Harvard University Press 1977) Chapter 10.

24. John Rawls's Kantian constructivism, especially as interpreted by *Political Liberalism* (New York: Columbia University Press, 1993) and Jurgen Habermas's discourse ethics both strike me as impressive and useful efforts in this direction.

25. This analysis relies in part on the conception of "law as integrity" developed in Ronald Dworkin, *Law's Empire* (Cambridge: Harvard University Press, 1986).

26. The concept of a "constitutional morality" has been developed in rich historical

and legal detail in David A. J. Richards, *The Foundations of American Constitutionalism* (New York: Oxford University Press, 1990). My argument does not rely on the specifics of Richards' account. The general notion may be found at work in diverse forms in Dworkin's works, cited above, and in Alexander Bickel, *The Morality of Consent* (New Haven: Yale University Press, 1975).

27. On the general issue, see David A. J. Richards, *Toleration and the Constitution* (New York: Oxford University Press, 1986). See also, Kirstie McClure, "Difference, Diversity, and the Limits of Toleration," 18 *Political Theory* 361, August, '90.

28. See, e.g., *Wisconsin v. Yoder,* 406 U.S. 205 (1972), in which the Court upheld the right of the Amish community to raise their children in accordance with a religious way of life which conflicted with state laws on compulsory education. Of course, such rights are not unlimited and will be balanced against conflicting interests as in the cases of religious objections to the provision of necessary medical care to children.

29. John Rawls, *A Theory of Justice* (Cambridge: Harvard University Press, 1971), "Kantian Constructivism in Moral Theory" 77 *Journal of Philosophy* 525 (1980).

30. John Rawls, *Political Liberalism* (New York: Columbia University Press, 1995).

31. John Rawls, *A Theory of Justice* (Cambridge: Harvard University Press, 1971), p. 331.

32. For a detailed argument analyzing the "due process" clause of the 14th Amendment in relation to the harm principle, see Richards, *op. cit.*, n. 27.

33. I am grateful to Cheshire Calhoun for raising this objection in response to an earlier draft of this chapter. See Cheshire Calhoun, "Sexuality Injustice," *Notre Dame Law Journal*

34. John Stuart Mill, *On Liberty* (New York: The Liberal Arts Press, 1956), p.13.

35. Ibid.

36. John Rawls, *A Theory of Justice* (Cambridge: Harvard University Press, 1971), p. 331.

37. For an extended account of this episode, see Ronald Bayer, *Homosexuality and American Psychiatry* (New York: Basic Books, 1981).

38. These issues have resonance far beyond questions about regulating homosexuality, especially in the fields of criminal justice and involuntary civil commitment. The psychoanalyst Thomas Szasz has devoted his career to producing books that argue for the continuing validity of Mill's harm principle despite the claims to scientific authority advanced by mental health professionals. The great strength of his position is his insistence that psychiatric evaluations of human behavior must be subject to the same scrutiny as any other ethical claim seeking enforcement by the state in opposition to the wishes of the individual affected. See, e.g., *The Myth of Mental Illness* (New York: Harper, 1961), *Law, Liberty, and Psychiatry* (New York: MacMillan, 1963).

39. See Henry Abelove "Freud, Male Homosexuality, and the Americans," in Abelove, Barale, and Halperin, eds., *The Lesbian/Gay Studies Reader* (New York: Routledge, 199) pp. 416–431; Kenneth Lewes, *The Psychoanalytic Theory of Male Homosexuality* (New York: New American Library, 1988).

40. See Chapter Two, section V below.

41. Daniel Ortiz, "Creating Controversy: Essentialism and Constructionism and the Politics of Gay Identity" *Virginia Law Review*, vol. 79 no. 7 (Oct. 1993), 1833–1858; Cheshire Calhoun, "Denaturalizing and Desexualizing Lesbian and Gay Identity." *Ibid*, 1859–1875.

42. Ibid.

43. See Ortiz, *op. cit.*

44. Jonathan Goldberg, *Sodometries: Renaissance Texts, Modern Sexuality* (Stanford: Standord University Press 1992), pp. 6–18.

45. See also Janet Halley, "Reasoning About Sodomy" *Virginia Law Review*, vol. 79 (Oct. 1993), pp. 1721–1780.

46. *Ibid.*

47. *Griswold v. Connecticut, Roe v. Wade.* This and related points are developed much more fully in Chapter Seven below.

48. This argument is fully developed in Chapter Seven below.

49. See, e.g., A. MacIntyre, *After Virtue: A Study in Moral Theory* (London: Duckworth, 1981); C. Taylor, *Hegel and Modern Society* (Cambridge: Cambridge University Press, 1979); M. Sandel, *Liberalism and the Limits of Justice* (Cambridge: Cambridge University Press, 1982). This debate has generated a rich and interesting literature. For an assessment, see Amy Gutmann, "Communitarian Critics of Liberalism" 14 *Philosophy and Public Affairs* 319 (1985).

50. Except for Sandel, discussed in Chapter Seven below, section IV, n. 57.

51. Patricia Cain has demonstrated the extent to which early gay rights litigation in the 1950's emphasized the associational rights of lesbian and gay citizens. Patricia Cain, "Litigating for Lesbian and Gay Rights" *Virginia Law Review*, vol. 79, no. 7 (Oct. 1993), pp. 1551–1642.

52. See especially, S. Benhabib, "The Generalized and Concrete Other" in Benhabib and Cornell, *Feminism as Critique* (Minneapolis: University of Minnesota Press, 1987). See also, S. M. Okin, "Reason and Feeling in Thinking About Justice," 99 *Ethics* 229, Jan. '89.

53. Mark Blasius, *Gay and Lesbian Politics* (Philadelphia: Temple University Press, 1994), especially chapters three and four; Shane Phelan, *Getting Specific* (Minneapolis: University of Minnesota Press, 1995).

54. Andrew Sullivan, *Virtually Normal* (New York: Alfred A. Knopf, 1995).

55. *Ibid.*, p. 143.

56. *Loc. cit.*

57. *Ibid.*, pp. 160–61.

58. Posner, *op.cit.*, n. 5, p. 323.

59. This and the preceding quotation are from Sullivan, *op. cit.*, p. 143.

Chapter Two: Historicizing Sexuality

1. I am especially grateful to Tom Schmid and Ellen Haring who provided detailed and timely responses to a draft of this entire chapter. An earlier version of sections I

and IV appeared as "Constructing Lesbian and Gay Rights and Liberation," *Virginia Law Review*, vol. 79, no. 7, October 1993, pp. 1877–1902. Reprinted by permission of the publisher. Thanks to Daniel R. Ortiz and Cheshire Calhoun, whose essays in that issue provided the occasion for my own reflections, and who responded to earlier drafts. Thanks to the following who provided comments on material now in section V: Judith Butler, Bonnie Honig, Tamsin Lorraine, Sharon Meagher, Sean O'Connell, Paul Robinson, Charles Shepardson, and David Stern. An early version was presented at the course "Rethinking Subjectivity: Identity and the Self" in Prague in May 1993. Thanks to Jean Cohen, Jodi Dean, Frank Michelman, and Linda Nicholson for their responses.

2. Quoted in Jeff Nunokawa, *Oscar Wilde* (New York: Chelsea House Publishers, 1995), p. 106.

3. Michel Foucault, *The History of Sexuality: Volume I: An Introduction*, trans. Robert Hurley (New York: Random House, 1978), p. 43.

4. Michel Foucault, *ibid.*, *The Use of Pleasure* tr., Robert Hurley (New York: Pantheon, 1985), *Discipline and Punish* tr., Alan Sheridan (New York: Vintage, 1977).

5. See among others, Mark Blasius, *Gay and Lesbian Politics* (Philadelphia: Temple University Press, 1994), David Halperin, *Saint Foucault* (New York: Oxford University Press, 1995), Shane Phelan *Getting Specific* (Minneapolis: University of Minnesota Press, 1995), Leo Bersani *Homos* (Cambridge: Harvard University Press, 1995), Jana Sawicki, *Disciplining Foucault* (New York: Routledge, 1991).

6. K. J. Dover, *Greek Homosexuality* (New York: Vintage Books, 1980).

7. Perhaps the best defense of a recognizable "homosexual type" among the ancient Greeks is John Boswell, "Revolutions, Universals, and Sexual Categories," in Duberman, Vicinus, and Chauncey, *Hidden from History: Reclaiming the Gay and Lesbian Past* (New York: Meridian, 1990). However, Boswell relies heavily on Aristophanes' speech in Plato's *Symposium*. Even if we abstract from the difficulties of taking the speech as evidence of contemporary attitudes, the myth that Aristophanes propounds would support the notion of *three* kinds of sexual orientation: heterosexual, male homosexual, and lesbian. See the detailed discussion, Chapter Two, section IV.

8. Metaphorically at least. The reference is not to physical position, but to *being* a top — a phallic penetrator rather than recipient.

9. David Halperin, "Sex Before Sexuality" in Abelove, Barale, and Halperin, eds., *The Lesbian/Gay Studies Reader,* (New York: Routledge, 1993), pp. 416–431; *One Hundred Years of Homosexuality* (New York: Routledge, 1990).

10. For a detailed discussion of ancient Athenian laws and customs in these matters, including some provocative comparisons with contemporary "Mediterranean" cultures, see David Cohen, *Law, Sexuality and Society: The Enforcement of Morals in Ancient Athens*, (Cambridge: Cambridge University Press, 1992).

11. Gayle Rubin, "The Traffic in Women" in Reiter, ed., *Toward an Anthropology of Women* (New York: Monthly Review Press, 1995), pp. 157–210.

12. Aristotle, *Nicomachean Ethics*, X.

13. Numbers in parentheses refer to the standard Stephanus pagination of Plato's

works. The translation quoted is that of Donald Watt in Trevor J. Saunders, *Early Socratic Dialogues* (New York: Penguin, 1987).

14. See especially, John J. Winkler, "Laying Down the Law," in *Constraints of Desire* (New York: Routledge, 1992), pp. 45–70.

15. Cohen, *op. cit.*

16. Freud comments in the concluding summary of *Three Essays* that the prevalence of male slaves in the upbringing of Athenian boys may have contributed to the incidence of homosexuality in the culture. (96)

17. See Plato, *Lysis* for a dramatic representation of Socrates' visit to a boys' lyceum on a festival day when it was opened to adults. Note also the role of the slaves at the conclusion.

18. For an excellent discussion of these issues, see David Halperin, "The Democratic Body: Prostitution and Citizenship in Ancient Athens," in *One Hundred Years of Homosexuality* (New York: Routledge, 1990).

19. Dover, *op. cit.*

20. Plato, *Symposium*, 182a–185c.

21. Dover, *op.cit.*

22. See especially, David Halperin, "Sex Before Sexuality: Pederasty, Politics, and Power in Classical Athens," in *Hidden from History*, n. 7.

23. *Ibid.*

24. J. G. A. Pocock, *The Machiavellian Moment* (Princeton: Princeton University Press, 1975).

25. Two interesting books have addressed the general question of the appropriation of the ancient Greeks in late nineteenth-century Great Britain. Richard Jenkyns, *The Victorians and Ancient Greece* (Cambridge: Harvard University Press, 1980); Frank M. Turner, *The Greek Heritage in Victorian Britain* (New Haven: Yale University Press, 1981). It is hard to overlook similarities between the situation of Athenian citizens and that of the Victorian gentlemen who reconstructed their lives as a source of emulation and legitimation; this resemblance extends to sexual as well as other political matters.

26. Linda Dowling, *Hellenism and Homosexuality in Victorian Oxford* (Ithaca: Cornell University Press, 1994).

27. Jeffrey Weeks, *Coming Out* (London: Quartet Books Ltd., 1977), ch. 4; Dowling, *op. cit.*

28. Benjamin Jowett, ed., *The Dialogues of Plato: vol. I* (Oxford: Clarendon Press, 1st ed., 1871), p. 486.

29. *Ibid.*, pp. 486–87.

30. John Addington Symonds, *Studies of the Greek Poets* (New York: Harper and Brothers, 1882), vol. I, p. 173.

31. Symonds, *op. cit.*, vol. II, p. 364.

32. *Ibid.*, p. 373.

33. Benjamin Jowett, *Collected Dialogues of Plato* (New York: Macmillan and Co., 3rd ed., 1892), vol. I, p. 534.

34. *Ibid.*, p. 535: the next quote, p. 408.

35. The definitive and detailed biography is Richard Ellmann, *Oscar Wilde* (New York: Vintage Books, 1987). A brief introduction, interesting although aimed at younger readers, is Jeff Nunokawa, *Oscar Wilde* (New York: Chelsea House Publishers, 1995) in the series "Lives of Notable Gay Men and Lesbians," edited by Martin Duberman.

36. E. M. Forster, *Maurice* (Toronto: The MacMillan Company of Canada Ltd., 1971) pp. 42–43.

37. *Ibid*, p. 50.

38. Alan Sinfield, *The Wilde Century* (New York: Columbia University Press, 1994).

39. I am grateful to Erin Carlson whose Jing Lyman Lecture at Stanford in the spring, 1994 first called my attention to this material.

40. Harry Oosterhuis and Hubert Kennedy, *Homosexuality and Male Bonding in Pre-Nazi Germany* (Binghamton, New York: Harrington Park Press, 1991),pp. 1–28; Barry D. Adam, *The Rise of a Gay and Lesbian Movement, Revised Edition* (New York: Twayne Publishers, 1995), 19–28, 53–59.

41. Eve Kosofsky Sedgwick, *Epistemology of the Closet* (Berkeley: University of California Press, 1990), especially ch. 1.

42. Recent work in feminist theory contest the validity of this distinction, arguing that "sex" is as much a social construction as gender. See Judith Butler, *Gender Trouble* (New York: Routledge, 1989).

43. Edward D. Stein, ed., *Forms of Desire: The Social Constructionist Controversy About Sexual orientation* (NY: Routledge, 1992) for a collection of material from this debate. For the argument in the text, see especially Stein's concluding essay, "The Essentials of Constructionism and the Construction of Essentialism." pp. 325–353.

44. See Hans G. Gadamer, *Truth and Method*, 2nd ed., tr. Joel Weinheimer and Donald Marshall (New York: Continuum Publishers, 1988); David Couzers Hoy, *The Critical Circle* (Berkeley; University of California Press, 1982).

45. Daniel R. Ortiz, "Creating Controversy: Essentialism and Constructivism and the Politics of Gay Identity," 79 Va. L. Rev. 1833, 1834–35 (1993).

46. Shane Phelan, *Getting Specific: Post-Modern Lesbian Politics* (Minneapolis: University of Minnesota Press, 1995). See also Judith Butler, *Bodies That Matter* (New York: Routledge, 1993); Diana Fuss, *Identification Papers* (New York: Routledge, 1995).

47. Audre Lorde, *Zami* (Freedom, CA: Crossing Press, 1982); Cherrie Moraga and Gloria Anzaluda, *This Bridge called My Back* (Watertown, MA: Persephone, 1981); essays by Tomas Almaquer, Philip Brian Harper, and Kolcra Mercer in Abelove, Barole, and Halperin, *The Lesbian and Gay Studies Reader* (New York: Routledge, 1993).

48. M. Duberman, G. Chauncey, M. Vicinus, eds. *Hidden from History* (New York: New American Library, 1988), pp. 129–149, 294–317.

49. Lillian Fadlemen, *Surpassing the Love of Men* (New York: Wm. Morrow, 1981), Carrol Smith-Dosenberg, *Disorderly Conduct* (New York: Oxford University Press, 1985), Martha Vicinus, *Independent Women* (Chicago: University of Chicago Press, 1985).

50. Shane Phelan treats the medicalization of lesbianism at some length in *Identity*

Politics (Philadelphia: Temple University Press, 1989), ch. 2.

   51. Foucault, *History*, vol. one, p. 101.

   52. One recent effort to do so in the context of political theory is Mark Blasius, *Gay and Lesbian Politics* (Philadelphia: Temple University Press, 1994).

   53. See Michel Foucault, *Discipline and Punish, The History of Sexuality. Volume One. An Introduction.*

   54. (Chicago, University of Chicago Press, 1983).

   55. *Ibid.*

   56. See Nicholas D. Kittrie, *The Right to Be Different* (Baltimore: The Johns Hopkins Press, 1971); Thomas Szasz, *Psychiatric Justice* (New York: Macmillan, 1965); Michael Foucault, *Discipline and Punish* (New York: Pantheon, 1977); David J. Rothman, *Conscience and Convenience* (Boston: Little, Brown, 1980).

   57. Bayer, *Homosexuality and American Psychiatry* (New York: Basic Books, 1981).

   58. Martin Duberman, *Cures* (New York: Penguin, 1991).

   59. For a full account, see Bayer, *op.cit.*

   60. Abelove, *op. cit.* in Abelove, Barale and Halperin, n. 9.

   61. Lewes, *The Psychoanalytic Theory of Male Homosexuality* (New York: New American Library, 1988), pp. 31–33.

   62. *Ibid.* pp. 32–34.

   63. 107 (1951):786.

   64. In Sigmund Freud, *Sexuality and the Psychology of Love* (New York: Macmillan Publishing Co., 1963), pp. 133–159, p. 137.

   65. After defining the aims of psychoanalysis in the language quoted above, Freud ends his letter on a curious note: he urges that in the unlikely event his correspondent decides to seek psychoanalytic treatment for her son on the terms proposed, she should bring him to Vienna to be treated by Freud himself. Henry Abelove has argued convincingly that this insistence, by a Freud with no dearth of patients, reveals his awareness that analytic practice in the United States had already departed from the understanding of homosexuality outlined in his letter. Cf. Abelove, *op. cit.*

   66. Lewes, *op. cit.*, p. 33.

   67. Foucault, *History, vol. one*, p. 129.

   68. *Ibid.*, p. 130.

   69. *The Uses of Pleasure* (New York: Random House 1985); *The Care of the Self* (New York: Random House, 1986).

Chapter Three: Eros Unbound

   1. I owe very special thanks to my friends Plato scholars Ellen Haring and Tom Schmid who took the time to provide me with detailed, timely and extremely helpful comments on an earlier draft of this chapter. My own romance with philosophy began with the study of Plato under Laszlo Versenyi during my freshman year of college. I was also privileged to study Plato with Nathaniel Lawrence at Williams and Robert Brumbaugh at Yale. The *Symposium* was an important text for all of them; I am sad-

dened that none of these teachers is alive to tell me what he thinks of what I've made of it here. Struggling over Plato has been a theme in some of my most important intellectual friendships. This reading is informed by conversations, in some cases beginning over thirty-five years ago, with Bob Anderson, Harry Berger, Ken Dove, Ellen Haring, Bruce Payne, Stanley Rosen, Tom Schmid, and Bill Torbert. The *Symposium* has come to figure importantly in my teaching as well. I am grateful to several generations of students at Purchase College who have engaged this text with intelligence and enthusiasm in my Plato seminar and in courses in Lesbian and Gay Studies. Two students, Kevin Monahan and Shelley Arneri, wrote senior essays focusing in part on that text. I was encouraged to include a chapter on the *Symposium* in this book by the example of Dante Germino who offered a paper on Plato as "A New Paradigm for Gay Identity?" at the American Political Science Association meetings in Washington, DC in September, 1993. I began this chapter in composing my response to his paper; George Kateb's comments as a fellow respondent also contributed to my reflections.

I have not addressed the secondary literature on Plato here. However, a few works have been important for my interpretation, even where I disagree on details. Stanley Rosen's early essay, "The Role of Eros in Plato's *Republic*" has influenced me since it first appeared in the 1960s. It is included in *The Quarrel Between Philosophy and Poetry* (New York: Routledge, 1993) pp. 102–118. His full-length study, *Plato's Symposium*, 2nd edition (New Haven: Yale University Press, 1987) is a fascinating and important work, much as I may quarrel with the general tendency of his argument. Rosen is a wonderful reader of Plato's drama, and he insists that questions about pederasty are central to the work's themes, both to defining philosophy as a way of life and to such distinctions as those between physis and nomos, praxis and poesis. David Halperin, a classicist who is also a major figure in lesbian and gay studies, has contributed some invaluable work, especially "Why Is Diotima a Woman?" in *One Hundred Years of Homosexuality* (New York: Routledge, 1990), pp. 113–151. Also of interest is Jerome Neu, "Plato's Homoerotic *Symposium*," in R. C. Solomon and K. M. Higgins, eds., *The Philosophy of (Erotic) Love* (Lawrence: The University Press of Kansas, 1991), pp. 317–335. Martha Nussbaum offers a provocative reading in "The speech of Alcibiades: A reading of the Symposium," in *The fragility of goodness: luck and ethics in Greek tragedy and philosophy* (Cambridge: Cambridge University Press, 1986) pp. 165–199.

2. The others have asked Apollodorus to recount the tale, of which they had recently heard a garbled version from one Phoenix. They mistakenly believe that the celebration was a recent event that Apollodorus himself had attended.

3. Named in the text as Glaucon, who may or may not be the brother of Plato who plays a major role in the conversation with Socrates we know as Plato's *Republic*. (173a)

4. Apollodorus appears in Plato's *Phaedo* as one of those friends in Socrates' cell on the day that he ended his life by drinking hemlock (in accordance with the sentence of the Athenian court). The intensity and character of his attachment to Socrates is exemplified there by his bursting into tears, for which Socrates chastises him, tellingly, for "acting like a woman." (59a, 117d) Plato, *Phaedo*, trans. Hugh Tredennicle, in E. Hamilton and H. Cairns, ed., *Collected Dialogues of Plato* (Princeton: Princeton Univer-

sity Press, 1961).

5. More accurately, *daimon*, according to Socrates' teacher Diotima (202e).

6. See especially sections VII–XI below.

7. Throughout this chapter, Eros is capitalized to indicate the allegorical figure of the god or daimon. In lower case, it refers to the phenomena of human love or desire. Although there is a rich literature contrasting Greek conceptions of eros with later conceptions of love in the Christian and romantic traditions, "eros," "love," and "desire" will be used interchangeably. Discovering the multiple meanings of "eros" within the text is a large part of the task of interpreting Plato's *Symposium*. As for the comparative question, see Martin D'Arcy, *The Mind and Heart of Love* (New York: Meridian, 1950) esp. ch. II.

8. All of these figures except Aristophanes, but including Alcibiades, also appear in Plato's *Protagoras*, where the two couples are also identified as such. Socrates, who narrates the dialogue, describes himself as the *erastes* of Alcibiades, but claims that he found Protagoras the elderly wise man more beautiful on that occasion than his young *eromenos*. In his book-length study, *Plato's Symposium*, 2nd edition (New Haven: Yale University Press, 1987), Stanley Rosen argues that the linking of each symposiast with a specific sophist as his teacher in *Protagoras* has implications for understanding their speeches in *Symposium*.

9. Where it is relevant to distinguish the parties to a pederastic relation, I will do so by using "beloved" for *eromenos* and "lover" for *erastes*. "Lover" may be used to refer to both where the distinction is not implicated in the context.

10. See section X below.

11. He quotes Hesiod, Acousileos, and Parmenides.

12. It is hard to read Phaedrus's speech in the light of recent public controversy about permitting lesbian and gay citizens to serve openly in the military without a strong sense of historical irony.

13. But not to all. See the discussion of *Der Eigene* in Chapter Two, section III above. Also for contemporary echoes, Richard Mohr, *Gay Ideas* (Boston: Beacon Press, 1993), chapter 6.

14. Numbers in parentheses indicate the standardized Stephanus pagination for Plato. All quotations from *Symposium* are taken from A. Nehamas and P. Woodruff, trans., Plato, *Symposium* (Indianapolis: Hackett, 1989).

15. There are ironies of Plato's own in the text. Phaedrus goes on to explain the extraordinary heroism of his lovers this way: "For a man in love would never allow his loved one, of all people, to see him leaving ranks or dropping weapons. He'd rather die a thousand deaths!" (179a) For Phaedrus, the courage inspired by eros is primarily a fear of shame and concern for one's appearance, rather than an intrinsic virtue. Such an approach, however plausible, is at some remove from Socrates' arguments in *Laches* or *Republic*.

16. Recall Ulrichs' "Urnings" and the homoerotic "Uranian poetry" produced by Oxford undergraduates late in the nineteenth century, discussed in Chapter Two.

17. And as the source of the "unwritten laws" to which Antigone appeals in defy-

ing Creon's edict in Sophocles' play.

18. "Contrast this with the love of the Heavenly Aphrodite. This goddess, whose descent is purely male (hence this love is for boys), is considerably older and therefore free from the lewdness of youth. That's why those who are inspired by her love are attracted by the male: they find pleasure in what is by nature stronger and more intelligent." (181c)

19. See John Winkler, "The Ephebes' Song" in Winkler and Zeittin, eds, *Nothing to Do With Dionysus* (Princeton: Princeton University Press, 1989).

20. See Halperin, "Sex Before Sexuality," for a discussion of the conventional linkage between male desire for women and sexual excess. Duberman, Vicinus, and Chauncey, *Hidden From History* (New York: Meridian, 1990), pp. 37–53.

21. One should be reminded here that although the laws of Athens did not penalize prostitution and its customs did not frown upon its patronage, it was a capital offense for a man who had been a prostitute in his youth to exercise the rights of citizenship. See David Halperin, "The Democratic Body: Prostitution and Citizenship in Ancient Athens," in *One Hundred Years of Homosexuality* (New York: Routledge, 1990), pp. 88–112.

22. Compare the speeches in praise of the non-lover in *Phaedrus*, 231a–241d.

23. The reference here is to *techne*, a Greek term encompassing a ranges of skills applied to the conduct of human life. It is hard to find a single word in English that captures the field of application, which included medicine, sculpture, various crafts, and professions, including both what later came to be called "fine and applied arts."

24. ". . . the love felt by good people or by those whom love might improve in this regard must be encouraged and protected. This is the honorable, heavenly species of Love, produced by Urania, the Heavenly Muse. The other, produced by Polyhymnia, the muse of many songs, is common and vulgar. Extreme caution is indicated here: we must be careful to enjoy his pleasures without slipping into debauchery — this case, I might add, is strictly parallel to a serious issue in my own field, namely, the problem of regulating the appetite so as to be able to enjoy a fine meal without unhealthy after effects." (187e)

25. "For what is the origin of all impiety? Our refusal to gratify the orderly kind of Love and our deference to the other sort, when we should have been guided by the former sort of Love in every action in connection with our parents, living or dead, and with the gods." (188c)

26. In a more political context, it must be noted that Eryximachus' vulgar love is devoted to the muse Polyhymnia, identified by Socrates in Plato's *Republic* with the regime of democracy. Once again, we cannot be sure to what extent Eryximachus, Phaedrus, and Pausanias are in fact at odds with contemporary Athens.

27. Freud's editor took his reference to a "poetic fable" in the opening paragraph of the *Three Essays* to indicate Aristophanes' speech in Plato's *Symposium*. Later scholars have suggested an Indian myth as the source that Freud has in mind for this "popular view." However, Freud explicitly addresses Aristophanes' speech from the *Symposium* in *Beyond the Pleasure Principle*. (1920). Given the acknowledgment of the

"divine Plato" in the preface to the third edition of *Three Essays* (also 1920), some "anxiety of influence" may be at work here. Sigmund Freud, *Three Essays*, p. 2; *Beyond the Pleasure Principle*, (New York: W.W. Norton & Co., 1989), pp. 69–70.

28. Sigmund Freud, *Three Essays on the Theory of Sexuality* ed., trans., J. Strachey, (New York: Basic Books, 1975), p. 2.

29. Aristophanes evokes and gives his own twist to Pausanias' revisions of the conflict between Uranian and Olympian orders: the hybris of our ancestors is linked to the efforts of the Titans to *recover* power from an upstart Zeus, although these well-worn tales are not mentioned.

30. Perhaps surprisingly, the comic poet's vision anticipates the love-death of a later tradition of courtly and romantic love. The beloved becomes the locus of all value and meaning in life; the lover seeks complete obliteration in union with the other.

31. Despite the presence of two couples comprised of adults at Agathon's banquet, such pairings were the exception rather than the rule for Greek pederasty. Officially if lover and beloved remained close after the beloved youth had crossed into adulthood, the relationship changed: the two became "friends." The beloved youth was expected to grow up to pursue younger men of his own, rather than remaining with the man who loved him when he was young. Of course, one can only speculate as to the actual relations men maintained.

32. Since Aristophanes' tale figures the object of desire as return to the unity of a primordial body from which one has been forcibly separated, it invites further comparison with psychoanalytic accounts of birth trauma, separation anxiety, and the longing to return to the womb.

33. Agathon's disagreement with Phaedrus is quite explicit: "And though on many other points I agree with Phaedrus, I do not agree with this: that Love is older than Kronos and Iapetos. No, I say that he is the youngest of the gods and stays young forever." (195c).

34. In Chapter Four, section V, I will consider Freud's discussion of the object of desire among Athenian pederasts. He could have Plato's portrait of Agathon in mind when he writes "It is clear that in Greece, where the most masculine men were numbered among the inverts, what excited a man's love was not the *masculine* character of a boy, but his physical resemblance to a woman as well as his feminine mental qualities, his shyness, his modesty, and his need for instruction and assistance." (*Three Essays*, p. 10.)

35. The reader of Plato will recall the Socratic dictum that it is always better to suffer than to commit an unjust act, and the ways in which Socrates' life demonstrated that one might well be faced with such a choice.

36. The ellipsis reads "so say 'the laws that are kings of society.'" (196c) This invocation of *nomoi* reminds us of Agathon's association with Pausanias and their common instruction by the Sophist Prodicus. Plato, *Protagoras* 315d–e.

37. In Plato's *Gorgias*, Socrates' questioning of the Sophist leads to an encounter between Socrates and Gorgias's students Polus and Callicles in which the Sophists' students explicitly defend the life of the tyrant against that represented by the So-

cratic principle that it is better to suffer than commit injustice.

38. See "Medusa's Head" in Sigmund Freud, *Sexuality and the Psychology of Love* (New York: Collier-Macmillan, 1963), pp. 212–13.

39. The portrayal of Socrates in ambiguous sexual/gendered terms appears elsewhere in Plato with no explicit reference to eros, as in the analogy with the midwife in *Theaetetus*.

40. Including an ability to recognize lovers when he sees them. Plato, *Lysis* (204c, 206a).

41. Some of these details recall aspects of Socrates mentioned by Aristodemus in telling of their arrival Agathon's banquet. Although shod for the evening, it was his practice to go barefoot; before arriving at the party, he stood abstracted under the sky. Readers of other Platonic dialogues will also recognize Socrates as "a lover of wisdom," and perhaps even "weaving snares," or dispensing "enchantments, potions, and clever pleadings." Among many others, see Plato, *Apology of Socrates*, *Charmides*, *Sophist*. When Alcibiades later draws an intimate portrait of his lover, the resemblances between Socrates and Eros become even stronger, but differences emerge as well. Diotima explicitly identifies eros with philosophy.

42. Reframing Socrates' question ". . . what use is love to human beings?" (202e), as, "What is the real purpose of Love?" Diotima declares, "It is giving birth in beauty, whether in body or in soul."

43. She points out that it sometimes happens that words may have both a general and particular use; where the generalized meaning is very broad, the term comes to be used in its more limited sense. Thus, all humans love, in the sense of seeking happiness, and many men are poets, in the sense of makers, creators: love comes to refer to a limited class of animating desires, and poetry to the kind of creativity practiced by a special group.

44. Socrates does not disguise the direction of her address, but rather emphasizes the difference between the position he attributes to her and that taken earlier in the dialogue by the comic playwright:

> "Now there is a certain story," she said, "according to which lovers are those who seek their other halves. But according to my story, a lover does not seek the half or the whole, unless, my friend, it turns out to be good as well. . . . I don't think an individual takes joy in what belongs to him personally unless by 'belonging to me' he means 'good' and by 'belonging to another' he means 'bad.' That's because what everyone loves in nothing other than the good. (205e)

45. This notion recalls the asymmetries of Freud's account of sexual difference: men seek to replace their mothers with a beloved wife; women console themselves for the "fact of their castration" with the boy child a husband may give them. See Sigmund Freud, "Female Sexuality," in *Sexuality and the Psychology of Love* (New York: Collier-Macmillan, 1963), pp. 194–211.

46. Plato's text includes a remark here that should lead the careful reader to follow

with caution. In reporting Diotima's identification of the search for immortality through offspring with the love of honor, Socrates comments that she offered those words "in the manner of a perfect Sophist." (208c) The argument that follows must be examined with some care, since Socrates is not often shown willing to receive instruction from "a perfect Sophist," although he does praise the beauty and defer to the wisdom of Protagoras in a dialogue which is referred to throughout the *Symposium*.

47. Diotima specifically mentions the actions of Alcestis and Achilles discussed by Phaedrus. She argues that they were not so much sacrifices on behalf of the beloved but as efforts to win immortality for themselves through their fame in future generations.

48. For a much more detailed examination of these issues, see David Halperin, "Why Is Diotima a Woman?" in *One Hundred Years of Homosexuality* (New York: Routledge, 1990), pp. 113–151.

49. Aristophanes invoked the net of Hephaestus to suggest that the culmination of our longing would be to share life with another to whom we remain united even in death. This refinding of a primordial wholeness is presented as a goal that the gods may grant us as a reward for proper piety. We are incapable of achieving it for ourselves. Aristophanes does not comment upon the fact that when we were once whole — rather than being satisfied, we took it upon ourselves to challenge the gods themselves. One might wonder why the gods should ever be disposed to test us again.

50. Scholars have taken this clue to imply some distinction between the views of Socrates and those of Plato in regard to this matter. The deepest teachings of Socrates' fictional teacher may be the discoveries of his historical pupil Plato. The question as to what was taught by the historical Socrates, what invented by Plato in his writings, is a notoriously difficult one and beyond the scope of this chapter.

51. "This is what it is to go aright, or be led by another into the mystery of Love: one goes always upwards for the sake of this Beauty, starting out from beautiful things and using them like rising stairs: from one body to two and from two to all beautiful bodies, then from beautiful bodies to beautiful customs, and from customs to learning beautiful things, and from these lessons he arrives in the end at this lesson, which is learning of this very Beauty, so that in the end he comes to know just what it is to be beautiful." (211d)

52. ". . . or in anything else, but itself by itself with itself, it is always one in form; and all the other beautiful things share in that, in such a way that when these other things come to be or pass away, this does not become the least bit smaller or greater nor suffer any change." (211b)

53. This is not the only place in Plato's texts where Socrates describes himself as the lover of Alcibiades; there are quite matter of fact references to their connection in *Gorgias* and *Protagoras*. Both Plato's readers and the characters in the dialogue would be expected to recognize the tie between them.

54. The rhetorical ploy of contrasting one's own unpolished reliance on telling the truth with one's adversary superior command of rhetorical skill is a favorite of Socrates himself. Plato, *Apology of Socrates* (198d, 199b).

55. This emphasis reminds the reader of the ambiguous status of appearance in Diotima's teaching. At first, she appeared to insist on the integral connection between eros and the beauty of its object. By the time she has turned to the higher mysteries, however, any image at all had come to seem inappropriate to a correctly guided erotic development. Not a beautiful image, but the underlying form of beauty itself, was the ultimate end of erotic striving. Alcibiades' insistence that he can speak of Socrates only through images marks his distance from the Beautiful itself.

56. Beneath the Dionysian imagery and the waves of self-flagellation, we recognize the Socrates who made a mission of questioning his fellow citizens and urging them to care for their souls. In Plato's *Apology of Socrates*, the philosopher on trial for impiety and corrupting the youth invites his jurors to ask the young men who had surrounded him what impact he had on the lives they led. Alcibiades here provides just such testimony. But it is ambiguous at best. Alcibiades credits Socratic speech with more power than that of Pericles, the greatest orator of democratic Athens. However, Socrates does not aim at political effects.

57. "Socrates is the only man in the world who has made me feel shame — ah, you didn't think I had it in me , did you? . . . I know perfectly well that I can't prove he's wrong when he tells me what I should do; yet, the moment I leave his side, I go back to my old ways: I cave in to my desire to please the crowd. My whole life has become one constant effort to escape from him and keep away, but when I see him, I feel deeply ashamed, because I am doing nothing about my way of life, although I have already agreed with him that I should." (216b–c)

58. See especially Books VIII and IX.

59. Plato scholar Robert Brumbaugh describes some actual objects that correspond to Alcibiades' image in *Ancient Greek Gadgets and Machines*.

60. This contrast illuminates the specific character of Plato's text however one resolves the disputed scholarly question which was written earlier. The author of the later text was clearly aware of the existence of the other. Thus, either Plato deliberately shifted the focus, or Xenophon set out to distinguish himself from Plato's work. Cf. K. J. Dover, "The Date of Plato's Symposium," *Phronesis*, X (1965), 2–20.

61. Xenophon, *Conversations of Socrates*, trans. H. Tredennick (New York: Penguin Books, 1990), p. 266.

62. Similarly, the other great dialogue devoted to eros, *Phaedrus*, is set outside the walls of the city in the countryside. There, too, city life intrudes in the form of the manuscript of a speech by the Sophist Lysias that Phaedrus carries with him and recites to Socrates.

Chapter Four: Psychoanalyzing the "Third Sex"

1. I am greatly indebted to Judith Butler, Bonnie Honig, Tamsin Lorraine, Sharon Meagher, Paul Robinson, Sean O'Connell, Charles Shepardson, and David Stern for comments on earlier drafts of this chapter. I have lectured on this material in the Jing Lyman Lecture Series at Stanford University, at Willamette University, the Cultural

Studies Series at U.C. Santa Cruz, the Philosophy Department Colloquium at Williams College, and the Humanities Colloquium at Purchase College SUNY. I am grateful to all who engaged me on those very lively occasions, especially Tom Kohut, Jerome Neu, and Chris Pye. Numbers in parentheses refer to Sigmund Freud, *Three Essays on the Theory of Sexuality* (New York: Basic Books, 1975).

2. Especially sections II, III, and V.

3. Michel Foucault, *The History of Sexuality: An Introduction, Volume One*, trans. R. Hurley (New York: Vintage, 1978), p. 43.

4. *Ibid.*

5. Michel Foucault, from whose work much of the attention to the construction of homosexuality in the nineteenth century derives, emphasized the extent to which the new discourse was accompanied by a "counter-discourse." *op. cit.*, p. 101.

6. See especially section IV.

7. See George Chauncey, "From Sexual Inversion to Homosexuality" in Kathy Peiss and Chistina Simmons, ed., *Passion and Power: Sexuality in History* (Philadelphia: Temple University Press, 1989), pp. 87–117.

8. See Jerome Neu, "Sexual Perversion" in Neu, ed., *Oxford Companion to Freud* (Oxford: Oxford UP, 1993). Also see, Davidson, n. 12 below.

9. Later Freud will distinguish perversion from neurosis, defining it as the "negative of neurosis."

10. Throughout this discussion, Freud acknowledges his reliance on data and some arguments from Havelock Ellis.

11. See Chapter Two, section V.

12. Arnold Davidson, "How to Write the History of Psychoanalysis: Freud's *Three Essays*," in J. Meltzer, ed., *Trial(s) of Psychoanalysis*, (Chicago: University of Chicago Press, 1989)

13. See Chapter Two, sections II–III.

14. See Chapter Two, section IV.

15. *E.g., Totem and Taboo, Civilization and Its Discontents.*

16. See Chapter Two, section V.

17. "Conclusion: The Essentials of Constructionism and the Construction of Essentialism," in Edward Stein, ed., *Forms of Desire* (New York: Routledge, 1992) pp. 325–383. For more detailed discussion, see Chapter Two, section IV.

18. Michel Foucault, *op. cit.*, p. 119.

19. See Chapter Two, section V.

20. Foucault, *loc.cit.* See also Sander Gilman, *Freud, Race and Gender* (Princeton: Princeton University Press, 1993).

21. It is an interesting and important question how far we may be able to conceive, much less imagine, a notion of sex or gender that does not eventually reveal itself to be dependent on some form of the binary opposition between male and female, masculine and feminine, which is inscribed in our culture. Differences with regard to this possibility inform the attempt to delineate relations between the "symbolic" and the "imaginary" in contemporary engagements between feminism and Lacanian psycho-

analytic theory. In another domain, Octavia Butler's sustained effort to envision alternative arrangements of sex and gender in her xenogenesis trilogy is worth some study. See section V of this chapter.

22. Numbers in parentheses in the balance of this section refer to page numbers in Sigmund Freud, *Sexuality and the Psychology of Love*, ed., Philip Rieff (New York: Collier Boods, Macmillan Publishing Company, 1963).

23. Among others, see Mandy Merck, "The train of thought in Freud's 'Case of Homosexuality in a Woman,'" *Perversions* (New York: Routledge, 1993), pp. 13–32; Diana Fuss, "Freud's Fallen Women: Identification, Desire, and 'Case of Homosexuality in a Woman,'" in Michael Warner, ed., *Fear of a Queer Planet: Queer Politics and Social Theory* (Minneapolis: The University of Minnesota Press, 1993), pp. 42–68 and in *Identity Papers* (New York: Routledge, 1995).

24. Otto Weininger, *Sex and Character*, English trans., (New York: G. P. Putnam's Sons, no date).

25. Jeffrey Masson, ed. and trans., *The Complete Letters of Sigmund Freud to Wilhelm Fliess 1887–1904* (Cambridge: Harvard University Press, 1985), p. 464.

26. *Ibid.*, p. 465 (July 26, 1904).

27. *Op. cit.*, p. 466 (July 27, 1904).

28. An earlier anticipation of this view appears in a letter to Fliess where Freud does not flinch from acknowledging its more radical consequences: "What would you say if masturbation were to reduce itself to homosexuality, and the latter, that is, male homosexuality (in both sexes) were the primitive form of sexual longing? (The first sexual aim, analogous to the infantile one — a wish that does not extend beyond the inner world.) If, moreover, libido and anxiety both were male?" *Op. cit.*, p. 380 (October 17, 1899).

29. See among others, Simone de Beauvoir, *The Second Sex* (New York: Vintage, 1974) and Luce Irigaray, *This Sex Which Is Not One* (Ithaca: Cornell University Press, 1985).

30. Judith Butler, *Gender Trouble* (New York: Routledge, 1990), pp. 60–61.

31. Masson, ed., *op. cit.*, p. 364. (August 1, 1899).

32. Thanks to Judith Butler for this variation.

33. Judith Butler, *op. cit.*, pp. 61–65.

34. Freud, *op.cit.*, n. 22, p. 140.

35. The failure adequately to recognize the role of fantasy in constructing the object seems to me to effectively undermine some of the ways in which object-relations psychoanalytic theory has been used to support a view of the infant/mother relationships conceived in terms of "reciprocal recognition" of real others. See Jessica Benjamin, *The Bonds of Love* (New York: Pantheon, 1988), as an example of this tendency.

36. Scholars have pointed out that Freud was misled by a faulty German translation. In Italian, the bird was not a vulture at all, but a kite. Sigmund Freud, *Leonardo daVinci and a Memory of His Childhood* (New York: W. W. Norton & Co., 1964), J. Strachey, ed.'s note, pp. 5–7.

37. There is not time to examine this familiar view in detail, much less relate it to

the other accounts which Freud will offer of the development of male homosexuality. This is the subject of a useful book by Kenneth Lewes, *The Psychoanalytic Theory of Male Homosexuality* (New York: Meridian, 1988), which recounts the vicissitudes of accounts of the genesis of homosexuality in the texts of Freud and his successors. For a sustained critique of Freud's alignment of homosexuality with narcissism, see Michael Warner, "Homo-Narcissism, or Heterosexuality" in J. Boone and M. Cadden, eds., *Engendering Men* (New York: Routledge, 1990), pp. 190–206.

38. Butler, *op. cit.*, 67.

39. *Ibid.*, 70.

40. Freud's deployment of narcissism in the explication of homosexuality, and the implication of this analysis with his account of sexual difference has been the subject of critical engagement and revision by a range of contemporary theorists concerned to delineate the contours of self-formation in the contexts of patriarchy and compulsory heterosexuality. These works include efforts to generate an imaginary alternative to those associated with the current regime of sex and gender relations. See especially Luce Irigaray, *op. cit.*, n. 29 and Judith Butler, *Gender Trouble*, and "The Lesbian Phallus" in *Bodies That Matter* (New York: Routledge, 1993), pp. 57–91. See also Michael Warner, "Homo-Narcissism," n. 37.

41. See Judith Butler, "Critically Queer" in Butler, *Bodies That Matter*, pp. 223–242.

42. As I was making final revisions on this chapter, I received the special issue of *GLQ: A Journal of Lesbian and Gay Studies*, vol. 2, n. 1–2, devoted to "Pink Freud."

43. Despite this assertion, Freud identifies male homosexuality with "feminine" passivity in the case studies of Leonardo and Schreber.

44. "Female Sexuality" in *Sexuality and the Psychology of Love* (New York: Macmillan Publishing Co., 1963), pp. 194-211; "Femininity" in *New Introductory Lectures on Psychoanalysis* (New York: W. W. Norton and Co., 1989), pp. 139–167.

45. Sigmund Freud, "Psychoanalytic Notes Upon an Autobiographical Account of a Case of Paranoia (Dementia Paranoides)" (Schreber) in *Three Case Histories* (New York: Macmillan Publishing Co., 1963), pp. 103–186, esp. 161–182; "A Case of Paranoia Running Counter to the Psychoanalytic Theory of the Disease" in *Sexuality and the Psychology of Love* (New York: Macmillan Publishing Co., 1963), pp. 97–106; "Certain Neurotic Mechanisms in Jealousy, Paranoia, and Homosexuality, *ibid.*, pp. 160–170.

46. See the discussion of Lord Devlin's position in Chapter One, section III. Certainly, the response to the question of permitting openly gay men and women to serve in the military is better understood in such psychoanalytic terms than it is as a rational debate about military personnel policy.

47. Freud's analysis challenges the reasonableness of Lord Devlin's appeal to feelings of disgust to test the intensity of a community's moral sentiments. See the discussion in Chapter One, section III above.

48. Eve Kosofsky Sedgwick, *Epistemology of the Closet* (Berkeley: University of California Press, 1990), esp. pp. 1–66.

49. Paul Ricoeur, *Freud and Philosophy* (New Haven: Yale University Press, 1970);

Jurgen Habermas, *Knowledge and Human Interests* (Boston: Beacon Press, 1971), ch. 10; Michel Foucault, *The Order of Things* (New York: Pantheon, 1970).

50. This utopian moment has been seized and developed in the work of figures like Reich, Marcuse, Deleuze, and Guattari. For works that engage specifically gay issues, see Guy Hocquenhem, *Homosexual Desire* (Durham: Duke University Press, 1993); Leo Bersani, *Homos* (Cambridge: Harvard University Press, 1995).

Chapter Five: Refiguring the Jewish Question

An earlier version of theis essay originally appeared in *Feminist Interpretations of Hannah Arendt*, Bonnie Honig, ed. (University Park: The Pennsylvania State Univeraity Press, 1995): 105–133. Copyright © 1995 by The Pennsylvania State University. Reproduced by permission of the publisher.

1. I developed this chapter during my tenure as the inaugural Rockefeller Foundation Fellow in Legal Humanities at the Stanford Humanities Center, 1993–94, partially funded by President's Junior Faculty Fellowship from Purchase College, SUNY. My interest in Hannah Arendt goes back almost three decades and has been nourished over the years by conversation with Robert J. Anderson, Seyla Benhabib, Richard Bernstein, Kenley R. Dove, W. Thomas Schmid, William R. Torbert, James Walsh, and Hannah Arendt herself. I was lucky to get to know her during the 1960s when we discussed both philosophical and political issues. Although we did not talk about a politics of gender or sexuality, I don't think anyone can predict her reaction had she lived through the political transformations of the last two decades. Frank Farrell especially encouraged me to pursue the analogy between homosexuality and the Jewish Question. At Stanford, Paul Robinson and Pericles Lewis commented on an earlier draft. Ken Dove provided a timely and pointed critique that proved very helpful in clarifying my argument. I owe Bonnie Honig very special thanks for her intensive efforts as an engaged, sympathetic, and critical editor to bring this essay to fruition. I presented this material in lectures at Stanford and San Jose State as well as panels at the American Philosophical Association, American Political Science Association, and the Center for European Studies at Harvard. Thanks to all who participated on those occasions, expecially Seyla Benhabib, Jane Bennett, Joan Cocks, Jean Cohen, Bill Connolly, Regina Gagnier, Stanley Hutter, Jeffrey Isaacs, Rita Manning, Meredith Michaels, Melissa Orlie, and Bill Shaw.

2. This understanding was based on her study of the effects of "statelessness" on those Jews and others who were stripped of citizenship rights before being exiled, interned, or murdered by the Nazis and their collaborator regimes in Europe. The first step in the loss of human rights was consignment to a status of second-class citizenship; for Jews in Germany by the Nuremberg Laws of 1935. It is a sober reminder of the history and continued vitality of racism in Western culture that these laws were based in part on the Jim Crow laws which mandated racial segregation in the South after the failure of Reconstruction in the last quarter of the nineteenth century.

3. Cf. Seyla Benhabib, "Hannah Arendt and the Redemptive Power of Narrative,"

Social Research, vol. 57, no. 1 (Spring 1990).

4. *On Revolution* (New York: Viking Press, 1962)

5. *Between Past and Future*, enlarged edition (New York: Penguin Books, 1968).

6. *The Origins of Totalitarianism*, 1958 edition.

7. Especially "Civil Disobedience" and "On Violence," included in *Crises of the Republic* (New York: Harcourt Brace Jovanovich Inc. 1972).

8. *Hannah Arendt-Karl Jaspers Correspondence 1926–1969*, ed., Lotte Kohler and Hans Saner, (New York: Harcourt Brace Jovanovich, 1992), 29. Numbers in parentheses in the remainder of this section refer to this text.

9. *Ibid.*, p. 70 (Dec. 17, 1946).

10. "The Jew as Pariah" in Ron Miller, ed., Hannah Arendt, *The Jew as Pariah* (New York: Harcourt Brace Jovanovich, 1978).

11. Hannah Arendt, *The Life of the Mind* (New York: Harcourt Brace Jovanovich, 1977), 192.

12. In the controversial essay on the school-desegregation crisis, "Reflections on Little Rock," some of which she later repudiated as a result of conversation with Ralph Ellison. *Dissent* vol. 6, no. 1. (1959).

13. *Eichmann in Jerusalem*, p. 7.

14. Hanna Pitkin, "Justice: On Relating Private and Public," *Political Theory*, vol. 9, no. 3 (August 1981).

15. Cf. Bonnie Honig, *Political Theory and the Displacement of Politics* (Ithaca NY: Cornell University Press, 1992). pp. 96–104.

16. In *Bowers v. Hardwick*, the United States Supreme Court held that constitutional privacy rights guaranteed to other citizens did not protect homosexuals from prosecution under Georgia's sodomy laws for acts performed by consenting adults in the privacy of the home. 478 U.S. 186 (1986). For an extended analysis, see chapters One and Seven.

17. Larry Kramer, *Reports from the Holocaust*, (New York: St. Martin's Press, 1989).

18. Eve Kosofsky Sedgwick, The *Epistemology of the Closet* (Berkeley: University of California Press, 1990).

19. I am indebted to David Bianco for calling Kramer's essay to my attention and for sharing with me his unpublished paper, "Eichmann in Washington? The AIDS/ Holocaust Metaphor and Larry Kramer's Reading of Hannah Arendt."

20. Kramer has been both founder and critic of the Gay Men's Health Crisis ("GMHC") and the AIDS Coalition to Unleash Power ("ACT UP"). His pre-AIDS novel *Faggots* was deeply critical of contemporary gay life and his plays "The Normal Heart" and "The Destiny of Me" address the AIDS epidemic.

21. See also Eve Kosofsky Sedgwick, *Between Men* (New York: Columbia University Press, 1985).

22. See Chapter Four.

23. Hannah Arendt, *Essays in Understanding, 1930–1954*, ed., Jerome Kohn, (New York: Harcourt Brace & Company, 1994), 11–12.

24. Numbers in parentheses refer to pages in Hannah Arendt, *The Origins of Totali-*

tarianism, (New York: Harcourt Brace Jovanovich, 1968).

25. "Intermarriage between leading families soon followed, and culminated in a real international caste system, . . . numerically no more than perhaps a hundred families. But since these were in the limelight, the Jewish people themselves came to be regarded as a caste." (63)

26. "But what drove the Jews into the center of these racial ideologies more than anything else was the even more obvious fact that the pan-movements' claim to chosenness could clash seriously only with the Jewish claim." (240)

27. See the discussion of Freud's critique of this approach in Chapter Four, section II.

28. See Chapter Two, sections III and V.

29. Sedgwick, *op. cit.*, pp. 213–51.

30. D. A. Miller, *The Novel and the Police* (Berkeley: University of California Press, 1988), p. 207, quoted in Sedgwick, *Epistemology, supra.*, p. 67.

31. Michel Foucault, *The History of Sexuality: Volume 1. An Introduction*, trans. Robert Hurley (New York, Vintage Books, 1977), p. 43.

32. *Origins*, 447–57.

33. Numbers in parentheses refer to pages in Marcel Proust, *Remembrance of Things Past: Cities of the Plain*, trans. C. K. Scott Moncrieff and Terence Kilmartin (New York: Vintage Books, Random House, 1981)

34. Michel Foucault, *op. cit.*, p. 43.

35. The narrator's definition of the "accursed race" deploys the conception of sexual intermediates introduced into nineteenth-century discourses of sexuality by Karl Ulrichs, developed by Otto Weininger in his misogynist *Sex and Character*, and promoted by the sexologist Magnus Hirschfeld in the defense of homosexual and women's rights. See the extended discussion of these views in comparison with Freud in Chapter Three above.

36. This formulation derives from Karl Ulrichs. Jeffrey Weeks, *Sexuality and Its Discontents* (London: Routledge and Kegan Paul, 1985), 93, 153. See also Sigmund Freud, *Three Essays in the Theory of Sexuality* (New York: Basic Books, 1975), 8.

37. See Chapter Four, section III above.

38. See particularly the discussion of Pausanias' and Agathon's speeches from the *Symposium* in Chapter Three, sections III and VI.

39. See Sedgwick, *Epistemology*, p. 233 *et. seq.*

40. Compare with Freud's speculations on the evolutionary origins of universal bisexuality in *Three Essays*, p. 7.

41. These ambiguities are not unknown to Freud. Consider his complex identifications with Plato and Leonardo, his remarkably sympathetic readings of Schreber, the Wolf man and the Rat man, and his repeated references to the homosexual component in his relations with colleagues.

42. Sander Gilman, *The Jew's Body* (New York: Routledge, 1991); *Difference and Pathology* (Ithaca NY: Cornell University Press, 1985).

43. Sander Gilman, *Freud, Race and Gender* (Princeton, NJ: Princeton University

Press, 1993), 5.

44. *Ibid.*

45. See Jeffrey Weeks, *Sexuality and Its Discontents* (London: Routledge & Kegan Paul, 1985), *Coming Out* (London: Quartet Books Ltd., 1977); John D'Emilio, *Sexual Minorities, Sexual Communities* (Chicago: University of Chicago Press, 1983); John D'Emilio and Estelle B. Freedman, *Intimate Matters* (New York: Harper & Row, 1988).

46. But then, something like this insight is at work in the account of a bureaucratic mentality in *Eichmann in Jerusalem.*

47. Julia Kristeva, *Powers of Horror* (New York: Columbia University Press, 1982); Luce Irigaray, *An Ethics of Sexual Difference, Speculum of the Other Woman, The Sex Which Is Not One.* (Ithaca, New York: Cornell University Press, 1993, 1985, 1985).

48. Elizabeth Spelman, *Inessential Woman* (Boston: Beacon Press, 1988) among many others. See the discussion above in Chapter Two, section IV.

49. Judith Butler, *Bodies That Matter*, (New York: Routledge, 1993), p. 116.

50. Gayle Rubin offers a powerful analysis of the tendency of sexual minorities to reinscribe hierarchies of acceptable sexual practices and identities in "Thinking Sex," in Abelove, Barale, and Halperin, *The Lesbian/Gay Studies Reader* (New York: Routledge, 1993).

51. Janet Halley has recently argued that this popular opinion does not reflect accurately the state of constitutional doctrine. To the contrary, she shows that the status of an "immutable condition" is neither a necessary nor a sufficient condition to secure constitutional equal protection of a minority. Janet E. Halley, "Sexual Orientation and the Politics of Biology: A Critique of the Argument from Immutability," *Stanford Law Journal* vol. 46, no. 3 (February 1994) 503–68. See also, Edward Stein, ed., *Forms of Desire* (New York: Routledge, 1992) for materials relating to the essentialist/social constructivist controversy about sexual orientation. More recently, Stein has persuasively argued that the ethical status of homosexuality is independent of scientific explanations of its origin, "The Relevance of Scientific Research about Sexual Orientation to Lesbian and Gay Rights," *Journal of Homosexuality*, forthcoming. Daniel R. Ortiz makes a strong case that the debate is primarily a political struggle over the definition of lesbian and gay identities in "Creating Controversy: Essentialism and Constructivism and the Politics of Gay identity" in *Virginia Law Review*, vol. 79, no. 5 (October 1993), 1833–57. In the same issue, see also Cheshire Calhoun "Denaturalizing and Desexualizing Lesbian and Gay Identity," pp. 1859–1875 and Morris B. Kaplan, "Constructing Lesbian and Gay Rights and Liberation," pp. 1877–1902. These issues are discussed in Chapter Two, section four.

Chapter Six: Queer Citizenship

1. An earlier version of this chapter was prepared for inclusion as an essay in Donald Morse, ed., *The Delegated Intellect: Emersonian Essays in Literature, Science, and Art in Honor of Don Gifford* (New York: Peter Lang, 1995). Reprinted by permission of the

publisher. It has been revised and expanded for this book. Section three is substantially reworked, section four, mostly new. I am indebted to Don Gifford, Professor of English and American Studies Emeritus at Williams College, for more than the occasion of its writing. He introduced me to Thoreau in the '60s: his unpublished lectures provided the starting point of my enquiry, which was guided further by *The Farther Shore* (New York: Atlantic Monthly Press, 1990). Giff generously commented on earlier drafts of the chapter; he continues to be a fine teacher and wonderful friend. I am also grateful for their comments to Alan Ryan and George Kateb; I was able to complete drafting the original essay during an NEH Seminar at Princeton in the summer of 1991. Portions of sections I-II were presented on a panel at the annual meeting of the New York State Political Science Association at Buffalo State on April 25, 1992. Thanks also to all who participated in a lively discussion on that occasion.

2. George Hendrick, "The Influence of Thoreau's 'Civil Disobedience' on Gandhi's *Satyagraha*" in Thomas, ed., n. 14.

3. Stephen B. Oates, *Let the Trumpet Sound: The Life Of Martin Luther King Jr.* (New York: Penguin Books, 1982), p. 62.

4. Richard Mohr, *Gay Ideas: Outing and Other Controversies* (Boston: Beacon Press, 1992), ch. 6.

5. Henry Abelove, "From Thoreau to Queer Nation," *The Yale Journal of Criticism*, vol. 6, no. 3 (1993), pp. 17–26.

6. Michael Warner, "Thoreau's Bottom," Raritan, vol. 11, no. 3, (Winter 1992), pp. 53–79. See Chapters Two and Four above for more on the historical and systematic issues around modern homosexual definition.

7. Warner, *op. cit.*, p. 62.

8. Don Gifford, "Thoreau on Civil Disobedience," unpublished lecture, University of Essex, England, 1970, emphasis in original.

9. This essay in indebted generally to the essays of George Kateb on democratic individuality, especially, "Democratic Individuality and the Claims of Politics," 12 *Political Theory* 331, (1984); "Democratic Individuality and the Meaning of Rights," in Nancy Rosenblum, ed., *Liberalism and the Moral Life* (Cambridge: Harvard University Press, 1989), pp. 207–226. These appear in revised form in George Kateb, *The Inner Ocean: Individualism and Democratic Culture* (Ithaca, New York: Cornell University Press, 1992), Introduction, chs. 3 and 10. The latter chapter, on Whitman, is especially important for the concerns of this book.

10. Don Gifford, "Address to the Danforth Graduate Fellows' Conference," South Lee, Massachusetts, unpublished, p. 7.

11. Thoreau wrote an essay favorable to Philips after the abolitionist's appearance at the Concord Lyceum in 1845.

12. See Staughton Lynd, *Intellectual Origins of American Radicalism*, (New York: Random House, 1969), pp. 100–129.

13. Perry Miller, "From Edwards to Emerson" in *Errand into the Wilderness*, (Cambridge: The Belknap Press of Harvard University Press 1981).

14. Numerals without a letter in parentheses refer to Owen Thomas, ed., Henry David Thoreau, *Walden and Civil Disobedience*, (New York: W.W. Norton & Co., 1966).

15. See e.g., John Rawls, *A Theory of Justice*, (Cambridge: Harvard University Press, 1971), sections 55–59.

16. Cf. Rawls, *op. cit.*, and Hannah Arendt, "Civil Disobedience" in *Crises of the Republic*, (New York: Harcourt, Brace, Jovanovich, 1972).

17. Quoted in Nancy Rosenblum, "Thoreau's Militant Conscience" in 9 *Political Theory* 81–110 (Feb. '81).

18. See section III below.

19. Although Prof. Rosenblum, n. 17, makes a powerful case for the "militant" and "heroic" aspects of Thoreau's conception of individuality, she overlooks the recurrent irony that undercuts these features of his self-portrayal. Similarly, she treats his use of paradox and contradiction solely in terms of rhetorical aggression, neglecting the extent to which these devices have been instruments of maieutic education since Socrates.

20. Ralph Waldo Emerson, "Thoreau" reprinted in Thomas, op. cit., n. 14.

21. See F. O. Matthieson *American Renaissance* (New York: Oxford University Press, 1941) for a discussion of the importance of formal rhetoric in the education of Thoreau's day. This context bears importantly on Thoreau's distinction between speech and writing discussed in section III of this essay.

22. Numerals preceded by the letter "G" refer to Wendell Glick, ed., *Great Short Works of Henry David Thoreau*, (New York: Harper and Row Perennial Library, 1982).

23. James M. McPherson, *Battle Cry of Freedom* (New York: Oxford University Press, 1988), 119.

24. James M. McPherson, *op. cit.*, pp. 152–53.

25. In an essay with explicit discussion of Brown's activities in Kansas, Thoreau does not mention the men fallen before the axes of Brown and his men at Pottawotamie.

26. Numerals preceded by the letter "D" refer to Jeffrey L. Duncan, ed., *Thoreau: The Major Essays* (New York: E. P. Dutton & Co., 1972). Compare Plate, *Phaedo* 118a.

27. The reading of *Walden* proposed here benefited generally from Stanley Cavell, *The Senses of Walden*, expanded edition (San Francisco: North Point Press, 1981), as well as from Gifford, *The Farther Shore*, n. 1.

28. See Thoreau's essay on "Friendship" in Glick, *op. cit.*, n. 22.

29. Abelove, *op. cit.*, pp. 17–18.

30. *Ibid.*, p. 26, citing Paul Goodman.

31. *Ibid.*, p. 24

32. *Civil Disobedience*, p. 243.

33. There is an affinity here with Socrates' position in Plato's *Republic* when, after constructing an allegedly ideal just city and arguing that it is probably impossible to achieve, he claims that the idea itself has value as a guide for individual ethical life.

34. Originally published in *Atlantic Monthly*, August, 1862. Reprinted in Thomas, ed., *op. cit.*, n. 14, pp. 266–81.

35. *Op. cit.*, p. 267.

36. *Ibid.*

37. *Op. cit.*, p. 266.

38. *Op. cit.*, p. 268.

39. *Op. cit.*, p. 267.

40. *Op. cit.*, p. 272.

41. See Chapter Three, sections VIII and IX.

42. See the detailed discussion in Chapter Three, section X.

43. In the context of *Walden*, the aestheticization of morality succeeds rhetorically in general terms whereas it failed dismally in the political context of "Slavery in Massachusetts," discussed in section III. This move in Thoreau's thought is reminiscent of Hannah Arendt's appropriation of Kant's *Third Critique*. She discusses Thoreau in her essay on "Civil Disobedience," n. 16, but I find no reference to him in *The Life of the Mind*, ed., Mary McCarthy, (New York: Harcourt Brace Jovanovich, 1978) despite the affinities in their analyses of thinking, conscience and judging.

44. See Chapter Three, section II.

45. See Chapter Two, section II.

46. Wendell Glick, ed., *op. cit.*, n. 22, p. 168.

47. *Ibid.*

48. *Ibid.*

49. *Op. cit.*, p. 169.

50. *Op. cit.*, p. 170.

51. *Op. cit.*, p. 165.

52. *Op. cit.*, p. 171.

53. *Op. cit.*, p. 172.

54. In *Love and Death in the American Novel* (New York: Criterion Books, 1960), Leslie Fiedler shows the pervasiveness within canonical texts of the theme of intense friendship between men of different races who escape together from the world of civilization — and of women — into the wilderness. He does not discuss Thoreau. Henry Abelove cites Thoreau's hostility towards the novel as another indication of his alienation from domesticity; this works for the sentimental novel, but Thoreau's own fantasies are reflected in the novels discussed by Fiedler.

55. *Op. cit.*, p. 163.

56. Warner, *op. cit.*, p. 62.

57. Glick, ed., *op. cit.*, p. 159.

58. *Op. cit.*, p. 160.

59. *Op. cit.*, p. 165.

Chapter Seven: Intimacy and Equality

1. This chapter is dedicated to Ed Stein, whose critical engagement with these issues provoked, challenged, and sustained my own efforts through several drafts and countless conversations. An earlier, shorter version was published in *The Philosophical*

Forum vol. XXV, no. 4, Summer 1994, pp. 333–360, and is reprinted here with some changes by permission of *The Pholosophical Forum*. Sections IV and V are new, developed in response to objections from several friends, especially Wendy Brown and Judith Butler. Work on this chapter was supported by grants from the Stanford Humanities Center, Rockefeller Foundation, the American Council of Learned Societies, and the President's Junior Faculty Fellowship at Purchase College, State University of New York. Earlier versions of this paper were presented to a Philosophy Department Colloquium at the State University of New York at Stony Brook; at a panel in the normative political theory section of the American Political Science Association; and in lectures at the University of California, Santa Cruz; at a Political Science Colloquium at the University of Washington; at the Stanford Law School; and at Willamette University. I am grateful to all of those who engaged me on those occasions, including Robert J. Anderson, Kenneth Baynes, Wendy Brown, Judith Butler, Christine de Stephano, Janet Halley, Eva Kitay, Smadar Lare, Sally Markowitz, Jason Mayerfeld, Jerome Neu, Joan W. Scott, and, especially, Cheryl Hall, and Marcos Bisticas-Cocoves, who were formal respondents. Many thanks to Cheshire Calhoun, Richard Eldridge, Don Gifford, Dan Ortiz, Alan Ryan, and Ed Stein for their comments on written drafts.

2. This chapter includes within its general construction of a right of intimate association the right of lesbian and gay citizens to raise their own children and to be considered for foster care and adoption on the same terms as heterosexuals. However, the specific issues that emerge in decisions effecting children will be not be treated here.

3. 478 U. S. 186 (1986). J. Blackmun, dissenting, cited Kenneth Karst, "The Freedom of Intimate Association," *Yale L. J.* 89 (1980) 624.

4. These thinkers have urged that privacy rights have been traditionally exploited to insulate families from state investigation of offenses against women and children by the male figures who have been their primary beneficiary. They argue that appeals to privacy reinforce the isolation of the nuclear family as an arena insulated against the claims of social justice. Oddly, this feminist critique intersects in its conclusions at least with a line of conservative argument which has attacked the constitutional right of privacy from its inception as an exercise in illegitimate judicial decision making unsupported by the text of the U.S. Constitution. Unlike conservatives who reject the right of privacy as an illicit extension of judicial power ungrounded in the text and history of the constitution, feminist critics of privacy rights have been insistent that a woman's right to abortion can best be defended by grounding it in terms of gender equality under the equal protection clause of the 14th amendment. See, e.g., Catherine A. MacKinnon, *Feminism Unmodified* (Cambridge: Harvard University Press, 1987), ch. 8. For a critique in the context of lesbian and gay rights, Kendall Thomas "Beyond the Privacy Principle," Columbia Law Review, October 1992.

5. Cf. Mark Blasius, "The Ethos of Lesbian and Gay Existence," in *Gay and Lesbian Politics* (Philadelphia: Temple University Press, 1994).

6. In an op-ed piece, Andrew Sullivan, former editor of *The New Republic*, has ar-

gued just such a case. The political argument seems to me to stand independently of the essentialism with which Sullivan partially defends it. Further, one can recognize the integrity of the position without endorsing its more general political stance. Andrew Sullivan, "Gay Values, Truly Conservative," *The New York Times*, February 9, 1993, A21. Sullivan makes the case more fully in *Virtually Norman* (New York: Alfred A. Knopf, 1995).

7. Paula Ettelbrick, "Since When Is Marriage a Path to Liberation," in William Rubenstein, *Lesbians, Gay Men and the Law* (New York: The New Press, 1993), 401–405.

8. 852 P. 2d 44 (Hawaii 1993).

9. Sylvia Law, "Homosexuality and the Social Meaning of Gender," 1988 *Wisc. L. Rev.* 187; Andrew Koppelman, "The Miscegenation Analogy: Sodomy Law as Sex Discrimination," *Yale L. J.* 98 (Nov. 1988) 145–164; William Eskridge, "A History of Same-Sex Marriage, *Va. L. Rev.*, 79 (Oct. 1993), 1419–1511; Cass Sunstein, "Homosexuality and the Constitution," *Metaphilosophy*, October 1994.

10. 388 U. S. 1 (1967).

11. In late December 1992, *The New York Times* reported that Stanford University and the University of Chicago had extended health benefits to the unmarried domestic partners of their employees. Stanford restricted such coverage to same-sex couples on the ground that they are denied the choice of marriage. In January 1993, Mayor David Dinkins announced the creation of a registry for unmarried domestic partnerships in New York City and the extension of some limited benefits to city employees in such partnerships. Although the movement to recognize domestic partnerships is an important trend, most such efforts fall far short of conveying the range of rights and benefits associated with marital status.

12. Kath Weston, *Families We Choose* (New York: Columbia University Press, 1991); Ellen Lewin, *Lesbian Mothers* (Ithaca: Cornell University Press, 1993).

13. This tension has been identified and amplified in the work of those feminist legal scholars and political theorists who have been profoundly suspicious of reliance on the right of privacy to secure a woman's right to abortion. They rightly insist on the importance of equality-based arguments which recognize the disparate impact of abortions rights on men and women. In addition, they have emphasized that privacy talk has been traditionally deployed to insulate patriarchal power relations within the family from scrutiny and intervention by the state. Cf. e.g., Mackinnon, *supra*, n. 4. My point here is to acknowledge the force of these critiques but to underscore the historical instability of this deployment such that the recognition of privacy rights has also systematically undermined the independence of the familial institution they are invoked to support. See particularly, the discussion of *Eisenstadt v. Baird*, below.

14. 381 U.S. 479 (1965).

15. 478 U.S. 186 (1986).

16. For a more detailed discussion, see Chapter One, section II.

17. 381 U.S. 479 at 482.

18. See Chapter One, section II.

19. *Pierce v. Society of Sisters*, 268 U.S. 510 (1925).

20. *Meyer v. Nebraska*, 262 U.S. 390 (1923).

21. 381 U.S. 479 at 482.

22. 357 U.S. 449 (1958).

23. 381 U.S. 479 at 483.

24. 371 U.S. 415 (1962).

25. See Chapter One, Section II, above.

26. 381 U.S. 479 at 485–86.

27. 381 U.S. 479 at 486.

28. 367 U.S. 497 (1961).

29. 367 U.S. 497 at 553.

30. 405 U.S.438 (1972).

31. 405 U.S. 438 at 453.

32. Ibid.

33. That bedroom had already suffered some profanation in 1969 when the Court decided in *Stanley v. Georgia* 394 U.S. 557 (1969) that privacy rights combined with the First Amendment to prevent the state from prosecuting a man for the possession of obscene material within his home. They recognized the individual's "right to satisfy his intellectual and emotional needs in the privacy of his own home." Not even the state's interest in regulating "obscenity," already acknowledged as exempt from First Amendment limitations, justifies such intrusion: ". . . a State has no business telling a man, sitting alone in his house, what books he may read or what films he may watch." 394 U.S. 557, at 565.

34. 410 U.S. 113 (1972).

35. 410 U.S. 113 at 153.

36. The Court goes on to establish a tripartite analysis of the State's interest in regulating these decisions from a minimal concern with defining conditions of medical safety in the first trimester through a more active concern for the mother's health in the second to an interest in the potential life of the fetus in the third trimester (or after viability). The weighting of competing interests focused on the mother's liberty and health and on the state's concern for the potential life of the affected fetus. Political controversy has combined with academic skepticism about the force of its arguments to undermine confidence in the quality of Blackmun's opinion in *Roe v. Wade*, even among those who support its outcome. I think that this view underestimates the statesmanship underlying its compromises: as a framework for working through the complex balancing that abortion requires, it has not been superseded.

37. 505 U.S. 833 (1992).

38. 478 U.S. 186 (1986).

39. See, e.g., Anne B. Goldstein, History, Homosexuality, and Political Values: Searching for the Hidden Determinants of *Bowers v. Hardwick*, 97 Yale L. J. 1073, 1081–89 (1988); Janet E. Halley, Reasoning About Sodomy: Act and Identity in and After *Bowers v. Hardwick*, 79 Va. L. R. 1721, 1750–67 (1993). The criticism extends across a broad spectrum of constitutional perspectives from left-republican Frank

NOTES

Michelman, "Law's Republic," 97 *Yale L. J.* 1493 (1988) to libertarian Richard A. Posner, *Sex and Reason* (Cambridge: Harvard University Press, 1993).

40. See the *Washington Post* story quoted in William Rubenstein, *Lesbians, Gay Men, and The Law*, n. 7, pp. 148–49.

41. The official version of these events has emphasized that the police were at Mr. Hardwick's home to enforce a warrant that had been issued because of his non-appearance in court on an unrelated matter. Michael Hardwick has offered a fuller and less benign picture of the events leading to his arrest. See W. Rubenstein, *op. cit.* pp. 125–131. Kendall Thomas has used this fuller and more convincing account of the episode in developing an argument about the role of sodomy laws in licensing homophobic violence. K. Thomas "Beyond the Privacy Principle" Columbia L. J. Oct. 1992.

42. 478 U.S. 186 at 196.

43. 478 U.S. 186 at 200 (Blackmun, J., dissenting).

44. 487 U.S. 186 at 190–91.

45. As to the right "to satisfy his own intellectual and emotional needs in the privacy of one's home" enforced as to the solitary enjoyment of pornography in *Stanley*, even White saw that it could not be said to "deal with" procreation, marriage, and the family. He devotes a separate paragraph to arguing that this is really a First Amendment case and not a privacy case at all, despite the acknowledged fact that the First Amendment does not protect "obscene" material outside the home.

46. See n. 39, supra.

47. 478 U.S. at 200 (Blackmun, J., dissenting).

48. Cf. Jonathan Goldberg, *Sodometries*, for an interesting historical and critical account of this and other anomalies of the sodomy laws. (Stanford: Stanford University Press, 1992) pp. 1–26.

49. 478 U.S. 186, at 194.

50. See Eve Kosofsky Sedgwick, *The Epistemology of the Closet* (Berkeley: University of California Press, 1990) pp. 6–7, 76–79; Kendall Thomas, "Corpus Juris (Hetero)Sexualis," *GLQ: A Journal of Lesbian and Gay Studies*, vol. 1, no. 1, pp. 33–52.

51. "Condemnation of those practices [homosexual conduct] is firmly rooted in Judaeo-Christian moral and ethical standards. Homosexual sodomy was a capital crime under Roman law. . . . Blackstone described 'the infamous *crime against nature* as an offense of deeper malignity' than rape,' the very mention of which is a disgrace to human nature,' and 'a crime not fit to be named'. . . ." 487 U.S. at 185-86. Anne B. Goldstein, *op. cit.* n. 39, has discussed the proliferation of historical errors and distortions throughout this case.

52. For a more detailed exposition, see section IV of Chapter One, above.

53. —U.S.—(1996) Decided in late May, *Romer v. Evans* is discussed in the Introduction above.

54. 478 U. S. 186 at 204 (Blackmun, J., dissenting).

55. For differing interpretations of Blackmun's dissent in relation to debates between essentialists and social constructivists about sexual identities, see articles by Daniel R. Ortiz, Cheshire Calhoun, and Morris B. Kaplan in *Virginia Law Review*, Octo-

ber 1993, devoted to "Sexual Orientation and the Law."

56. 478 U.S. 186 at 205-06 (Blackmun, J., dissenting).

57. Michael Sandel has argued that the invocation of privacy on behalf of lesbian and gay rights in the *Hardwick* dissents shares a generic liberal proceduralism which avoids substantive ethical argumentation with its necessary reference to conceptions of a good life. Sandel's claim seriously mistakes the force and direction of Justice Blackmun's argument. The redefinition of private rights as protecting freedom of intimate association does more than trigger the protections of the due process clause. Michael Sandel, "Moral Argument and Liberal Toleration: Abortion and Homosexuality," 77 Cal. L. Rev. 521 (1989).

58. The notion that a plurality of forms of shared life represents a positive good rather than simply a political retreat from substantive ethics has been an important component of liberal thought from the Federalist papers through J.S. Mill to Isaiah Berlin.

59. For an effort to portray a distinctively lesbian and gay ethos in this context, see Mark Blasius, *op. cit.*, n. 5.

60. 478 U.S. 186 at 211. (Blackmun, J. dissenting).

61. Although the right to marry belongs to individuals and requires state action for its fulfillment, it distinctively depends on mutual and joint decision making for its realization. At the same time, the married couple enjoys a special status vis-à-vis both state and society. The family unit created by marriage comes to have independent status even in relation to those individuals who created it. Until the wave of reform in states' divorce laws since the 1960s, and even today in some jurisdictions, state authority has made it quite difficult to dissolve a marriage once formed. Indeed, nowhere is it as easy to end as to initiate a marriage, and this remains true even where there are no children whose welfare may be at issue. One reader of this paper insisted that he would go along with the argument for lesbian and gay marriage so long as it was clear that there would also be a right of lesbian and gay divorce.

62. See Lenore Weitzman, *The Divorce Revolution* (New York: The Free Press, 1985); Martha A. Fineman, *The Illusion of Equality* (Chicago: University of Chicago Press, 1991); Susan Moller Okin, *Justice, Gender, and the Family* (New York: Basic Books, 1989) chs. 6 and 7.

63. See articles cited in n.9.

64. "Homosexuality and the Constitution," *Metaphilosophy*, October 1994. I develop a more detailed critical response in "Why *Does* Sexuality Matter to Philosophy — and How? Mutual Interrogations" in the same issue, which includes the papers and commentary from a Symposium, "Why Sexuality Matters to Philosophy" sponsored in 1993 at the eastern division of the American Philosophical Association by the Society for Lesbian and Gay Philosophy,the Society for Women in Philosophy, and the Society for the Philosophy of Sex and Love.

65. Especially the work of Catherine MacKinnon.

66. The most forceful and influential articulation of this position is Adrienne Rich, "Compulsory Heterosexuality and Lesbian Existence," in Abelove, Halperin, and

Barale, *The Lesbian-Gay Studies Reader* (New York: Routledge, 1993).

67. An important exploration of the relations between gender and sexuality, feminism, and queer politics, to which I am indebted is Gayle Rubin, "Thinking Sex," in Abelove, Halperin, and Barale, *The Lesbian/Gay Studies Reader* (New York: Routledge, 1993).

68. Henry Abelove, "From Thoreau to Queer Nation," *The Yale Journal of Criticism*, vol. 6, no. 3 (1993), pp. 17–26; Richard Mohr, *Gay Ideas* (Boston: Beacon Press, 1993), pp. 93–102.

69. See among many others, Eugene V. Rostow, "The Consent of the Governed," *Virginia Quarterly*, Autumn 1968.

70. Plato, *Gorgias*, tr. D. J. Zeyl (Indianapolis: Hackett Publishing Company, 1987), p. 52 (482c).

71. John Rawls, *A Theory of Justice* (Cambridge: Harvard University Press, 1971), p. 364. See *op. cit.*, pp. 363–391 for Rawls's definitions and justifications of both civil disobedience and conscientious refusal.

72. *Ibid.*, p. 365.

73. *Ibid.*, p. 375.

74. Hannah Arendt, "Civil Disobedience" in *Crises of the Republic* (New York: Harcourt Brace Jovanovich, Inc., 1972), p. 94.

75. Hannah Arendt, "On Violence" in *Crises of the Republic, supra*, pp. 103–198.

76. Hannah Arendt, *On Revolution* (New York: Harcourt Brace Jovanovich, 1963).

77. Hannah Arendt, "Civil Disobedience," n. 74, p. 101.

78. See the studies by Weston and Lewin cited in n. 12.

79. Michel Foucault, *The History of Sexuality, Volume One. An Introduction* (New York: Vintage, 1978); *Discipline and Punish* (New York: Pantheon, 1977).

80. The many issues raised by Foucault's work as to sexuality and identity as historical forms of social control are approached from a variety of perspectives in Chapters Two and Four.

81. The analysis offered above converges with and is influenced by Mark Blasius's discussion of the normalizing dimensions of gay community in his *Gay and Lesbian Politics* (Philadelphia: Temple University Press, 1994), He also focuses on the ethical potential of queer sexual practices and institutions although with different emphases.

INDEX

A

Abelove, Henry, 179, 182, 194–5, 200, 227, 241n. 39, 246n. 65, 263n. 54
abortion, 35–6, 216, 219, 220, 264n. 4, 265n. 13. *See also Roe v. Wade*
Achilles, 200
ACT UP, 178
Aeschylus, 87
African Americans, xi, 15, 40, 41, 43, 227; and Civil Rights Movement, 48, 70, 73, 227–8
Agathon, 82–4, 86, 89, 92–9, 104–5, 107, 109, 250n. 33, 36
AIDS, x, xiii, 9, 16, 38, 48, 72, 159–60, 178, 211, 223, 236; and safer-sex education, 236–8
Alcibiades, 52, 57, 82, 95, 97, 104, 106, 107–11, 198–9, 248n. 8, 252n. 53, 253n. 56, 57
Alcott, Bronson, 180
American Journal of Psychiatry, 75
American Psychiatric Association, 33, 74, 122; Diagnostic and Statistical Manual, 33, 74
American Psychological Association, 33–4, 74
American Revolution, 20, 193
androgyny, inner, 63–4, 69, 70
anti-slavery movement. *See* African-American
Anzaldua, Gloria, 68
Aphrodite, 86, 98, 99, 249n. 18
Apollodorus, 83, 247n. 2, 4
Arendt, Hannah, xii, xiii, 8, 9, 27, 40, 48, 125, 147, 184, 188, 191, 223, 226, 227, 231–6; and "Civil Disobedience," 155; and *Eichmann in Jerusalem*, 157, 159, 160, 172; and Foucault, 154, 156; and Freud, 155, 173; and homosexuality, 151–76; and *The Human Condition*, 153, 155, 173; and the Jewish Question, 151–76, 257n. 2, 258n. 25, 259n. 26; and *The Life of the Mind*, 155, 157; and "On Violence," 155, 233; and *The Origins of Totalitarianism*, 152, 159, 164; and *Rahel Varnhagen*, 158, 172, 174; and Thoreau, 177
Aristodemus, 83, 104, 110
Aristophanes, 53–4, 82, 84, 88, 90–5, 99, 101–2, 104–5, 110, 134, 243n. 7, 248n. 8, 250n. 29, 30, 32
Aristotle, 38, 51
Arnold, Matthew, 56
autonomy: individual, 22, 27, 29, 31–2, 34, 36, 37, 216, 219; moral, 5, 22–31, 32–6, 118; women's, 9, 127, 216